THE MIND IN EXILE

The Mind in Exile

THOMAS MANN IN PRINCETON

STANLEY CORNGOLD

PRINCETON UNIVERSITY PRESS

PRINCETON & OXFORD

Published by Princeton University Press
41 William Street, Princeton, New Jersey 08540
6 Oxford Street, Woodstock, Oxfordshire OX20 1TR

press.princeton.edu

All Rights Reserved

Library of Congress Cataloging-in-Publication Data
Names: Corngold, Stanley, author.
Title: The mind in exile : Thomas Mann in Princeton / Stanley Corngold.
Description: Princeton : Princeton University Press, 2022. | Includes bibliographical references and index.
Identifiers: LCCN 2021018405 (print) | LCCN 2021018406 (ebook) |
    ISBN 9780691201641 (hardback) | ISBN 9780691229676 (ebook)
Subjects: LCSH: Mann, Thomas, 1875–1955—Exile—United States. | Mann, Thomas, 1875–1955—Political and social views. | Mann, Thomas, 1875–1955—Homes and haunts—New Jersey—Princeton | Mann, Thomas, 1875–1955—Friends and associates. | Princeton (N.J.)—Intellectual life. | Authors, German—20th century—Biography.
Classification: LCC PT2625.A44 Z544197 2022 (print) | LCC PT2625.A44 (ebook) |
    DDC 833/.912 [B]—dc23
LC record available at https://lccn.loc.gov/2021018405
LC ebook record available at https://lccn.loc.gov/2021018406

British Library Cataloging-in-Publication Data is available

Editorial: Rob Tempio, Matt Rohal, and Chloe Coy
Production Editorial: Mark Bellis
Jacket Design: Layla Mac Rory
Production: Erin Suydam
Publicity: Alyssa Sanford and Carmen Jimenez
Copyeditor: Jodi Beder

Jacket photo by Fred Stein © fredstein.com

This book has been composed in Arno

Printed on acid-free paper. ∞

Printed in the United States of America

10 9 8 7 6 5 4 3 2 1

CONTENTS

PREFACE

THIS BOOK DESCRIBES the extraordinary exile of the German writer Thomas Mann in Princeton, New Jersey, where he lived for two and a half years, from September 1938 to March 1941. They frame a crucial historical juncture, the beginning of World War II, spanning the Nazi dismemberment of Czechoslovakia and the intensified bombing of England.[1] Fascism was rampant both outside and inside America. Mann lived through this low, dishonest triennium in varying moods of outrage, and hope for a constructive outcome. He wrote articles and speeches expressing his horror at the Nazi desecration of his homeland and his belief in the "Coming Victory of Democracy," a topic with no mean relevance to the debacles of today.[2]

Mann arrived in Princeton as the widely praised author of the novels *Buddenbrooks, the Decline of a Family*, for which, in 1929, he received the Nobel Prize, and *The Magic Mountain*, on which many a young reader has cut his or her intellectual teeth; and the great novellas *Tonio Kröger* and *Death in Venice*. It might be enough to say at this point that his first novel and stories were loved by Franz Kafka. Along with Albert Einstein (1879–1955), Mann, who was Einstein's elder by four years—Mann was born in 1875 and died several months after Einstein in August 1955—was the most famous of the refugee intellectuals who lived in or near Princeton during these years. They were eminent figures in a "circle," broadly speaking, that included Mann's best friend, the cultural historian Erich Kahler (1885–1970); the novelist Hermann Broch (1886–1951), who was Kahler's best friend; the Princeton University physicist Allen Shenstone (1893–1980) and his wife Mildred (Molly) (d. 1967), a special favorite of Mann's wife Katharina (Katia) Pringsheim Mann (1883–1980); and solid acquaintances from the Institute for Advanced Study, among them the mathematician Hermann Weyl (1885–1955), the logician Kurt Gödel (1906–1978), and Mann's translator H[elen]-T[racy] Lowe-Porter (1876–1963) and her husband, the Russian-American paleographer Elias Avery Lowe (1879–1969), who also held a post at the Institute. The propinquity of these scholars was at once mental and physical: Hermann Broch lived in Einstein's house for a time and thereafter in Kahler's mansard, where he wrote his towering novel *The Death of Virgil*. Kahler and Einstein lived only a few streets away from Mann, whose own distinction survives in the unmasterable volume of the work of high quality he produced, let alone the volumes upon volumes of criticism dealing with this work. Toward the end of his life in 1952, Mann wrote to the Yale Germanist Hermann Weigand: "Even in these times it is possible for a man to construct out of his life and work a culture, a small cosmos, in which everything is interrelated, which, despite all diversity, forms a complete personal whole, which stands more or less on an equal footing with the great life-syntheses of earlier ages."[3] He was entitled to think that his own achievement had met this standard, and everything he accomplished at Princeton belonged to it.

Mann's exile in Princeton lasted until 1941, when he moved to Pacific Palisades, an elegant neighborhood of Los Angeles, attracted by the climate and the presence of even more stimulating refugees, including the "movie gang."[4] Under close surveillance by the House Un-American Activities Committee, he abandoned America definitively for Europe in 1952, settling first in Erlenbach and then in Kilchberg, Switzerland, both just outside Zurich, where he lived until his death in 1955. He had made a few postwar forays to Europe, one with quite resounding effect in 1947, when, at the PEN Club in Zurich, he delivered a speech titled "Nietzsche's Philosophy in the Light of Our Experience."[5] The speech was often repeated and later became a much-quoted essay: on the first occasion of its delivery, it was broadcast all throughout Switzerland. At its close, Mann plangently rejects Nietzsche's celebration of raw, ecstatic life in the name of its opposing principle—morality—inviting "us" to suppress a sort of elite aesthetic defiance of common decency and goodness. Goodness is "the spirit" of what Mann had called, in a telegram to President Roosevelt (which note), "all that is loyal, honest, and decent in a world of falsehood and chaos."[6] When Mann criticizes Nietzsche's glorification of life, of instinct, of power over others—unchallenged by reason, untrammeled, unrefined—he is criticizing an unscrupulous politics, sustained by manifestations of naked will. Recent history, Mann declares, referring to the rise and fall of a Third Reich that he ultimately reviled, had exposed the reprehensible thrust of Nietzsche's aesthetics of power. In his lecture, Mann had no qualms calling it "fascistic."[7]

At this moment of writing, winter in America, we are subjected to an exercise of power, as once in Mann's Germany, by a persistent invocation of crisis. "Crisis" means "things separating," things coming apart, embroiled in perpetual change. Like it or not, we have achieved the ambition of a Faust, who "dedicates" himself to the turmoil of incessant inner commotion, "the most painful excess / enamored hate and quickening distress. . . ."[8]

Beset daily through the social media by manifestations of willfulness without circumspection, without prudence—without grammar!—an ongoing sequence of crises—the frenetic changes of the news cycle, the bewildering storm of disconnected bits of information whose disconnect is importantly owed to an absence of perspective, more precisely, to a dwindling historical memory of—and care for—past experience as a principle of organization,[9] we are suddenly well informed on reading Mann's notes from Rostovtzeff's "Social and Economic History of the Roman Empire"; for here Mann cites "the downfall of ancient civilization, its main phenomenon being the gradual absorption of the educated classes by the masses, the 'simplification' of all functions of political, social, economic, and spiritual life: barbarization."[10] We can read an account of our crisis by the cultural anthropologist Claude Lévi-Strauss—which Mann did not read, but which he could have read in Switzerland (both connoisseurs of mythical thinking) in the year of his death in 1955. For Lévi-Strauss, our spasmodic "barbarization" figures as an "insidious leakage from contemporary mankind, which has become saturated with its own numbers and with the ever-increasing complexity of its problems, as if its skin had been irritated by the friction of ever-greater material and intellectual exchange brought about by the improvement in communication."[11] Finally, there is Erich Kahler—clairvoyant in 1961—for a last word on crisis and friction: "[A] crisis develops through the increasing friction between an elaborately established, less and less flexible and receptive order and the ever growing perpetually onrushing life material. A crisis is [a] final breaking point, the overpowering of the controlling form by the discontinuous multitude of life."

In regard to "all former . . . locally or substantively restricted" crises,

> they lack the present panicky simultaneity and therefore immediate universality and comprehensiveness of crisis, which is mainly due to the technological unification of our world, the rapidity of world-wide communication, the crowding of events and reactions to events. The incessant advances of our technology and science have, moreover, brought about an inner crisis of man, by promoting conformity and standardization, by alienating individuals from each other and from themselves by besetting human consciousness with continuous material changes, by sweeping away traditions and memories and thus endangering personal and communal identity.[12]

And so, I want, as a modest defense, to awaken the memory of several historical junctures, beginning with the decision in 1938 by Thomas Mann (at that time termed "the greatest living man of letters") to immigrate and anchor his American exile in Princeton as Lecturer in the Humanities at Princeton University.[13] Here, he would accomplish his exemplary itinerary of thought and feeling: the transformation from arch European conservative to liberal conservative to ardent presenter of democratic socialist ideals.[14]

For these two and a half years, Mann was astonishingly productive as author, university lecturer, and public intellectual. With Princeton as his home base, he traveled throughout America, delivering countless addresses in defense of humanistic values. His university lectures on Goethe, Freud, and Wagner were each attended by nearly 1,000 auditors.

Mann fulfilled what has been called "his stupendous capacity for work" (Hermann Broch) in a circle of friends, subsequently celebrated as the "Kahler-Kreis," in which the dominant players, at the time, were Kahler, Einstein, and the same Hermann Broch. And so, in the course of describing the mind of Thomas Mann, I hope to revive something of the intellectual atmosphere of an extraordinary place and constellation. Its significance is not only historical but also contemporary: in a time of a troubling transatlantic alienation, a meditation on Mann's American exile will remind us of a quondam "alliance of European and American intellectuals and traditions that might be an inspiration for the present" (Heinrich Detering).[15]

Mann's epochal friendship in Princeton with Erich Kahler remains of special interest. Kahler lived nearby, having settled in Princeton, on Mann's urging, in late 1938, supplying a welcome familiarity and neighborliness to Mann's at first precarious perch in the New World. Kahler's superior erudition provided Mann with countless impulses and ideas: Mann's entire political education was shaped by his decades-long contact with Kahler, almost a member of Mann's family. In a letter to Kahler dated May 25, 1941, shortly after Mann had left Princeton for Pacific Palisades, Mann laments having had no news from his friend: "For we often speak of you among ourselves, since we have the habit of comparing everyone here with whom we are on a friendly footing with you and saying, 'But Kahler was better!' or 'Everything would be fine if only Kahler were here!' Believe it or not."[16]

Kahler, Broch, and Einstein were not Mann's sole "educators" during his Princeton years (I use the word as flying the colors of Nietzsche's "Schopenhauer as Educator"). Add on the occasional but very lively visits of Mann's son-in-law, the fiery anti-Papal, anti-Fascist Giuseppe Antonio Borgese, a political philosopher at home at the University of Chicago. Borgese and Broch were extraordinarily intense thinkers and conversationalists: together with Mann and Kahler they crafted a plan for world government (see, in chapter 2, *The City of Man*). In a letter to Mann, Kahler suggests their type: "Anyone who has ever been really obsessed with a many-layered project understands that craving to get to work, and to do nothing else! The feeling is comparable only to physical thirst. And he knows also the animal fury that flares uncontrollably against anything that detains him from work."[17]

My chief concern in this book, then, is to shape a cultural memory of Thomas Mann during his American exile in Princeton—a link, by memory, to a continuum between "our" past and present. And here I shall take the liberty of translating Mann's phrase "*our* experience" ("*unsere* Erfahrung") in his essay on Nietzsche, mentioned above, as "*my* experience" ("*meine* Erfahrung"). I have a vested interest, not entirely innocent, in choosing this period of Mann's life and work as a fit object of study. For many years at Princeton University, I have taught Mann's major novels to undergraduates and graduate specialists in German literature. Now, in the perspective of my own experience, I want to describe something of general importance in Mann's past and even recent reception. I am concerned with "was bleibt!"—with what can be remembered of Mann's work and personality in Princeton today.

Caveat: A Very Personal Addendum

In spring 1966, as I was writing my doctoral dissertation in Zurich, I received a telegram offering me the position of assistant professor of German at Princeton, contingent on my finishing my doctoral thesis. It was signed by Victor Lange, the Chair of the Department of Germanic Languages and Literatures—now, with good ecology, called simply: the Department of German. I was thrilled to accept.

I arrived in Princeton on a Sunday afternoon in late August 1966 and found my way to a neo-Gothic building and up the marble steps to the Department Office. I knocked at the lit-up door, where I was asked in by a handsome, smiling man, who was taking handfuls of books down from a high shelf behind his desk. He was preparing to give a talk, it emerged, on Goethe at the Aspen Institute in Colorado. He greeted me in wonderful, accented English: "Aha, you're Mr. Corngold. I was about to leave, but now I have the good luck of meeting you. Come with me. I'll show you to your office." He led me down the corridor to the far end and opened the door to a small, beautifully shaped room with a gleaming oak floor, an octagonal ceiling of dark, sumptuous wood, and high leaded-glass windows. "I've saved this room for you," he said, and, beckoning toward the window, added, "I thought *you* might enjoy the view on the piazza." I looked out onto a stone square in front of another huge Gothic building, very likely the library. I glanced at my chairman: he looked a bit like Goethe and also a bit like my father.

The gentleman was Victor Lange, who taught a course titled, fittingly, "The Romantic Quest." He soon explained to me that although I'd been hired as a lecturer in German (my thesis being unfinished), with a specialty in comparative literature, I would have to bide my time. Princeton did not yet have a program of comparative literature, so I would be asked, like every other professor in the department, to earn my living by teaching what he called "Sauerkraut"—basic German. But there would be the opportunity to "precept" in "The Romantic Quest"—I would lead one of the discussion groups run on the "Socratic model." The idea would be never to impart information to a preceptee but rather *elicit* it, to coax it out of his mesoplasm (Princeton was still an all-boys school) in subtle, ingenious ways—a remarkable feat, indeed, when the information was under no circumstances to be found there.

Victor Lange was to tell me that it had not been easy to get faculty approval for "The Romantic Quest," since it had originated in the *German* Department; and, although bookended by Goethe's *Faust* and Thomas Mann's *Doctor Faustus,* it also included such titles as *Don Juan, The Charterhouse of Parma, Père Goriot, The Sentimental Education,* and *Notes from Underground.* There were territorial incursions involved. In fact, this initial assault on departmental integrity was not going to pass unnoticed. On one occasion, Lange continued, a distinguished and elderly professor of English, Willard Thorp, had waved across campus to him and, referring to the faculty's agitated discussion that day, confided, "Victor! I'm about to introduce a new course in the English Department: The Modern Lyric. And it's going to include 'Wilkie'!" He had in mind the German poet Rainer Maria Rilke. And so, the gist of it all—I would be "precepting" in a course including *Faust* and Thomas Mann's *Doctor Faustus!*

Mann conjured that portal to intellectual life that I, like so many, have passed through: it can be a single great book. For many young readers of my generation, which takes us back to the middle of the last century, it was Thomas Mann who waited at the gate to take us in, our Virgil. His book? *The Magic Mountain.* And so, my encounter with Thomas Mann begins long before my setting out to write this book, long before a half-century of teaching Mann's novels at Princeton. Like many a teenager, in summer, as a high school student, I had lain on a couch and devoured *The Magic Mountain*, Mann's best-known work.

In a fine study, *Thomas Mann, der Amerikaner*, Hans Rudolf Vaget relates with a certain awe a feat attributed to the late, ineffably brilliant critic Susan Sontag. He considers the fact that she actually read *The Magic Mountain* while still a teenager to be a sign of her remarkable precociousness, her burgeoning genius.[18] In fact, the feat of reading and loving *The Magic Mountain* as a teenager was not rare in America in the 1950s and certainly not—alas!—an unambiguous sign of personal genius.

On the brink of our going to college, fascinated by Europe, *The Magic Mountain* served many of us as an introduction to European intellectual history and its leading idea of dialectical process. (Since I am talking about myself, I will avoid repeating the mantra "many of us" to make me seem better than I am.) I am thinking particularly of the thrust and counterthrust between Settembrini and Naphta—this latter figure held to be a noble parody of the Jewish-Hungarian Marxist György Lukács (whose memory, at this writing, is being extinguished in Budapest). In his diaries, Mann cited the preceptorial on *The Magic Mountain* that he held for Princeton students one spring evening in 1940: "Today I let myself be tempted to tell the boys that *The Magic Mountain* was prophetic and the present war to some extent the world-political realization of the dialectical quarrels of Naphta and Settembrini."[19]

In college, owing to a disadvantageous chronology, I did not have the luxury of attending a Mann-led preceptorial, but nonetheless I did read Mann's elegant turn-of-the-century stories in German: "The Clown" and "Little Herr Friedemann" and "Tristan," the story that features a standoff between the faint-hearted aesthete Detlev Spinell and the boisterous businessman Anton Klöterjahn; and then, inevitably, *Tonio Kröger*, whose artist hero longs for the qualities—or lack of qualities—of his blond, horse-loving counterpart Hans Hansen. I confess that I—as well as my cohort at *The Columbia Review*, students of the humanities with artistic longings—could not quite parse this war of types. In the American tradition, following Philip Rahv, we were accustomed to refer to our "paleface" authors, before and after Henry James (1843–1916) and Edith Wharton (1862–1937), let us say; and to our "redskins," thinking immediately of Jack London (1876–1916), Stephen Crane (1871–1900), and Ernest Hemingway (1899–1961).[20] We "wild Indians"—as my parents, at any rate, called us—were quick to identify with the latter; and thus we imagined our literary success, before our longings ever approached reality, without the benefit of the dialectic that served Mann so well. (Incidentally, Mann had literally something of the "wild Indian" in him, as his mother was the daughter of a Portuguese woman from Brazil with South American *Indian* blood, described by Mann in his autobiography as "Portuguese-Creole-Brazilian.")

I return to "meine Wenigkeit" ("my humble self") as a graduate student of comparative literature at Cornell. Now, we read very little of Mann there, because my influential teacher, Paul de Man, considered him a bourgeois realist and hence negligible to his deconstructive project, which required "texts" of a higher degree of poetic self-consciousness—or, better, a higher degree of unintelligibility—than Mann's stories and novels allegedly possessed. De Man's dislike of Mann was overdetermined. As a result, an entire wave of young literary theorists from the 1970s did *not* read Thomas Mann, even though he had been canonized as a modernist, along with James Joyce and Marcel Proust, in the years of Professor Harry Levin's famous course on literary modernism at Harvard.[21] More precisely, Mann was canonized at Harvard until ca. 1948. Shortly thereafter, Levin published in *The New York Times* his scathing review of *Doctor Faustus*, finding (reprehensibly) the myth stale and the manner pedantic, whereupon Levin changed the title of his course on literary modernism to Proust, Joyce, and . . . Kafka! Mann, I hasten to add, was very unhappy on hearing this news, despite his personal admiration for Kafka; it is unlikely that his appreciation of Kafka, though it was considerable, went *that far.* In this way, Levin, who was actually de Man's teacher, but no friend of deconstruction, contributed, regrettably, to Mann's general loss of prestige. For him, once more, *Doctor Faustus* was "a portentous commentary" and not "a work of sustained imagination. . . . In contrast to the humanistic insight, the cosmopolitan breadth of Mann's ripest works, this book harks back to his earlier anxieties over the artistic temperament and the Germanic tradition."[22] (These very important earlier anxieties inform Mann's Zurich lecture on Nietzsche's philosophy.) Mann complained stridently to Erich Kahler of Levin's betrayal.

I still intend to requite the loss of an historical consciousness by reviving our cultural memory of Thomas Mann at Princeton.[23] And so, in 1966, some three decades after Mann's arrival in Princeton, I would be acquiring a heightened sense of Mann by helping to keep his memory alive. What a splendid task! In the following years, I would inherit entirely "The Romantic Quest," the course originally conceived by Professor Victor Lange—this charismatic and morally admirable *Grossgermanist* and, I will now add, since I have only recently found out this fact, a well-liked acquaintance of both Thomas Mann and, especially, of Erich Kahler. (When, in former times, Lange had been chair of the

Department of German Literature at Cornell University, he had appointed Kahler a professor of German literature, and, moreover, had been encouraged by Kahler to recommend *his* friend Hermann Broch for a Nobel Prize.)[24] It was this very Professor Lange who organized the setting of the stone tablet in the brick wall at the front of the house on 65 Stockton Street, in which Mann lived. It was placed there in 1964—that is, nine years after Mann's death—and reads, simply, "THOMAS MANN LIVED HERE 1938–1941."[25] "At its dedication, [Professor] Lange . . . expressed the hope," one reads in Alexander Leitch's *A Princeton Companion*, "that as 'a lasting reminder of Thomas Mann's presence in Princeton,'" this tablet "might 'strengthen the spirit of courageous humanism among us and reaffirm the vision of a community of free men to which his life and work bore such eloquent testimony.'"[26]

In 1975, the Princeton Library commemorated the centenary of Thomas Mann's birth by putting memorabilia on display. It included letters exchanged with Kahler, who—when he was some eighty years old and finally invited to lecture to a larger audience at the university—was introduced by classics professor Robert Fagles as "a one-man youth movement." In one such letter, Mann, thinking of the bumbling petty bureaucrats he'd encountered at a local post office in Pacific Palisades, wondered how it had ever been possible for "us" to win the war (Mann became an American citizen in 1944). Kahler was really the one intimate friend in Mann's distinguished circle at Princeton: the other members were respected acquaintances and at best good neighbors. More than the others, Mann saw something of the eminent novelist, critic, and philosopher Hermann Broch, who, along with Mann's son Klaus and the composer Roger Sessions, was chosen as one of the main witnesses to the marriage in Princeton, on November 23, 1939, of Mann's daughter Elisabeth ("Medi") to the much older but very well-preserved Giuseppe Antonio Borgese.

At Princeton, Mann also exchanged infrequent visits with Albert Einstein, who did, however, prefer conversations with the less, shall we say, venerable Heinrich Mann and, above all, with the mathematician Kurt Gödel. With Mann's increasing admiration for Kafka (Kafka greatly admired Mann's work as well), it is reported that Mann was moved to give a copy of Kafka's *The Castle* (*Das Schloß*) to Einstein to read, which Einstein returned not too many days later, remarking, it is alleged, "I couldn't read it for its perversity; the human mind isn't complicated enough."[27] There are detailed reasons to disbelieve this story, *ma se non è vero, è ben trovato.*

At the Princeton exhibit one saw what at first seemed a trivial curiosity, a library card with Thomas Mann's signature on it. He had taken out a scholarly work on ancient Egypt. As Victor Lange told me, in those days, in order to borrow a library book, you needed to write your name in a card in a little pocket at the back of the book. When Thomas Mann, recognizable, with his erect and patrician air, stood at the counter, signing out his books, others gathered round to glimpse their titles. As a result, a month later, when these books had been returned to their shelves, the observers could find cards on which Thomas Mann has written his name. This situation prompted Katia Mann to declare, allegedly, "Tommy, you are cheapening the value of your signature!" Thereafter, she arranged to have some nonentity borrow books for Tommy. To commemorate this exhibition, Lange, the late Theodore Ziolkowski, and I collaborated on a short book with the following chapters: "Thomas Mann the Novelist" (Lange); "Thomas Mann and the German Philosophical Tradition" (Corngold); "Thomas Mann as a Critic of Germany" (Ziolkowski); "Thomas Mann and the Émigré Intellectuals" (Ziolkowski); "Thomas Mann in Exile" (Lange); and "The Mann Family" (Corngold).[28]

I have remarked that I taught *Doctor Faustus* a dozen times; *pace* Harry Levin, students were mostly entranced. Of course, when many foreign students—Asian students foremost—began arriving at Princeton, especially in the 'nineties, and having been instructed by their parents that it would be sensible to take at least one course in Western culture, my "Romantic Quest" began to be frequented by students with very little background knowledge of the world of Thomas Mann, Serenus Zeitblom, and Adrian Leverkühn. So, when at the outset, I sketched out the trajectory of the course, saying that in *Doctor Faustus* students would encounter an artist who intended to *take back* Beethoven's Ninth Symphony (on account of its "Ode to Joy" and its appeal to "Universal Brotherhood"), one intense Chinese American student, as I recall, looked at me, with panic in his eyes, and wondered, "Is *that* going to be on the midterm—this *taking back* of—what was it—'Beethoven's Ninth'"? But imagine how many of us might have reacted being asked, on the first day of our introduction to the history of Chinese literature, to anticipate Kao Hsing-chien's *taking back* the work of Chao Shu-li—a genuine event in that history.

Mann, I want to stress, is very much alive at Princeton, even as I write; our advanced graduate students of *German* now read Thomas Mann, invariably concentrating on *Der Zauberberg* (*The Magic Mountain*) and again on *Doktor Faustus,* partly for their paraphrasable content—a history of ideas (grounds for such critics as Vladimir Nabokov to consider them not novels at all). Just last year, a *first-year* graduate student in our Department of Comparative Literature, a Mann enthusiast, organized, along with Professor Michael Wood, an expert, a graduate seminar devoted to Mann. At this moment, even in retirement, I am supervising the senior thesis of a Chinese American student of comparative literature on *Doctor Faustus* and selected works of Yukio Mishima, also an ascetic artist, a self-tormentor.[29] Teachers and students at Princeton, otherwise barely aware of Thomas Mann, have recently grasped from the work of elite journalists the timeliness of Mann's battle for democratic values; and they are reading his essays and his formidable novels of ideas, two of them—*Lotte in Weimar* (*The Beloved Returns*) and *Joseph the Provider*—products of his Princeton exile. In a recently published family memoir, writer Alexander Wolff—Princeton class of '79 and afterwards, Ferris Professor of Journalism—reprints a scintillating review of *Lotte in Weimar* written on December 9, 1939, for *Die Zukunft*, a Paris-based German exile newspaper. The author? Alexander's grandfather, the urbane publisher Kurt Wolff:

> Written on the shores of Lake Zurich and in southern France, in the cabin of an ocean liner and in an American college town, excerpted in a Swiss magazine, printed in Holland, graced with cover art by an illustrator from Prague, published (by Bermann-Fischer) in Stockholm—can the story of a book possibly be any more "far-flung," any more grotesque a reflection of the diaspora of German intellectual life in our time? Yet no work by Thomas Mann is less distended than this, none more collected, more dense, or imposing, and we bow in awe before the moral achievement of this writer, who in times like these has created a work that so supremely captures the era. For *Lotte in Weimar* is a book of the highest relevance, a book that stands as a radiant and persuasive monument to the German genius, a book to tell the world of the stakes that Europe fights for today.[30]

Indeed, it speaks of the stakes that we are all fighting for today. The review was headed *Habent sua fata libelli* (Books have their destiny). How *timely*!

ABBREVIATIONS FOR MANN CITATIONS

B   *Thomas Mann: "On Myself" and Other Princeton Lectures: An Annotated Edition Based on Mann's Lecture Typescripts*, ed. James N. Bade. Frankfurt am Main: Peter Lang, 1996.

BR.H   *Letters of Heinrich and Thomas Mann, 1900–1949*, ed. Hans Wysling, tr. Don Reneau, with additional translations by Richard and Clara Winston. Berkeley, CA: University of California Press, 1998.

BR.M   *Thomas Mann und Agnes Meyer: Briefwechsel 1937–1955*, ed. Hans Rudolf Vaget. Frankfurt am Main: S. Fischer, 1992.

C   *The City of Man: A Declaration on World Democracy*. New York: Viking Press, 1940.

D   *Thomas Mann Diaries 1918–1939*, tr. Richard and Clara Winston. New York: Harry N. Abrams, 1982.

E   *Essays*, ed. Hermann Kurzke and Stephan Stachorski. 6 vols. Frankfurt am Main: S. Fischer, 1993–97 (volume and page numbers are indicated in Arabic numerals).

EF   *An Exceptional Friendship: The Correspondence of Erich Kahler and Thomas Mann*, tr. Richard and Clara Winston. Ithaca, NY: Cornell University Press, 1975.

GKFA   Thomas Mann, *Große kommentierte Frankfurter Ausgabe—Werke, Briefe, Tagebücher*, ed. Heinrich Detering, Eckhard Heftrich, Hermann Kurzke, Terence J. Reed, Thomas Sprecher, Hans Rudolf Vaget, and Ruprecht Wimmer in collaboration with the Thomas-Mann-Archiv of the ETH, Zurich. 17 vols. Frankfurt am Main: S. Fischer, 2002– (volume and page numbers are indicated in Arabic numerals).

GW   Thomas Mann, *Gesammelte Werke in dreizehn Bänden*, ed. Peter de Mendelssohn. 13 vols. Frankfurt am Main: S. Fischer, 1974 (volume and page numbers are indicated in Arabic numerals).

H   Klaus Harpprecht, *Thomas Mann: Eine Biographie*. Reinbek bei Hamburg: Rowohlt, 1995.

L   *The Letters of Thomas Mann, 1889–1955* [a selection], tr. Richard and Clara Winston. New York: Knopf, 1970.

LW   *Lotte in Weimar, Roman*, ed. Werner Frizen. GKFA 9.1. Frankfurt am Main: S. Fischer, 2003.

LWA   *The Beloved Returns: Lotte in Weimar*, tr. H. T. Lowe-Porter. New York: Knopf, 1940.

N   *The Letters of Thomas Mann to Caroline Newton*. Princeton, NJ: Princeton University Press, 1971.

T3   Thomas Mann, *Tagebücher 1937–1939*, ed. Peter de Mendelssohn. Frankfurt am Main: S. Fischer, 1980.

T4 Thomas Mann, *Tagebücher 1940–1943,* ed. Peter de Mendelssohn. Frankfurt am Main: S. Fischer, 1982.

TB Tobias Boes, *Thomas Mann's War: Literature, Politics, and the World Republic of Letters.* Ithaca, NY: Cornell University Press, 2019.

VA Hans Rudolf Vaget, *Thomas Mann, der Amerikaner. Leben und Werk im amerikanischen Exil 1938–1951.* Frankfurt am Main: S. Fischer, 2011.

V Hans Rudolf Vaget, "'The Best of Worlds,' Thomas Mann in Princeton." *The Princeton University Library Chronicle* 75, no. 1 (Autumn 2013): 9–37.

THE MIND IN EXILE

1

Thomas Mann in Princeton, 1938–41

A MAN OF QUALITIES

Yes, the homeless one has found a home. A new home in Princeton, in America. His gratitude is great. And since the desire to give is inseparable from such abundant taking, I shall pray my good genius that my gratitude may bear fruit.

—THOMAS MANN

Precisely when everything has assumed such vile form, an international sphere of freedom and the intellect will take shape, a private circle of betters who will always assure us a vital setting for our thoughts and works.

—THOMAS MANN

DURING THE FIRST TWO AND A HALF YEARS of his American exile, from September 28, 1938, to March 17, 1941, Thomas Mann lived with his wife and several of his six children in a spacious Georgian house at 65 Stockton Street in Princeton, New Jersey.[1] His feelings about his new home changed in different seasons. The first winter of his exile had its share of disturbances in the form of illness and public criticism;[2] and so, in summer 1939, Mann set sail for Europe, meaning to reinvigorate himself at a seaside resort in Holland and finish writing his novel *Lotte in Weimar* (*The Beloved Returns*). But as the political climate darkened, in September, on his return to Princeton, on board the SS *Washington* en route from Southampton to New York, he wrote in his diary, "It will be a good thing to follow—and await—the unforeseeable development of the war, its vicissitudes and terrors, in my Princeton library" (T3 472). Six months later, in Princeton, on March 24, 1940, having had his fill of joyless days—weary and often in pain, depressed by nasty weather—Mann exclaimed in his diary, "Princeton bores me" (T4 49). But on the first of May 1940, still in Princeton, having slept well and woken to a sunny day, he noted briefly, but with feeling, "The beauty of blossoms. Magnolias" (T4 68). Finally, a year later, on the first of June, 1941, after leaving Princeton for Pacific Palisades, California, Mann declared in a letter to Erich Kahler, "In this, my favorite season of the year, it is lovely here, although I liked it better in Küsnacht [on Lake Zurich] and even in Princeton" (EF 53).[3] In this sequence of brief epiphanies, we have a picture of Mann's Princeton experience in the years 1938– 41—a wave motion of moods of anguish, contentment, and monotony.[4]

Before settling in Princeton, having arrived in spring 1938 in New York from his home in Switzerland, Mann set out on a cross-country trip, delivering vigorous antifascist speeches in twenty-three cities.[5] His talks in defense of democracy were extraordinarily popular: a feature article in *Life* magazine includes a photograph of some of the more than 2,000 members of the audience in Tulsa, Oklahoma, who "jammed Akdar Theatre, a former Shrine Temple, to hear him speak for an hour on *The Coming Victory of Democracy.*" That evening, March 18, 1938, Mann noted in his diaries that he had "spoken with liveliness and with no mistakes, [to] the greatest attentiveness and with great applause" (T3 192). But two nights later, in a less exalted mood—having absorbed the "tension and panic" in Europe following Hitler's annexation of Austria (T3 190)—he concluded that "whether war comes or not, it seems increasingly *in*advisable for us to return to Switzerland. If things continue as they are, the monster will soon stop at nothing" (D 295). To leave America, which had been so hospitable, for Switzerland, would be to risk assassination by Nazi agents. There were precedents for such murders.

In fact, the idea of an American immigration was not entirely new. The prospect of a convenient stay in Princeton had already been put into Mann's mind by his determined patroness Agnes E. Meyer, of whom Mann declared himself the *protégé*; and so "it was both developments, the deterioration of the general situation in Europe as well as the prospect of Princeton as a future residence, that ultimately decided Mann to settle in America" (BR.M 39).[6]

On May 5, 1938, Thomas and his wife Katia began the immigration formalities. Since all applications had to come from outside the country, they took the night train from Cleveland to Toronto in order to visit the American consulate the following day. Their move was eased throughout by the moral and financial support of Mrs. Meyer, an influential woman active in Republican politics, and her wealthy husband, Eugene Meyer, publisher of *The Washington Post*. Though Mann's speeches had been well paid, and he received good royalties, Agnes Meyer undertook to find the gainful employment for him that he and his large family needed. She negotiated on his behalf with Harvard University and floated the idea of residence in Boston—she wanted him at all costs on the East Coast, within visiting distance—but the offer never came.[7] Meanwhile, Princeton had become an inviting prospect, and, owing once again to Meyer's mediation, Mann received and accepted a Lectureship in the Humanities at the university. Meyer then won a substantial one-year's grant for him from the Rockefeller Foundation to support the appointment (B 9).[8] On May 26, 1938, Mann wrote to Kahler his pleasure at his good luck:

> My trip from East to West . . . has shown me how much trust, sympathy, and friendship are given us here. . . . For the autumn I am making an arrangement with Princeton for a kind of honorary professorship that will not impose an excessive burden upon me and will provide a basic livelihood. . . . The place has the advantage of being rural, with very good connections to New York. (EF 18–19)

At the end of September, Mann moved into his Princeton villa and immediately began to prepare to deliver his first lecture at the university, eight weeks later, on Goethe's *Faust*. His choice of Princeton, at that point a small, "dignified" city choked with trees,[9] would confirm him in his preferences: as he wrote to Kahler the following year from his beach chair in a Dutch spa, "I have always appreciated the connection of the elemental and the comfortable" (EF 20).

His pleasure in the place emerges in the course of his urging Kahler to settle in Princeton.

> The happiest news I gathered was your growing resolution to come over here. Do so! What's the sense of staying now? And how fine it would be to live as neighbors. Our house . . . is very comfortable and an improvement over all those of the past. I think it important always to fall upstairs. The people are well meaning through and through, filled with what seems to me an unshakable affability. You would breathe easier among them, would be touched and happy. The landscape is park-like, well suited to walks, with amazingly beautiful trees which now, in Indian summer, glow in the most magnificent colors. At night, to be sure, we already hear the leaves trickling down like rain, but people say that the clear, serene autumn often continues until nearly Christmas, and the winter is short. (EF 21)

Mann was ready to call a halt to his travels and—in anticipatory good spirits—
to settle in.

But fully settling in proved impossible. The very day after his arrival, on hearing news of the Munich Agreement between Hitler and Neville Chamberlain,
he was struck by moods of outrage and depression.[10] "This entire 'peace,'" he
wrote, "is surely a rotten lie (*eine gemeine Lüge*)—and [the profit] of it [is] the
monstrous strengthening of Germany, a crushing blow to the democratic idea."
His depression even made him afraid of his new life (T3 301, 303). But there
would be no question of his cutting himself off from the European crisis for
the sake of an artificial serenity. The crisis was forced by Germany—his once
beloved country, in which he has the deepest imaginable roots.

And yet, at the same time, he could not respond with the same intensity to
every outrage—nor did he want to. He was foremost the author of great novels
and immersed in the writing of two more—*Lotte in Weimar* and *Joseph and His
Brothers*—eager to complete both projects, writing them in German to maintain his *Deutschtum* ("Germanness"). "The next few chapters [of the final volume, *Joseph the Provider* (*Joseph, der Ernährer*)] must progress rapidly at
Princeton," he wrote, stressing the Apollonian side of the writing mania: "The
worldly adventures that come may not disturb their calm and their cheerfulness" (T4 185). At another time, we hear of the rather Dionysian side of the
writing drive: "*Excitation*. When will this tricky, life-annoying and life- and
art-related demonism expire? Probably not until the very end . . ." (T4 199).[11]
As Hans Rudolf Vaget observes: "The consciousness of being 'a German writer
and servant of the German language' was and always remained the deepest
root of his exile-existence."[12] His greatest concern, announced on the very first
day of his arrival in Princeton in a letter to Agnes Meyer, was that of "a German
writer" who, despite the sympathy and trust he was receiving as an exile in
America, cries out: "Where will my primordial German language (*mein ur-
sprüngliches deutsches Wort*) still be heard?" (BR.M 133).[13] Some months later,
in writing to her, he described his endless obligations (and honors): "Next year
I am going to have cards printed, with the resistant message: 'I am a writer
(*Dichter*) and I have to write (*dichten*)'" (BR.M 159).

As a result, expressions of his indignation at the Nazi horrors were necessarily selective, and not every visitor to Princeton was content with this
triage. His muted response to what is reprehensibly called "Reichskristallnacht," which he termed a merely temporary aberration in the great history
of Germany—or, rather, Germanness—dismayed one scholar, Professor Sol
Liptzin, who had visited Mann precisely in order to be encouraged by his reaction. On the other hand, Mann's diary for that day does plainly reveal his

dismay, and so his visitor's disappointment might be traced to Mann's prudence and patrician—not quite American—reserve.[14] And it should be added that on other occasions, he denounced anti-Semitism everywhere, as he did with persuasive fury in a March 3, 1940, radio broadcast titled "The Dangers Facing Democracy," sponsored by the United Jewish Appeal for Refugees and Overseas Needs, when he named by name the Nazi extermination of the Jewish people in Eastern Europe (T4 709).[15]

On his arrival in Princeton in 1938, Mann was sixty-three years old. In 1933, after the Nazi seizure of power, being abroad in Switzerland, he chose not to return to his once beloved country. The new regime saw him as its ideological enemy: in the years following the First World War, Mann made a number of public speeches critical of fascist values. His opponents recalled his former support for a war in 1914 on behalf of a uniquely precious German *Kultur*; they could not tolerate his reversal, a defense of Anglo-Saxon and European values enshrined in a democratic Weimar Republic. His change of heart turned heads—hotheads.

His first arguments were addressed to so-called conservative-national ideologues, as in his pivotal address on October 13, 1922, on "The German Republic," which harvested the values of romanticism (Novalis), vitalism (Nietzsche), aestheticism (Stefan George), and homoeroticism (Walt Whitman) as political supports.[16] In the following years of great danger, he spoke directly to the Nazis, in 1930 bravely outfacing an audience of Nazi thugs with "An Appeal to Reason," which identified and repudiated the fanaticism of the movement. On February 13, 1933, barely two weeks after the Nazis' seizure of power, at the admitted risk of being misunderstood, he discussed the work of the conservative cultural hero Richard Wagner as an "amalgam of dilettante accomplishments." Indeed, the caveat merely provoked an outraged Nazi press.[17] With this intervention, he would become persona non grata with the Reich.

In 1936, the Nazis stripped Mann of his German citizenship, condemning him to permanent exile (and probably with the risk of being murdered if he made a clandestine return). Soon afterwards, he received a letter from the dean of the Faculty of Philosophy at the University of Bonn, informing him that in light of his expulsion from Germany, his honorary doctorate from that university would also be revoked. In a memorable, widely circulated reply, which he composed on New Year's Day, 1937, Mann wrote: "I could never have dreamed, it could never have been prophesied of me at my cradle, that I should spend my later years as an émigré—expropriated, outlawed, and committed to inevitable political protest. . . . I was born to be a representative and not a martyr."[18] It is a tribute to an extraordinary strength of character that he never thereafter relented in his sense of the importance of his life's work as author and *citizen* in the face of the unspeakably vile attacks on him that now flowed from the sewers of Nazi agitprop, chief among the hacks one Ernst Krieck.[19] (Mann wanted him punished after the war.) Even in Switzerland, Mann had reason to fear for his life, despite his aery denial, on August 6, 1938, while inviting his brother Heinrich to Küsnacht: "I have never felt endangered here for as much as a moment" (BR.H 216). His friend, admirer, and gift-giver, the American psychiatrist Caroline Newton, reports that other attentive personalities thought differently. In the late winter of 1937, she was asked by Christian Gauss, then dean of the College at Princeton, whether she knew Thomas Mann. "'Why does it matter?' I asked. 'It matters damnably,' he said forcefully. 'His life is not safe in Switzerland. The Nazis will murder him, stage an automobile accident or send over some poisoned food'" (N 4).[20] By the spring of the following year, Mann had evidently come around to Gauss's view, writing to Agnes Meyer, "Quite apart from [my] emotional (*psychisch*) resistance, Switzerland would not even offer me physical security" (BR.M 115–16). There would be the rumor of lethal danger even in the short flights across Europe he took during the summer of 1939: it was said to be unwise to occupy a window seat, since German warplanes had been seen "looking into" passenger planes with the intention of shooting passengers if they had been identified as serious opponents of the Reich (H 1112).

At Princeton, as eager as Mann was to continue writing *Lotte in Weimar*— but obliged by his "honorary professorship" to compose important lectures for the university and conduct "preceptorials" for the "boys"—his insistent moral sense required him to speak out, to the point of alleged exhaustion, against the horrors in Europe. A diary note on Saturday, November 19, 1938, reports "Poor appetite, tendency to nausea." (His hypochondria, as more than one observer has noted, helped assure him a long, productive life.) But he continues in a major key: "Stronger mental state today, serious and willing to speak powerfully (*eine große Sprache zu reden*) in the name of the moral world and to strike a blow against the vermin" (T3 323). It had never been his intention to practice what the psychoanalyst Jacques Lacan calls "une politique de l'autruiche"(French: "ostrich" = "autruche"; "Austria" = "L'Autriche").[21] The pun is timely: in his letter to Kahler of May 26, 1938, Mann had registered

the shock of the crime against Austria, [which] was severe; the parallel with 1933 forced itself upon us; we felt it as a "seizure of power" on the continental scale, and again we had the sensation of being cut off, as in 1933. All this may prove to be exaggerated or premature. Nevertheless, we cannot regret our decision and our act of "immigration"; there are too many good reasons, in Europe and here, for making this country our residence at least for a time, although we shall keep in touch with the old continent as much as possible. (EF 18)

Mann then mentions the warm reception his book *Joseph in Egypt* had received in the United States—with this book he had completed the first three volumes of the tetralogy and would brood about and then begin the fourth in Princeton—and stresses again the friendship he had experienced in traveling across the country. "Friendship" is a key word in his moral vocabulary; it abounds throughout the pages of his fiction and polemics; it may be the highest good. He wrote, "If I have a wish for the posthumous fame of my work, it is this: that it would be said of it: it is life's friend although it is aware of death."[22]

There is a touching irony in this statement. Friendship was not Mann's strongest suit: his "few friends," wrote Janet Flanner, in a notorious *New Yorker* profile, "[are] less numerous than the members of his own large family."[23] Aside from Erich Kahler, Mann's diaries suggest that he and Einstein were "good friends," a claim that all scholarly commentators hitherto have repeated. But that is merely wishful thinking. Peter de Mendelssohn, the devoted editor of Mann's diaries, has found *le mot juste*: their relation was little more than "freundnachbarlich," good-neighborly (T3 701).[24] When Mann speaks of "new pleasures of love and [a renewed] zest for life," he has in mind not new human acquaintances but rather the gift from Caroline Newton of "the delicate poodle (with the unexpected name *Gueulard* = 'Big Mouth' or 'Glutton') and the prospective first-class musical apparatus" (T3 494, 496). The poodle, a standard black—soon to be miniaturized and Germanized with the name Niko—will replace all others for a time as the central figure in Mann's diaries (T3 495).[25] No one else, with the possible exception of Katia Mann, is mentioned so consistently. When the poodle, "gone wild and confused," runs away, Mann is devastated, and when Niko returns, "although in a muddied state," his master is overjoyed.[26]

A delicate drama unfolds: will the poodle be allowed into Mann's study, mornings, like Faust's, when Faust is engaged in translating the New Testament and when the poodle will be unmasked as Mephistopheles?[27] True, on the very afternoon of Niko's arrival—a "mute, shy, noble creature"—the poodle is allowed to sit at Mann's feet while he is at work; but the work is only of a secondary kind, as Mann takes notes for his Princeton lecture on Goethe's

Werther (T3 494). And so, Mann's poodle does sit beside young Goethe's other proxy—not Faust but Werther—but he does not growl, and he is not unmasked as a hellhound. Before too long the poodle is invited into Mann's study even during the sacred morning hours of Mann's devotions, though here Mann is still at work on his *Werther* lecture and not yet on his new Indian novella *The Transposed Heads* (T3 495).

In those days, he had been giving "much thought to *The Transposed Heads* and its whimsical (*wunderlich*) possibilities." Writing on January 28, 1940, seated in the New York Pennsylvania Station (!), Mann noted this

> first approach to the French-surrealistic sphere (Cocteau), to which I had long been drawn. A reading like "Eheglück" [Tolstoy's "Family Happiness"] in its realistic and moral seriousness of course does not encourage it. [One] feels the gap between this healthy-serious sphere and frolicsomeness and fantasy, which is much more afflicted (*leidend*, also "ailing") than that naturalism. The attempt is to be continued. (T4 16)

It might now be a delicate decision for Mann to risk the effect of the (*French*) poodle—*Gueulard*—on his new form of imaginative writing; or would precisely its "whimsical" way of being serve as an inspiration? We will have to wait until August 18, 1940, during Mann's summer holiday in Brentwood, Los Angeles, to hear the phrase, "Niko as a roommate" (T4 134).

Meanwhile, Mann would have to suffer the knowledge that pet love never did run smooth, and so we have him writing at some length about a "disagreeable quarrel about his disobedience following the discovery of disagreeable things." Whereupon Mann catches himself and writes of his "resolve, no longer to worry about such things" (T4 5). (He does literally "worry" about that other addition to a zest for life—"the overloud bass-resonance of the new gramophone" [T3 502].[28]) But this is not to say that his concern for Niko will vanish entirely: he will worry when the poodle shows signs of being ill and will be relieved when the creature is well. And he will suffer again when Niko is attacked by Erwin Panofsky's "nasty poodle" (T4 5), although Niko himself is not altogether without a malicious bone in his body, for, as Mann reports, he will not be allowed to spend the night in the library, since, "as recently when we were in New York, he chewed up a philosophical work by Ernst Cassirer" (N 69).[29] There is an entire engaging short story buried in these diaries and letters, inviting the title "Herr Mann und Hund."

In Princeton, Mann craved order and seclusion—the conditions of his continuing literary production—but these were wishes out of season. His time in

Princeton is charged with constant changes and portents of change. Europe is in convulsion, a product of Hitler's territorial aggressions, which Mann registers daily in his diaries. On October 8, 1938, a week after settling in, he recorded "the ghastly news of the deportation to Germany of the German émigrés in Prague. . . . [I am] confused, distracted, depressed, and revolted by the course of events in Europe, worried about America, weary" (T3 307). He had to be especially disturbed by the news as both a German émigré and a *Czech citizen*. He phoned the news to Einstein, who had once lived and taught in Prague and was now in Princeton, at 112 Mercer Street, a mere few city blocks away. In his diary Mann took rare note of Einstein's admission that "never before in his life had he been so unhappy" (T3 303).

When we follow the days of Mann's life, we watch feelings of grief and sympathy crystallize into action. Despite complaints of ill health and the overwhelming demands for help made on him, he could rely on reserves of energy and devotion to the good cause. The "good cause" was actually two, demanding two different kinds of support: one, practical, moral, aiming to shore up democratic ideals of friendship and justice against the barbarism of the times; the other, being, in words reported by Ernst Lothar, by means of his *novelistic* writing, "to wash off the stain that had sullied the German Geist."[30]

And so, soon after his telephone conversation with Einstein, he wrote a detailed, precise, and heartfelt plea to Cordell Hull, the Secretary of State, asking Hull for his intervention in a tragic knot that was entailing heartbreak and anxiety. Mann pleads for aid on behalf of the German émigré intellectuals in Czechoslovakia whose lives were now in danger and who had turned for help to members of the Thomas Mann Society in Prague. There was an agonizing bureaucratic obstacle blocking émigrés' safe passage to the United States. As Mann wrote to Hull: "The American consul in Prague is certainly only doing his duty when he demands that those concerned present birth certificates and evidence of good character from Germany," since—stated with a certain irony—"under the circumstances [of the Nazi seizure of power], such documents simply cannot be obtained" (L 284).

———

Mann's efforts on behalf of American democracy were for the greatest part appreciated in his adopted country. We will learn about the exceptions in "Contra Thomas Mann the American" in chapter 2. On November 10, 1938, *The New York Times* featured an article with a dramatic headline and subheadlines: "Munich Pact Saved Fascism, Says Mann / So-Called 'Democrats' Acted Deliberately, He Tells Parley of Booksellers / Deplores Curb on Truth / Contrasts Atmosphere of His Native Land with U.S., His Adopted Country":

> Calling the dismemberment of Czechoslovakia a drama "in which European statesmen who still call themselves democrats went consciously and deliberately about to save fascism from its approaching fall," Thomas Mann, Nobel Prize winner and exile from Germany, defined before several thousand persons yesterday what it meant to him to live in a country "where thought and expression are free."
>
> "[There is a general feeling] that the atmosphere of truth is healthier for man's spiritual lungs, and more nourishing to his moral blood structure than an atmosphere of lies," said the German author, who immigrated here recently and is now engaged in a lecture course at Princeton University. . . .
>
> Drawing a parallel between life in America and life in Europe, he found that the fundamental difference was "exactly the difference between the [belief and the disbelief in truth as an inalienable human value]," and that regarding the Munich agreement "truth was subjected to a most careful embargo."

Mann appealed to the nation: "In a desolate and morally leaderless world, may America stand the strong and unswerving protectress of the good and the godlike in man. [May she] do so . . . scorning violence and the lie."[31]

Mann's polemical legacy lives on. Some eighty years later, on December 14, 2017, *The New York Times* published a brief essay by David Brooks titled "The Glory of Democracy." Brooks deplores the degradation of democracy, especially in America, and seeks to reawaken consciousness of its value. He adverts to first principles and writes:

> I'm going to start with Thomas Mann's "The Coming Victory of Democracy." . . . Democracy begins with one great truth, he argued: the infinite dignity of individual men and women. . . . Democracy, Mann continues, is the only system built on respect for the infinite dignity of each individual man and woman, on each person's moral striving for freedom, justice and truth. It would be a great error to think of and teach democracy as a procedural or political system, or as the principle of majority rule. It is a "spiritual and moral possession." It is not just rules; it is a way of life. It encourages everybody to make the best of their capacities—holds that we have a moral

responsibility to do so. It encourages the artist to seek beauty, the neighbor to seek community, the psychologist to seek perception, the scientist to seek truth.[32]

A democracy, which, as its first principle, would encourage "the artist to seek beauty," must allow him to do so and protect him from harm during his "search." Again, and again, Mann, as "one who needs order so very much," sought such protection for his work within the elliptical whirl of events of which he himself was one axial point.[33] The thought that the *German* personality would need to battle forever for stability, for *une assiette ferme*, being uniquely vulnerable to radical change, was scarcely alien to him. In an earlier letter to Mann, Kahler summarized the gist of his important but never quite finished study of the German character in European history, a work that Mann admired:

> With Germanness what is involved is a still fluid type, one which has not yet reached its specific character, which is still in the process of becoming. If, therefore, it is to be grasped as an organic whole, it must be excavated from its historical conditions and supplemented by imaginary possibilities. This dynamic folk cannot be represented in terms of essential traits but rather only in potential traits (*nicht in Wesenszügen, sondern nur in Werdenszügen*). (EF 4)[34]

These "potential traits" might be realized in imaginative writing and bring about a precarious stability to the incessant flow of possibilities. Mann himself noted succinctly in a later diary entry "the complex [character] of the German nature and tradition, which is expressed in my work and gives it its variety" (T4 174).[35] But this variety is not (only) intrinsic to the German "artistic-character" (*Kunstcharakter*) of Mann's literary practice. His political and ideological career is marked by sudden openings and sudden turnabouts, some self-determined and some owed to the force of events.

In due course, and with a certain painful, historical irony, Mann answered Kahler's analysis with a lesson in steadfastness. On October 19, 1938, in the one letter Mann wrote to Kahler while in Princeton (almost all of their discussions were in person), Mann paints a mood darker than the moods in May.

> You can imagine how I have been living; first the disturbing days of uncertainty in Paris, then the week of depression along with the painfully inadequate news aboard ship, then the hours of tense hope after arrival here, culminating in a gigantic mass meeting in Madison Square Garden, at which I spoke and witnessed tremendous demonstrations; then [the]

Munich [Agreement] and the realization at last of the filthy play which was being performed all along. The dénouement came when the "democratic" governments transmitted Hitler's blackmail threats of war to their own people. . . . The shame, the disgust, the shattering of all hopes. For days I was literally sick at heart, and in these circumstances, we had to install ourselves here.

The letter takes a turn.

Now I am over the worst of it, have accepted the facts, whose meaning and logic is only too despicably clear. And now, I am tempted to think by magic, my desk stands in my study with every item arranged on it exactly as in Küsnacht [on Lake Zurich], and even in Munich. I am determined to continue my life and work with maximum persistence, exactly as I have always done, unaltered by events which injure me but cannot humiliate me or turn me from my purposes. The way that history has taken has been so filthy, such a carrion-strewn path of lies and baseness, that no one need be ashamed of refusing to travel along it, even if it should lead to goals we might commend if reached by other paths. (EF 20–21)

Mann might be imagining the ultimate tightening of bonds of decency among nations, the outgrowth of the experience of their common resistance. But that would clearly take decades.

Meanwhile, one is dealing with Hitler and a naively treacherous American press, publishing scurrilous comments on . . . [President Roosevelt] from the Italian and German papers. Impossible situation. Hitler also hand in glove with the Roosevelt opposition. Never against a nation as a whole, but always dividing it, pitting one group against another, subverting it, calling his partisans "the American people," while branding all the others as Jews, Marxists, and warmongers. (T3 318)

How very perceptive of Mann to have detected a tactic evidently valid for demagogues at all times and places.

The current of change that runs through him and his circumstances, resisted by the effort of keeping a semblance of continuity, also shapes his situation in America as something between adaptation and assimilation—until the end, if we may look ahead, when, hounded by J. Edgar Hoover and his vassals as a Communist sympathizer, he left California in 1952 for Switzerland, not wishing to be buried in this now "soulless soil." The effort of assimilation might have gone even further than his assuming American citizenship in 1944 if, of course, Mann had fled Europe sooner and if, of course, he had not been the object of malicious political machinations at the time of America's *chasse aux communistes*. According to Alice Kahler, the second wife of Erich Kahler, Mann's leaving America was owed to

> a tragic story from the McCarthy era. In that witch-hunt, Thomas Mann was accused of signing the so-called Stockholm Peace Petition, which was a Russian venture. At the Thomas Mann exhibition at Rutgers University, which [in 1975] commemorated his hundredth birthday, it was interesting to see where his son Michael showed, enlarged, this petition. I know Thomas Mann's signature very well; it was obvious that this signature had been falsified. Since he did not want to return to Germany, he went back to Switzerland, where the Manns bought the house in Kilchberg. The tragedy was that he no longer felt safe here.[36]

Mann's grandson, Frido Mann, stresses that Mann's flight to Switzerland was not dictated by the prospect of enjoying once again the treasures of spoken German. Not at all! He had been traumatized by the repetition in America of a "politically barbarous situation" comparable with the German situation that had originally forced him from his homeland. "This catastrophic political development [in America] 'finished' him, and that is why he had to leave."[37] Detailed, sinisterly enthralling accounts of Mann's tribulations with the FBI, with Henry Luce, the publisher of *Life* magazine, and with the House Committee on Un-American Activities during his last years in America are accessible to the happy few Germanophone Mann-lovers in two of the best biographies—Hans Rudolf Vaget's *Thomas Mann der Amerikaner* and Klaus Harpprecht's *Thomas Mann: Eine Biographie*.[38]

———

Despite his immersion in the academic and political trials of the day, Mann was steadfast in continuing his life as a writer. At Princeton, Mann completed one novel before beginning two others: he had written the first six chapters of *Lotte* in Switzerland and only then embarked on the difficult seventh chapter, the first appearance of Goethe in propria persona. In his diaries, Mann wonders how this material can best be represented—perhaps as a "monodrama and monologue" (T3 311). In a letter to his brother Heinrich, he remarks: "It would not be a novel at all, but something like a monograph in dialogue, were it not for an element of excitement in the initial conception that seems to have been retained in the execution" (BR.H 232–33). After a serious struggle, he did finally complete this and the subsequent two chapters, writing, on October 26, 1939, "[I] introduced corrections into the finished copy of the final chapter, put the complete manuscript of the novel in order, and laid it aside" (T3 494). He then went on to the Indian novella *The Transposed Heads* (*Die vertauschten Köpfe*) and several "Hauptstücke" ("Principal Parts," even, grandly, "Center-pieces") of the last volume of the *Joseph and His Brothers* tetralogy. Although he wrote the best part of *The Transposed Heads* in Princeton, he would not finish the novella until August 1940, while spending the summer in Brent-wood, California. At this time, he called the novella a "diversion and an inter-mezzo," a quality perhaps dictated by the mood—"the paradisiacal climate"—of the place: "Our house," he wrote, "is charming and looks directly out onto an almost Tuscan hilly landscape. We do not lack good friends and good music, and if one did not constantly have the smell of the fire of world history in one's nostrils, and in one's ears the SOS calls of the dying, life could be pleasant" (N 71–72). It was in the equally paradisiacal Pacific Palisades, Cali-fornia, that, "writing the final lines" on the morning of January 4, 1943, he would complete *Joseph the Provider* and therewith the grand tetralogy *Joseph and His Brothers* (T4 520).

During his years in Princeton, Mann was often away from home, lecturing in New York or at far-flung continental points (Iowa, Texas). He would brood on the value of these many journeys undertaken mainly out of a sense of moral and political responsibility, and regret as well even the time spent writing *The Transposed Heads*:

> Always, between the torments and burdens of this social inevitability, the now pessimistic and incredulous thoughts of the outcome of the political process mingle with the question of the success of the personal life, the problem of mood and resilience for the completion of *Joseph* after the rather redundant novella digression. Travel like this is also a problem: very time consuming, but perhaps necessary to escape the monotony. (T4 36–37)

"Monotony"? But he has his literary work to do—his intensely imaginative writing—every morning—*without fail*, true—but that has always been his practice, and it is almost always rewarding, both in the doing of it and the reso-nance it will have. After lunch, usually in distinguished company, Mann can read the countless letters and essays about his work and personality that with few exceptions are laudatory at the highest pitch. His many public appearances are, at least in his view, resoundingly successful; and there is the endless stream of visitors of distinction and family and local friends to entertain him at every single meal and tea. Add to this steady encouragement and recognition, he has the company of Niko, the poodle, to spell the gloom—Niko, whom, when Mann travels, he "longs to see . . . again," "of whom I even dream about at night." (T4 37).

And so, is the charge of monotony proof of Mann's distinctively Faustian—read: insatiable—character (when, even in Brentwood, in Los Angeles, in the summer of 1940, following a dinner party with the Aldous Huxleys and "others," he declared himself "exhausted for tedium") (T4 122)? Or is his tedium proof of the underlying character of Everyman—in Walter Kaufmann's phrase, his "ontological privation"?[39] Among his other acquaintances in California—not quite brilliant or vivid enough to curb his ennui for long—were Charles Boyer (whom he did like very much), Charles Laughton, Lotte Lehmann, Basil Rathbone, and Bruno Walter, among others. This is merely to skim the surface of the celebrities prepared to acknowledge Mann's distinction. Frido Mann adds another ingredient to this mix: he was asked, "Wasn't it his wife Katia and his daughter Erika through whom the *American way of life* first became attractive to him, right up to going to the movies?" Frido Mann replies: "Movie going was something, I think, inborn in him, like visits to the circus, which he liked very much. For that reason too, he wanted to get out of Princeton. Princeton was too boring for him, provincial and half-asleep." There it is, a grandson's view of Mann's case, but I doubt that Frido's gaze covers the full canvas.[40]

On this topic of boredom, not to be dismissed lightly, Mann is himself a privileged commentator—as Martin Heidegger, for one, agreed;[41] and Mann has a quite brilliant thing or two to say about the monotony he did indeed feel, once especially keenly, while struggling to untie a knot in the narration at the beginning of the fourth *Joseph* volume. It is a fine chip from the writer's workbench. In a letter to his patroness—and plague—Agnes Meyer, he remarks,

I am worried about *Joseph*, who now presents me with artistic difficulties. Perhaps it would have been wiser to choose a vague, fabulous Pharaoh instead of Akhenaten, whose figure brings with it the danger of a historical, biographical heavy weighting of the book. The political and the religious aspects are not completely resolved when put into dialogue, scenic display, and indirection. Again, investigative, reportorial, and so to speak instructive interpolations are necessary; and as much as one tries to beware of dryness, poetically it always remains a questionable, vulnerable thing. By the way, as for my scruples, perhaps simply exhaustion and a certain weariness with the old, preserved material are in play. If, however, I think of how Tolstoy got bored with *Anna Karenina*, I may say that my boredom does not necessarily prove that even the reader will be bored. It may even be useful as a compulsion to invent innovative stimulations (*Neuigkeitsreizen*). (BR.M 256)

Here, tedium might itself be a stimulant to the imagination: it is not clear whether that is the lot, at best, of the author or the reader. But boredom is not always so promising. In a letter some weeks later to "Mrs. Agnes," Mann puts his weariness in a drearier light. How does the writer take his way through boredom to excitement? Recall Mann's sense of the Dionysian excitement of writing when it has gripped him. Mann has returned to Princeton with a debilitating cold contracted in the "metropolis"—that is, New York City, where he had seen a liberating *Fidelio*—and has the feeling that he just ought to take to his bed. "Lately I've paid a little too much homage to the principle of 'Despite everything!' and from time to time I'm reminded of Goethe's saying: 'Unconditional activity in the end bankrupts you.' *But how does one begin to be inactive?*"[42] There is no likely interval available—for him!—in which to lodge and draw strength and newness.

———

Mann forever brooded on the looming disturbances to his routine, which is more than a routine: it is a *mythic* devotion to his writing. Distraction is an ongoing worry, not only in the form of his entire world-historical program of lectures and visits and meetings but, of course, by everyday material distractions. His struggle for his writing is worsened by the very imminent departure of the Manns for California, which means, now, in mid-March 1941, the physical tearing apart of their Princeton house. "It lies on my chest like a weight of stone, the homeless, confused weeks ahead, in which one must also hold one's own at lectures and banquets, and the doubt in one's heart whether what one is doing is right and reasonable" (BR.M 259).

But there is still another worry at work: his crushing sense of responsibility—to his art and to his country fighting for its democratic life—that tends to blind him to the suffering he might be inflicting on his family and friends. Precisely at the time of this correspondence, Agnes Meyer alerts him to the pain he can have caused to those especially devoted to him. Mann is moved to answer:

If I already make my friends suffer, what does it mean to be married to me! You have shaken my conscience in respect of my poor wife, who has had to put up with this for thirty-six years. Well, I have weighed down the earth for the longest time, and that's a good thing for me too, because, believe me, I am often thoroughly weary and look with liking to the time when only that portion of me will be there with which I tried to make people happy and "to help them live." (BR.M 259)

This question of taedium vitae to one side—in its manifold areas: poetics, hygiene, family, and the time on earth put in—Mann's decision to move to California was quasi-inevitable: it was already urgent some fifteen months after his arriving in Princeton. The impulse had mythic dimensions, having struck him on his very first visit to California in the spring of 1938. Speaking of California's Pacific coast, he wrote to Agnes Meyer of the "enchantments of this region": "A slight silliness [there] is outweighed by the hundredfold charm of nature and life. Whether we won't settle here one day?" (BR.M 153). California might be the permanent antidote to boredom and, more, be really entertaining (a delusion, as we have seen). "Future settlement plans, California, also the vicinity of Boston [sic], Hollywood, Santa Monica, strongly attract me for the climate, a more cheerful environment, [as a place] to write the fourth Joseph." Princeton had gotten on his nerves. "But the long-distance move, anything new at all, also scares me again" (T4 49). And so, it was Katia, his organizer, "the dragon at the gate," who—despite her grief at leaving Princeton, whose academic ambience suited her, and above all her friend and co-secretary Molly Shenstone—arranged the move.[43]

True, it was under a serene and cheerful Californian sky—"so like that of Egypt"—that, two years after his permanent move, Mann would find the "lust and love" to finish the Joseph tetralogy.[44] It shone on his power of invention. One of the book's more engaging feats is Joseph's economic policy, directly reminiscent of Roosevelt's New Deal. That is not surprising: the extent of Mann's fascination with Roosevelt has become a much-appreciated topic, especially in light of his several meetings with the president, the first on an earlier visit to the United States. On June 29, 1935, shortly after receiving an honorary degree from Harvard, he dined at the White House with the president and Mrs. Roosevelt.[45] Thereafter, he wrote to Kahler about "the very interesting dinner" he had had with them: "The meeting has greatly reinforced my bias in favor of this man" (EF 13). On a more casual note, Mann, the epicure, did take pains to comment in his diary on the dinner itself, which was rather poor.

Mann, let it be known, had a very lively relation to good food and drink: In his diaries the patrician can suddenly seem very human, *un homme* (even a bit more than) *moyen sensual,* as when he mentions dinner with Saul C. Colin, a film director, "in a kosher restaurant on Broadway, with excellent food, then a very funny Marx brothers' film" (what an engaging set of pictures!) (T3 309). Or when he describes taking pleasure in an "uncommonly juicy and tasty dish of mutton with beer in jugs" in a dinner in a private room in a New York restaurant (very likely a privatissimum in the Lincoln Room at Kean's Chophouse) before going to see Robert Sherwood's *Abe Lincoln in Illinois* (T3 352).[46] Then there is lunch with the "Rabbi" in Detroit "in a Russian restaurant: cabbage soup, vol-au-vent, and roast mutton" (probably lamb) and in the evening a "jam-omelet"—and yet he remained forever whippet-slim, an effect no doubt owed to his otherwise ascetic habits and continual smoking of cigarettes and cigars (T3 371).

Despite the mediocre dinner at the White House, Mann's admiration of President Roosevelt never flagged. On November 1, 1940, he

> listened to another, strongly socially focused election speech by Roosevelt, which was greeted with the strongest acclaim. His reelection is of paramount importance for the development of all things. The character of the era makes it unlikely. It would be [for me] the first political joy and satisfaction for seven and a half years. On the other hand, here for once the leader motif and the mass motif come together with the higher and spiritual interest—this could lead to satisfaction and beat Nazism. (T4 173)

Mann once again had the good fortune of staying at the White House on January 13 and 14, 1941.

> Taken by his presence. Lively conversation. The main theme of his inauguration speech: the political-moral point of view before the economic. Story of Litvinov and God. Naivety, faith, cunning, acting, amiability. Considering the power and importance, it is very interesting to sit by his side. (T4 210–11)

His impressions of Roosevelt conveyed to Heinrich Mann two weeks later are vivid and incisive:

> The most interesting episode on the trip I mentioned was a two-day stay at the White House—the three of us, including Erika. The president is decidedly a fascinating man, sunny in the face of his handicap, spoiled, cheerful, and clever, also something of an actor. Nevertheless, he is a man of

profound and unshakable convictions, the born counterpart to the European miscreant, whom he hates as much as we do. He suffered more than a little over not being able to make his views public sooner. To have done so would have put his reelection at risk, which, with complete justice, was his first consideration. (BR.H 243)

The high point of Mann's visit remained "a cocktail with the president in his office." During the entire period of his American exile, Mann felt quite free to send a telegram to Roosevelt to plead for fair treatment of the exile community, who were in danger, during the war, of being declared enemy aliens (L 389–90).[47] If Mann had not had a Czech passport and been treated as a German alien, he would not have been permitted to live on either coast. Mann's empirical attachment to Roosevelt was informed all along by his covert faith *only* in that form of democracy that was headed by a strong, charismatic leader, bound—it goes without saying—to humanistic values, to a belief in the rule of "spirit" (*Geist*).[48]

———

Even during all Mann's travels in his years at Princeton—and despite the "difficulties" they caused him—Princeton was never far from his mind. In Omaha, Nebraska, on a walk with Katia at noon, noting the landscape, he was reminded, presumably happily, of Princeton (L 380). In Paris at the home of his friend the writer Annette Kolb, while champagne and coffee were served, he lounged on her sofa (paint the scene!), reading in the Basel *National-Zeitung* an article by a certain J.W. titled "Bei Thomas Mann in Princeton." Two days later, at the Dutch bathing resort of Noordwijk, he recorded his "agitation and depression at the loss of the key to his Princeton desk," which led to a brief tirade against "Zurich doctors" . . . and "all the rest": it was only after swallowing "the red capsule" that he could sleep (L 421–22). At this point he stresses the strenuous effort to adjust to the climate of the Dutch seashore following the aforementioned "difficulties of Princeton"—presumably *that* labor of climactic adjustment, both literal and symbolic of his transplantation from Europe—which had indeed translated itself into an outbreak of shingles! And as if that thought were unkind, for Princeton is also a place of safety and of one strong friendship, he sets about writing to Kahler, his "dear friend": "It is really time that our thoughts of you . . . were set on paper" (EF 23)—a "beginning" important enough for him to note in his diaries as an event and producing, the

next morning, a rare "relinquishing" of Mann's task as an author, and his favorite beach chair, to finish the letter quite formally at his desk.

Mann attended to a high literary level in writing to Kahler: many of its sentences deserve citation as winged words, as, for example, the lines previously
cited: "I have always appreciated the connection of the elemental and the comfortable" (EF 20). He teases Kahler about something Kahler had "on the tip of
his tongue" to write about the great, difficult chapter 7 of *Lotte in Weimar*—
Goethe's monological stream-of-consciousness—asking Kahler . . . well, to say
it. We will soon be exploring Kahler's canny observation of the secret passage-
ways in which Mann, writing *as Goethe,* had secreted small revelations about
himself, "highly personal statements" (EF 29).[49] Mann's game repeats Goethe's
own enjoyment in playing hide-and-seek with his identity.[50] But here we are
again at the high point of Mann's feelings for Princeton. In the days following
his confession to his diary that "the future is very dark," he declares, "It will be
a good thing to follow—and await—the unforeseeable development of the war,
its vicissitudes and terrors, in my Princeton library" (T3 472).

If I referred earlier to the abundance of trees in Princeton as the "elemental"
factor, in Holland we have a factor evidently more powerful in Mann's imagination: the sea. Mann's feelings about oceans deserve a monograph; the pull of
the waters helped bring him to California. He was explicit about one sort of
feeling he harbored for the sea a half-century earlier in a great set piece in *Buddenbrooks*. Here, the older Thomas Buddenbrooks addresses his sister Tony
while meditating on the kind of (modern) decadent—the artist-type—who,
like Mann himself, prefers the ocean to the mountains:

> What sort of people prefers the monotony of the sea . . . ? It seems to me
> it's those who have gazed too long and too deeply into the complexity at
> the heart of things and so have no choice but to demand one thing from
> external reality: simplicity. It has little to do with boldly scrambling about
> in the mountains, as opposed to lying calmly beside the sea. But I know the
> look in the eyes of people who revere the one [the mountains] or the other
> [the sea]. Happy, confident, defiant eyes, full of enterprise, resolve, and
> courage scan from peak to peak; but when people dreamily watch the wide
> sea and the waves rolling in with mystical and numbing inevitability, there
> is something veiled, forlorn, and knowing about their eyes, as if at some
> point in life they have looked deep into gloomy chaos. Health or sickness—
> that is the difference. A man climbs jauntily up into the wonderful variety
> of jagged, towering, fissured forms to test his vital energies, because he has

never had to spend them. But a man chooses to rest beside the wide simplicity of external things, because he is weary from the chaos within.[51]

That is one sort of the seductiveness he felt coming from the sea—one of endless variations. In spring 1938, months before his move to Princeton, while
staying at Caroline Newton's summerhouse in Jamestown, Rhode Island, he
registered "the extraordinarily stimulating and exciting effect on the senses of
the sea air," "an aphrodisiac, especially in damp weather" (H 1010).

On March 17, 1941, Mann left Princeton for Pacific Palisades—*and* the
Pacific Ocean. The motive for his leaving Princeton was overdetermined—
the reasons are confidently described in his diaries and letters. Foremost is
the distraction of lecturing and teaching at the university, for which, at any
rate, in 1941, funds were no longer available. And then there is the climate, the
"continental" weather on the East Coast, with its freezing winters and humid
summers. Bernard Berenson is said to have judged a permanent residence in
New Jersey tolerable only on the condition that one be affluent enough to
summer in Maine and winter in Florida. Such dislocations for Mann would
have been out of the question. There were other reasons: the boredom of a
circumscribed routine and a smallish social circle in a university town, to
which now add on a possible motive less sublime and rarely mentioned by
other biographers. On September 3, 1940, Mann writes in his diary that he has
read a frightening article in *The Nation*,

> written from the perspective of American military experts: extreme pessi-
> mism in the matter of England's situation and the threat to America, hope-
> fully meant primarily as propaganda for the draft. The cessation of English
> resistance predicted for the end of this month.—The issue of a settlement
> is being much considered *here*. It seems reasonable because a quick turn-
> around for the good in Europe is not to be expected; in the best case,
> England will be on the defensive for a long time; war and uncertainty may
> go on for years. (T 4 143; emphasis added)

Short text: if "here" is meant to include Princeton, just fifty miles from New
York, it would be safer to live thousands of miles away from the East Coast and
its proximity to German submarines and airplanes. Earlier that year, in the
manifesto *The City of Man* that Mann helped to write, one could read: "Forerunners of Nazi Germany, as early as forty-odd years ago, anticipating the great
wars, had said already, 'Some months after we finish our work in Europe, we
will take New York.' The Nazi conquerors today manifestly envision this

time."[52] On the other hand, buying a house on the Pacific Coast brings its own worries in tow: after receiving a disturbing letter from his brother Heinrich, Mann notes, on March 3, 1941, two weeks before his planned departure,

> Shattering of the California resolutions, or at the least . . . doubt; half a mind to walk away from it. On the other hand, our stay here [in Princeton] has outlived its purpose. What disturbs me is the neighborhood there, settling permanently in such uncertain times, the thought of negative possibilities when conditions in the country become more parlous. (T4 227)

The thought that "conditions in the country" might well become more parlous was not strange to him. In a letter to Agnes Meyer, he wondered in 1940 about future "developments" in America: "I do *not* believe in this country—and have not for a long time. It is undermined, paralyzed, and ready for a fall like the rest of so-called civilization. It may not offer us security much longer" (H 1149).

————

Two years after Mann's move to Pacific Palisades, Mann would plunge into his turbulent, self-involved, self-incriminating *Faustus* epic. It is no wonder that he often went to look at the ocean further north, above the city of Santa Monica. He would take long walks on the Ocean Boulevard promenade or be driven along it to a bluff overlooking the beach and the ocean. He loved to look at the waves, something he had loved to do ever since his childhood stays at Travemünde on the Baltic Sea.

But that is least of all the full horizon of Mann's activity. For, every month, during his stay in California, until May 1945, with few interruptions, he was driven from his home to Hollywood for his political broadcasts—*Deutsche Hörer* (Listen, Germany!)—transmitted via the BBC to Germany (see in chapter 2, "*Listen, Germany!*" *infra*) (E 5:351). They are splendid, vigorous, courageous polemics, conveying Mann's fury with dazzling virtuosity. They infuriated Goebbels, who, in his diaries, after hearing the first of Mann's talks, jeered venomously at his "many political metamorphoses since 1914," which was supposed to make Mann an unreliable commentator.[53] In fact, the frequency and incisiveness of Mann's denunciations of the Third Reich do much to overpower the cultural memory of Mann's early hesitations and later contradictions. It is true that in his first years in exile, Mann was undecided about what position to take toward the new Nazi regime. After all, the audience for his books and the guardian of his distinction was the good Germany, still possibly alive under the barbaric hide of the New Order. Mann's son Golo wrote rather cruelly in his diary, "The old man wavers back and forth like a headless wasp."[54] Mann's wavering became the*"unerhörte Begebenheit"* ("the startling occurrence") of *The Decision,* a novel by the Dutch senator Britta Böhler, whose account has been criticized as insensitive to Mann's "towering complexity."[55] The book might have been called *The Agonizing Decision;* the choice was surpassingly difficult for Mann, even under the relentless pressure of his children.

During the years of his Princeton exile, Mann's polemical writings turned consistently on a set of moral and political themes.[56] Authentic Germany, the genius of German literature, is to be found where its guardian dwells—Thomas Mann—and never mind on which continent. At the same time, this treasure—and burden—cannot erase the sorrow of exile from one's country, which meant, for Mann, the loss of home, wealth, friends, readership, and more. His predicament leads us back to its source: the vicious inhumanity of a fascist regime forever bent on war. Until December 1941, Mann had needed to tell the world of what was in store for it, and now this terrible promise is alive. The "world" that needed to be told included Germany proper: the first of the sixty-one speeches to *Deutsche Hörer,* composed shortly before Christmas in late 1940, warned the Germans that their misguided loyalty to a barbarous regime would cost them dearly at the end—an end whose horror one could barely imagine. It is unlikely that these speeches had the desired effect of inducing listeners to "rise up," to "revolt." But Mann was tireless and prolific in issuing one vivid, outraged assault after another, stressing again and again the un-moveable "opposition of the cultural totality of humanity to the political to-talitarianism of the State."[57]

Many of Mann's tirades were dropped as leaflets over Germany by the RAF and the US Air Force. No other exiled German author engaged in so persistent and forceful a propaganda attack against Hitler's regime, although it was Mann's singularly lofty prestige in both Britain and America (considering his Nobel Prize and numerous honorary doctorates) that gave him that opportu-nity. At the same time, he never stopped making bold use of it. He would also have enjoyed the free play of his rhetorical gifts it offered him: in the manner of a schoolmaster, congenial to him, he could convey facts concealed by the Nazis, and he could also unfurl a furious satire against that "menagerie" of Nazi rulers—Goebbels the liar and Goering the fat.

In many of his writings during his first years in America—but not in the radio addresses—he attempted to distinguish between Nazi and Soviet totali-tarianism to the slight credit of the latter. But his sympathy for a genuine socialism, which he could not entirely detach from the ruling clique of the Soviet Union, would cause him immense trouble in the years after Princeton. He imagined—articulately—a social democracy somehow not at odds with individual freedom, but it was beyond his abilities to advance a plan to realize this ideal. Germany had never experienced a popular revolution, and so no one could judge its possible efficacy. The core of German intelligence had, in the modern period, been sequestered in culture, inwardness, romantic yearning, myth, untouched by something like a canny social-political pragmatism bent on realizing a free, equitable, and just society. This "spirit" (*Geist*), which Mann attaches, exemplarily, but certainly problematically, to the German "bourgeoisie" of the nineteenth century, was powerless to resist the "botching" (*Verhunzung*—literally, "the going to the dogs") of these very qualities in a fascist political mythology. Running through these tensions between an inner and an outer world was a deep and long-standing conflict at the heart of the country's history: never an organically developing nation, Germany obtained its unity, following Mann, at the price of its internal liberty. Along with this felt deprivation, it was quick to develop an aggravated sense of how the freedom of the individual might be constrained in a society posited on the equality of its members—an opposition Mann cast directly as that between "democracy" and "socialism." So, how could a *democratic socialism* be imagined taking root in this rift? And yet, side by side with the fierce "militarism" of Mann's opposition to the Nazis, he conjures "a fundamental ethics, a 'socialistic' political theory, although one rather vague, illusory, and impossible to realize."[58]

In the years following the end of the war, Mann no longer commanded the media of radio broadcasts or an increasingly irreproachable political dossier. In a country now driven by paranoid suspicions of sabotage, he was at the mercy of the media, just as in our own days: "the cynicism of power once again dictates the values at large; whoever controls the media-driven public world is in the right; and foreignness presents itself as a threat."[59] In 1952, under the threat of investigation by the House Un-American Activities Committee, as we now know, Mann left America for good, for Erlenbach and thereafter to Kilchberg near Zurich. He died, three years later, in 1955, at the age of eighty, just three months after the death of his Princeton neighbor and occasional friend Albert Einstein. The third great antifascist exile in America, Arturo Toscanini, died a little more than a year later. What a loss in human distinction there was!

2

Reflections of a Political Man

My work is still in the making and, I venture to hope, still reflects the present and its problems.

—THOMAS MANN

Prologue

Mann composed most of the ethical and political essays in this chapter between September 1938 and March 1941 during his stay in Princeton. At the time, he was considered by many knowledgeable Americans to be Germany's, if not the world's, greatest living writer.[1] He was also consulted as a savant—a moral and intellectual authority—and was repeatedly asked for essays on the current moment by serious journals, such as *The Nation, The New Republic, The Saturday Review of Literature*—and the *New York Herald Tribune* as well. Few of his biographers have described in detail the variety and scope of these pieces, which display a breathtaking eloquence—especially in the German in which they were first composed—and a perceptiveness entirely cogent today in rallying a humanist resistance to populist totalitarianism (the seizing of absolute state power by a minority).

And still, there is no consensus about how good these writings are. The division of opinion was already vivid in a cluster of full-length biographies published two decades ago.[2] The Mann scholar T. J. Reed describes the skeptical stance that critics took toward Mann's earlier (ca. 1930) political writings—a skepticism extending even to the antifascist writings ca. 1940. Mann was dismissed "as out of place, out of his depth in politics, naive, unrealistic, ineffectual"; but, Reed adds, "the assertion often rests simply on the fact that he was a mere writer rather than on analysis of what he wrote. No critic has yet shown [as of 1996] that Mann's assessment of the intellectual climate was wrong, that his warnings were irrelevant, that his appeal had no effect."[3]

A decade later, the eminent historian Manfred Görtemaker appears to have internalized this conflict of interpretations. Writing in 2005, he declares, "There is scarcely any other German writer who took a public stand more often and in a more engaged manner than Thomas Mann."[4] These words sound like high approval, but his praise of Mann's "engagement" is soon withdrawn. Görtemaker turns out to disbelieve in any such thing as a heartfelt conversion to *democracy* on the part of this aristocrat of the spirit, this literary aesthete. It would be ipso facto impossible; it must be—the critic declares—at best a role.

The reaction of Mann's American audience during his Princeton years is an ostensive refutation of this complaint. The striking number of enthusiastic listeners speaks to their power, joining their approval with Mann's sympathetic biographers Donald Prater (1995), Anthony Heilbut (1996), and Reed himself.[5] Indeed, another scholar, Tobias Temming—writing some years after Görtemaker—concludes, "Lately, there has been an *increase* in the voices calling for a revision of the image of Thomas Mann as a political dilettante . . . and a wider receptive stance [of his writings] among professional historians."[6]

In an incisive study of Mann's reception in the United States, Tobias Boes notes that "the ordinary people who came to hear the author speak by the thousands were not primarily drawn by the promise of intellectual nuance" but rather by his celebrity as a rather splendid "antifascist émigré, which lent his pronouncements a kind of authenticity that was clearly an attraction in its own right" (TB 139). Mann's spoken arguments might not have made the clearest sense they do when close-read under a lamp at midnight. But on the wings of his fastidious, old-world elegance, listeners were bound to feel his *Suada*, his persuasive eloquence, even when, as was sometimes reported in the newspapers, he seemed otherworldly and abstruse. All this to give some color to my decision, produced at first by affectionate admiration, to give readers the opportunity to look at these papers in detail.

Adding to the charm of their rhetorical power is their relative rarity—the fact that they were written at all when you consider how often Mann had to resist invitations to publish his thoughts. In his fluent, detailed biography of 2,256 pages, Klaus Harpprecht discusses Mann's dilemma:

> Thomas Mann—[in September 1938] at the height of his fame—saw himself besieged by invitations to lectures and readings, by solicitations to contribute to all sorts of newspapers and magazines, by well-intentioned

requests to accept this and that honor. The registry of his letters, which can scarcely be called complete, lists eighty-five "Regrets . . ." sent to a variety of institutions from the time of his arrival at Princeton on September 28 through to the end of 1938. Mann began to complain about the "colossally naïve, zealous and demanding land" that was overwhelming him with endless benefits and kind gestures (which, at the same time, he undoubtedly enjoyed). He moaned over the torrent of letters, which he read with increasing resistance. "Supersaturation & mutiny," he wrote in the diary. He confessed to Kuno Fiedler: "I hardly touch the things if I do not recognize the handwriting." (H 1035)

For various conceptual and editorial reasons, I will treat only the pieces Mann published during his stay in Princeton. It goes without saying that he wrote powerful ethical and political pieces while in America both before and after that period—foremost, "The Coming Victory of Democracy," which he read throughout the States in spring 1938 and in the years following. On the other hand, the widest in scope of the first papers—*This Peace*—protesting the West's feckless acceptance of Hitler's dismemberment of Czechoslovakia, was drafted on September 29, just one day after Mann arrived in Princeton and only hours before the Munich Agreement was signed.[7] And so, the time line for this presentation of his papers has a certain world-historical cogency. The September date marks decisive proof of Hitler's lust for abusive conquest; and Mann's talk in late 1940, "Listen, Germany!" (*Deutsche Hörer!*), begins a series of radio addresses of that name that amount to the sharpest, fiercest denunciation of the Nazi predations ever written by Mann—or others. Boes informs us that "Mann's importance as an interpreter of the current situation in Europe easily outpaced his role as the author of demanding and culturally prestigious fiction." During the years 1938–45, for instance, along with the publication in America of five of his novels, five new volumes of his speeches and essays appeared—and sold! "The lecture transcript *The Coming Victory of Democracy*, for instance, sold more copies even than *Joseph in Egypt*, the most widely acclaimed literary work that Mann published during his American exile" (TB 15).

Almost all Mann's political talks and essays were conceived in the so to speak colloquial atmosphere available to him in Princeton—Mann in conversation with the sharp-witted members of his family and extended family and other refugee scholars. They are shaped by his long-achieved political perspective—his "conversion" to democratic socialism dating nearly two decades before. But the main extrinsic impulses came from the world-historic convulsions of the time and the books and newspapers he read, filtered through conversations with Erich Kahler and, to a lesser extent, with Hermann Broch, Giuseppe Antonio Borgese, and (minimally) Einstein.

Mann's visits with Kahler make up a regular feature of his stay in Princeton. He attended to the political and moral judgment of this polymathic intellectual historian, "his judgment being, as a rule, calmer and soberer than [Mann's] own."[8] In the period November 5, 1938 until March 18, 1941, from Kahler's arrival in Princeton until Mann's departure for Los Angeles, Mann's diaries record some thirty meetings—many others presumably unrecorded—in which they discussed contemporary politics and German and world history. Mann read his own manifestos and polemical pieces to Kahler and listened carefully to his opinions: they "discussed" in Mann's library on 65 Stockton Street until very late at night. Kahler in turn read his political and historical essays to Mann; and he was a deeply engaged and published critic of all Mann's work.

It's noteworthy that their conversations also included a good deal of what Germans call *Rede und Widerrede* (statement and counterstatement), especially stemming from Kahler's legacy of historical vitalism—his fascination, often celebratory, with bursts of historical life never mind their ethical bearing—and Mann's stern adherence to rational republicanism.[9] Even so, wrote Mann, "every conversation with him occurs on an agreeable (*wohltuend*) niveau."[10]

In the pieces that follow, I want to evoke the argument and flair of Mann's papers, with only occasional interventions when I feel the need to emphasize a point. I keep to a minimum judgments about what's good or less good— what's heartfelt and what seems contrived—about these lectures: I think that response belongs to the engaged reader.[11] I prefer not to dictate affects or supply the sort of abbreviated conclusions useful in passing examinations, with a wry nod to the aesthetic of André Bazin, which requires "a new form of reality . . . dispersive, elliptical, errant or wavering, working in blocs."[12] Employing this approach appears to be the modern writer's duty, though I shall not be making excessive use of it.

So, let us see and savor, as his audience, what Mann wrote in his moment. As readers, we join the greater jury, which has yet to deliver a final judgment on the sincerity of Mann's calls and declarations. There shimmers over his commitment to democracy in these writings—*he agreed*—an irremovable glaze (*Lasurfarbe*) of irony.[13] What is certain is that no simple judgment is possible. All of Mann's decisions arise from a complex of *associations*: the latter word is one he literally *loved*![14] But quite apart from such speculations as to Mann's heart of hearts, there is the fact of the survival of these beautiful, compelling, often furious lectures and essays. We can learn from them![15]

"A Brother"

Mann composed this tour de force in 1938. It was published a year later in English in *Esquire* magazine with the title "That Man Is My Brother" and, in an extraordinary temporal and spatial sequence of events, reprinted almost immediately thereafter in German, in a Paris-based German exile newspaper.[16] "That man"—"my brother"—is Hitler!

The piece, which aims to humiliate an *enemy* brother, succeeded in too dangerous a fashion to be published in Europe in 1938. Its aim is political, but its nerve is artistic: it is boldly imaginative and has a visionary accuracy, qualities that Mann himself acknowledged as unique among his political writings, which were otherwise rather *brav* ("correct," "well-behaved"). One is fascinated and appalled by the artistic courage needed to descend into the depths of a putative likeness between oneself and a detested enemy. This conceit, demonically inspired, proposes that Hitler—though *unnamed* throughout—is himself an artist of sorts, a failed artist.[17] In an interview in early 1938, Mann is said to have said that *that man* "had delivered a fatal blow to German culture, 'incorporating it into his idea of a totalitarian state. You see, Hitler was a paperhanger. He sees himself as an artist. Therefore, all art must agree with his ideas.'"[18] But in "A Brother," Hitler's appetite is more ferocious than one that merely craves agreement: Hitler has turned—literally—*endlessly* vindictive for his failure, and he will punish the world for it.

We shall learn at one point that Einstein visited Mann for the express purpose of telling him his opinion of "A Brother." Mann had sent him this fugue on an "abundantly painful relationship," based on "the Hitler-phenomenon" as a gross distortion of artistic sensibility and achievement.[19] Mann does not record what Einstein said—it would be rewarding to know!—though throughout his diaries Mann is the least productive recorder thinkable of anything that Einstein can have said. Being of a peaceable disposition, Einstein might have been shocked by the savagery of Mann's essay, as it excoriates this "unpleasant and mortifying brother," but mollified, too, by Mann's initially irenic approach to this monster. "I will not disclaim it," writes Mann:

> For I repeat: better, more productive, more honest, more constructive than hatred is recognition, acceptance, the readiness to make oneself one with what is deserving of our hate, even though we run the risk, morally speaking, of forgetting how to say no. . . . I will not decide whether history has ever produced a specimen of mental and moral baseness accompanied by the magnetism we call genius, to compare with this one to which we are the

amazed witnesses. . . . The phenomenon of the great man has, after all, been most often an aesthetic, not an ethical phenomenon. . . . [But] I like to think . . . that a future is now on the way in which art uncontrolled by mind, art as black magic, the issue of brainlessly irresponsible instinct, will be as much condemned as, in humanly frail times like ours, it is reverenced. Art, certainly, is not all sweetness and light. But neither is it all a brew of darkness, not all a freak of the tellurian underworld, not simply "life." (157, 159–60, 161)

In attending to this devil, Mann does not mean to suppress the hatred this brother deserves, "which is the only right reaction from those to whom our civilization is anywise dear."[20] One continues to hope for his speedy and, inevitably, disgraceful erasure. Mann's revulsion invites a discourse on emotion, love, and hate—interestingly. And it may be more than wordplay when Mann finds at the root of expressions of love and hate an agency he calls "interest." His definition of "interest" is surprising: he strips away any connotation of aggressive *self*-aggrandizement in favor of "a desire for self-discipline, inclining to be humorous, ascetic; to acknowledge similarity, even identification with oneself, to feel a sense of solidarity. And all this I find morally superior to hatred" (154). Still, this success requires that the air that interest breathe be "freedom, objective contemplation"—in a word, the *irony* that is the hallmark, Mann writes, of "all creative art" (and here we have a long-awaited, thirsted-for clarification of Mann's notorious irony).[21]

Let's get down to the bottom (if there is one) of this miscreant himself:

Here is a man possessed of a bottomless resentment and a festering desire for revenge; a man ten times a failure, extremely lazy, incapable of steady work; a man who has spent long periods in institutions; a disappointed bohemian artist; a total good-for-nothing . . . who has learnt nothing, and in his dreamy, obstinate arrogance would learn nothing; who had neither technical nor physical discipline, could not sit a horse, or drive a car, or fly a plane, or do aught that men do, even to begetting a child—he develops the one thing needed to establish a connection between him and the people: a gift of oratory. (154–55)

But every part of his success depends on the readiness of his vast audience to receive his hysterical rant; there is a psychic crater in them to fill. After the war's defeat, they crave the restoration of their "honor." He excites this craving: he digs into their wounds with his wild and whirling words. He "understands" their resentment: has he not felt this massive resentment in his own personal humiliation, his own "insulted grandeur" (155)? Oh, "they" will pay for this insult! "We" have been wronged, and those who have wronged us will pay— with their death! His rage, and the promise of extravagant compensation, touches masses of men: first in Germany, and then in other parts of Europe, whose exhaustion and fear of war make them receptive to the hysterical energy that promises that all will be made glorious again with no shot fired. The observer is helpless not to admire the success of this masterful charlatan— the political animal *sui generis*.

This man's success is fostered by famous myths—"the simpleton who wins the princess and the kingdom; the ugly duckling who becomes a swan" (156). Mann is a stunning cultural psychologist—his specialty Germany, with "its folk tradition, mingled with debased and pathological elements." Consider "the Sleeping Beauty surrounded by a rose-hedge . . . and smiling, as her . . . hero awakens her with a kiss." Is this not the *colored* background of the Nazi motto *Deutschland erwache!* (Germany, awaken!)?[22] And who, then, is Prince Charming in this fairy tale if not "our political medicine-man" . . . as painful as this allegory might seem? Now, it is an irresistible impression—there is something of the artist in this creature, this brother. It is mortifying to imagine, but it is there, sprung from "the lazy, vegetating existence in the depths of a moral and mental bohemia: the fundamental arrogance which thinks itself too good for any sensible and honorable activity, on the ground of its vague intuition that it is reserved for something else," something much higher, infinitely high, to be stormed through anger, through the sense of all the wrong that has been done to it. It craves fulfillment of a deep, crazed wish for compensation that would have the world at its feet, begging for redemption (156). For all his inspired frenzy, for whatever in Hitler's personality sparks this madness, it would dissipate if it were not amplified by all the technical tricks now available in the dawning age of domination by mass media. The historical, political factor is crucial—"the *medium* and sphere of activity of the political or demagogic method which it wields to sway whole populations and the destinies of masses of people, with much accompanying noise and destructiveness" (emphasis added; 157). But there is no escaping the imprint of the deranged artistic personality behind it all; and it is impossible to resist Mann's eloquence in discussing this connection. He has identified the pattern both intrinsic and extrinsic to this "successful hysteric":

> the insatiable craving for compensation, the urge to self-glorification, the restless dissatisfaction, the forgetfulness of past achievements, the swift

abandonment of the price once grasped, the emptiness and tedium, the sense of worthlessness as soon as there is nothing to do to take the world's breath away; the sleepless compulsion to make one's mark on something. (157)

How stunningly relevant to the type of "Führer" that the world has come to know.

Mann proposes a morality of hatred: it requires haters—if they are courageous enough—to inquire into the resemblance (with themselves!) of the others who provoke their hatred. This does not mean losing all feeling for *difference.* One detects a parallel between the artist's easy access to his unconscious feelings and what Mann calls the absence of any limit whatsoever "to the extent that the unconscious can go in effective projection of itself upon reality." Witness the upsurge of primitivism in the contemporary European mass mind (158). It might be supposed that the artist would be bemused by and pleased to share in this anti-intellectualism, but this is where a sense of difference and revulsion come into play. Mann has lived through the reign of ideas—types of vitalism—contrived to defy the "psychologism of the age"; but the age failed to note the danger when these ideas had "degenerated into the political sphere and wreaked their violence on a plane where professors enamored of the primitive and literary lackeys of the anti-intellectual pose were the only ones who did not fear to tread" (159). We will hear this complaint again in Mann's "Mankind, Take Care!" A muddled "life philosophy" has become part of the conceptual baggage of the street, providing easy access to a thuggish politics. Mann speculates boldly, wondering whether "the élan of [Hitler's] march on Vienna [in March 1938] had a secret spring: it was directed at the venerable Freud, the real and actual enemy, the philosopher and revealer of the neuroses, the great disillusioner, the seer and sayer of the laws of genius" (159). It is noteworthy that Mann himself had "marched" to Vienna in June 1936 to read to "the venerable Freud," in his office on the Berggasse, Mann's lecture "Freud and the Future"![23] The fantasy that the Nazi annexation of Austria was "sprung" by its rage at Freud is easily accommodated by this essay—a *jeu d'esprit*—since, as Mann declares, earlier in the piece, that "the moral sphere"—here the sphere of irrefutable knowledge—"is really not altogether the artist's concern" (157).

Is Hitler, then, a genius of sorts? "If genius is madness tempered with discretion . . . then this man is a genius." On the other hand, it is once again moot "whether history has ever produced a specimen of mental and moral baseness accompanied by the magnetism we call genius to compare with this one to which we are the amazed witnesses" (159–60). Mann alleges to have heard people say, "Well, we know that Napoleon was a boor too." The comparison is untenable! We do not have here what Hegel called "the world-spirit on horseback." Along with the times' botching of such concepts as "nationalism, socialism, myth, philosophy, irrationalism, faith, youth revolution," could we really have expected to do without a botching, a distortion, as well, of *genius*? (160).

Mann may have been stimulated by the "horse" above—the horse that the world-spirit bestrides—to draw on his good acquaintance Robert Musil's disquisition on the modern genius in *Der Mann ohne Eigenschaften* (*The Man without Qualities*), published in 1931, seven years before Mann composed this essay in German. Following Musil, the "gymnastic" form of genius would allow for the notorious apotheosis of a "*racehorse* of genius," something the hero of Musil's novel has read in Vienna newspapers ca. 1913.[24]

Mann concludes his essay, as he began it, by raising the question of morals. Earlier, on approaching the task of turning his hatred of Hitler into a "fraternal" identification, he called the exercise "a *moral* flagellation" (153; emphasis added). But why? This enterprise was born from recognition of "the bald and sorry facts" of Hitler's success, who "passes unopposed from one triumph to another." A perceptive reader of Mann's essay, Morten Høi Jensen, interprets these phrases strongly, writing:

> What is so thoroughly moving about this essay is that it is filled with self-reproach—a "moral self-flagellation," as Mann puts it. His prosecution of German history was equally a prosecution of himself. He never stopped atoning for his political errors during the First World War, and, apparently, for waiting so long to become the international face of German opposition to Nazism in the late 1930s and '40s.[25]

We will soon be acquainted *in detail* with this conundrum (see "Contra Thomas Mann the American," later in this chapter), and this scholar is right to see it as a crucial vexation of Mann's moral sensibility, even when Mann lays stress on a decidedly "ironic approach."[26]

But there is, finally, another dimension to this "moral" question; it is age-old and not Mann's alone—namely, the morality of art. Mann's closing *condemnation* of what he has just done by way of "artistic" identification could not be sharper—or more distressing: "An artist, a brother. But the bond, and the recognition of it, are an expression of art's contempt for itself." This means that Mann's "salvo of novelistic genius" (Jensen) is not meant to be taken quite seriously. He appears to be on the verge of admitting, despondently, that this essay—a "political article" but also a piece of art building on symmetry and mimesis—is without pragmatic value in a desperate, world-historical matter (161). In a later interview, he would declare, rather grandly, that there is *no contradiction* here. When he abandoned his earlier "unpolitical stance," it was because "a writer, for whom the most natural thing is to assert his powers productively in . . . art, cannot be content today to strive in art for what is right, good, and true; he must do this in the political-social world as well and unite his thoughts with the political will of the time."[27] This joining of what is right, good, and true in art with the goals of moral action may be more difficult, more problematic than what is being supposed here, as we have learned from Mann's "A Brother."

———

A Postscript. The following citations amount to a brief *summa* of the salient points of Mann's Hitler profile:

> The shattering blow to his [Hitler's] self-esteem [was] delivered when the Vienna Academy turned down his application to study art. . . . He had been fanatically certain that he would get in, and the wound of that rejection, perhaps his only solid grievance, never ceased to hurt. A whole human generation was punished for it. . . . His weapon was oratory: Hitler's one tremendous gift and his only natural talent. . . . He couldn't drive or swim or dance. . . . The discovery of this gift of rhetoric, and the techniques to intensify its impact, set Hitler on his way. . . . He was the supreme practicant and product of the "self-magnifying" craze, the genre of little-man literature . . . on how to "bend others to your will." . . . A box of tricks was available to overcome the "little man's" sense of powerlessness in times of slump, hyperinflation and political chaos. . . . Fear of war also helped to bind the German masses to Hitler—and all the more so as his foreign policy grew more aggressive and riskier.

Mann did not write any of these sentences: they are taken from an essay on Hitler by Neil Ascherson, an expert scholar of the German mentality, published in June 2016. After eighty years of research and writing about Hitler from the date Mann composed "A Brother," his *jeu d'esprit* reveals an extraordinary knowledge and insight.[28]

"I Believe"

Mann contributed this dense, tightly woven essay to an anthology of personal credos by several of the leading writers and intellectuals of his time, none less than W. H. Auden, E. M. Forster, Jules Romains, Albert Einstein, John Dewey, and George Santayana. His piece brings together in brief compass religion, the artist, God, Goethe, Christianity, nature, and the new, "third" humanism, an inventory of centering concepts that today would be called "logocentric" and thence "put under erasure" in a deconstructive gesture forecasting everything *except* "the new humanism" and ushering in, instead, the new "posthumanism." But let us stay with Mann's quest, in this piece, to find his conclusion—his thought twistingly en route to its leading idea: the proclamation of a new humanism attuned to the age, with an appetite for negativity more capacious than an older sort; for the new humanism sees itself as mediating between the good of man—his art and science and religion, his ideals of justice and goodness— and the spectacular evils—"the fantastic vileness"—of the present age.[29]

Mann takes his cue from the assigned topic: to present his "living philosophy," a task that he promptly inflects to his views on religion. He makes this turn, no doubt, because foremost in his mind at this time is the completion of his "Jewish epic," the missing fourth volume of *Joseph and His Brothers*, which he forever intends to get to, with myriad responsibilities standing in his way; but these responsibilities are unavoidable, as he will state sternly in this essay.

The concept-word "religion" is rooted in the Latin word *religio*, which might derive from the verb *relegere* or *religare* and "means originally in its profane sense to take care, to pay heed, to bethink oneself." Mann will sustain a profane sense of religion throughout this credo, "temporarily divested of its priestly garment and contenting itself with the humanly spiritual" (189).

His intellectual pleasure is palpable in his recent discovery that "the word *religio* seems to have retained throughout the Latin age this sense of conscientiousness, of conscientious scruples . . . without necessary reference to religious, godly matters." This concept, in a word, of *care* (the italics are Mann's) is crucial: it will lead him to the defining faculty of the artist, who is par excellence "the careful human being" (on Mann's example, one might add, in the spirit of this enterprise, the caretaker of the *word*). In this sense the artist is "a religious man" (190). Mann, however, will refer the artist's attention to something "higher" than words. This thought gesture involves a grandiose, somewhat opaque leap to a loftier order of being, attributing the artist's guide to nothing less than

> the will and activities of the universal spirit; to change in the garment of the truth; to the just and needful thing, in other words to the will of God, whom the man of mind and spirit must serve, heedless of the hatred he arouses among stupid or frightened people, people obstinately attached by their interests to obsolete or evil phases of the age. (190)

How is one to understand this exalted drama of the artist's "attention," if not as Mann's commitment in his own writing to values *superior* to those which at the moment are historically triumphant—those of fascist Germany foremost? And who are these despicable followers—"these stupid or frightened people"? They must be the inert Germans of the homeland, loyal to their regime, about whose hatred for him and his political tirades he is continually informed.

Mann is not alone among modern writers whose "care [is] not only for his own product but for the Good, the True, and the will of God." Consider the writer, his contemporary, whom he greatly admired—Kafka—who declared in his diaries that he had felt passing satisfaction from works like *A Country Doctor* but happiness only if he could raise the world into "the Pure, the True, and the Immutable." When Mann comes to write a preface to the first American translation of Kafka's *The Castle,* he will stress, with satisfaction, that the work is a religious quest and a sure reflection of the artist's higher will, which Mann describes as his proper concern.

We have the refrain: "For me and my kind [the artist's kind], the religious is lodged in the human" (191). This is not to conjure a religion *of* man, as if the human race invited prostrated admiration: its creativity in vileness is all too apparent. And yet, despite this evidence, "we must not . . . forget [humanity's] great and honorable traits, revealed in the shape of art, science, the quest for truth, the creation of beauty, the conception of justice" (191). To ignore this mystery—worse, to treat it with scorn and contempt—is only to invite spiritual death. The "harsh and bitter fact" is that the world is in crisis, when the very definition of man is contested and must be fought for—and the field of this fight today is ineluctably political. The artist, quite particularly, courts inanity, stuntedness, if he is not prepared to bring a decision *for* humanity into his work.

The human being is mysterious in the sense especially that "in him nature becomes conscious of itself." This is Mann's variation on the teachings of the German idealist legacy, marked by the philosopher Hegel and his schoolmate, the poet Friedrich Hölderlin, whose exquisite poetic claim about "the gods" reads: "For as / The supremely blessed feel nothing themselves / Doubtless another must / If it is permissible to say such a thing / Feel in their name, in sympathy / And that someone they need."[30] In Mann, "Nature" comes to be articulated, "spiritualized," in the single suffering human being, whose vivid exemplum is the artist, the mediator between spirit and life. "She [Nature] seems to have brought man forth . . . to lay herself open in him to the spiritual"—and now Mann goes Hölderlin one higher—"as in a being who is at once herself [Nature] and a creature of a higher order." This creature evinces the superiority of conscience to innocent nature.

In a side panel, for our contemplation, we have the elaboration of this conceit in Mann's *Joseph and His Brothers*: God creates man as a mirror of Himself. And however sorely tempted God is to destroy this creature, with whom evil came into the world, He has not—thus far. The unwitting commentary of Mann's Princeton neighbor Albert Einstein is apt: "What has perhaps been overlooked is the irrational, the inconsistent, the droll, even the insane, which Nature, inexhaustibly operative, implants in an individual, seemingly for her own amusement."[31] Ergo, God-Nature has chosen to leave man to his own devices, but also, according to Mann, to a higher end, "because a mirror is a means for self-recognition and because He would then see the consciousness of that ambivalent creature [man] reflected in one son of man, in a certain Abirâm or Abraham—see it as a means for His own self-awareness."[32]

Forgetting Einstein, Mann proceeds, logically by his own lights, to hail *Christianity* as the basic character of Western culture, emphasizing faith as the noble adversary to "the half-educated mob that today sets itself up to 'conquer Christianity.'" He is alluding to the dismal ideologues of the Third Reich but is careful throughout this piece not to name by name "Brother Hitler" (let us say) and his retinue; he has been asked to keep to the generality of "the philosophical" (192). At the same time, he is preparing for a humanism that will constitute a philosophical advance on Christianity, a view to which he brings his best energy:

> Equally strong is my belief that the humanity of the future—the new human and universal feeling now in process of birth, drawing life from efforts and experiments of all sorts and kinds and striven after by the choice and master spirits of the age—that humanity will not exhaust itself in the spirituality of the Christian faith, in the Christian dualism of soul and body, spirit and life, truth and "the world." (192–93)

Mann will boldly align all his own analytic and creative work with this movement: his sense of participation is the justification of "his own strivings." I shall paraphrase Mann's aim in the words of an excellent critic, the late Morton Dauwen Zabel, writing on Mann's representation of Goethe in *Lotte in Weimar*: "In its patent autobiographical references, it brings Goethe to take his place anew in a time of confusion and violence comparable to his [Mann's] own and even more desperately in need of his inspired sanity and passionate defense of human destiny."[33] With an implicit caustic domination of the "third" in Hitler's Third Reich, Mann develops his commitment to "a new, a third humanism." One might wonder how this humanism distinguishes itself from all previous humanisms, presumably the German humanism of the early sixteenth century (viz. Reuchlin and Pirckheimer and Melanchthon) and the so-called new humanism of the mid- and late eighteenth century (viz. Lessing, Herder, Goethe, Schiller). It will *not* declare a large-hearted, unequivocal friendship with humanity: it has seen too much of the horror that this humanity has caused—an entirely new experience of the "demonic," an incomparable viciousness. And yet it will "understand" it—presumably, endure it—encouraged at the same time by its admiration of man's "spiritual" powers. "The new humanity will be universal, and it will have the artist's attitude; that is, it will recognize that the immense value and beauty of the human being lie precisely in that he belongs to the two kingdoms of nature and spirit" (193). It will not look at this conflict romantically or stress it as a tragic dualism, but on a Goethean model, it will aim for *combination*—of the demonic and the urbane. Mann foresaw its example in the figure of Joseph in his "life's work"—the epic tetralogy *Joseph and His Brothers*—for Joseph is "blest with blessing from the heavens above and from the depths beneath," whereupon he is the representative, for Mann, of "the most compendious possible formulation of an ideal humanity [or human nature]"—namely, the human being, "as artist," a sojourner, with "art as his guide on the difficult path toward knowledge of himself" and hence toward a "happily balanced humanity [or human nature]." Here we see Mann refurbishing the second-stage humanist ideology of aesthetic education.

Blessed is he that believes. The British scholar Jeremy Adler remarked of his father, H. G. Adler, who experienced on his living body all the horror that might ever assault the new third humanist in the grip of the Third Reich: "The prisoner became an observer, the observer a theorist, the theorist a witness, and the witness an admonisher. What binds those roles together . . . [is the] conviction that a system of beliefs, ethical values, and the basic political concepts of human rights and democracy do make sense. Their abuse, however terrible, did not destroy them."[34] The testimony that Adler's novels bring is an agonized confirmation of Mann's hope, for, as Mann's credo ends, "Art is hope" (194).

"Mankind, Take Care!"

> The *petit bourgeois* learned by actual experience that reason had been
> liquidated and that mind may be insulted with impunity; that . . . in some
> way . . . socialism, internationalism, and Judaism were to blame for his plight.
>
> —THOMAS MANN

Mann published this scathing analysis and urgent warning in 1938 in *The Atlantic Monthly*, a journal always hospitable to his reflections. The civilized world is at a critical juncture. One sees with dismay an entire generation—"the youth of the world"—abuse the democratic privilege of assuming a militant point of view in order to reject the finest achievements of their culture—art, intellect, idealism.[35] These young people are all actual or virtual pupils at the school for barbarians established in the fascist states. We shall hear again and again of Mann's furious repudiation of fascism's mass man—though *no* mass man escapes whipping—who feeds on the propaganda of "blood and soil" and the shabby ecstasy of marching in lockstep. A widespread flight from the ego does not choose carefully which of the half-educated to ensnare. No objective observer can fail to note the degradation of a hard-won culture once in love with truth, with painstaking works of art, with integrity of purpose—but no longer. I will add that this reader, and I imagine many others, will come away from this essay with renewed respect for Mann's soaring intellectual energy and moral and political drive.

The essay arises from a literal *shock* of the view on the "younger world" in 1939 that prompts the duty of criticizing it. Mann turns to categories in Goethe, just as we might find Mann's criticism uncannily apt to our own "younger world": "the scorn of the young for higher and better things" (read: besotted with visual and acoustic media); "the unspeakable pressure from without" (read: angry demagogy); "and 'the monstrous acts by which men express their fury at themselves and each other' [Goethe]" (read: the world at war) (178). Goethe speaks briefly of the culture it takes *to listen*—presumably, to audible signs of a degradation of norms of just and decent behavior, mediated, perhaps, by the cautionary *words* of wiser, more experienced heads. This trigger word "culture" prompts Mann to reach for his most plangent rhetoric.

> Culture! . . . It refers, of course, to the cherished goal of our whole liberal bourgeois outlook . . . [to] liberalism, good citizenship! . . . As though, whether as a matter of form, as desire for freedom and truth, as the conscientious guiding spirit of life, as endless painstaking, it were anything at all but the moral discipline itself! . . . in its higher and deeper sense: of work for its own sake, of individual responsibility, of individual painstaking. (178–79)

Here, Mann draws on his sense of himself as conscientious artist, implicitly opposing lonely artistic craft and reflection to what today is called "group thinking"—a collectivism of ideology and one or another sort of drug-fueled ecstasy.

This taking refuge in the group informs the essay as a signature degradation of an ideal: ecstatic liberation from the everyday self. Here, once more, we witness the *Verhunzung*—the botching—of "elements long understood and reverenced in Europe"—a concept that Mann often applies to pieces of the New Germany's spurious revolution. What are some of these disgraced ideas? Consider the articles of faith of "the bourgeois age . . . of the nineteenth century . . . [which] believed not only in the blessings of liberal democracy but also in socialism—that is, in a kind of socialism which would raise and instruct the masses and bring them science, art, education, the good things of culture" (180–81).

It is not crystal clear which thinkers and which national tendency Mann has in mind. Goethe, certainly, was no socialist, nor Schopenhauer (1788–1860) . . . nor Kierkegaard (1813–1855) . . . nor Nietzsche (1844–1900) . . . but we do hear of a good, an idealistic Karl Marx, who struggled "for the sake of a new truth and justice . . ." (!). And this creative bliss, which Nietzsche described as "Dionysiac ecstasy" (Nietzsche goes unnamed in this essay; in 1938 he is an unsavory figure in the American reception of German ecstasy), now surfaces as "debased, in the collectivist intoxication, in the purely egotistic and hedonist craving of youth to march together, keeping step and singing songs which are a mixture of degenerated folklore and propaganda." Mann has the Hitler Youth in mind but does not refer specifically to Nazi Germany; in fact, at no point in this essay does he write the words "Germany" or "National Socialism." He must not be thought of as forever carrying out in public his quarrel with the authorities that harmed him. Instead, he means to address a nearly universal phenomenon—a mass mentality; he even gives his target a local habitation in alluding to (a bad) intoxication by jazz.

Mann is frankly indebted to Ortega y Gasset's *The Revolt of the Masses*, and he is certainly influenced by Erich Kahler's preoccupation with the loss of the human personality in the mass man. Behind the thinking of both are the ruminations of Hermann Broch on the phenomena of mass hysteria. This pathology is drastically visible in the New German politics, even if this pointer goes unnamed; Mann means to diminish the claims of a particular political ideology, for the youths who march do not have a head full of ideas; they are bent not on understanding what they are marching *for* but on maintaining the intoxication. "The main thing [is] . . . the release from the ego, from the obligation to think—in short, from moral and reasonable obligations altogether" (179).

This general degradation is often represented as the effect of World War I. But war is not its sole cause, however much the decay was exacerbated by its carnage and destruction. The fall is also the result of the previous century's spiritual and intellectual generosity, which is to say: its liberal ideas, which have once again been botched, distorted, and degraded. To participate in a civilization, one must have a fair idea of its "highly complicated antecedents," such as ideals of "freedom and truth." If you do not *know* them, you will not respect them—and that is the case with the half-educated masses.

Mann had recently attended a performance of Ibsen's *The Wild Duck* and was shocked by the crassness of the reactions of an audience consisting mainly of younger people. This sort of shock is not unknown to many spectators, then as now. There were nuances in the meaning of the play that simply went unheard, but more disturbing were the serious moments that excited derision and laughter. It is not difficult to guess which moments Mann was referring to. We have the illusions of the bewildered character Hialmar Ekdal, who lies or fabulates to give himself authority. His father, Ekdal Senior, has gone to prison for a financial crime. Hialmar describes his own attempted suicide in the hour of his father's shame:

> HIALMAR: It was in such an hour that Hialmar Ekdal pointed the pistol at his own breast. . . .
> GREGERS: But you did not fire?
> HIALMAR: No. At the decisive moment I won the victory over myself. I remained in life. But I can assure you it takes some courage to choose life under circumstances like those.

GREGERS: Well, that depends on how you look at it.

HIALMAR: Yes, it takes courage. But I am glad I was firm: for now, I shall soon perfect my invention. . . .[36]

Here, I presume that some in the audience laughed loudly, as Hialmar can supply no details whatsoever as to the nature of his invention—which is surely only an "invention." And yet Mann's point is, and Ibsen surely means to make it, that no one can live without illusions; it the bread of hope; the fit object for a sort of loving irony and no cause for laughter.

Neither does the tormentor Gregers Werle escape humiliation in the cutting description offered by Relling, a doctor, to Gina Ekdal, Hialmar's wife. Gregers has something urgent on his mind:

RELLING: He is suffering from an acute attack of integrity.

GINA: Integrity?

HEDVIG [Gina's daughter]: Is that a kind of disease?

RELLING: Yes, it's a national disease, but it only appears sporadically.[37]

One can hear the raucous laughter that Mann reports.

That hilarity does rather recapitulate Mann's argument *in nuce*: it is the contempt of "today's" youth for the good qualities of character and idealism fostered by their elders. "In the nineteenth century there was a society capable of grasping the European irony and innuendo, the idealistic bitterness and moral subtlety of such a work. All that is gone. . . ." Instead:

Modern man is at once the product and the prey of wild, distracting impressions which assault him, intoxicate his senses, and stimulate his nerves. The amazing development of technology, with its triumphs and disasters, the noisy sensationalism of sports records, the fantastic adulation and overpayment of popular stars, the boxing bouts before hordes of people for million-dollar stakes—these things and more like them make up the picture of our time, together with the decline and obsolescence of civilizing, disciplinary conceptions such as culture, mind, art, ideals. (180)

How prescient, how apt, after eighty-odd years, to the state of the nation in 2021!

A dominant nineteenth-century ideal, especially in the German history of thought, is *Bildung*, education of the self—self-formation, self-enhancement—but what Mann sees (in 1938) is the supersession of the will to educate and be educated by the desire to lord it over others—most visibly in demagogues bent on power over the masses, their willing subjects. Education means

stimulating rational thought in oneself and others; but "today we have convinced ourselves that it is both easier and more important to dominate the
masses, developing . . . the clumsy art of playing on their emotions—in other
words, of substituting propaganda for education." What accounts for the readiness of the masses to subject themselves to propaganda? In its brutal simplicity, propaganda unifies; it is an agent of organization, which the individual in
flight from himself craves, "even in the spirit of violence. Violence is an extraordinarily simplifying principle: no wonder that it is understood by the masses"
(181). There is an underlying relation between the inducement to violence and
life lived in an industrial age, which levels differences—violently if necessary—at the same time that this "movement"—Mann means Nazi Germany—
"rails at the industrial age—with which it is one." Fascism picks up and abuses
the romantic debris of *Volk* and *Blut und Boden* (blood and soil) in the half-
baked manner with which it "thinks." There is a paltry remnant of intelligence
in this youth, who are just able to be emotional and "philosophical" about the
submerged "darkly creative, holy-conceiving, mother-world" that marching in
lockstep might reawaken (181).

The conatus, ill informed, of the generation of young people anno 1938
feeds on a mistake: they have misunderstood, cannot understand, the subtlety
of the attack on reason flowing out of various forms of "life-philosophy" (*Leb-
ensphilosophie*) abounding in the decades before and after the turn of the twentieth century. It was not necessary for Mann to have read Heidegger's claim
that "thinking begins only when we have come to know that reason, glorified
for centuries, is the most stiff-necked adversary of thought": there were nuanced, aestheticized forms of irrationalism in plenty for him to refer to; he
need only turn the pages of his "educator" Nietzsche.[38] But what elite thinkers
of the irrationalist turn were blind to were its implications as soon as it was
seized on by demagogues and the half-educated—"implications" which in
their full barbaric accouterment are on display in the fascist armies of Europe
and its bleak imitation in the not yet conquered democracies. This is Mann's
leading and strongest idea.

Certainly, in the higher echelons of thought there had been a surge of anti-
idealist, anti-rational thought—but it had been idealistic in its own way. Returning to *The Wild Duck*, Mann concludes that "the nineteenth century loved
truth with such vehemence that through the mouth of Ibsen, it even declared
that illusions were indispensable to life" (181). But admitting the lie (of the
ideal) with the melancholy awareness of its necessity is not the same thing as
dismissing it with thuggish contempt. *That* is the deplorable outcome of the

trickle-down of a higher order intellectualized anti-intellectualism. And now ... we taste the rule of the half-educated, in whose mouths language—the Word—is suffering an abuse from which it may not recover (182).

Can something redemptive be said on behalf of the masses? Christianity also begins with the revolt of simple people, the poor in spirit, "the humble, the fisherfolk, the publicans and sinners." But Mann imagines a different sort of bond among them: brotherly love—from a world-historical perspective, a decent sort of compensation for their "abasement of science, learning, and culture." But now we have a different sort of mass and a malignant result, "a mass aggregation of the poor in spirit [who] applaud with pathological frenzy that abrogation of human rights which has been proclaimed to them through a loud-speaker from on high." They claim a "heroic" attitude inspired by a love of violence, including, foremost, a hatred of truth—the most lethal, the most detestable part of their program. Such hatred is a sin against "the will of God ... which the intellectual man must serve," like it or not; he or she must be prepared to confront "the hatred of the stupid, the fearful, and the insensible, of all those interested to uphold the domination of the false and evil." (This, I'll note, borders on the sort of comminatory biblical rhetoric that "scientific" opponents of fascism would reject as futile; see "Contra Thomas Mann the American," later in this chapter.) Mann may be more incisive when he inverts the unnamed Nietzsche's aperçu "Only the life-promoting is true," a view that sanctifies the *lie*. Mann writes *à rebours*: "Only truth is truly life-promoting" (183). Disinformation is not an invention of the reign of Trump. Truth versus the lie: this is the epochal struggle—truth in all its difficult mutability, requiring the finest sort of discernment in the intellectual, who must nonetheless *act* without hesitation, for the opponent is deadly, "setting up the lie as the single, life-giving, history-shaping force" with the inevitable consequence of a catastrophic war for the fate of civilization (183–84). Meanwhile, the "older cultural group" appears to underestimate the gravity of the moment. "Dazed and abashed, with an embarrassed smile, it abandons one position after another, seeming to concede that in very truth it 'no longer understands the world.'" How cogent the metaphor: the abandonment of the moral and metaphysical high ground had its exact correlative, in 1940, in the West's abandonment of territorial positions—the Saar, the Rhineland, Austria, Czechoslovakia. Mann knows of what he speaks. The philosopher Peter Sloterdijk, among others, has observed that liberal humanism has always had an aggressive face: it stands poised to *attack* barbarism.[39] But Mann deplores the feeble benevolence that also inheres in it, "bound up with ... [this very] hatred of fanaticism, its tolerance and love of skepticism. . . . That weakness may become its nemesis." Where is its militant face? "What we need today," at the cost of losing Europe, "is a militant humanism, conscious of its own virility" and sworn to protect "its principles of freedom, tolerance, and skepticism. . . . If the ideas of European humanism are incapable of a militant rebirth . . . then it will be destroyed" (184). We will see these principles affirmed and such admonitions proclaimed in vivid detail in *The City of Man* (discussed later in this chapter). The haunting question remains: What form might Mann's called-for militancy take to be effective, short of tanks and guns? Only inside a war, one would think, is there a workplace for "soldiers of ideas."

This Peace

Mann wrote and published *This Peace* in an articulate spasm of fury and dismay at the Munich Agreement of 1938.[40] It is a beautifully printed pamphlet of thirty-six pages fired by an outraged moral imagination. It castigates the peace of weakness produced by the Munich Agreement, which gave much of Czechoslovakia to the Nazis on the very day following Mann's arrival in Princeton. The coincidence can only have inflamed him as a fatal disturbance. He would have no peace in Princeton—an ocean away from Munich but part of the world plunged by this event "into profound disillusionment, discouragement, and even despair. We have been the shocked, disgusted, and cruelly bewildered spectators at proceedings of far-reaching and decisive significance."[41]

These events have worked entirely to the advantage of the Nazis, a fact calling for outrage . . . and response. The representatives of the so-called democracies of Europe, at that very moment in a position to humiliate the Nazis, chose to support them; the betrayal of democratic ideals by the British ruling class above all is flagrant—and contemptible. Czechoslovakia was abandoned—"betrayed, sold out, sacrificed . . . [to] German fascism on its march toward European hegemony" (8).

What does this dire fact *mean* in light of all the political and polemical work that had been done to stop and destroy this march? (Mann names himself as such a worker.) Addressing an audience of an erudition one can no longer presuppose, he quotes the Latin *Victrix causa diis placuit sed victa Catoni* from Lucan's *Pharsalia* and leaves the tag untranslated. Its literal sense is not entirely helpful: "The victorious cause pleased the gods, but the vanquished pleased Cato." The point is that Cato the Younger, a Stoic of impeccable character, aligned himself with a forlorn (Republican) cause and thereafter—rather than submit to the tyranny of Caesar, the victor, if even to accept his pardon—chose "the freedom" to commit suicide. Mann's sad commentary reads: "In these words of philosophic resignation, the spirit reserves its right to freedom at the expense of success."

He continues, in a perhaps all-too-personal celebratory vein, evoking "the spirit" (*Geist*) as it reveals itself to *him*: "It feels no despair over its defeat in the actual, no chagrin or remorse, but rather prides itself on having espoused the cause of righteousness even though it was destined to practical failure at the start" (9). This paean to the spirit, even as actuality has failed it, is one of Mann's recurrent supports throughout these desperate times. He cannot believe that rational protest even *sans* force of arms can fail to have a liberating effect. James T. Farrell, the hard-bitten realist novelist, refused to sign one of Mann's manifestos some months later, sensing that in Mann's language, "spirit" is being radicalized as a *weapon* for the good: "Thomas Mann's claim that Fascism will wither away because writers, intellectuals and other men of good will condemn it is a *non sequitur*."[42] We know by now the subtext to Mann's defense of a momentarily ineffectual spirit: spirit is staged as a protagonist while the real protagonist rests, coiled, underground: a *war* to be declared by the democracies against Hitler. Still, the work of the contrarian spirit—his—arises from an inescapable "duty to humanity." It is also conceived, raising the martial tone, as an answer to the demand that "the movement must be *fought*" (10; emphasis added).

Fascism is an ideological swindle, effective through its propaganda: it claims the role of "a breakwater . . . to hold back the forces of socialism," and it makes this claim after it has looted bolshevism for elements of its demagogy. What is to be done? What culture-sustaining counterforce is at hand, able to defend an "ideal of humanity and human dignity"? It is the party to which Mann has joined in spirit, "a voluntary union of the traditionally cultural bourgeoisie and the forces voicing the social demands of the hour" (11). But his cause has been betrayed by the traditionally bourgeois nations of France and England, who have helped Hitler to his victory.

Germans of good will, both inside and outside the country, have had their hopes broken by that Europe of which it had always been a part: the expected moral support did not appear. The awful conclusion to this Munich crisis is the realization that Europe "did not *in the least desire* the overthrow—several times almost within our grasp—of the National-Socialist dictatorship" (12). There had been a time when the Nazis had laid no claim on the rest of Europe but—with Mann stating his charge with full rhetorical power, which comes to a head in his speeches to Nazi Germany in wartime—

> the world cared not a whit for the fate of the German people, for the atroci-
> ties of the concentration camps, the tortures and murders, the persecution
> of Jews and Christians, the rejection of spirit, the cultural reign of terror,
> the domination of a philistine bolshevism at the heart of Europe, threaten-
> ing the very foundations of Occidental civilization. (14)

Hitler and the National Socialists claimed credit for the return of the Saar to Germany, but the return was made on the basis of a national plebiscite, by no means identical with the voice of the "Gestapo government." The same trickery was in play when the Nazis claimed credit for the advantages of the naval agreement between Germany and England. The agreement was con-cluded without the participation of France, who was supposed to have allied herself with English and not German interests. Here we have the beginning of a refrain recurrent in Mann's politics at this time: "Nowadays we have learned to doubt whether France was really betrayed, [or] whether indeed the con-spiracy of the fascist sympathizers was not even then already maturing" (15).

The German Army occupied the Rhineland in defiance of the Versailles Treaty. How was this possible? German officers allegedly held orders for their retreat at the first show of French military action. It was not forthcoming. The occupation could not have succeeded without the covert approval of the French and English, since the dire effect of its success could have been fore-seen—a tipping of the balance of power in Central Europe, which would lead, in fact, to the German annexation of Austria en route to the complete "fasciza-tion of the Continent." In seeking an answer, Mann cites the putative "guilty conscience [of the Entente] in respect of the Versailles Treaty," leaving observers—especially in England—to forget "what a German peace might have been, imposed by a victorious Germany in 1918." For many, the success of the German occupation of the Rhineland was an outcome of the sense of fair play of the English, who were willing to ease the harshness of the treaty; but there was something else—and worse—really in play: the machinations of "a set of people who had their corresponding group in France—reactionary, pro-fascist, opposed to the Russian alliance"—who were prepared to blink at the prospect of a fascist Europe (16).

Reading *This Peace* today, we learn a great deal of political history from Mann's aggrieved essay—that, for one thing, the German annexation of Austria by 1938 came as no surprise. Given the disintegration of the Austrian Empire, the fusion of the remaining German-speaking piece with the Reich "had come to seem only a matter of time"—but only after the overthrow of the German Republic, which had never considered a union of Austria with Germany an interesting object for either country (16–17). What saddens and infuriates Mann is his belief that England's ruling class was in spirit behind the annexation and at the least gave it its blessing. With what right?

> The Austrians were no German tribe, like the Pomeranians and Saxons, but the integrated product of a specially desirable cultural mixture, with a special cultural and humanizing mission. The denaturing of Vienna—which took place, of course, under the most repellent and infamous circumstances—her degradation into a German provincial town, was a cultural disaster. (17)

This German coup was inspired by a reason hidden to most: it was a *diversion* from serious problems at home—foremost, economic. The Sudeten crisis, too, needs to be read as timely: according to Mann's sources, morale was low in a country far from being economically self-sufficient.[43] The behavior of this government should always be read as a thrust to the East in search of wheat and oil and, not least, the wealth of the Skoda munitions works; and Austria borders on Czechoslovakia, and Czechoslovakia on Hungary, and Hungary on Rumania. England evidently had no material dog in this fight; it could care less about the fate of the non-Germans in the Sudetenland, let alone the German-speaking opposition. Far worse, "it wanted and was working for the preservation and reinforcement of the National Socialist regime." A Nazi government in the East would be a physical bulwark against feared and detested Russia (18). And France was part of the foul game. France's foreign minister, a certain Pierre-Étienne Flandin, declared that "German expansion eastwards was conformable to natural law, and France must fraternize with the Third Reich" (18). Flandin was identified from the start as a notable appeaser of the Nazis. There would be no hope for the democracies—not from France or from any of the remaining capitalist democracies—when the West harbored

> a sentiment stronger than any antipathy for Nazi Germany's mob rule and gangsterdom, for the debasement of moral standards, its shattering effect on cultural values; a sentiment stronger even than its fear of the anarchistic theory of nationalism, so perilous to the security of all established states. I mean the nightmare of bolshevism, the dread of socialism and of Russia. This it was that brought about the capitulation of democracy as a political

and intellectual concept, and drove it to affirm the Hitler thesis, the division of the world into two camps, fascist and communist.

It is appalling—it was unforeseeable—that this false state of affairs would be exactly reproduced in the rest of Europe. Tragedy repeats itself as . . . tragedy. "It is uncanny to see how the wretched figure of von Papen, the conservative who delivered up Germany to Hitler, recurs again in the English Chamberlain" (19).

Under what meretricious pretext could Chamberlain have accomplished his trick? The fear of war—but in truth, since no war was ever intended, the threat was "a monstrous abuse, a cruel practical joke played on . . . [the people's] nerves and heart-strings and their justified and universal fear of war" (22). It may be that Hitler—alone among the Nazi satraps—was truly prepared to destroy Czechoslovakia—and himself, because, in the case of his armed intervention, Russia and France, and its ally England, were obliged to respond in force. But at some point, Hitler was restrained and even made aware—confident of England's good will—that conquest by other means was possible. And so, "Treachery was indicated [in lieu of] less explicit forms of attack and betrayal." Instead of war, the National Socialists, in collusion with England, provoked the *fear* of war: "Czechoslovakia must be sacrificed, or the world would be plunged into the horrors of war. It was an ignoble trick" (25–26). There would never have been a war, and the outcome is a "peace" that is not one.

The opportunity to secure peace on its only real basis—the destruction of Hitler and his regime—"was to be had . . . [but] only if the western states, certain of the moral support of America, had stood shoulder to shoulder with Russia for the protection of Czechoslovakia" (26). Mann recalls, on the strength of his own experience—three days before the infamous pact—the sense that a countering force to this treacherous masquerade might have come from the indignation of decent people everywhere. He is not so modest as "to forget the roar of applause from 20,000 throats that greeted my words, in Madison Square Garden on September 26: 'It is too late for the British government to save the peace. They have lost too many opportunities. Now it is the people's turn. Hitler must fall! That alone can preserve the peace!'" Nor has he forgotten his prediction, in his letter to the dean of the Faculty of Philosophy of the University of Bonn—in which, we recall, he rued his role as martyr and not as representative of the real Germany—that "at the decisive moment, Germany would stand alone," abandoned by Mussolini (27). At this juncture Hitler's threats would have been exposed; "the hero of Germany could neither advance nor retreat"; he would have been overthrown (28). "The very revelation that his mission had been nothing more or less than to lead Germany into a suicidal war with the whole world . . . would have been enough to prove its bankruptcy. . . . Twenty-four hours of firm resolve on the part of the mild-mannered democracies . . . and the corrupter of Europe would have played out his hand; European fascism would be physically, mentally, morally finished. . . . It was not to be" (28–29).

Along with the Hitler regime, Britannia is the chief culprit.[44] She was not about to go to war, *not* because she was convinced of her defeat by Germany but because her defense of Czechoslovakia against armed aggression would have provoked Russia's entry into the Central European battlefield—and that *joint* victory she did not want. Russia's victory would mean the triumph of communism over fascism, anathema to the governing classes of England, who did not want fascism defeated for any reason whatsoever. Mann again cites his notorious letter to the dean of the Faculty of Philosophy of the University of Bonn stating that "war will not be permitted" to Germany (29). Yes, the prophecy has fulfilled itself—but with a twisted logic: "Hitler was not 'permitted' to bring about the ruin of fascism": he got everything he wanted, escaping his own ruin by nonviolent means, and "Bohemia was returned to an empire to which it had never belonged." The terms? A promise of incalculable human suffering. "Czech districts 'with more than fifty percent of German inhabitants' were delivered up to German domination, *along with German-speaking democrats, socialists, and Jews*" (30; emphasis added). What would have been the fate of Franz Kafka, I will add, had he been alive in 1938?

The Munich Agreement spells the end of this last eastern bastion of democracy, "destroyed or deliberately converted into a broken-spirited dependency" of a Gestapo government. And the profit? "This peace" (!) (31). If the peace founded until now on the one-sided unkindness of the Treaty of Versailles was held to be insecure, what of *this* peace? What peace can be in store for a world still held in thrall by the heroic posturings of a tawdry regime, with its concentration camps, its racial persecutions, its debasement of all civilized norms? It is not as if we now observe a general disarmament or a surge of concern by the Germans for the misery that its government is preparing for it: we saw that effort briefly in the run-up to the Munich Agreement, not now.

Mann advances one curious and one wrong conclusion: he will emerge as a false, if well-meaning, prophet. A curious statement repeats his opening salvo: "One may be right a thousand times in the name of all reason and morality," like those people who were right in detecting everything vile about "this peace" and now consider it a mere truce, an interregnum—"and yet not end up right in the end." These thinkers of good will could not stop the Munich plot; and now they are certain that a terrible war will come—but a war *need* not come. Mann's commentary: "Is that not at once our everlasting shame," namely, not to have been right in the end, after all, if an unwanted war should come, no matter who the victor and who the vanquished? One consolation remains—the moral logic of the Latin tag *Victrix causa diis placuit sed victa Catoni*, which provides the consolations of defeat. In this instance, the "defeat" lies in the fact, "hard to comprehend, why those who did not want war, when it would scarcely have had to be waged, should wish or be forced to wage it under conditions of far greater difficulty" (32).

The meaning of the "abiding consolation" of the Latin tag may lie in one of two senses: it may be the realization that right reason—the "spirit"—has once again been thwarted by a malicious actuality whether or not war should come. Or it may be something simpler and more nearly material: the fact that war will *not* come. In either case, one need no longer feel the fear of war that enveloped the Munich Agreement or to live now in fear of a greater war.[45] The anxious observers are wrong: "Armaments," Mann prophesizes, "are no longer accumulated to wage war, but only to levy blackmail and to counter it" (32). He has intuited the logic of assured mutual destruction; but one year later, and until 1945, his knowledge did not prevent the mutual destruction of much of Europe and the Far East.

Mann bases his optimism on what he believes the Munich crisis has actually brought about. First, there is the definitive end to "the bad conscience of the democracies over the peace of Versailles." Their policy of appeasement has "put Germany where she would have been if she had been victorious in 1914 [!]. More they cannot do to atone for the blunders and stupidities of the peace." Second, there is the outpouring of antiwar sentiment from the German people, which was apparent even prior to the crisis: so much for the martial discipline inflicted on them since 1933. "The extravagant joy and thankfulness with which Germany, too, greeted the peace would . . . have been just as great if it had brought no territorial aggrandizement with it" (33).

A third consolation has the form of an unusual argument. The complete fascization of Europe will bring about a malevolent unity of the nations. Fascist totalitarianism, involving, as it does, "moral and spiritual sacrifices of freedom, civilization, and human dignity," nonetheless spells the end of the nation-state (34). The thrust of fascism being perpetual war, the vast empire will run out of objects to conquer; its aggressive dynamism will come to a halt; and "just as fascism excludes peace, so peace excludes fascism" (35). Once halted, its "trashy ideology which served as vehicle on the road to such a goal might have become superfluous, or even useless, and more humane conceptions would again obtain a hearing" (34–35). The happy outcome would be a United States of Europe, an institution that can prevail as a culture of human dignity, respect, and fruitful work. A certain version of this prediction would in fact be realized, only after the world war, yet one that Mann could glimpse (he died, in exile from America, in 1955). As Ian Buruma reminds us, "After the war was won, Churchill gave a famous speech in Zurich [on September 19, 1946], in which he called for the creation of a United States of Europe."[46] Add on the decent fraternization of France and Germany in the European Coal and Steel Community and the founding of the United Nations. Mann might have realized, too, to his immense satisfaction, that the great promulgator of this vision of a comity of nations at the end of the war, together with Churchill, was his beloved Franklin Delano Roosevelt.[47]

Furthermore, historians currently argue that the Nazi movement, in no wise a revolution, did, via its destruction, bring about quasi-revolutionary changes in German society. Neil Ascherson deals productively with this question: The Nazis called their movement a "'national revolution.' Does it deserve the name?" He cites one authority, Volker Ullrich, who, like Thomas Mann, thinks not. For Ullrich,

> it was a change brought about by the alliance of traditional elites with the Nazi mass movement; it led to no replacement of elites or fundamental remaking of society.... With the challenge from the left destroyed, Hitler went on to crush two of the conservative social groups that had brought him to power: the titled landowners and the officer class. [However,] [...] by eventually destroying these old governing elites with all their institutions, [Eric] Hobsbawm, in *The Age of Extremes,* writes, the Nazis unwittingly helped to lay foundations for the future "bourgeois democracy" of West Germany....[48]

And so, Ascherson concludes, "Hitler was a modernizer as well as a genocidal tyrant. His perceived legacy is a burden of unbearable horror and humiliation. It's a difficult thought that the Third Reich also contributed to postwar Germany's success in unacknowledged ways: a robust sense of social equality, a stronger sense of common German identity co-existing with the restored federal structure, an imaginative provision for working-class welfare and leisure."[49]

It is interesting to note that in an interview on February 1, 1940, hence, a year before America entered the war, Mann commented that with the passing of the Nazi regime, "the true character of the German people (*des deutschen Volkes*), one inclined to love the world and the productions of other peoples, would overcome narrow nationalistic ideas." And he would view a United Nations of Europe as a "splendid" thing for Germany.[50]

Mann's argument deploring the failure of the Western democracies to stop the Nazis in a timely way was repeated—independently, of course—by Churchill in the most famous of his later speeches. On March 5, 1946, in the "Iron Curtain Speech"—"The Sinews of Peace"—Churchill declared,

> Up till the year 1933 or even 1935, Germany might have been saved from the awful fate which has overtaken her, and we might all have been spared the miseries Hitler let loose upon mankind. There never was a war in all history easier to prevent by timely action than the one which has just desolated such great areas of the globe. It could have been prevented . . . without the firing of a single shot. . . .[51]

In an essay referring to Churchill's speech, Ferdinand Mount appositely cites a Churchill biographer: "It is never difficult to speak grandly of a policy of 'firmness'; it is less easy to spell out where, when and how such a policy can best be applied."[52] Mount continues: "What exactly, for example, should or could Britain have done about Hitler in 1933?" Thomas Mann was appalled, of course, by Chamberlain's appeasement in 1938, but a few diehard defenders argue that in this way, as Mount observes, he could "buy a precious extra year," so that a better prepared British Army could declare war on Germany over Poland rather than the Sudetenland. But "the old questions" remain difficult to answer.[53]

Contra Thomas Mann the American

Despite his best efforts, Mann was not always appreciated in America: his work on behalf of the good cause could be considered ill-conceived and un-entitled.[54] That he was not well loved by all the parties in Germany who had got wind of his books and speeches goes without saying. Nazi newspapers could gleefully report in March 1940 that Mann was sitting captive in an English concentration camp (BR.M 198). The notoriously bold chapter 7 in *Lotte in Weimar*, in which Mann's Goethe fulminates against the political stupidity of the Germans, produced hate mail, as in this one sordid instance: "A card, a vile slander, in the mail, in Jewish jargon, with the presumption that I had caused the English bombardment of Weimar—as [Martin] Gumpert told me;

I would not have read it, just that the sender was spitting 'contemptuously into my face.' The reason is the reviews of *Lotte in Weimar*" (T4 144).[55] But these slurs were preceded by disturbing events in December 1938, only three months after Mann's arrival in Princeton. He could count on the cruel invective coming out of Nazi Germany but was unprepared for the hostile reaction of the American Trotskyite novelist James T. Farrell, who had been asked to sign on to Mann's manifesto "To the Civilized World" (*An die gesittete Welt*), which aimed honorably to strengthen the spine of a democratic resistance to the Nazi triumphs (GW 13:672–79).

And so, Mann's first Christmas in America was in part a grievous time: he was very angry at Farrell's accusation that his rebuke to fascism was feckless on grounds of its abstraction and high-flown literariness. To Mann's fury, he and all the world could now read Farrell's objections in a letter to the *New York Herald Tribune* of December 23, 1938; other readers of Farrell's piece joined in with their complaints. The complaints became far-ranging, putting into damnable question Mann's authority to speak on behalf of democratic ideals, a serious matter that requires our close attention. How had this contretemps come about?

In late 1938, at the suggestion of a group of concerned intellectuals—foremost, Dorothy Thompson, the author, broadcaster, and celebrated enemy of Hitler—Mann composed "To the Civilized World," his diatribe against Nazi totalitarianism. He was ready to undertake the task in a straightforward effort to heighten the morale of a world in shock at the succession of apparent Nazi triumphs. But the story unfolded in an unpredictable manner.

Mann wrote "To the Civilized World" as a jeremiad, composing it on a high plane of moral indignation. Its rhetorical style did not suit Farrell, a naturalistic novelist and socialist journalist. I reprint a version closest to the English text that Farrell read—a *composite* translation. I would ideally like to print the original translation of Mann's German text *pur sang*, which was presumably made by Molly Shenstone, an intimate friend of Katia Mann. Though regarded by Mann as "provisional," the essay was nonetheless circulated, to his indignation, among the would-be signatories. I have seen this rather rough, though exalted, version, the one that prompted Farrell's criticism, but it may not be published in its original form.[56] So, what follows is a *later* English version of the original, one that Mann subsequently embedded in a speech titled "Der Feind der Menschheit" (The Enemy of Mankind), which, despite its title, was delivered in English on April 3, 1939, in Beverly Hills, California, before the American Committee for Christian German Refugees (GW 13:645–55). This polished version departs in crucial ways from the translation that Farrell saw. After these

unhappy events, Mann anticipated circulating a revised version, but the
damage—Farrell's polemic—had already been done. In the composite translation below, fragments of the typescript (its word choices indicated in brackets
in *italic*) will allow us to capture something of the tone of the original, whose
hauteur provoked Mann's critics. The first paragraph is identical to the original; the rest reprints the relevant sections from "The Enemy of Mankind."

To the Civilized World
A Manifesto
By
Thomas Mann

Shall only those speak who, since they brazenly usurped control of it, have
identified language with the lie; who have made speech to share the mar-
tyrdom which is today the lot of all that is good, or noble, or eager to rise
unto God and the fullness of the ideal of man; who have crucified the word,
head downward, because it was never anything more to them than a means
with which to set the moral universe topsy-turvy in smudgy satanic glee
(which one must not marvel at weakly, just because it seems so utterly inconsistent with the level of our time), and to dishevel, maim and poison life
in the very spiritual depths out of which life rises?

Shall we listen only to the enemy who says "peace," when he means
"war," "order" when he means "anarchy," "elevation" [in the original translation: *resurrection*] when he means "deepest degradation," "freedom" when
he means "servitude," manliness" when he means "bestiality," "culture"
when he means the terror of vindictive stupidity. He possesses the knack
of the rogue to wrest the verdict from the hands of non-plussed truth, and
before the latter can emit a sound, with a foresight of insanity, he roars at
those who are opposition-minded against his infamous march of conquest
and death, every name and every reproach that rightfully is his: robber,
murderer, cheat, destroyer [*perverter*], poisoner [*brute-man (Untermensch)*,
omitted] and finally "war-monger." [...]

Language is the possession of mankind that unites not only man with
man, but man with intellect [*the spirit (Geist)*].[57] Language is the medium
of prayer, of confession [*profession*] of faith, and of literature [*poetic insight*].
This possession shall not be delivered to those alone to whom lamentably
peoples and countries are being delivered, in another attempt, a last one, to
prevent the enemy from drowning the world in blood. It is insufferable [*we
find it intolerable*] to think of this monstrosity among humans [*deformation*

of the human essence], whom by all the laws of nature nothing but icy silence is due, this dark brood, blind to all morals and human dignity, blind to the most moderate righteousness [*the most primitive norms of justice*], blind to the most fundamental logical decency, without which life holds nothing [*life becomes impossible*],—it must not come to pass that this creature shall be the sole spokesman, to the end that he may dishonor the spoken word, distort it, drag it through the mire and thrust into despair [*until*] a mankind that hears nothing else than this creature's abhorrent dialect, sees nothing else but the triumph of baseness [*its vulgarity*], devoid of all consideration [*be led to despair of its own life*]. Much as human judgments [*the human faculty for giving names to things*, omitted] may be tempted to capitulate before this creature's deeds and words, much as the designation given to works that are a failure [*utterly misshapen works of art*], namely that they are "below criticism," applies in this instance also and much as reason will have left only derisive laughter for the no longer adequate, for the senseless infamy,—nevertheless they must be told, the spoken word, still linked to honor, meaning and humaneness, must not be renounced, muted and banned from the world [*disappear from earth*] during its grotesque march through an age of brainless decline [*definable only as a mad stampede*]. Where this word is still free, has not been trampled under foot, where it has not been thrust back into a frightened spirit by physical [*raucous*] threats, it must raise its voice,—not for a discussion with the enemy—there is no regulated language in which discussion with him could be possible—but rather its voice must be raised with inalienable authority, granted by God and reason, to protect the human spirit against the onslaught of devilish lies [*satanic untruths*] and confusion which it suffers. Its voice must be raised in definitely comforting accents [*with utterance of manly comfort*] to save this spirit from a despair that endangers its very life. [. . .]

We men and women from several countries of Western and Eastern culture, who, with our honorable work in the fields of knowledge and art, have achieved names that redound to human honors [honored of humankind], confirm the sense and intention of the following words [preceding nine words cut from original]: we are not politicians, and this is not a political manifesto.]

It is no longer a question of politics [*It is a long time since the issue at stake has had anything in common with political action*], it is no longer a question of statement and counterstatement of political or even world-view [*philosophic*] opinions; it is a question of the foundation and the fundamental terms of civilized and intellectual [*moral and spiritual*] life, it is a question of culture itself, which to us is no idle-presumptuous pretension to beauty, but humanity itself: the expression of eternal approach of man to his ideas [*Man to his Idea*], his inborn obligations to decency before God, to reason, truth, and right—his craving for perfection, of which artistic endeavor [*creative effort*] is at once the brightest and most severe symbol.

Among us there are conservatives and revolutionaries, for this antithesis, too, is eliminated in that common bond that vaults above it! The conservative values and protects that which survives, that which endures in human life, the customs of his forbears [*what in human life is enduring, perennial, tested by experience:—the customs of the fathers*], venerable traditions of manners and morals; the revolutionary values and protects new formations, the will for a new order of things, the active betterment and purging, even the enthusiastic overthrow and faithful re-beginning. One sanctifies the past, the other the future—but both are concerned with the human being, his welfare, his dignity, his happiness, his divine [*Divine*] calling; and therefore in the last analysis they fight on the same ground and ultimate understanding between them is possible. It is not possible with that which has nothing in common with honor, reason and kindness, such an understanding is not possible with intellectual filth [*the muddy residue from which the spirit has flown*], with the distorted mask, with the diabolical [*Satanism*], with the arch-criminal or the profligate [*implicit banditry, the everlastingly outcast*]. Just as in a free state the most diverse opinions [*of the common good*] may be engaged in contact, it matters only that they are devoted to its welfare [*that good*]. It would be madness, however, it *is* madness, to admit treason itself, the negation of the idea of fellowship [*the community*], the enemy of the state to its councils. This is true also when it is no longer a question of the state but of humanity proper and its greatest concern, civilization: the entire moral world must unite against the *enemy of mankind*, it must speak, for that right belongs to mankind, not to the enemy [*so that the misdeeds of this enemy may be stigmatized*]. In entering this protest against the enemy's misdeeds, the moral world must bring solace and strength to disturbed mankind in order to save it from despondency and secession [*apostasy (Abfall)*]. For at the spectacle of the enemy's victories, mankind no longer knows what to think and believe. The word which he stole and that he used for his lies has brought him acclaim [*given him his strength*]; this very same word may also fell him—not at once; in reality he may continue along these same lines for a while and boast of his successes, successes in which he is being aided by weakness, short-sightedness, lack of understanding for his true nature, as well as interest and treason; that will only be a reprieve, which we can await. When the best among us [*the best spirits of the time*], those who are intellectually decisive, have passed sentence upon him, he will waste away and ultimately perish from this wound, which the free word of the intellect [*spirit*] has inflicted upon him, although he does not seem to feel it now.

Have no fear![58] What you now see will pass away. Do not believe what appearances would like to teach: that right, truth, human standing and all higher aspirations have come to an end: these, so they say, were frail illusions [*have been weakling delusions of fancy*], but what is to rule now, that to which one must conform, that by which one must be governed, that is the lie [*prevarication*]. Violence [*force*], the battering down of the weak to the accompaniment of scornful laughter, the filthy lust for degradation of human beings, the cowardly barbarism of venting one's anger on [*whets the steel of its courage on the bodies of*] defenseless people. All this is the affair of the enemy of humanity; he believes and wants it, he thinks it is only natural. But the intellect [*the spirit (der Geist)*] is nature also, at least that is true of human beings, and in the nature [*this spirit*] of man there are energies that categorically and definitively do *not* want this and sooner than he expected, with unexpected momentum and dignity, they will give the lie to the sub-human world-picture of the opponent [*proof of the falsehood of the enemy's faith*].

Have no fear! Do not let the propaganda lies [*propagandistic fables*] that have aided him in playing his game, intimidate and bewilder you; these lies will help him for a little longer, thanks to the folly of many and mighty ones. He tells you about "bolshevism." You must choose, so he maintains, between him and "bolshevism;" in his opinion he is the only stronghold against "bolshevism" and therefore everyone must seek refuge with him, the world must fall to his share, so as not to be devoured by the red specter [*Red Spectre*].— Very well, we know that you, too, whom we approach and who are irresolute, shaken [*and cowed*], impressed by the success of this evil spirit, believe half-heartedly at least in this lie, the most effective purposeful lie of this enemy of mankind. Do you want to hear the truth? This "bolshevism" which he means and which you mean also, when you speak the word or hear it spoken, that "bolshevism" of course exists in the world; he who threatens you with this "bolshevism," who uses it as a subterfuge for his infamous acts, who extorts his victories from this same "bolshevism," he knows exactly where this "bolshevism" is located: *he is this "bolshevism."* Here again, and particularly here, is demonstrated the diabolical [*demoniacal*] and therefore the morbid as well as laughable bondage to which he is subject. It is this that makes him shout to all the world all what he is and what he knows himself to be in his deepest misery, from a fear, that infuriates him, [*drives him mad*] not as though he were speaking of himself but of someone else. Whatever you may visualize at the mention of the apocalyptic names of bolshevism: violence, anarchy, blood, incendiary and mastery by rabble, religious persecution, most infamous cruelty, the reversal of all conceptions, the desecration of right [*rape of justice*] and reason, the insolent, ridiculously infamous distortion of truth, inciting to basest action [*the fanning into flame of every base instinct*, omitted], disintegration and dissolving of the order of states,—all this disseminated over land and sea; undermining the farthest corners of the world with money, bribes, dulling perceptions [*deafening talk*], endless spy- and agitator-systems, until everywhere resistance is broken, order collapses and the globe becomes the uniform grave of freedom, over which the flag of stupid servitude flies,—he, and he alone, is this "bolshevism;" and if wars, more destructive and more barbaric than the Thirty Years' War come over Europe, blow it into atoms and leave it thrown back for centuries, he, the enemy of mankind, will have been the instigator of all this.

However, while he asserts that not he is bolshevism, but the exact opposite, namely salvation from such bolshevism, he plays the part of the great revolutionary, the renovator of the world, and intimidates the faint-hearted, bribes the youth with his boast that he is making "history." Every time he has slapped the face of mankind by some particularly crass misdeed, so that indignation and opposition lift their hands in such countries where an open moral movement is possible, he limps to the microphone and says: "You should be ashamed, you drowsy and fearful ones, those of you imbued with a prejudice for the old and the stale, you eternal ones of yesterday, why cannot you understand the new order we bring you, the great historic-revolutionary revival, whose active prophets we are!" The word "eternal ones of yesterday" he has stolen from the noble-minded poet, whose aim it was to educate the people for the better through beauty and who little dreamed, just as other endeavoring intellects [*zealous spirit*], that one day he would have to serve the enemy of mankind as a crown-witness. However, it is not a question of yesterday and today, of old and new, it is the question of the eternal and inalienable that God-Nature himself has instilled into man and which the enemy of mankind treads underfoot. Can you believe in a revolution that will cast off the sense of right of man, his struggle for truth, his natural-intellectual [*natural-spiritual (natürlich-geistige)*] obligation for that which is good, with the result that henceforth art and perception, every free joyous effort, insured by intellect [*spirit*] and ennobled by it (*geistversicherte und geistgeadelte*), will be done for? You should laugh at the rodomontades of these low scoundrels, instead of letting them shame you.

Politically you are told about "right" and "left,"—the "Left," they try to establish [*want to say*], everything connected with progressive ideas, belief in betterment, the will for liberation from superfluous, stale sufferings, has become obsolete; the "Right," so they say, has taken over the leadership and only through this "right" may the revolutions of the future be brought about. What is the obvious truth? "Progress," moral, intellectual, yes, technical development has led mankind to pacifism, as a matter of principle. The peoples, the average man, the man on the street, will have nothing of war; they see through it, are satiated with it, no longer will they be made fools of by war or for it, they have reached that point. And this pacifistic state of mind and conviction [*of humanity*, omitted)], finally arrived at and dearly paid for, is being misused and exploited by those morally in arrears [*defective*] who mock this natural progress and simultaneously speculate upon it. The love for peace, the just unwillingness for war of the people [*which stirs in the hearts of the peoples*] must serve them as a rampart in their crimes; they lean on them, exact them by violence, with their help they inflate compulsory states, gigantic [*gargantuan*], armament-studded citadels [*that gleam with weapons*] of human enmity, behind whose bastions they believe themselves safe, to sneer at all opposition to their daily contemptible acts [*every attack on his abiding worthlessness*]. That is the leadership which they exercise, the revolution they bring, the "history" they make. But it is a knavish [*childish*], void, senseless and anachronistic sort of history. It will explode before your very eyes [*his eyes*] and then you will see whether you were right that you knew no fear and that you opposed the lies of the Antichrist with the resistance of your hearts [*still uncorrupted*] that have remained steadfast.

We are only workers of the intellect, without any direct influence upon the happenings of the world. Nevertheless, our words of comfort, our joint admonition, should not be evaluated too lightly. The intellect [*spirit of man*], devoid of material power, has a quiet, yet irresistible efficacy on earth, an efficacy that is both annihilating and constructive, and its decisions are of importance [*originally are carried out*]. When it turns from a matter, that matter is doomed. The enemy of mankind knows this full well. His deep, howling fury, that no success can still, emanates from just this knowledge: he knows that intellect [*the spirit*] has passed judgment upon him. You, too, should know it and should not fear. No matter how much he may swagger [*though his glory may be lordly*] today, no matter how far-reaching his policy of intimidation is, no matter how much misery he has caused [*of which he has been the artisan*], how great [*the endless expanse*] the dishonor, depravity, blood, tears, despair and suicides on which he looks down from his mountain seat and in so doing feels great and [*venture[s]*] *thereupon to esteem himself*] "historical," his fate is sealed [*his staff is already broken*]. Nothing [*not a jot or tittle*] will remain of his works, because they are false and hollow, and his posthumous glory [*fame*] will be disgrace [*shall be infamy*] [1938].

The original text—a late German draft presumably translated, as noted, by Molly Shenstone, Katia's best friend and helper—was distributed among several prominent writers and intellectuals for signatures without Mann's full knowledge or consent. It could seem an unproblematical invitation for anti-fascists to underwrite its sentiment while enduring its rhetorical oddities (as consider especially the final paragraph above): they merely had to sign on. The outcome, however, as we have heard, was unexpected—and for Mann extremely disturbing. He found himself at the receiving end of Farrell's blunt criticism and, still worse, of a highly publicized attack in the *Herald Tribune* just before his first Christmas in Princeton.

Farrell criticized Mann's text on rhetorical and "scientific" grounds. He found the summons abstruse, a compilation of glacial abstractions—goodness versus evil—with no scientific understanding of the political and economic factors underlying the Nazi coup. Here are the main features of Farrell's rebuttal:

Mann's Manifesto against Fascism
James T. Farrell Writes That He Cannot Accept It

In the name of abstract and frozen good, . . . [Mann's pamphlet] thunders against evil in a manner more befitting the Jehovah of the Bible than a modern man seeking to discuss crucial contemporary issues. . . . It does not even name Hitler and Fascism. It erects a *devil-theory-of-Fascism* [!] [emphasis added]. . . .

Mann states that his manifesto is not a political document and that "it is a long time since the issue at stake has had anything in common with political action." I refuse to accept this statement and the conclusion drawn from it, a conclusion isolating "moral and spiritual life" from politics. Any attack on totalitarianism is and must be a political attack. When I sign a political manifesto, I do not believe in declaring that I am signing something else. . . .

Thomas Mann's claim that Fascism will wither away because writers, intellectuals and other men of good will condemn it is a *non sequitur*. Fascism establishes a régime of reaction with arms in hand and state power in its control. When in history has reaction, with such powers, withered away instead of being overthrown? This type of counsel of patience is false and delusory.

I am neither a religious nor a mystical man, and I believe in no appeals to God and spirit. I cannot sign a manifesto containing such appeals. This manifesto contains various statements concerning the relationship of language to spirit, the word, and the like which are without the slightest scientific warrant. These run counter to everything that I have written and thought. They are irrelevant in the crucial issues of Fascism and the kind of a threat against modern culture which Fascism constitutes.[59]

Vaget's summary of Farrell's full polemic is on point: "Farrell advances both stylistic (the text is vague and abstract) and substantive objections: the confusion of the terms 'conservative' and 'revolutionary'; the implicit criticism of the Russian Revolution; the failure to discuss the 'important causative factors of Fascism'; the recourse to religious and mystical ideas; the tendency to rely on patience rather than struggle" (BR.M 852). Farrell would not sign on. His *public* attack killed the project. Moreover, it provoked an entire discussion of the merits of its arguments, printed, to Mann's dismay, in the following issues of the *Herald Tribune*. What was worse, the criticism of Farrell and the like-minded soon metastasized into an attack on Mann's role *tout simple* as a spokesman for democracy. Energized readers raised with a vengeance the compromising specter of Mann's First World War polemics, the most forceful being one Thomas A. Baggs, a scholar of propaganda, who, in a biting, mainly well-informed letter, acquired the distinction, for the first time in America, of raising the incriminating ghost of Mann's dark, "conservative" past. Here is Baggs:

ECHOES OF MANN'S MANIFESTO
James T. Farrell's Refusal to Sign Discussed by Readers
Election to the Academy

Three lusty cheers for James T. Farrell's letter in the *New York Herald Tribune* of December 23 expressing dissent from the manifesto which Thomas Mann, the German writer, has addressed "To the Civilized World."

It is a timely service, for the newspapers of December 22 report Thomas Mann's election to an honorary corresponding membership of the American Academy of Arts and Letters, and concurring in his election are a great American humanist, Nicholas Murray Butler, and a great American biographer, Van Wyck Brooks, both of whom doubtless were moved to do so by reason of their admiration for Mann the novelist and not Mann the political pamphleteer.

* * *

The distinction has to be made, for even our best minds are prone to act under the urging of some emotional cataclysm, such as the current wave of anti-Nazi revulsion.

Reason as well as feeling revolts at happenings in Germany today, but that surely is no reason why an American literary institution of standing should lose its sense of proportion, and without adequate background information do honor to Thomas Mann for "defending the basic idea of our civilization, perhaps more powerfully than any other writer"—Thomas Mann, who only a score of years ago declared himself in favor of militarism and kultur and the things that have spawned into the Nazist philosophy of the present day: Thomas Mann, who declared his faith in "the German soul which is too deep to accept civilization as its motivating force."

Consistency is for little minds, it is true, but surely it is not expecting too much of a mature writer that he do not completely turn about-face without offering an explanation.

Thomas Mann was in his fortieth year in 1915 when he delivered himself of these edifying thoughts on Germanic kultur. He was not the most prolific of German apologists during the war, but he was unequivocally on the side of kultur and all it meant in the early years of the great war, as any careful student of propaganda must remember. He sided with his fatherland— and that cannot be held against him—though he showed the same mental quirks and the same verbal looseness in attacking "civilization" then as in defending it today.

* * *

In manner, certainly, if not in matter, he is the same Thomas Mann, the discursive pamphleteer as distinct from the discerning novelist. Read his

"Friedrick und die Grosse Koalition" [*sic*] (Berlin 1915)—there's a copy in the New York Public Library—and observe the "sea-change" that has in recent years transmogrified his political theorizing.

Here, for instance, are some typical thoughts from the book's second essay, entitled "Gedanken im Kriege":[60]

Kultur and civilization are not the same but opposites. . . .

The Germans are not so enamored of the word "civilization" as their Western neighbor-nations . . . they have preferred kultur as word and ideal. . . . Truly, there is something in the feeling and opinion of weaker nations that the German soul is disturbing, disquieting, and strange even to the point of appearing disgusting and savage. It is her militarism, her conservatism, her soldierly moral strength—an element of the demoniac and heroic that has made Germany refuse to recognize the civic spirit as the last and worthiest human ideal!

A pretty philosophy for democracy's Galahad! So, by your leave, President Nicholas Murray Butler and Academician Van Wyck Brooks, I prefer to find a champion whose background and breeding are beyond all question native American. I may admire immensely parts of "Buddenbrooks" and "The Magic Mountain"—although I find both entirely too otiose in style—yet I do not expect their author to turn out a pamphlet on Democracy or peace of [*sic*] Fascism which will be a marvel of its kind and every whit as convincing and as acceptable. I find much to debate in "The Coming Victory of Democracy" and "This Peace"—much, too, that reminds me of that "windy suspiration of forced breath" which annoyed Hamlet.

These are some of the reasons why I second James T. Farrell's motion of entering a *caveat* against accepting Thomas Mann as the champion of democracy. Loose thinking and flaccid psychologizing are enemies instead of aids to a better popular understanding of the institutions of government. Clear thinking and "modern instances" are first essentials—and I submit we can find them at home among native Americans without drawing upon the talents of a kultur propagandist lately turned anti-Nazist.

THOS. A. BAGGS

NEW YORK, DEC. 27, 1938.

A devoted friend and admirer of Mann and his work, Harry Slochower, a professor of German at Brooklyn College, stepped into the breach and added a positive "echo" to this discussion—a defense of Mann's political science.

Sees Mann Misunderstood[61]

Mr. Farrell's attack on Thomas Mann's anti-Fascist manifesto "To the Civilized World" (*New York Herald Tribune*, December 23) contains an astounding misrepresentation of Mann's position on the relation between the spiritual and political realms. Farrell writes that he refuses to accept Mann's "conclusion" in which he isolates moral and spiritual life from politics. Everything that Mann has written since "The Magic Mountain" refutes Farrell's characterization. Mann's recent "The Coming Victory of Democracy," in particular, employs the term "democracy" precisely in the sense of a union between poetry, morals and politics. More recently, Mann stated: "The political and social is a part of the human and [to] be included within the human" [Lecture at the German Day Festival, December 4, 1938; GW 11:946].

Mann is also clearly cognizant of the social factors involved in Fascism, as anyone acquainted with his current pronouncements knows. In this manifesto, he avoids raising controversies over interpretations of social doctrines, preferring to emphasize that over which there is widest agreement, namely, the moral and spiritual values involved. His appeal on human grounds is in the interests of rallying the largest number of people against the imminent menace of Fascism. And, since Thomas Mann does not share Farrell's "devil theory" of "Stalinism," he recognizes that, in international politics, Russia is on the side of the democracies.

Furthermore, Mann, as an artist, lays stress on the power of the word, as symbol. Farrell writes that Mann's appeal to spirit and his belief in the relation between language and the spirit "run counter to everything I have written and thought." This is doubtless true.

HARRY SLOCHOWER

BROOKLYN, DEC. 24, 1938[62]

After Baggs, however, Slochower's response reads as somewhat abstruse and no longer keenly relevant to Farrell's, let alone to Baggs's attack. In a woeful letter, Mann thanked Slochower for his loyalty in this "hateful disturbance," although Slochower's brief defense had not been enough to "calm and console him": this public discussion amounted to a catastrophe for the entire project, which had mattered very much to Mann and cost him work. Now, without mentioning Baggs's insinuations, or even contemplating writing in self-defense, Mann discussed the origin of the affair: it had come about, in many of Mann's words, when a number of people whom he admired had suggested to him that the time was ripe for a manifesto that might be backed by "outstanding representatives of the entire moral and spiritual world." Its aim would be to bring "strength and consolation to a world which had been put in a state of grave moral confusion by the most recent triumphs of [Nazi] violence and injustice." The idea was not new to Mann; he had had it in mind for some time, and so he declared himself ready to write the manifesto. But it soon became apparent that what Mann had had in his heart to say could not be said in a few lines, and the envisioned single page became eight pages.

At this point Mann perceived the trouble with a "manifesto" of such a length, which was actually the personal confession—the reflections of an awakened political man. He noted that few presumptive and desired signatories would be able to *identify* themselves with so big a text of such subtlety and complexity—and then simply sign on. So, what Mann had in mind was to invite those "representatives of the moral and spiritual world"—and certainly not including Farrell, in which "circle" Mann had never envisioned him—to contribute a general endorsement. But Mann was not in charge of this project, and he did not supervise its process. The translation made its way into the circle but not into the public world. In yet another letter to the *Herald Tribune*, under the heading of "Echoes of Mann's Manifesto: Calls Statement Premature," Albert H. Gross explained that it is he who "has been acting for a group of American writers in presenting for signature to outstanding intellectuals in the United States the manifesto against Nazi barbarism, 'To the Civilized World,' by Thomas Mann." Gross defends the evident propriety of the document, which had now been enthusiastically welcomed by such luminaries as "William Rose Benet, Van Wyck Brooks, Charles Beard, Paul Vincent Carroll, Edna Ferber, Sidney Howard, George Jean Nathan, Carl van Doren, Maxwell Anderson, Owen Davis, Ford Madox Ford, Paul de Kruif, W.E. Woodward and Robert Sherwood," among others. But Farrell's attack has cut right through all of them.

In a bold essay, the critic Paul Fussell once took arms against writers who were vexed and indignant when their published work was treated badly in the press. Fussell merely pointed out that no one had ever *forced* them to put their work "out there." It would invite praise and encouragement in the best case; it could just as well invite dislike, and who would the author have to blame for his chagrin if not himself?[63] Another letter to the *Herald Tribune* added to Mann's distress: the writer, Bernard Rosenberg, like Baggs, supported Farrell's thrust. The letter contains a perfectly trenchant objection from the side of a free thinker. Rosenberg focuses on Mann's invocation and celebration of the "spirit" (*Geist*). Writes Rosenberg, "Mr. Farrell is not alone in his contention that mysticism and 'spirit' have nothing to do with the issue, the threat of Fascism to modern culture. Spirit is a word which is used to clothe the nakedness of the nonexistent. Spirit is the nightgown of nescience." (Interestingly, in the later working through of Mann's manifesto that we have seen, Mann often translates *Geist* with the less provocative word "intellect.") Rosenberg ends, more bluntly: "Mr. Farrell's letter is an appeal for each to think for himself. That [being] the habit, we need fear no extirpation of individualism which is the only possible antidote to totalitarianism of whatever ideological shade."[64]

It needs to be stressed that, like Baggs, Rosenberg was completely ignorant of the manifesto proper. What Mann, in his letter to Slochower, called a "senseless and impermissible polemic against a text that wasn't even 'in the world'" could be seen as deeply unjust precisely because of its provisional character. The indecency of its being submitted to public discussion before it had even been published *is* galling. As Gross writes, "Criticism of an unrevealed document is a one-sided game at best."

Mann was not a lame player in this game. He soon answered the demand that he account for his conversion to democracy by publishing such an account on an invitation from the journal *Survey Graphic*. Here, he implicitly replies to Farrell and Boggs by frankly reproducing parts of the content of the disputed manifesto "To the Civilized World." Now, in "Culture and Politics," Mann takes the opportunity—a felt obligation—to lay out his credentials as a responsible spokesman for democracy.

In a letter to Agnes Meyer, on hearing of her passionate support, Mann outlined his thesis with admirable concision: it centers on the conflict in the *Reflections of a Nonpolitical Man* between a German, politically neutral, culture-immersed intellectuality (*eine deutsche politik-freie Kultur-Geistigkeit*) and the duty owed to politics and to the social order. It will be profitable to read this text in full, because we do want to know how Mann's conversion proceeded and why it had been necessary in the first place. It is decisive for the manner in which Mann treats his own career, not with self-regard, but as an exemplary error, as an aberration typical of the German bourgeoisie. He cites luminaries from the German tradition like Schopenhauer to build his case, in many instances, with a dazzling conciseness and precision. The piece was republished in the volume *Order of the Day* with minor corrections, where it has been read by many; but I find the original *Survey Graphic* article of 1938, which I want to reprint in its entirety, to be the more compelling.[65]

CULTURE AND POLITICS
by Thomas Mann

Herewith a 38'er and his evolution as an exile for democracy's sake. That is in line with a great tradition left by the 48'ers and after, such as Carl Schurz and Dr. Jacobi, Goldmark, Lasker, Brandeis, Kudlich, Siegel. Readers of "Buddenbrooks" know Dr. Mann as a keen analyst of the old German stock from which he sprang. There he told the story of a burgher family, brittle, broken. Here he tells that of a whole class, the why of its surrender and degradation. Yet not utterly without hope, for with it he tells his own story—the rise of a fighting faith which makes him today, in turn, an American-in-the-making.

[—THE EDITORS]

MY PERSONAL ALLEGIANCE TO DEMOCRACY RESTS UPON A CONVICTION which I was obliged to acquire, since it was basically foreign to my bourgeois-intellectual origins and upbringing. I mean the conviction that the political and social are parts of the human; they belong to the totality of human problems and must be drawn into the whole. Otherwise we leave a dangerous gap in our cultural life.

Perhaps it sounds strange that I should so simply equate democracy with politics and define it, with no more ado, as the political aspect of the intellect, the readiness of the intellect to be political. But indeed, I did that twenty years ago, in a large and laborious work called "The Reflections of an Unpolitical Man." And therein my definition was not only negative but even belligerently so. I defined democracy as the political functioning of the intellect, and I opposed it with all my power, in the name of culture—and even in the name of freedom. For in accordance with my intellectual traditions, what I meant by freedom was moral freedom. Of the connection between moral and social freedom I understood little and cared less. The book was written during the war. It consisted of a passionate self-examination and revision of principles—in short, of all my traditional values, which were intellectual, bourgeois, German and unpolitical. Culture for me meant music, metaphysics, psychology; meant a pessimistic ethic and an individualistic idealism in the cultural field. From it I contemptuously excluded everything political.

Now That I Have Become Political

BUT SELF-EXAMINATION, IF IT IS THOROUGH ENOUGH, IS NEARLY ALWAYS the first step towards change. I was to discover that no one who learns to know himself remains just what he was before. The book itself, in its urgent haste to talk about everything all at once, was the expression of a crisis, of a new situation evoked by profoundly upsetting outward events. Thanks to these, the question of each of us as a human being, the problem of humanity as a whole, began to challenge both my mind and my conscience more sharply than ever before. I came to see that there is no clear dividing line between the intellectual and the political; that the German bourgeoisie had erred in thinking that a man of culture could remain unpolitical; that our culture itself stood in the greatest danger wherever and whenever it lacked interest and aptitude for the political. In short, an acknowledgment of democratic feeling rose to my lips. Despite all the inhibitions of my anti-political upbringing this was not to be suppressed. I did not suppress it—and for that I am grateful to my good genius. For where should I stand today, on what side should I be, if in my conservatism I had clung to a Germany which in the end has not been saved by all of its music and all of its intellectualism, from surrender to the lowest form of worship of power, nor from a barbarism which threatens the foundations of our Western civilization?

The unhappy course of German history, which has issued in the cultural catastrophe of National Socialism, is in truth very much bound up with that unpolitical cast of the bourgeois mind, and with its anti-democratic habit of looking down the nose from its intellectual and cultural height at the sphere of political and social action. Not long ago I was made freshly aware of this when I happened to re-read the works of a very great German thinker and writer—Arthur Schopenhauer. He was an extraordinary brain. Schopenhauer was the forerunner and teacher of Nietzsche's anti-intellectualism. He was a revolutionary reactionary—who thrust reason from her throne and made her the creature and tool of the "Will," of blind and sinister instinct. He was the strongest opponent of Hegel, and declared that the Hegelian system—with its apotheosis of politics and its "bee-hive" theory of the state as the culminating point of all human striving—was the grossest philistinism. For his part, Schopenhauer regarded the state as a necessary evil. He would neither criticize, he said, nor mix into the affairs of those whose thankless task it is to govern men—an addlepated lot at best—in order to preserve order, execute the laws, and protect the rights of the propertied classes against the countless hordes who had nothing to boast of but their physical strength.

Today we know the inhumane horrors of a code wherein it is the end of man to be consumed in the state. We can understand very well any objections to the absolute power of the state, which, as Schopenhauer put it, "snatches the lofty goal of existence away from our eyes." But the conception of the state as an institution created for protection of property—does that not smack as much of the philistine as Hegel's idolatry of the state, as such? And our small capitalist philosopher's ironic disclaimer of any ambition to mix in politics— might not that be regarded as a refusal to entertain any spiritual passion for the rights and happiness of mankind? Now it was Schopenhauer who declared that his motto in life was not to worry about the Holy Roman Empire. For this, he flippantly said, he thanked God every morning! One can scarcely know how to credit such a philistine evasion of responsibility in so doughty an intellectual fighter as Schopenhauer surely was.

IN OTHER WORDS, EVERY SURRENDER ON THE PART OF THE INTELLECT is an error and a self-deception. One does not get clear of politics that way. One only approaches politics from the wrong side—and with so much the more violence. To be a-political simply means to be anti-democratic; but we scarcely realize, save in a crisis, what a suicidal position the mind has thus taken. Schopenhauer's attitude in the revolution of 1848 was tragi-comic; it was both shabby and grim. His heart was not at all with those presumed fanatics who hoped to guide German public life in a direction that might have changed the course of European history for the better and happier. That should have been the interest of every man of intellect, and it was in the direction of democracy. But Schopenhauer called the common people the "*souveräne canaille*." When from the window of the philosopher's house an officer was reconnoitering the men on the barricades, Schopenhauer ostentatiously handed over his own opera-glasses that he might see better to direct the fire. Is that being superior to the political? No, it is simply reactionary passion—the grounds of which are, indeed, intellectually quite clear to us.

It would take us too far afield to inquire into the roots of Schopenhauer's anti-revolutionary bias. But this much is plain: that it arose logically and by process of thought from his conception of the world; that it had its roots, also, in his temperament, his fundamental trait of ethical pessimism. His was the characteristic mood of "the Cross, Death and the Grave" which by psychological law feels revolted by rhetoric, by enthusiasm for freedom, and by the cult of humanity. Schopenhauer became, then, a political anti-revolutionary because of his melancholy and his critical spirit, his reverence for suffering and his hatred alike of "indecent optimism" and progress-preaching demagoguery. But all this only makes him a perfect specimen of the old familiar type, the German bourgeois: German precisely because that type is intellectual and because of its subjectivity, its conservative radicalism, its absolute remoteness from democratic pragmatism; its geniality, also, and its profound and foolhardy indifference to freedom. All these are quite specifically German, orthodox—and dangerous.

Will Germans Profit from Hard Experience?

THIS POLITICAL PASSIVITY AND REMOTENESS FROM DEMOCRACY HAS frightfully avenged itself. Germany has been sacrificed to a state totalitarianism which has robbed her not only of civic but of moral freedom. If we identify democracy with the recognition that the political and social are constituent parts of the human; if we say that democracy, in defending her civil freedom, defends her ethical freedom as well; then the opposite of democracy—into which the anti-democratic arrogance of intellect dialectically transforms itself—is that theory and that fundamentally anti-human practice which makes the political dominate the whole field of human affairs to the exclusion of everything else. There is a ruthless and tragic consistency in its operations from knowing nothing but the state, thinking of nothing but power, sacrificing the human being, to sacrificing all that pertains to humanity itself and making an end of freedom once and for all. The absence of political experience on the part of the intellectual German bourgeois and his contemptuous attitude towards democracy, his scorn for freedom—which to him was nothing but libertarian cant—all this resulted in nothing less than the enslavement of the citizen to the state and to power politics. It made of his life and labor a mere function of totalitarianism, and so debased him that one asks how he can ever again hold up his head before the world.

Granted that he escapes with his life from this frightful experience; granted that German culture—which, following Goethe, we are fain to believe must always be a bourgeois culture—survives the degradation called National Socialism, we must hope that the disastrous consequences of his political blindness have served him as a harsh but wholesome school. Often, I have said: "Before things can get better in Germany, they must reach the point where when they hear the word freedom, Germans burst into tears."

They do not seem to be far from that point now. After six years of the Gestapo state, it looks as though the German bourgeois is coming to understand the meaning of the words freedom, justice, human dignity, duty and conscience. And to understand that these words are more than the humanitarian mouthings of a cheap revolutionarism. But certain things are more easily lost than found again. The outcome remains a doubtful question, the answer to which depends not alone on the duration of the present catastrophe, on its character as episode or as epoch, but on whether the bourgeois intellectual of Germany will be able to profit by his hard experience.

FOR THE MOMENT DESTINY TAKES ITS COURSE. WE WITNESS THE paradox of the decline of that German mind which was scornful of politics. The bourgeois anti-revolutionary understood revolution only on the religious or the intellectual plane. In the end he has been impressed into service as the *sans-culotte* standard-bearer of the most extravagant revolution the world has ever seen. Certainly, one cannot call this revolution intellectual; one can scarcely call it human. It is directed against everything that occidental civilization has taught us to call either mind or humanity. No, it is a revolution of absolute and deliberate destruction and disintegration of all the foundations of morality, in the interest of the one idea of power.

Yes, this is the essence of it, of this thing which calls itself the German revolution. It knows no intellectual, moral, human bond; only the false and hollow will to power and mastery. Every idea, every conviction, every doctrine or conception of the world we live in, is good only to serve as a screen, a pretext, a technique of trickery in the pursuit of a goal empty of all moral content. So much must gradually have become clear to those who, in Germany and outside of it, thought they saw in National Socialism a bulwark and shelter against disruption, if only of the capitalistic economic system. If the Western powers continue to give way, more will be lost in this revolution than the capitalistic economy. Indeed, before that destruction, revolution, absurdly enough, might pause; but for the sake of retaining power, Nazism is ready with the completest cynicism to fly any flag. Today, as a hundred signs betray, it is even ready to fly that one from which it promised to protect the bourgeois world: I mean the Bolshevist flag.

Enemy of Humankind

THE BOURGEOISIE OF EUROPE—AND EVEN OF THE WORLD—HAVE BEEN taken in by the pretense of this thoroughly dishonest and cynical movement, that it was a bulwark against bolshevism. The bourgeois literally trembles at this word. The time is probably past when it would do him any good to recognize his error. It is an inexcusable error. For no sound instinct could fail to realize that this movement, with its nihilistic goal—though it began by assuming various idealistic disguises, such as nationalism and lower middle-class conservatism—is nothing else than what the bourgeois mind conjures up as bolshevism. All the horrors associated with that apocalyptic word: bloodshed, mob violence, arson, pillage, the filthiest cruelty; the subversion of all principles, the persecution of faith, the shaming of reason and justice, together with the shameless, ridiculous and diabolical perversion of truth; the exploitation of the baser elements among the people; the dissolution and disintegration of international order—all these we see. And we see the attempt to spread to the corners of the earth—corrupting and undermining with money, with an endless, deafening propaganda, and the activities of spies and agitators—until opposition everywhere breaks down, the order of things gives way and the whole world becomes the grave of freedom, with the standard of a stultifying slavery floating above it. If this is bolshevism, National Socialism, and National Socialism alone, is this. If wars, more barbarous and destructive than even the Thirty Years' War, are to sweep over Europe leaving it devastated, pulverized, set back for centuries, then it is National Socialism which will be responsible. National Socialism, the enemy of humankind

Enemy of Humankind! To this has the German spirit come with its anti-democratic cultural pride. This awful name, a name accursed, has become its name. The intellectual German bourgeois could never have dreamed it, and thinks he is dreaming now that it has become the truth. But true it is. His refusal to realize that politics are part of the human problem has issued in political frightfulness, enslavement to power, the totalitarian state. The fruit of his aesthetic bourgeois culture is barbarism: a savagery of convictions, purposes and methods like to nothing in the world before. His elegant disdain of democratic revolution has made him the tool of another revolution; an anarchic one, running amok to threaten the foundations and props of all our Western morality and civilization; a world revolution to which no invasion of the Huns in olden times can even be compared.

Hope for the Future

THE GERMAN BURGHER COULD BE ANTIDEMOCRATIC BECAUSE HE WAS ignorant. He did not know that democracy is just another name for those foundations and props. He did not know that democracy is nothing but the political stamp of occidental Christianity; that politics itself is nothing but intellectual morality, without which the spirit perishes. And yet, let me say this: Outwardly we live in an epoch of retrograde civilization, wherein treaties are worthless, lawlessness and disloyalty are the contagious mode. But there is an inward spirit among men which has entered upon a new moral epoch: one of simplification, of humble-minded recognition of the difference between good and evil. That is *its* way of returning to the primitive and renewing its youth.

Yes, we have learned once more to know good from evil. For evil has revealed itself to us in a naked crudity which has opened our eyes to the simple dignity and beauty of the good. We have laid hold upon it; and think it no shame to our sophistication to admit the fact. Again, we dare to take upon our lips such words as freedom, truth and justice; being weaned from our embarrassment and skepticism by the sight of so much baseness. We hold them out before the Enemy of Humankind, as the medieval monk held out the Crucifix before Satan in person.

And all that the times call on us to bear of anguish is outweighed by the youthful joy of the spirit, at finding itself once more in its chosen role: the role of David against Goliath, of St. George against the old dragon of violence and lies.

The matter rested for a while until no one less than James T. Farrell reappeared a year later, keen to test Mann's politics, and once again about to displease him intensely. In a letter of November 22, 1939, he demanded from Mann an explanation of the German-Soviet Nonaggression Pact! Mann declined, in the only letter of his I have seen rather coldly rebuffing his correspondent. He did set down his view on Farrell's demand in his September diaries, a week after the German invasion of Poland:

Radio message of Russian partial mobilization, which excited in me far-reaching, sorrowful thoughts about the course of the war. Will the regime be overthrown? In Germany a profound revolution has taken place, which has completely *de*nationalized the country, in the matter of its "national allure," according to all older concepts of Germanness. Nazi Bolshevism has *nothing* to do with Germanness. The new barbarism has very naturally found contact with the seemingly opposite Russia. If this bloc of nearly 300 million people stands together, it is almost unthinkable that "civilization," which in a long war also does not remain itself, could so defeat it that it can set its conditions. The events in Germany are unlikely to be reversed. The future is very dark. (T3 469)

———

Christmas 1938 had been unkind to Mann's past; he would have mixed feelings about Christmas 1941 in Pacific Palisades, California. Around this date, there appeared the first and second installments of an extensive *New Yorker* "Profile" by the brilliant journalist Janet Flanner, ironic throughout and not overly awed. (The dates of Flanner's piece—and that of other critics of Mann—fall outside our optic—the years of Thomas Mann's stay in Princeton—but they contribute vividly to the insistent, disturbing question of Mann's "conversion" to a faith in democracy.)

The second of Flanner's profiles tips the scales in the direction of what Mann called a nasty "disturbance," for she repeats and enlarges Baggs's insinuations without acknowledging him as the vindictive pathfinder to Mann's militantly "conservative" past. Her piece has the provocative title "Goethe in Hollywood"— its source is a snarky remark by Bertolt Brecht, who was furious about Mann's fame—and it makes for incisive, acerbic reading.[66] Flanner points out that Mann was fiercely partisan—to say the least—on the German side of the First World War. She then cites the very same sentences as did Baggs from *Gedanken im Kriege* (Thoughts in war) included in Mann's notorious 1915 volume *Friedrich und die grosse Koalition*—sentences that justify a war on behalf of German culture against the corrupting values of the Entente: democracy, politics, newspapers—in a word, "civilization," in a growingly pejorative sense. Mann's remarks flame up on behalf of a German morality at once "inner-directed" and soldierly—deep and stern in its readiness to protect its culture of metaphysics and music from "civilian" dilution. (Mann had already summed up these features of the German mind in the essay "Culture and Politics" that we have just read.)

Despite Flanner's tone, Mann felt that he had emerged from the entire portrait with his dignity intact, yet her piece is through and through mischievous, skeptical, and deflating. It remains to stress that Baggs's letter in December 1938 fully anticipated her account of Mann's first "political attitude" and her exasperation with the slowness of his "metamorphosis": "It took Mann exactly twenty-three years [i.e., until 1941, 1918 + 23 years] . . . to become the militant liberal . . . that he is today [December 1941]."[67] This happens to be an absurdly unfair account of Mann's conversion, which, as we saw in "Culture and

Politics," began no later than 1922 with his speech "On the German Republic." Here, he declared his loyalty to the parliamentary democracy of Weimar and discussed the many impressive way stations of his development. In Mann's own words, "For ten years before Hitler's assumption of power [i.e., in 1923], I fought against the rising nationalistic tide in Germany. Exposed to the most poisonous attacks and with the constant sacrifice of my peace and personal comfort, I sought for a decade to ward off the evil that I saw coming. And in the end, I paid for this fulfillment of my duty with exile, with the loss of my German reading public, with the loss of home and fortune."[68] Flanner actually mentions "On the German Republic," so her numbers compute badly.

The late summer of 1943 would bring news as distressing as Baggs's and much of Flanner's Christmas writings had been. Recalling Mann's distress means once again advancing the date stamp of our story but will serve to emphasize the way in which his political past was *repeatedly* excavated in order to renew the charge that he was unqualified to educate anyone in democratic ideals. On August 21, 1943, a surprising—and by this time for us, and for history, otiose—protest by the Spanish minister Luis Araquistáin appeared in the "Letters" to the *London Times Literary Supplement*. Unknown to him and his readers, his letter was a mere reprise of Baggs and Flanner; and Araquistáin, too, had certainly not read Mann's account of his political education in *Survey Graphic*. The minister's polemic concludes hoarsely: "Who is the real Thomas Mann, the author of "Gedanken im Kriege" . . . ? Who knows? Perhaps not even himself. In any case we have this latest Thomas Mann—and the other, not precisely a democrat, but a democratic full-blooded militarist." [69] Araquistáin's letter was then rather unattractively adverted to by the Irish Francophile and professor of French literature at Oxford Enid Starkie, who wrote of *her* indignation some weeks later, on September 10, 1943, in *The Spectator*.[70] Her letter is, again, a reprise of the arguments we have heard—from Baggs to Flanner to Araquistáin. As the Allies' cause, following the defeat of the German armies at Stalingrad earlier that year, seemed stronger and stronger, the issue arose of Germany's war guilt and her putative reeducation. A writer, a "Miss Bottome"—thus Professor Starkie—"suggests that Thomas Mann and 'the best German refugees' in our country and America should start a committee to choose the teachers for this purpose. Those of us, however, who read Mr. Araquistain's letter in *The Times Literary Supplement* of August 21st will not feel so confident that Mr. Mann is the wisest choice as educator." Starkie then reprints the same flaming citations from Araquistáin's letter: "War is a purification, a liberation, an enormous hope. . . . Germans are far from being in love with the word 'civilisation.' They have 'Kultur' . . . [etc.]."[71]

It was not long before Henri Peyre, another professor of French literature—at Yale—would have the poor sense to take up the gage for his colleague Dr. Starkie. On the invitation of the editors of *The Atlantic Monthly*, in May 1944, Mann published a seemingly irreproachable, certainly heartfelt essay titled "What Is German?"[72] The invitation reads: "On this the tenth anniversary of the Burning of the Books, it seems appropriate to invite Thomas Mann, Germany's most distinguished author, to examine for us the temperament of the German people." It is very interesting to read this crystallization of Mann's political and cultural views long since formed in Princeton. We have encountered these views in "Culture and Politics" and in the lectures discussed in previous pages and in others that we will soon discuss. But enter Professor Henri Peyre and his conviction of Mann's insincerity in espousing democratic ideals. The dusky light of Mann's scandalous *Reflections* of 1918 continues to glow, and Peyre is inclined to conclude that Mann, in "What Is German?," is implicitly exonerating a nation of Nazis and calling for a "soft peace."[73]

Mann would find the attack outrageous, although it could not entirely surprise him or dismay him as deeply as had Baggs's in 1938. Peyre's weak repetition of a charge that had been bruited about for years cannot have differed much from a Mr. Smith's slapping Beethoven on the back and saying, "How are you, old man?" (In "What Is German?" Mann had instanced this slap on the back as a familiarity not at all implied by the democracy he was advocating.) Mann now launched a striking and really triumphant rebuttal titled "In My Defense," published in *The Atlantic Monthly* and bringing the contretemps to a decisive end. As the editors write in a preface to this piece, Professor Peyre "raised the question: 'If a man of his eminence and of his wide culture could think and speak thus in 1915–1918, how can he now expect his readers readily to dissociate the German people from the Nazis?'"[74] Mann's answer included the plaidoyer that one hopes shamed Peyre: Mann wonders whether Peyre

is probably not without some feeling for the inappropriateness of tripping up with the cudgel of ancient quotations a man who is exerting the vital powers of his declining years to play a rightful part in the current struggles of humanity, and to combine his duties as a world citizen with the task of furthering and completing a life's work that may have some value for many people. He is probably aware of the inappropriateness of persistently reminding such a man of statements that he made in an entirely different phase of history and of his own life, and of forcing him to justify himself with regard to them. . . . If I was in error at the age of forty, I do not imagine that I possess the Truth today. It can never be a possession, but only an eternal aspiration. May it be said of each one of us that he spent his life honestly and restlessly striving for the true and the good.[75]

The scandal of the alleged hypocrisy of Mann's belief in democracy in light of his militantly conservative past appears to end here, whereupon the attack on his political probity would be taken up by "anti-Communist" persecutors, foremost in the FBI, who would harass Mann on opposite grounds and help to drive him out of the country. This second exile—or return to the homeland—was in fact urged by a variety of motives. There was Mann's wish to be close to his daughter Erika, whose return visa from Europe to America would be denied. There was the venerable desire he described, as follows, to his Swiss friend, Otto Basler: "Say nothing of politics! It doesn't really play a role. Rather, I refer to my repeated previous statements that I wish to spend the final part of my old age in Switzerland." And then there was the more mordant concern he expressed to the German writer Hans Carossa, "I do not want to rest in this soulless ground, to which I owe nothing and which knows nothing about me." Meanwhile, we may recall the view of Frido Mann, Thomas's grandson, who rather stressed the contrary motive: Mann's desire *not* to abandon the "Egyptian sunlight" of Pacific Palisades, where he had been so productive: "Those were fruitful years," Mann wrote. "There I wrote the final volume of the Joseph-Tetralogy, there the *Faustus* and the *Erwählte* (The Holy Sinner)—and productive time, that is for me, in retrospect, happy time."[76]

"America and the Refugee"

In a perceptive review of Britta Böhler's *The Decision*, a novel dramatizing Mann's wavering decision to denounce the Nazi regime—Mann did not do so publicly until 1936—Morten Høi Jensen criticized the author of the novel for her failure to appreciate Mann's "towering complexity."[77] Such richness is evident even in the short piece "America and the Refugee," which Mann composed for the *New Republic* soon after publishing *This Peace*.[78]

Mann assumes the voice of the desperate refugee—for many refugees had written to him about their plight—but not before declaring the privilege he enjoys. Unlike them, he has found a place in America to pursue his work in peace even while observing "the growth of a cordial and vigorous relationship [with] . . . the intellectually interested public." His exceptionalism prompts him to speak out on behalf of those German exiles—he never specifies that they are mainly Jews—who have written him letters expressing their grief and frustration at not finding honorable work. They have not found a place in the American economy, let alone in American society. Most refugees in America have had little experience of a "paradise of individualism"; and while they must be careful not to criticize their hosts, who have saved their lives, on the other hand, these hosts have done little to help make their lives productive or enjoyable. It is hit or miss if refugees can live with any dignity or satisfaction, since they are entirely dependent on private sources—chiefly family—for their support.

The predicament of the refugee is part of a more general trouble afoot in the land. Even as a newcomer, Mann will take the liberty of writing about its faults, encouraged by the very *freedom* that is also at the root of the impediment that in the last decade has stalled "the continuous progress of a century and a half." He calls the impediment "strange"; the thrust of his essay suggests that that impediment is an unbridled individualism, which knows little or no duty to society as a whole. Freedom and democracy, as "rule" of the whole, are opposite principles: Mann will explore their tension in future writings. Here he merely assumes the freedom to speak for that "good" emigrant who murmurs, "I like them, these Americans, and they behave magnificently toward us, but fundamentally . . . we are not wanted *even here.*"

Mann introduces a correspondent, whose plaint might read *literally*:

> In the six years of the Hitler regime not more than about 100,000 Germans and Austrians have immigrated permanently, yet there seems to be no place for them, even in this huge country. Vast stretches of Oregon, Washington, and Alaska lie fallow and unpopulated, but what could I take up in Oregon? I'm too weak alone to solve the problem. Who is to tell me, us, what we should do? Who will force us, if it must be, on the right road, so that we develop from fugitives into citizens, from birds of passage into Americans?

This complaint gives Mann his opening—he believes in democratic socialism, a society in which individuality nurtures a love for the whole. I will add that Mann knew well Goethe's distich from that eminent anthology of epigrams—the *Xenien*—that he and Schiller put together and which contains the commandment "*Leb' im Ganzen*" ("Live in the whole"), which is to say: live a life oriented toward the being—indeed, the well-being—of the whole of your society, a society wider than a nation, the whole of humankind, if this is thinkable.

In the meantime, Mann proceeds pragmatically; he is struck by the wide-ranging social innovations produced by the administration of his idolized President Roosevelt (some of which will appear in the *Joseph* tetralogy, in

Joseph's economic policies in Pharaonic Egypt). Mann cites the "impressive public works in the Tennessee Valley, at Boulder Dam" as an instance of benevolent state intervention. Ergo, might not a suitable "public works" be devised for the émigrés, since the problem is no longer an individual one? We are not in the year 1890 at a time of wildcat immigration, when "the moment the emigrant leaves the pier he disappears in the crowd." We cannot ignore the complex social problem of the fittest use of a considerable human potential: the problem requires *organization* from above . . . but it may not be to the taste of every American."[79]

Here, Mann's complexity comes to the fore. With a great novelist's power to envision the Other, Mann undertakes to speak on behalf of that "host" who admits his guest—the emigrant—but offers him no material support. Qua preceptor, Mann will teach the dismayed emigrant what he is up against—humanly speaking—and then invite his patience and understanding. With native intricacy, Mann articulates the standpoint of the established citizen: "This mosaic of peoples [in America] has taken on a quite definite and unalterable national form in the course of generations, which like every other product of historical evolution, insists on the maintenance of its *physiognomic* character" (emphasis added). Here, we have a much edulcorated voice of elements in America committed to the worst excesses of rhetoric and commotion in order to keep the nation white. Where in the posited uniformity of the *face* of the nation that Mann conjures are the features of African and Asian Americans? In fact, there is little to suggest that in his heart of hearts he would join with the nativist party to protect the "physiognomic character" of the American nation—but for the wrong reason. After witnessing an entertainment in Washington, D.C., some months later, Mann remarked: "Huge crowd . . . Pan-America, socially remarkable, not without a lesson, but humanly-racially ugly" (T4 65). Additional physiognomic protection of the nation's face would be otiose.

Mann's next formulation on behalf of the anti-immigration party might be judged merely obscurantist—or worse: "The idea of an over-infiltration of foreign elements, which plays such a large role in little Switzerland, has—with all the differences involved—*its justification in America as well*, at a time when the 'Kulturpropaganda' of certain European states has at least retarded the effectiveness of the 'melting pot'" (emphasis added).

That the humanist sensibility behind this proposition is at best murky hardly needs discussion. The reader of this squib might well want to know with what right *Germany's* propaganda on behalf of racial purity may play a role in the

American reception of refugees. Having previously espoused the cause of the desperate emigrant, who numbers only one or two hundred thousand, how can Mann give even lip service to the preposterous idea of an "over-infiltration"—or is he merely striving to be objective on behalf of "the old stock"? Really, the kinder way to attempt to understand these lines is to invoke Mann's celebrated "irony" as he taps into the unconscious of the Other.

What makes this fugue still difficult to understand—one does not wish to attribute it to Mann's own unconscious, although other commentators will—is that the *next* argument for the host country's tepid welcome to its immigrants appears to be sound—or sounder.[80] It is not ironically meant. Mann asserts the real dearth of possibilities for "pioneering" achievement in a country that has long been thoroughly—quaintly put—"motorized," i.e., industrialized. (How cogent, once again, to today's industrial predicament!) Mann is entirely convinced of the *inevitable* expansion in America of what appears to be, at least in part, the effect of a social and economic safety net—described vaguely as "a deepening and expansion of the social and cultural structure." If we are still in the unconscious of the grudging nativist, that would be a good thing, but in fact an unannounced break in the argument introduces the nativist's resistance to this development. We now have "the American of the old stock" expressing his *dislike* of precisely this increase of opportunity: "He has a vague [*sic*] feeling that the new arrival receives the privileges and fruits of historical accomplishments too much as a matter of course; it is the American's heritage and not his." Mann takes his disconsolate emigrant by the collar: "You understand already what I am aiming at: our relation to the New World is, to a very great extent, a problem of tact. Tact and patience, a great deal of patience—." That would be a virtue easier for Mann to practice, while living in near splendor in Princeton, than the less accomplished, unluckier guests of the nation.

This War

This War is a compendium of Mann's main motifs of political argument during his first years at Princeton.[81] He wrote this short book in the late months of 1939, following the German invasion of Poland on September 1, as a "companion piece" to *This Peace*. It is less furious than that essay—more reflective (analytical, even ironical) and more hopeful. What *This Peace* left open as a world-historical possibility has now been realized: the world is at war. The fear of war has been changed into the fact of war—however "phony" at the time of writing, as the bizarre interregnum between September 1939 and spring 1940 was called. The quarrel with a pacifist alternative is over.

Four topics recur:

(1) A description of National Socialism as a debased and violent regime that means to bring this truth home to the Germans, who, at this juncture, are treated as distinct from their "Gestapo government." Mann keeps them in reserve as valuable pawns and bishops and knights for the endgame of revolt, in which they (must) overthrow their enslaving and enslaved Führer king and his queens.

(2) A benevolent address to England—the largest turnabout thinkable in Mann's wartime thought, recalling his sustained assault on perfidious Albion in *This Peace* for consenting to, or far worse, arranging the Munich Agreement's dismemberment of Czechoslovakia. But England, now the more powerful of the Western Allies at war with Hitler, is the single liberal-humanist hope of a redemption, its "treachery" forgotten.

(3) A further warning to the Germans to come to their senses, to find the kernel of sane reason in their grotesque and aery imaginings of a German racial empire somehow immune to the attrition that an outraged *human* world is preparing for it. They are to rebel in the name of their better nature before they are plunged into the depths of ruin and suffering.

(4) Mann's hope for a new European organization to arise from this war—a variation on his long-held idea that at the moment a fascist empire no longer had further territories to bomb and destroy, the gathering of captured peoples would throw off the makeshift ideology of their masters and form a better, more perfect union, a confederation of states no longer nation-states but cooperative parties of a united government (cf. *The City of Man, infra*).

Let us look at these factors of argument in slower motion, meaning especially to bring Mann's tenacity and eloquence to light.

There had been talk of England's "wishing nothing better for herself than to come to an understanding with Nazi Germany in order to march jointly with her against Russia."[82] This, says Mann, is nonsense. After Germany's invasion of Denmark and Norway, neither England nor France will contemplate "peace" with Germany. What hurts Mann so deeply is the vision of his people unwilling to revolt against the monstrosity that has been imposed on them:

"What can be their purpose in risking all that they have and are, to labor for the victory of a bloodstained and morally purblind, universally contemned and discredited régime?" (187). Even if its plan to conquer half the world succeeds, it could never be tolerated or maintained.

The Allied cause, *in principle*, is not to "destroy" Germany. What would be the sense of threatening its ruin when the cooperation of the German nation is crucial to a civilized Europe? Mann will systematically distinguish between the vicious immorality of the regime and the puzzling moral failure of the people. In his heart of hearts, he remains a German and no doubt wishes to maintain the good will of the people and, not incidentally, their interest in his books now and in the eventuality of his return. The goal, rather—he continues—is to bring this people to their senses, to encourage them to cast off their criminal regime; and yet, the melancholy fact remains that the government has the support of this misguided folk who "for the last seven years have dedicated all their capacity, strength, patience discipline, and devotion"—qualities, one might add, that characterize Mann's relation to his art—"to this coarse, crude despotism" (187–88). It is all the more vexing since, in principle, they are a decent, honest, straightforward folk (Mann's choice of a hero, in *The Magic Mountain,* is the decent, honest, straightforward Hans Castorp). So, how is it that they continue to subject themselves to this murderous pack while seeming to admire it, content with its machinations (consider: the Reichstag's fire and the trial—a travesty—that followed it) and awarding it their conviction? How much longer can they endure—more, cheer on—"a country whose entire internal policy has been in the nature of a Reichstag fire and nothing more . . . a record of betrayal and beastliness [that] leads inevitably to war"? "Force within and peace without—that is an impossible conjunction" (190). They pay fealty to a regime that murders communists in its midst while allying itself with the Soviet Union! (Recall that Mann is composing these lines almost a year before the German invasion of Russia in June 1941.) Can this exhibition of cruelty and force, in open pogroms and barely hidden blood-cellars and concentration camps, ever have had any purpose other than war? How were these people bribed, when not beaten into submission, except for being granted the assurance of racial superiority?—after all, they are not Jews, they are "Aryans."

True, there have been other compensations for them, foremost a spectacle of continual "victories." The party of the National Socialists has restored their "honor" (they have been told). This party (of criminals) "tore up the shameful Treaty of Versailles; they forged a mighty armament for Germany, as a result of which the problem of unemployment, which so baffled the Republic, was miraculously solved; they secured military freedom for the Rhineland, built the West wall, took Austria, planted the Swastika banner on the Hradschin, destroyed Poland, and incorporated half of it in the Reich" (193). Mann treats us to his irony: "In return for all this greatness, is a certain amount of individual suffering and disaster, some slight collective curtailment of old-fashioned liberal privileges, such as freedom and justice, too high a price to pay?" If only this tone were still audible in the homeland. And it is moot that Latin sententiae would have much carrying effect: *Oderint dum metuant* (Let them hate as long as they fear): this is the vehicle of German diplomacy—in short form, its relation to what remains of the civilized world (193). But in the end this adventure will cost the people dearly, for a war, with all its local deprivations, is on; and Germany will now face proper adversaries, no longer weaker neighbors, formidable in material and moral resources.

Mann turns again and again to his countrymen: they are the better hope. Let them be taught that they never lost their honor: they lost a war and not their honor. Mann alludes implicitly to the tag that he cited in *This Peace*, to which *This War* is a companion piece: *Victrix causa diis placuit sed victa Catoni* (We recall: "The victorious cause pleased the gods, but the vanquished pleased Cato"). Now consider: "Defeat may serve honor, not destroy it" (194).

The grounds for this potential "new acquist / of true experience" (Milton, *Samson Agonistes*) are bold and surprising. Germany's loss of the Great War might be reckoned a healthy atonement for an empire that was acquired by brutal conquest. Modern Germany is a creature of wars: "from the Austro-Prussian, Prusso-Danish, and Franco-German wars Bismarck's Empire emerged. It was a sinister empire . . . and viewed objectively, a defeat was what was needed to atone for that origin and history . . . to conciliate humanity and reconcile her to a world scarce able to cope with this massed force within its midst" (194–95). Here one hears Erich Kahler's instruction: consult, for instance, his book *Man—the Measure*, where something of his vast learning was set down:

The new Germany confounded nationality with the acquisition of material power, with the functioning and aggrandizement of the state. She tried to offset her intrinsic weakness and instability by material power. [In due course,] she became a rude intruder on every part of the already fragile world system. . . . The combination of a disproportionately powerful army . . . with a mighty navy and an aggressively expanding industry: this combined challenge of the respective supremacies of various nations, constituted a threat of unlimited scope. . . . [83]

REFLECTIONS OF A POLITICAL MAN 85

Germany in 1939 has the opportunity of promoting a peace movement in Europe; instead she has plunged back into a crippling, repudiated mode of nationalistic thinking, killing off any impulse for community and shored up by the "monstrous and perverted social philosophy . . . [of] National Socialism" (196). But surely in their heart of hearts the German people are conscious that the path their regime has taken will lead to no good; no less than their antagonists, they want peace. "Civilization felt that it could endure war no longer, it definitely recoiled from war—how profoundly has been shown today by the extreme reluctance of the warring powers to embark on all its horrors in good earnest."

I (SC) stress again that this essay is being written in the midst of the *Sitzkrieg, le drôle de guerre*, the "phony war"—quasi an interregnum—but one that would end shockingly enough in the months to come, in May 1940, with the crushing German invasion of France and the Low Countries. Mann continues to write hopefully of the German *people*: "They are known as disciples of culture—they could scarcely acquiesce with pleasure in the destruction of the fundamental values of Western civilization, which was conducted in their name" (198). A small point, perhaps—but this English translation is misleading. In the original, Mann does not employ the German for "Western *civilization*." It may be that Mann does not write it because it would too graphically, too vividly constitute a reversal of everything he had written in the time of the First World War in opposing the values of German *culture* to those of French and English—that is, Western—*civilization*—an opposition worth more than a mass, worth, in Mann's view at the time, a war. The words Mann writes in *This War*—here translated as the "fundamental values of Western *civilization*"— are the "Grundwerte abendländischer *Gesittung*," namely, the "fundamental values of [the] Western *ethos*" (E 5:93). Mann has come full turn in his political philosophy, but it must not be exhibited in such blunt terms, inviting precisely the scorn about the authenticity of his conversion to democracy that excited the critics we discussed in "Contra Thomas Mann the American," *supra*.[84]

Mann's flair for contradiction, dialectic, indeed "deconstruction," is on display. He continues his scathing account of the German mentality under its murderous regime: "They will now let themselves be persuaded, and persuade themselves, that the guilt of this war lies with others—whom, at the same time, in the crassest contradiction to this assertion, they have been taught to regard as decadent and outmoded pacifists no longer capable of any historic deed" (199). How grotesque to imagine that in England, let us say, or in France, *as in Germany*, we find "war exalted, peace despised, pacifists and socialists martyred and destroyed" (199). Mann cites from his notorious, powerful letter to the dean of the Faculty of Philosophy of the University of Bonn his analysis of a society whose sole justification lies in the goal of producing a nation outfitted for war. There must be war: no peace offering from a threatened nation can be accepted; it would stop the dynamic, bringing an "ideal and physical suicide for a regime" that would choke on the air of a Europe truly at peace (200). Can the Western nations not have grasped this point—the futility of concessions to Hitler, as if at one point he could be turned into a normal statesman, bent on European harmony? And yet for capitalist eyes there remained the illicit promise that here was a "bulwark against bolshevism," which one might encourage—a stance that explains, in part, the evident reluctance of England and France to fight (201). The rape of Czechoslovakia was not incentive enough; only the plain brutality of the German invasion of Poland made a fight inevitable.

In Germany, an alleged *revolutionary* spirit is bruited about: there is talk of a young nation bent on replacing the older, decadently refined nations of France and England. But that alleged youthfulness and health reveals itself solely in violence and cannot understand that "refinement can produce a kind of tenacity that, when the crisis comes, is beyond the reach of violence" (204). Mann may be building on the point, well known to political philosophers from at least Rousseau's *The Social Contract* on, that as the disparity between a nation's *moeurs* (habits, customs) and laws increases, so does the likelihood of violence. A vital, active tolerance and an energetic skepticism—appanages of civilization—also know how to draw the lines. England, now Germany's great adversary, declares that it is waging war against a ruling clique and not on the heads and bodies of the Germans. But the regime will not allow its people to hear what England has to say; surely, "perfidious Albion" is lying, and has only the one aim in view: to annihilate Germany. But the regime's denial is "a vulgar legend, which the German people is expected to accept from men, who, for their part, believe nothing at all, for whom any sort of ideology is merely a means of propaganda and an instrument of power, and to whom words, and even thoughts, are known solely as a disguise for deliberate political deceit" (206). This point leads Mann to a philosophical reflection in the Schopenhauerian vein: the (political) intellect is the servant of the will. First comes interest; then comes its intellectual—better—ideological embellishment. There may be a good deal of luck (or destiny) involved if it should turn out that the object of one's interest is also the good and the true and can be justified in the rhetoric of humanism. In this instance, "the warring democracies are today in the morally agreeable position of being able to defend the right in serving their own ends." (Here, we have the notion of the "good war.")

Meanwhile, Mann's portrait of the German character is fraught. In its "deeper" sense of the "tragedy of life" and in much that follows, we shall in fact hear echoes of his earlier views about the moral superiority of (German) "depth" and pessimism—in short, German *Kultur*—but now we do not have Mann espousing it; on the contrary, he deplores it, and in doing so he implicitly deplores the person—himself—who once stood by it:

> The German people are inclined to believe in this moral superiority of harsh and repellent ideas over those of a gentler and more benevolent cast; it is in consonance with their deeper sense of the tragedy of life, and the inevitability of evil in the world, which they love to set in sharp confrontation to the "shallow" pragmatism of the West, with which also their pessimistic view of interest as the motive of all thinking is involved. (207)

Briefly put, in the present context of war, the Germans "deny that there can be any contact between politics and morality," and so they inevitably pursue power before knowledge—a pursuit (of power) that is blind to the knowledge that this entire mad adventure has been provoked by envy of England and its empire (208). The curious feature here is the different ways both nations regard the achievement of an empire and the responsibility for governance it lays on its builders. Mann invokes British understatement and alleges having heard an Englishman say, "We got our Empire in a fit of absence of mind." Such a remark underscores the difference. No German at home, he writes, would ever mouth such a quip; for such a man—the German—"the effort to achieve great things" is "fierce," is "tense . . . and he speaks very freely of his successes, not with any sort of deprecation but in the most thunderous tones of self-applause" (209).

Mann concludes his analysis of the British Empire, the object of Germany's envy, by affirming what can only be called "colonialism"—as long as it is under British aegis. He is not appalled by British power, since it is so little like the German concept, which is "darkly emotional; . . . [for] power, in English eyes, implies no emotion—the will to power is a German invention—but a function" (210). This is well and good, but now, carried away by *parti pris* and a will to refinement, Mann offers propositions contestable from the ground up. Of British imperial power, he writes, "They exercise it in the gentlest and most unobtrusive manner, with the least possible display and safeguarding as much freedom as feasible" (*sic*; 210). What is missing is a glance under the cloak of the "Liberalism" that Mann celebrates, which would find the British tolerance for the famines in India in 1896–97 and 1899–1900 that cost the death of millions; the concentration camps of the Boer War; the Amritsar massacre of 1919; and comparable atrocities. Granted, Mann attributes to English Liberalism an elastic, "an infinitely adaptable quality": it is not historically bound. He conjures an empire en route to abandoning capitalist colonial exploitation in favor of "an education in freedom . . . and the liberal relaxation of the administrative structure." What we will then have is a "politico-economic symbiosis," which, already active "in the post-Liberal period, has become an example to the world" (211). Mann's much loved vision of a confederation of nations here overwhelms his insight; in fact the empire would become a spectacle of dissolution, drawing and drowning in blood, as consider, also, the Bengal famine of 1943, resulting in four million deaths; the partition of India, in 1947, allegedly drawn up over a single lunch by a certain Viscount Radcliffe, which uprooted ten millions and resulted in a million deaths; the detention and torture of the Kikuyu during the Mau Mau Uprising of 1952–60, and more. But we are still in the year 1939, when Mann could hope for virtuous results achieved by odious means—through England's (and perhaps America's, devoutly to be wished) destruction of the behemoth of National Socialism.

Associated with Mann's newfound admiration for the British Empire ("destiny" has obliged him to it, England being the only live adversary of the Germany that has disenfranchised and humiliated her) is his admiration of the English language; this relation becomes ever more pronounced during the years of Mann's stay in America, as his relation to American literature deepens. The British Empire, he writes, "is the Empire of the English language—a quiet but powerful language with a unifying, binding, colonizing force with which no others, though they have also produced great literature, neither German, nor Italian, nor French, can enter into competition" (212). There is some truth to this statement, as long as it is made clear, I will add, that that "colonizing force" is the language spoken by soldiers with rifles and administrators with poison pens, as witness the compulsory renaming of Irish places with British stereotypes—a means to empty out the history embedded in the original Gaelic.[85]

Mann ponders a novel dimension to this war: if England is sincere in claiming that its war with Germany is with *the German regime* only—as the keepers of a vile ideology—it has thankfully broken with a time-(dis)honored principle of noninterference. At the bottom of the notion of noninterference are ideals of freedom and democracy: let come to pass what will behind the walls of nationhood; it is no other nation's business. But the present crisis reveals that the relation of democracy and freedom to social justice is by rights a variable one, appropriate to the age and its circumstances. Social democracy, not individual freedom, is the order of the day—an argument we will hear Mann making in his speech on "The Problem of Freedom" in April of that year at Rutgers. "Only in this form," Mann continues, "as a socialized security . . . which retains the individual values by voluntary concessions to equality, can democracy continue to exist—nationally and internationally" (214–15). Where individualism is unrestrained, you have anarchy; where you have impermeable national sovereignty, you have a Europe under threat. A wild individualism must make way for "a community of free but inter-responsible peoples under a moral law that binds them all" (215). What is implied here and, moreover, has been stated explicitly by Lord Halifax as Britain's war aim (according to Mann) is not only a radical change in Germany but in her enemies as well. The victory of the Allies intends a social, political, and economic change basic for establishing a permanent peace. Mann's hope for this future is eloquent and deserves citation:

> It consists in adherence of the European states to a commonwealth, which would represent a new and creative synthesis of freedom and reciprocal responsibility, in the cultivation of national character and of social equality; a league to which all states would have to offer sacrifices of their absolutism and their right to self-determination in order to enjoy the advantages of ease, security for their labors, and the due meed of prosperity which only a real community can provide. (217)

This is the program embedded in "The Problem of Freedom" and afterwards fully developed in *The City of Man*. The development it receives there is stimulated, in large part, by Mann's contribution.

Now, in *This War*, Mann goes on to contrast this league of equals with a National Socialist incorporation of weaker states into its empire as slave states, a condition of humiliation on which their German masters are in turn slavishly dependent as their only concept (218–19). Mann takes up the language of "Goethe's" political ruminations in the remarkable chapter 7 of his *Lotte in Weimar* (see chapter 4): "Dark and bitter will be the way to the goal that they ['a handful of perverted and bloody-minded men'] have set before you, and terrible indeed will be your state when it is reached. All that you most deeply value, all that was easy and natural to you, your need to love and to be loved, you must disavow and destroy" (219).

Does the German nation not realize that its aim of subjecting parts of the world has no natural end? One conquest must follow the next, until there are no more parts of the world available as booty—and then the war will need to be conducted from within against "a world subjected but not won ... in eternal revolt against its infamous oppressors" (220). Was there ever an "eschatology" more futile, less practicable—a "conclusion" in perennial war? A humanitarian vision of nations willing to sacrifice pieces of their sovereignty for the sake of a better union, rooted in a love of peace: need it be scorned as "optimistic"? And yet

> an optimistic, human, kindly vision which promises ease, freedom, justice, individual happiness, and the enrichment of culture, and for that very reason—strange indeed is the bitterness and self-contempt of humankind—stands at a certain spiritual and moral disadvantage as against the tragic, pessimistic, and realist concept of a black, bloodstained, and violent future. (221)

Here Mann is reaching back again to that fund of anthropological distinctions between the German and the Western, democratic mind that he belabored in his earlier writings, in the First World War time of his *Reflections of a Nonpolitical Man*. The core distinction is German "depth" versus Western "life at its surface." But there are some important refinements to be made inside this notion of German "depth," which, once again, is being botched by German conservative ideologues. There is "a great moral difference ... between the pessimism that comes from the sufferings of life ... and that which is itself evil and an inhuman disavowal of any principle of betterment." That deliberate enterprise of promoting pain and brutality is not inspired by a well-founded pessimism with regard to utopian hopes but by a "plain diabolism," which, under the guise of heroism and fate, "does its best to make sure that [the hope of 'happiness and honor'] shall be blacker and bloodier ... than ever" (222). Is there a core of misapprehended love in all this defiance—the craving *to be loved and admired*—at bottom in the German soul? That is, so to speak, a reasonable desire, but to find reason in the German soul today, says Mann—wittily—you must go really deep. The Germans must be encouraged to grasp that the obstacle to the path of genuine satisfaction lies in their attachment to this regime. In their own country they have been encouraged to think of this attachment as noble and, any rate, inalienable; but this is once more an ideological degradation of the truth that they are in principle free to cast off "their present rulers, who are really enemies of humanity, hating and hated." Mann is seductive on behalf of the good cause, but is he telling the truth on declaring that "the whole world holds desperately to the distinction between the German people and their destroyers" (223)? He will struggle to maintain this distinction all during the war years; but as German crimes grow exponentially and there is no or little sign of popular resistance, he will abandon it. But is inducing the Germans in 1939 to take their destiny into their own hands a blameless gesture? It is a lot more fraught than being merely seductive on behalf of the good cause: it is irresponsible. Mann is not deaf to the cry that the terror that governs the state—a "fearful mechanical power"—makes this action impossible. But with his word choice of the "machine," he has already declared his idealistic hand. No machine can stop for long the unified will of men, he asserts, in ever richer rhetoric: a genuine will to revolt cannot be held in check. There will never be enough terror at work to suppress a people's decision to be free. Certainly, there are strategic considerations in play. But the claim that "we" Germans must wait for Germany's military defeats before acting is wrong: if we do so, we are accomplices in this havoc. Waiting to see means, furthermore—Mann continues, thinking very likely of the First World War—"that we shall, through a long, bloody, and destructive war, destroy the hopes of that peace for which Europe is ripe." But if Germans were to act *now*, casting off their regime, it could participate freely in the constitution of a new and peaceful European order. To leave that project to the victors, excluding a crushed and broken Germany (presumably steeping in resentment), is merely to portend new horrors (224). Should the Germans nevertheless prefer to wait and see whether additional conquest and terror will justify what their rulers have done to them—which is to have turned Germany into "a formless and distracted 'living space,' held together by police terrorism"—they will regret their fecklessness and reap a reward of guilt and misery. But if they will act, take to the streets, refuse "injustice, evil, villainy, and madness!" they will have assisted at another future, "a Europe that can live in a free community of interests and devotion to the arts of peace . . . the world wherein the German people, so unpolitically-minded, are destined to find happiness and love and fame" and the nurturing of the "really great qualities" in her, of which the world is well aware (225). Here ends Mann's elegant mix of flattery and doomsaying.

———

Mann's own commentary on the piece, published in 1942, deserves to be cited:

> What had to come, came. We bitterly disillusioned ones could have counted on the inborn *inability* of the German gangster regime to keep the peace. On the terrible rape of Czechoslovakia followed the onslaught on Poland;

and then the public morals of England drove the semi-fascist governments of the Western powers to battle against the nations with which they would have preferred to combine against the liberties of the people. It was in the days of the "phony war" that I wrote the article which I include here as documentary supplement to the account of the Munich betrayal. After it appeared, a British friend said to me: "Naturally, it is pleasanter reading for us than 'This Peace,' but you did the better job the other time." He was right. Are pain and anger deeper and more burning incentives than hope to make one take up the pen? Or was hope sicklied over and its pinions made to droop, by unconfessed fears touching the fate of France, undermined as she was by fascism?[86]

"Mediators between the Spirit and Life"

In May 1939, evidently craving distraction and a fresh topic, with an eye, too, on its practical benefit, Mann spoke to a banquet for booksellers. With rather high-flown eloquence, he likened the "noble business" of both entities— booksellers and authors—to one another . . . but quickly stipulated the plain difference, "for production is something different from dissemination."[87] Still, as mediators, they have a common interest at the point "when the spiritual work has detached itself from the originator and must make its way into life; when dream and vision have assumed the form of a mercantile and industrial object which is in need of distribution, if it is to have its effect."

Mann quotes wittily and to good effect a line spoken by Mephistopheles in Goethe's *Faust* at the time of the signing of his pact with Faust: "Blood is a quite peculiar juice." The relevance? Just as books are a quite peculiar—a higher!—sort of mercantile and industrial object, so is the "blood" of the author that has flowed into these objects: they are paid for with the author's life. The "height" of books lies in their nearness to "the spirit . . . the world of ideas and art." By dealing in "the creative and the spiritual . . . he [the bookseller] mediates the human needs" (*sic*; 1886). At which point Mann compliments the sellers grandly, invoking as their patron no one less than "the beautiful ethereal god with winged sandals—Hermes or Mercury . . . the god of trade and traffic, of exchange and commerce, but likewise the messenger of Zeus . . . mediator between heaven and earth . . . between the spirit and life." One might wonder how this audience of businesspeople would feel about having "spirit" assigned exclusively to their opposite number, to authors, of whom, for the moment, Thomas Mann—although not with winged sandals and almost certainly in evening dress—is appearing as their patron.

Mann contrasts the egotism of the author (in no ignoble words) to the sociality of the bookseller. The author "may cultivate this [personal] talent to a lofty height; he may draw ever more of the world into his spiritual life; within human limitations it may become comprehensive in scope." And yet he still may envy the bookseller—and, here, the publisher, too—for consider the "happy vital advantages the mediator has after all over him who is producing individually" (1886–87). The bookseller and the publisher can take the products of the creative effort of single makers—tormented "soloists of spiritual exertion," hemmed in by their individuality—and hurl them collectively "into the battle of life against the powers of ignorance and barbarism." And while the life of these noble tradesmen might not be without its troubles, Mann means to leave them with the impression of the incomparably greater torment of the author, who knows "the torture and frailty of all individual productivity." (Here, Mann is delivering lines from Thomas Buddenbrook's pastiche of Schopenhauer's draconian views on the ego.)

The trouble the publisher and bookseller might be experiencing is the crisis created by the competition of the book with the emerging media of radio and film (how relevant!). They are products of the ongoing mechanization of the world. But the machine is as such innocent until abused, and it was a machine—the printing press—that enabled the growth of intellectual and spiritual liberty and, in due course, a modest acquisition of political liberty. "The death of the soul through mechanization becomes questionable, one could say, in that moment when the mechanism is imbued with the spirit." In lecturing on the resistance that invention engendered at its birth, and consistent with his own personal decorum—described by one scholar as joining the austerity of a Spanish cardinal to the stiffness of a Prussian general—Mann favors his crowd with a Latin tag, "*Pulchrum est paucorum hominum*," put in the mouth of an imagined adversary of Gutenberg: "Beauty is [after all] for the few" (1887).[88] Given the extreme irregularity of Mann's pronunciation of English words, it is no leap to suppose that his Latin was any the less incomprehensible. But supposing there were among this bookish crowd a few happy linguists, they would have understood that Mann was encouraging them not to fear the new machines for mass entertainment—movies and radio. To conjure the "I"-word often on Mann's lips—"irony," as, for example, in his citing the "irony of world events—[for] it was, after all, a German who brought the printing press into the world"—we recall that Mann was himself a passionate devotee of movies and classical radio music, as he frankly confesses: "I do not find that the joy of reading suffers from the susceptibility with which one meets the stimuli of the film."

These tools are in principle democratic: it is once again a cruel irony that "the enemies of the spirit and culture have made more clever use of these democratic tools than democracy itself." Elsewhere, Mann would appeal to democratic forces not to neglect mass media propaganda for the good cause, and even to make "militant" use of it. But film and radio do not constitute threats to the perennial appeal of the book. It is interesting to hear Mann cite the German passion for books before 1933 in his fine, rousing conclusion:

> In Germany, a country well adapted to the modern technique [*sic*], even intellectually difficult and expensive books could, before 1933, if they touched the nerve of the period, go through mass editions of hundreds of thousands of copies. If today the book plays a lamentable role over there, it is because of the terrorism of the regime which misuses the word and has robbed it of all power to inspire confidence.

Nevertheless, even under the Nazis, declares Mann, translations of the works of authors writing in free countries are passionately sought after. The future of the book is assured, its mission is intact (1888).

Mann's prophecy has stood the test of time, at least until the present constellation, when subliterate autocrats serve as role models for millions.

"The Problem of Freedom"

On April 18, 1939, at Rutgers University, Mann accepted one of his eight American honorary doctorates and responded with a dense and passionate speech on the question that gnawed at him—"the problem of freedom" (VA 297).[89] Individual freedom is sustainable, paradoxically, only in a democracy—a rule of the *many*, in which the many are held to be *equal*.[90] But at this historical moment (April 1939), the ideals of both freedom and equality are deeply endangered, since they are nurtured, according to Mann, only in a "secular Christian" democracy, whose very survival is at stake. The acceptance of fascist rule in Europe means, for the moment, "the downfall—the end of Democracy on earth."[91] And so, the urgency of defending democratic socialism must not be compromised by the belief that individual freedom and social equality cannot coexist.

Mann's opening reproduces the argument of *This Peace*, which deplored the response of the democratic nations of the West to the dismemberment of Czechoslovakia. On the basis of a flimsy idea of national sovereignty and non-intervention, the democracies turned feckless in the face of the criminal violence inside and outside of a Germany under the rule of "Der Führer" ("that dubious individual" [3]). So infrequently does any real demonstration of a belief in democracy—a militant belief!—come to light at this time that, Mann declares, it might be an empty effort even to address this concept as a topic. But he will make the effort, with passionate conviction.

This talk contains many of the claims and figures of thought that recur in Mann's political writing of the time: along with *This Peace,* it recalls his address "To the Civilized World" and, as we shall see, *The City of Man.* But for the first time in the political writings we have looked at, we have Mann's extreme emphasis on the *Christian* root of democracy. It is a claim that leaves one to wonder how heartfelt this argument can be. Mann's beloved, preferred "educator" Goethe, in 1831, the year he wrote the ending to *Faust,* described the Christian cross, as Mann knew, as "the most disgusting thing under the sun, [which] no reasonable human being should strive to exhume."[92] Again, one will wonder about the accuracy of Mann's thesis of the Christian basis of late bourgeois democracy. Is there nothing in it of Athens? or the Hebrew Bible? Unlike Walter Benjamin's claim that "no poem is intended for the reader," Mann's eloquent speech—today, a book—feels very much designed to captivate a Christian audience. He is bent on arousing a detestation of National Socialism and will cite the most impressive reasons for it: its war on both religion (Christianity) and democracy. The appeal to Christians in the Rutgers audience is of a piece with his appeal to declared congregants in his speeches to Christian organizations and seminaries, part of the assumption that their sympathy for the persecuted churchmen in Germany might somehow embolden German Christians to revolt. There is nothing in this speech about a "*Judeo*-Christian" tradition of community, a rhetorical strategy that might be best—if oversimply—"explained" by Mann's reluctance to be seen as pleading for "militancy" on behalf of the persecuted Jews of Europe. Nevertheless, in the course of his speech, he does attack the vile pogrom of the ill-named *Reichskristallnacht* ("Night of broken glass"). Let us look more closely at the grain of his arguments.

We hear about the sinister underbelly of the Nazi's seizure of power—a catastrophe enabled by "the revolting swindle of the Reichstag-fire and the farce of the trial which was to follow"; these abuses were tolerated by the European democracies, who will, one fears, pay dearly in the future for their weakness (3). Or was it something internal to weakness that enabled the Nazi success: sympathy for a people so badly oppressed by the Versailles Treaty? Some in the West are willing to give credence to Hitler's claim "that the world cannot always remain divided into Have and Have-not nations," but that claim lacks precision; and one is not inclined to give credence to the claims of self-interest in the mouth of a liar (4). (How evocative!) If the West were otherwise moved by sympathy to relax some of the harshest features of the Versailles Treaty, it could have done so in conversation with the German (Weimar) Republic fifteen years before the Nazi coup.

The slackness and bad conscience of the West appear to be buttressed by a (false) political calculation, which reads: if we let Hitler have the East of Europe, he will leave the West alone. The idea is psychologically obtuse. You are dealing with a regime whose entire dynamic is to possess *everything*: its vindictiveness, its thirst for revenge, has no limit. But Mann appears to be under the sway of the notorious German tag (from Christian Morgenstern)—"*Nicht sein kann, was nicht sein darf*" (freely: "What *may* not be [for it would be unjust], *cannot* be").[93] Mann declares:

> Just . . . because of our conviction that it *cannot* be the meaning of history and of the world's spirit, to make one Hitler the ruler of the world, we may be quite sure that the very boundlessness of National Socialism will lead to its disaster, one way or another, and that the eternal and fundamental values of our Occidental civilization *will* win in the end against the barbaric theories and practices of the fascist régimes. (5; emphasis added)

We detect the sheer incredulity of Mann, and of every decent observer, that at this modern, this progressive historical juncture, a pack of criminal barbarians can be in possession of half of Europe—shadowed only by a feeble show of resistance by the bourgeois democracies.

The values we cherish, Mann declares, are *eternal*; on the other hand, they will not be won back without an *existential* fight. To bring these two views on our values together—on the one hand, the *eternal* character of such values as Christian sociality and "faith in goodness, in freedom and truth, in justice and in peace" (16), and on the other hand, the fact that they have been trampled into the dust in Europe—might call, predictably, for some casuistry. This reader is inclined to take the modifier "eternal" not as a qualifier of duration but of exaltation. Talk of Christianity invites talk, however indirectly, of God, who, if anything, is *eternally* present—or absent—as the case may be.

Inspired now by the rhetorical choice of "eternal" as qualifier, Mann is moved to stress National Socialism's war not only on democracy but on Christianity as well. And yet he cannot be ignorant of the cooperation of the Lutheran churches with the Nazi state; so Christianity in Germany—as here too, in America—needs to be understood as a certain secularized, value-laden attitude toward the world. It is only then that "Democracy may be called the political expression of our Christian feeling for life, of Christianity on earth" (6). In the following, Mann repeats the surely contentious claim, as I have noted, that Christianity is the single root of democratic freedom. The philosopher Walter Kaufmann is such a "contester" and judges the claim that "Christianity discovered the infinite worth of every human soul" to be a deplorable cliché. This original idea of the infinite worth of *every* human soul, writes Kaufmann, is found in the Hebrew Bible.[94] And has Mann never registered the brutal Christian inegalitarianism of the saved and the damned?

At this juncture, Mann "gets real," expanding the virtual social economy of Christianity to include real socialist thought, which he situates as a tendency alive at "the beginning of the nineteenth century, the childhood of bourgeois Democracy" (6). This is the vision of Henri de Saint-Simon, called Saint-Simonianism, which, at its close, did explicitly build on a Christian notion of brotherly love. Saint-Simon gives support to Mann's presentation of democracy and socialism as joined at a common Christian root: all stand or fall together. Once again, this connection does not exclude an apparent contradiction, which Mann himself foregrounds: a philosophy of *personal* freedom does not imply a comity of *equals*. What should my stance be toward another, the exercise of whose freedom impinges on mine? Where and when does the value of a socialist "tendency"—acknowledging the equivalent rights of others—begin and end? Mann's solution to this dilemma occurs in the optative mode: really, there *ought to be* no conflict between these parties, for "logic has not a final nor the highest validity for life, and in human . . . ethical requirements, freedom and equality are not a real contradiction. . . . A human synthesis, a reasonable and just synthesis, *must* be possible between freedom and equality, individual and society, the person and the collectivity" (6, 8; emphasis added). A cooler pragmatic view notes that they do often cooperate. At the back of Mann's mind is the example, which he will enlist at the close of his talk, of his *own* sacrifice of the freedom he most cherishes—a freedom to write imaginative works of literature—for the sake of a duty to act in public on be-half of the welfare of his society, as witness his present oration.

But more to the "problem of freedom," which need not be one, Mann de-clares, for it is patent even to elites that "a purely individualistic . . . humanity is incomplete and dangerous to culture." And with an assertion that will figure as a refrain throughout his writings in years to come, especially when he has been attacked for his former apolitical cultivation of "the spirit" (*Geist*)—his devo-tion to a privileged German *Kultur* of inwardness—Mann affirms that "political and social activities are a part of the humane: . . . it is not possible to separate them from spiritual and cultural activities. Nor is it possible to devote oneself to culture and declare that one is 'not interested' in politics" (8). If one under-stands by "politics" no slight regard for the pragmatic material-economic basis, then among "woke" intellectuals today, I will add, it is rather the opposite that is the case. And it may be possible to detect, in the faintly feckless "nor . . . not" structure of Mann's claim, some lurking inner resistance to its necessity.

As a result of these highly personal ruminations, Mann is ready to refine his notion of freedom: "The just and reasonable division of emphasis between the individual and the social element in man, the limitation of the political and social to their natural and necessary share in humanity, culture, and life—that is freedom" (8–9). At such moments, less enraptured listeners might be in-clined to mutter, "humanist essentialist cant." From the skeptical viewpoint—from the existentialist viewpoint—there is nothing "natural and necessary" about human ideals of one single type, viz. Jean-Paul Sartre, for one: "Exis-tence precedes and commands essence." But Mann commands the rhetoric of humanism, which is ready to hand for such compulsory occasions. And, more-over, there is a war on.

The greatest danger facing the West is internal to democracy: the weak-ness of self-doubt; it is on the lips of "the cultured person" who fears the drift to an egalitarianism that could empower the worst tendencies of socialism—"the tendency to exaggerate the mechanization and regimentation of society and to sink the individual and the group in a practical uniformity and in mass movements" (7). In this way, with little self-awareness, the "cultured person" co-opts the Nazi rhetoric, in which its regime figures as the sole bulwark against bolshevism, hoping to make democracy, the alleged precursor to socialist communism, "ripe for assault" (7–8). (In an interview conducted precisely one month earlier, asked whether he foresaw the coming of totali-tarianism to America, Mann replied that he believed "the roots of democracy" were too firmly planted but . . . if it were to come about, it would be "in the guise of freedom"—*verb. sat.*[95]) Fascism is in reality a totalitarian seizure of power over the many by a few. "In the anti-human will toward this political absolutism, fascism and communism meet" (9). But. . . .

Here, Mann trims this claim with a fine distinction between the two dictatorships to the advantage of communism—precisely the gesture that will ruin him, in America, a decade later, during Washington's pursuit of "subversives." There is, thus Mann, a difference in the "moral level" of the two systems—a difference ripe for a fall, one adds from hindsight, since now, in April 1939, he considers "communist Russia . . . a peace loving power and . . . one of the strongest supporters of the League of Nations" (!). Think of the peace of death it will administer to Poland five months later, on September 17, 1939! Perhaps the absence of a formal declaration of war on the part of the Soviet Union, until it was invaded by Germany in June 1941, continues to qualify Stalinist Russia as committed to world peace. But Mann, who was often prescient, is not clairvoyant, and builds his claim on the provable contrast between Germany's *foreign* territorial aggressions during the preceding six years and Russia's few or none.[96]

Individualists should be clear: It is not as if fascism, unlike communism, aims "to protect private property and an individualistic economy. Especially in its economic policies, National Socialism is nothing but Bolshevism"—a bolshevism on the right or a fascism on the left. In a memorable trope, which Mann regularly employs, the two systems are "hostile brothers of whom the younger has learned almost everything from the elder, Russian, brother." Nazism, too, is bent on the sequestration of citizens' property, whereupon Mann astutely exposes the economic subtext to the persecution of the Jews in Germany: "It is quite certain that the expropriation of the Jews is only a prelude to more comprehensive acts of this sort which will be wholly free of any race-ideology." And he adds, repeating a point he has made before, "Particularly if the concept of Bolshevism is understood in its popular, mythical interpretation as the epitome of terror and raging destruction, no better picture of it can be imagined than that which was exhibited in the German pogroms" (10–11). Mann will have known that the Nazis confiscated the insurance payments meant to have been paid out to Jews whose property was damaged in the *Reichskristallnacht.*[97]

This "revolution," as the Nazis term their movement, does not deserve that name: "It is a revolution such as has never existed, a revolution of absolute cynicism without relationship to any kind of faith and filled with lust for the degradation of men and of ideas. What it means economically may leave us comparatively indifferent. But morally its purpose is extermination"—not yet of the Jews; the Wannsee Conference was held nearly three years later, on January 20, 1942. Here, however, we could invoke Mann's clearsightedness: *one year later*, in the speech on March 3, 1940 cited in chapter 1, Mann would allude to "the unspeakable horrors which . . . [anti-Semitism] is perpetrating on a scale putting all previous atrocities in the shade." And he names by name the mass murders of Jews in the East. In the Rutgers speech, Mann is referring more "generally" to the Nazi "extermination of the foundations of civilization" (11–12). But, once again, the speech on March 3, 1940, plainly connects the two criminal ideas: "The anti-Semitism of today . . . is no end in itself; it is nothing but a wrench to unscrew bit by bit the whole machinery of our civilization."[98] Or in the present address, "The final meaning of . . . [National Socialism's] anti-Semitism is not the foolish idea of the racial purity of the German people but an assault upon Christianity itself." (Mann's bloodline, as we know, includes Brazilian Indian, and his six children are the offspring of a Jewish mother.) For Mann, the assault upon Christianity is an assault upon the "source" (he alleges) of the values of "freedom, truth, justice, reason, human dignity" (12). What, I wonder, would the professors of history and philosophy listening to this address have made of this claim? Luther . . . and *reason*?

Mann makes the point that democracy, which in Europe was inspired by revolution, is today a conservative force—a conservative bulwark against barbarism. "But in order to do justice to this new responsibility, it must, to a certain extent, return to its revolutionary state: it cannot merely *be*, it must give battle. For without battle, it will cease to *be*." It must rouse "the will to concentrate and to resist, the will to call a halt, to *command* a halt, the will to defend civilization against the corrupting onward march of force" (12). A *militant* democracy is the need of the day.

But, one will ask, does not a militant democracy—democracy in the state of war—imply loss of the tolerance that defines it? That is the cost in principle, but it is smaller than the practical cost of tolerating those who aim to destroy democracy. What is momentarily at issue is not the preservation of every sort of freedom; it is a case of self-preservation. And if this distinction has given rise to debate, it becomes clear that freedom has always been a problem; and so Mann calls for "a voluntary restriction and a social self- discipline of freedom" (13).[99] Current readers will be surprised to learn that this discipline alone, in Mann's parlance—"severer and more binding social forms"—"can help freedom to survive *liberalism*," by which he understands the weak generosity that masks self-interest, a *laissez-aller*, which he has already castigated in *The Magic Mountain*. There are more and less appropriate forms of liberalism; they are suited to the times; but the ideal of a disciplined freedom transcends time and place. And it is this discipline empowering "the social"—a passion for justice and equality—"that is now the order of the day." Consider the present speaker, Thomas Mann, who has straitened his freedom as an imaginative artist to fulfill a duty to "*Social Democracy*" (14). "Is it not, therefore, significant and symptomatic that today an artist should feel obligated to apply these standards [drawn from his craft, 'the right, the good, and the true'] to . . . the political will of the times . . . ?"

These values are being trampled on. "The spirit," ever alert, in Mann's hands, to its own advantage, even—or especially—in times of empirical failure, finds a new strength in a *moral simplification*. The distinction between good and evil is profound and clear. "Evil has been revealed to us in such crassness and meanness that our eyes have been opened to the dignity and the simple beauty of the good." The moment might be reckoned a spiritual rejuvenation, and with this connotation Mann returns to America—its "youth" and, as he will have it, its "moral vigor" (16). He is not always ready, as in his diaries, to attribute this virtue to his new homeland; he wrote of his "brother" Hitler, "Thanks to his own baseness, he has indeed succeeded in exposing much of our own."[100] There would be no impediment, however, in his audience at Rutgers, which consisted predominately of "youths," to receiving Mann's attribution of virtue. Mann concludes the appeal, as he has concluded appeals before, with the formulaic hope (see chapter 1): "May America stand forth in an abandoned and ethically leaderless world as the strong and unswerving protector of the good and the godly in mankind" (16). America would indeed declare war on Hitler's Germany on December 11, 1941, but only *after* Germany had already declared war on America.

"The War and the Future"

"The War and the Future" is Mann's representative and quite possibly richest political lecture while at Princeton. It rephrases beautifully many of the positions of his other lectures and speeches. Originally published in *The Atlantic Monthly*, it was included in Mann's compendious *Order of the Day: Political Essays and Speeches of Two Decades* where, as Mann notes, "it constitutes the final form of addresses which I made on various lecture trips, in colleges and town halls, before and after this country entered the war."[101] That is the text before us now. We will concentrate on the arguments and aperçus that we have not yet seen.

Mann begins modestly: he wonders aloud what he could possibly add to the awareness of the threat to democracy that has already been produced by the work of the American "intelligentsia." Then, in the surprising, worrisome modality of a *j'accuse,* he warns his audience that, if the free world should shatter under the "onslaught of evil, if freedom and justice should perish and slavery be the fate of mankind, then America must bear its share of the guilt." Ignorance of the gravity of the threat is inadmissible: "What the great daily press, . . . the books, pamphlets, and lectures have done to analyze events in Europe, to explain their significance for America, to define the values which we defend against . . . [the enemy]—all this has been simply admirable, and without its equal in any other country" (238). It is not hard to hear an autobiographical resonance in this claim: at considerable personal cost, Mann has contributed a good deal to the achievement of this awareness; and indeed nothing like the role that he has fulfilled will be found in any other country.

As an *artist,* he has fulfilled his task with the clearest possible awareness of the non-distinction, especially in these parlous times, of the spheres of art and politics. "In whatever sphere . . . truth and freedom are denied, violated, trampled upon; there art and every decent artist must be gravely affected. He cannot live, cannot breathe, cannot work; he must degenerate, or he must flee" (241). During the war, artists who had remained in Germany knew of Mann's feelings about them; during and especially after the war, when he refused to immigrate to his homeland, he would reap their scorn and rancor.

Mann relates a fascinating anecdote involving the world-historical context of an article about his work.

> On the day when the German troops marched into Russia, my works were mentioned in a broadcast from Moscow. For two years, since the date of the Russo-German treaty, it was not allowed to mention me in Russia. The article dealing with my works had probably been prepared for some time, but as long as the treaty lasted it could not be used. When the treaty was broken, the article was promptly unearthed. (242)

This anecdote throws light on an intriguing incident noted in Mann's diaries at the time (T3 428, 814). On May 29, 1939, Mann delivered a version of "The Problem of Freedom" at Hobart College, which was reported in *The New York Times.*[102] Getting wind of the piece, Runa, a clandestine communist news agency, discovered to its ideological horror that Mann had once again described the Nazis as "Bolshevism's younger brother." Runa was furious—but evidently out of step with Moscow policy. According to Erika Mann, "Moscow," through its agencies, then interceded and defended Mann from Runa's scabrous description of him as a phony fascist and an ignorant anti-Stalinist. Stalin's ideologues believed that Mann was not yet convinced of Stalin's irremediably vicious character and was not to be reckoned among his enemies. Here is decisive evidence that even in the months leading up to the treaty, Moscow had no quarrel with Mann as long as it had a quarrel with Germany.

Mann's strongest new point in the present talk is the development of a brief against *nationalism*. He makes vivid the fact that on all fronts the current war cuts through nations, and his own alienation from Germany is his leading example: "My heart is passionately engaged in this struggle, not at all on the German side . . . my own fate is symbolic of the fate of the national idea in general and of the dwindling of its power to bind and enforce." Mann has grown dramatically less concerned about the well-being of the German citizenry; or so one can understand his wish "that . . . [his] misguided and brutalized country will receive the frightful and final lesson which alone can restore it to reason and bring about an inward conversion" (243). Only a crushing defeat can open its eyes to "its share of the guilt . . . if the world should really succumb to the onslaught of evil [and] freedom and justice should perish." Indeed, there have been few signs in Germany of anything like the enlightened awareness of danger that Mann claims to have seen in America (238).

Reflecting on the dissolution of national frontiers, on "this war, which divides minds far more than it does nations," Mann instances the emigration of genius from the Axis nations—Germany and Italy—to the United States: "All the important representatives of German literature are here in America; so are all the important Italian physicists and historians, all the representative European musicians. Members of the same nation fight against each other on the battle fronts, as the Free French fought the troops of General Dentz [in Syria and Lebanon]" (244). In this light, can we ever again talk about the unassailable sovereignty of individual nation-states?

An alternative vision of the future has been advanced in Hitler's "half-educated, oracular harangues": Europe will be a single Germanic empire founded on a notion of racial purity—hence, on the marriage of a tawdry mysticism and machines (tanks and airplanes!) (244–45). But this is not what the future holds in store for us; rather "the kingdom of the world, the city of man has now been born as idea; it will not rest until it has achieved actuality" (245). In America the slogan "America First!" is afoot. Have its proponents not realized that a "world civil war" is raging, one having the beneficent effect of dissolving the boundaries of any nation seeking deliriously to go it alone? Doesn't

Mann's concern speak to us today? The point for right-thinking sloganeers in America would be "Democracy First!"—here and throughout the world. The future of this ideal is in the hands of America—and Russia. Mann proclaims an idea of American and Soviet unity that will ruin his stay in America some ten years later: he links the Russian Revolution with American "evolution." "Evolution" is the odd word choice here: Mann is presumably disinclined to call attention to the old "Anglo-Saxon" rift—the American *Revolution*, since today "Russia and the Anglo-Saxon peoples . . . fight shoulder to shoulder against the enemies of freedom and human dignity." This external link suggests "an inner and deeper truth: socialism and democracy" belong together.

Questions upon questions: does Mann truly believe—rather than hope—that there is an affinity between his imaginary democratic socialism and Stalinist communism? Indeed, "we are inevitably influenced by wishful thinking in our visions and projects for the future." The Russian system, although no less the American, requires "adjustment." Nothing less than "the hope of the world depends on the social reform and rejuvenation of western democracy, and the humanization of eastern collectivism by . . . a recognition of the values and rights of the individual" (246). A station of Mann's very first visit to Germany after the war in summer 1949 was a Goethe celebration in Weimar in the Soviet Zone! This gesture excited the rancor of those Germans who had practiced a merely "*inner* emigration" in the West, meanwhile content to breathe the atmosphere of the Third Reich for nine years.

Admittedly, the proper development of democratic socialism in East and West might be the product of wishful thinking, but here Mann speaks in the accents of his friend Erich Kahler in lauding "man's belief in his power to shape events by his hopes and desires. After all, history is not a mere mechanism; it is made by human beings, human passions affect it; the fatalistic renunciation of all hope of influencing history would mean the abdication of the human spirit" (247). This is *in nuce* the "argument" of Kahler's masterwork *Man—the Measure*, "an attempt to write history as the biography of man and from it to gain a view of the future of man."[103] Mann and Kahler will have discussed this philosophy of history throughout all the years of their friendship.

What is the indispensable groundwork of any decent future? The answer is *law*—"personal security under the law . . . a man cannot exist without confidence in the bond and the security of the law; that without this confidence and without respect for contracts life becomes a hell." Mann chooses rather boldly—others would say imprudently—to speak in the accents of Metternich, for we would be conjuring here, at least in part, a restoration: "a Holy Alliance of governments and peoples bent on raising the concept of law from its present dreadfully fallen state would mean a restoration in the best . . . sense of the word" (249). One wonders how much of the spirit of Metternich's Holy Alliance is meant to shape Mann's new alliance of nations, since Metternich's was thoroughly repressive, aiming to quash in ca. 1820 the liberal reform movements within Central and Eastern Europe, which, he alleged, would threaten the stability of the empires—which is to say, undermine the powers of the princes. The successor to the Holy Roman Empire, Metternich's German Confederation—a prelude to the Holy Alliance—consisted to a large extent of the Austrian Empire. It is fitting that Grillparzer, the Austrian dramatist, should be the one to best sum up the modern European experience: "From humanism via nationalism to bestialism." How stunningly cogent to Mann's time and our own!

Respect for the law means the abrogation of "absolute" personal freedom. That concept of freedom has run its course: it cannot be granted to persons or states. The Nazi debacle gives an example of the destructive "insistence upon the unrestrained sovereignty of the national states" (252). We have seen Mann's analysis of the "problem of freedom" in his talk of this name at Rutgers: freedom must learn to live with a burning recognition of the claims of "social ties and democratic discipline"; this is Mann's continual, passionately felt concern (250). A proper future would be realized, not in "Hitler's misanthropic, daemonic New Order ['the evil Utopia'], based on the megalomania of a single race," but, as we shall soon see, in the good Utopia, "The City of Man" (253; see *The City of Man* in this chapter). The latter must include a purged and chastened Germany, which, after the defeat of Nazism, will work with other nations in the light of its better traditions, its truer self. "May wisdom, imagination, and courage make a peace which shall reconcile the freedom of the nations with their equality before the law binding them all" (256). "*Before the law*," it might be pointed out, is Mann's crucial provision as to the sort of equality of men and women he is prepared to concede. Recall his struggle in "The Problem of Freedom" to coordinate freedom, implying the bold and dangerous life of the exceptional man or woman, and equality, implying, against all evidence, equivalent talents throughout society. Certainly, this problem continues to haunt us, especially in its variant: the putative right of persons aligned in groups to claim the advantages that they allege are enjoyed by all other groups—which is no solution at all.

A Typical Evening's Reading: Nizer and Mumford

It was Mann's custom, before going to bed, to read; he never failed to do so. His days were symmetrical: the morning was invariably devoted to writing one creative page; his evenings were rounded with a read. His diary for October 22, 1940, contains the entry: "[Read] in Nizer's book, in Mumford's" (T4 169). He is thinking, first of all, of Louis Nizer's *Thinking on Your Feet: Adventures in Speaking* (1940).[104]

You come very close to the person of your interest when you read the very pages he read. You see him motionless, attentive, beside you; you are one with him. But it remains for you to know beforehand just what pages he was reading. The choice in Nizer's book is easy: Thomas Mann is richly acknowledged there.

Thinking on Your Feet aims to give instruction on how to make short speeches: it contains many examples of Nizer's own prowess, and several of these mention Mann by name. In one instance, Mann is introduced as guest of honor, in words like those that came especially easily to his publisher Alfred Knopf: "the greatest living man of letters."[105] On two other occasions, Mann is represented as part of the intellectual treasure that Hitler expelled from Germany (Nizer is a learned, eloquent anti-Nazi). Those pages would have interested Mann very much but probably not so much as the page describing himself and his wife Katia in life— this is presumably the reason why Mann had been encouraged to read Nizer. The page figures in a brief encomium to Albert Einstein:

> From one dark little corner of this world [namely, Nazi Germany] he has been exiled. Sometimes I doubt that Einstein and Reinhardt and Thomas Mann have been exiled from Germany. Rather I think Germany is in exile from them. . . . On a later occasion I [Nizer] met him [Einstein] at Thomas Mann's home in Princeton. The newsreel cameramen are there to take motion pictures of Einstein presenting Mann with a medal for high achievement. . . . Mrs. Mann, a woman of nervous energy and staccato torrent of words and thoughts, which one might better understand in her brilliant and frail-looking husband, observes that Einstein is wearing no socks. It is bitter cold out. He has come without a hat. A simple sport coat which buttons high in the neck relieves him of the necessity of wearing a shirt or tie. With motherly solicitude she condemns him for not wearing socks. Without the slightest trace of humor, he replies that he never does, because he has trouble with them when they get holes. His simplicity staves off laughter. We all maintain an acquiescent silence.[106]

I am not sure whether the very urbane Mann was amused by this cameo. He might have been only slightly better pleased by the casual horror of the text "I Pity Germany," which begins:

> Shall we hate Germany, or shall we pity it?
>
> I think of German literature—of Goethe, Schiller, and Heine, and Grimm and Sudermann and Hauptmann and Thomas Mann.
>
> Then I realize that today no German writer can retain his integrity without fleeing from his country or being thrown into a concentration camp where he is starved and beaten with a steel-tipped whip, until pronounced dead from pneumonia.
>
> I pity German literature! . . .
>
> It was Emerson who said that talent alone does not make a great writer. There must be a man behind the book. And in the case of our guest of honor, Thomas Mann, without resort to a fortuitous play on a word, there is a man behind the book.
>
> We can all take comfort in the fact that when the guns of Hitler have been silenced, as were those of Charlemagne, Torquemada, Gomez[107] and Napoleon, the works and ideas of Thomas Mann will live on triumphantly. The pen is the tongue of the mind and the word is still mightier than the sword.
>
> I pity Germany![108]

Nizer's final piece, "Let Them In," contains a solid argument, which puts his many-sided intellect on display. He makes the intriguing, relevant case for immigration even at a time of drastic national unemployment. Contrary to the commonplace prejudice, it is the fact that

> economic history has shown that prosperity increases as our population increases, and that we suffer depressions when our populations decrease. . . . Yes, the answer to the question, "How can we afford to admit hundreds of thousands of refugees to compete for our jobs?" is that they will create jobs and help solve our economic problem; that we need an increase in population; that it is in our own selfish and economic interest to admit the refugees.
>
> We owe a great debt to immigrants. If the Puritans had not been compelled to emigrate because of the Anglican Church, we would never have had a George Washington, a Benjamin Franklin or a Thomas Jefferson. If Samuel Lincoln, a Quaker, had not been driven from England by Samuel Fox, we never would have had an Abe Lincoln; nor in literature a Longfellow,

Hawthorne, Poe or Whitman; nor in science a Morse, Edison or Fulton. And I suspect that Germany has paid her debt to us in better currency than gold, when it sent us Einstein, Mann, Reinhardt, Klemperer, [Willy] Ley, Grosz and many others. When Ferdinand and Isabella of Spain drove out the Jews, they received the following note from their traditional enemy the Sultan of Turkey: "I thank you from the bottom of my heart for having enriched my country while impoverishing yours."[109]

The citation from Mann's diaries on October 22, 1940, which notes the authors he was reading, adds to "Nizer" the name of the eminent critic and philosopher [Lewis] Mumford. And then, without further explanation, Mann concludes: "German culture: Luther and Hitler. Fichte, Nietzsche, Wagner—and Hitler. . . ." This sinister thought would have emerged from his reading both these books; in fact, it is an almost direct, unattributed quote from the chapter "Force, Grace, and Reason" in Mumford's *Faith for Living* (1940).[110] This eloquent essay is a diatribe against a certain class of "pragmatic liberals"

who have been incapable of making firm ethical judgments or implementing them with action. Their color-blindness to moral values is the key to their political weakness today. Hence, they cannot distinguish between barbarism and civilization.

Worse than this: such color-blindness leads many of these liberals to pass a highly favorable verdict upon barbarism, because of the superior capacity it has shown for reorganizing its economic institutions so that they may serve exclusively for military conquests, putting through public works that gratify the egos of their dictators, and multiplying the engines of war, so that these egos may be further inflated by the tribute exacted from conquered nations. It is more than a sneaking admiration for Nazi barbarism that shows itself in the callous utterances of a Lindbergh—that flattered receiver of Nazi "honors." . . .

This tenderness toward fascism shows where the hearts of such "liberals" really lie: many of them covertly worship power and cringe before it; they esteem success, and do not concern themselves with the evils sponsored by the successful. One needs no gift of prophecy to see how quickly their liberal coats will turn inside out should fascism ever invade America's shores.

Refusing to recognize the crucial problem of evil, the pragmatic liberals are unable to cope with the intentions of evil men. They look in vain for mere intellectual mistakes to account for the conduct of men who have chosen deliberately to flout man's long efforts to become civilized. In the case of Germany, they look to the Treaty of Versailles—itself a work of marvelous magnanimity and high justice, compared with the treaties already inflicted by Stalin and Hitler—for explanations of conduct and ideas that have nothing to do with the first World War or the economic depression that started in 1929.

The fundamental ideology of fascism was first formulated clearly in the sermons, letters, and exhortations of Martin Luther; for Hitler's program today as applied to the world as a whole is little more than Luther's original doctrines, including the fantastic Nazi doctrine of national autarchy, with the top dressing of Christianity removed. . . . The raucous hatred that shouts on every page of "Mein Kampf" received its first classical utterance in Luther's denunciation of the Peasants' Rebellion; and the direct line of connection between Luther and Hitler, through Fichte, Nietzsche, and Wagner, is familiar to all those who know the history of German culture.[111]

It is a very interesting fact, which offers us a window onto Mann's learning and accumulation of ideological tropes, that in a letter written a year later, on August 8, 1941, to Graf Carlo Sforza, Mann writes:

I have determined that "the good old Germany of culture and learning is more or less an American fiction" [*this clause in Mann's own English*] and that one would have to drive pretty far upstream along the course of German history before one found no sign of that spirit which today has reached the last degree of baseness and threatens to barbarize and enslave the world. At least as far as the Middle Ages; for Luther . . . already had decidedly Nazistic traits. And what horrors are to be found in Fichte! What menaces in the music, and even more in the writings of Wagner! What a muddle of clarity and obscurity in Schopenhauer and Nietzsche![112]

We have identified the text—Mumford's—that helped inspire this formulation. But there is more in Mumford's writings that would have interested Mann, would have stuck in his memory, and would have shaped in depth and detail his understanding of the Nazi state. One reads in Mumford's major opus *The Culture of Cities* (1938), a book that Mann had in his library, a description of a metropolis in crisis—and, by implication, a nation going to its ruin. Mann would have been struck by the pertinence of this passage from "The Decadence of Cities":

Fifth stage: Tyrannopolis. Extensions of parasitism throughout the economic and social scene: the function of spending paralyzes all the higher activities of culture and no act of culture can be justified that does not involve display and expense. Politics becomes competition for the exploitation of the municipal and state exchequer by this or that class or group. Extirpation of organs of communal and civic life other than the "state." Caesarism. Development of predatory means as a substitute for trade and give-and-take: naked exploitation of colonies and hinterland: intensification of the cycles of commercial depression, following overexpansion of industry and dubious speculative enterprise, heightened by wars and war-preparations. Failure of the economic and political rulers to maintain the bare decencies of administration: place-hunting, privilege-seeking, bonus-collecting, favor-currying, nepotism, grafting, tribute-exacting become rife both in government *and* business. Widespread moral apathy and failure of civic responsibility: each group, each individual takes what it can get away with. Widening of the gap between producing classes and spending classes. Multiplication of a *Lumpen proletariat* demanding its share of bread and shows. Overstress of mass sports. Parasitic love of sinecures in every department of life. Demand for "protection money" made by armed thugs and debased soldiery: organizing looting, organized blackmail are "normal" accompaniments of business and municipal enterprise. Domination of respectable people who behave like criminals and of criminals whose activities do not debar them from respectability.

Imperialistic wars, internal and external, result in starvation, epidemics of disease, demoralization of life: uncertainty hangs over every prospect of the future: armed protection increases all the hazards of life. Municipal and state bankruptcy. Drain of local taxes to service increasing load of local debts. Necessity to appeal to the state for further aid in periods of economic disorganization: loss of autonomy. Drain of national taxes to support the growing military establishment of the state. This burden penalizes the remnants of honest industry and agriculture, and further disrupts the supply of elementary material goods. Decrease in agricultural production by soil-mining and erosion, through falling off in acreage, through the withholding of crops from the city by resentful husbandmen. Decline in rate of population—increase through birth control, abortion, mass slaughter, and suicide code: eventual absolute decline in numbers. General loss of nerve. Attempt to create order by external military means: rise of gangster-dictators (Hitler, Mussolini) with active consent of the bourgeoisie and systematic terrorism by praetorian guards. Recrudescence of superstition and deliberate cult of savagery: barbarian invasions from within and without. Beginnings of megalopolitan exodus. Material deficiencies and lapses of cultural continuity: repression and censorship. Cessation of productive work in the arts and sciences.

Sixth and final stage: Nekropolis. War and famine and disease rack both city and countryside. . . . [113]

Mann greatly valued Mumford personally, who was, according to Vaget, "undoubtedly one of the most remarkable and important Americans with whom Mann came into contact." Hence, we have more than ever reason to suppose that Mann drew on Mumford's writings.[114] On November 14, 1941, shortly before departing for Amherst College, where Mann would lecture on *The War and the Future,* he spent a remarkable evening with Mumford in Borgese's summer home in Amenia, New York.[115] Mumford, who lived in Amenia as well, was invited. Mann had met Mumford before, once in Munich as early as 1932, where, as Mumford relates in his autobiography—*Sketches from Life: The Autobiography of Lewis Mumford, The Early Years*—the two had an enthusiastic conversation. Mann had been told that Mumford had read *The Magic Mountain* "three times," a claim that was to some extent true. Mumford's account of their cordial meeting in Munich is preceded in his memoirs by a less happy report:

> In 1914 [*Mumford was at most 19!*], I did not realize how deeply these militarist assumptions had penetrated the whole German population. Years later I was profoundly shocked to find that perhaps the greatest of contemporary German writers, a European of the Europeans—Thomas Mann, in fact— had without blushing made the same insufferably juvenile claims for *deutsche Kultur.*[116]

"Years later" certainly refer to the years after 1932 and Mumford's first of several conversations with Mann: "When I rose to take my leave of Mann at the end of the stipulated half-hour, Mann begged me to remain, for he had been reading Ernest Hemingway, with admiration for his laconic style, so different from his own; and it also developed that he, too, appreciated Kipling's prose."[117] I am inclined not to take the preterit "begged" too graphically; it is part of Mumford's rather mandarin diction in a book of memoirs published at the age of eighty-six.

Thereafter, Mann met with Mumford and other notables, including Borgese, at the first "City of Man Conference" at Atlantic City from May 24 through May 26, 1940 (T4 81). Borgese, along with the historian Gaetano Salvemini, was the inspiration behind the project and its organizer; Mann's

Princeton neighbors, Kahler and Broch, were involved, though to different degrees: Broch very decisively (he was responsible for the economics side of the proposal, and was literally present at the conference), Kahler, indirectly, as Broch's advisor and confidant. The purpose of the conference, like that of many small groups coming together spontaneously at the time, was, in plain words, citing Mumford, "to awaken their countrymen to the threat that Hitlerism and Stalinism then posed to democratic (representative) government." In describing the meeting, Mumford stressed "the split of our committee into militants and pacifists, [which] showed how quixotic Borgese's original hopes were." Borgese's idea had been, years before,

> to bring together a group of representative intellectuals, who would pool their wisdom and exert their authority to make clear the issues democracy now faced. Borgese, indeed, dreamed of formulating measures which might *forestall or circumvent* the world-wide totalitarian threat. . . . [But] both our strength and our weakness were well revealed in our first and only publication, "The City of Man," which bears Borgese's unmistakable stamp.[118]

The City of Man: A Declaration on World Democracy (C) is a militant appeal outlining the principles and values of democracy; warning against the lethal threat posed by Nazi-fascism; and calling for the unconditional defense of these principles and values in their ideal embodiment: a unity of all nations under one world government.[119] Readers today will find its stunning intelligence and dazzling rhetoric to be relevant. The Declaration is a rich harvest of historical knowledge and political thought as this intellectual substance might bear productively, even militantly, on the historical crisis anno 1940: the victory of Nazi-fascism in Europe (the Old World) and the threat it represents to the New (America!). The document assigns the strongest possible defensive role to America, which might join hands, in 1940, with England, the last remaining bastion of antifascism. It lays out the antithetical directions dividing the city of man, even as they divide us today: the paths of barbarism—wildcat individualism—and democratic socialism. "The *emergency of democracy* must be the emergence of democracy."[120] "We address our words . . . to the American youth, whatever the differences of racial origins and social status among them. They all . . . will reject the guidance of a false education," one that makes barbarism attractive; "the teachings of a degraded science," which invests its intellectual capital in weapons and technological diversions; and "the sophistry of the irresponsibles"—read: the idioms of the deplorables.[121] For all its majesty, Mumford subsequently described *The City of Man* as a merely "vain attempt to open our countrymen's eyes to the inimical dangers that threatened the world."[122] (Readers will find a fuller account of this book in the pages that follow.)

Mumford gives a touching picture of Mann's contribution to the conference at Atlantic City: "Thomas Mann, grave, genial, aloof, a little shy still because of his English, was silent most of the time: but his deep feeling in the reading of his paper on democracy impressed everyone: at one point he could hardly keep back his tears."[123] I'll add that Mann would have been moved and then especially pleased to sign a paper stating, in respect of "the continuity of ancient and modern wisdom" flowing in from an authentic Europe: "Here, and almost nowhere else, is Europe."[124] He would have felt confident of his contribution to the manifesto on reading, on December 15, 1940, Harold J. Laski's incisive *Where Do We Go from Here?*, especially the chapters "What Fascism Is" and "What Are We to Do Next?"—thoughts consistent at every point with the text of *The City of Man* and possibly helping to shape it.[125] Mann subsequently sent *The City of Man* to Eleanor Roosevelt, which he describes, in turn, as "a little book, which a group of us prepared in all sincerity and humility as an attempt to outline the future world democracy and a contribution to the solution of the fundamental problems facing all nations today. If the book appeals to you and you think it would interest the President, perhaps you will show it to him. Yours very sincerely, Thomas Mann."[126]

Mann's meetings with Mumford also give us a vivid picture of Mann's public persona. This time the report is less empathetic. We return to Borgese's birthday party on November 14, 1941, at his summer home, to which the Mumfords had been invited. Mumford reports:

> Thomas Mann and his wife were up for the briefest of parental visits . . . so perhaps you think I'm going to tell you about the meeting of four great minds, and of all the jewels that dropped from the creator of Joseph, who always . . . carries with him the indefinable aura of a true German prig, an aura conveyed best by the tone of his voice: just a touch of fussiness and unction, like the German rentier I met once on a train going from Zürich to Innsbruck, who meticulously put on a pair of elegant silk gloves as soon as he entered the compartment. I did have a few brief snatches of conversation with Mann, not about Joseph or Hans Castorp but about Shakespeare. We agreed that he was a very great writer! More, that he had pre-figured the entire modern world. Mann had just been to a dress rehearsal of Macbeth and was struck by its contemporaneity. But what a difference, he observed, there was in the ruthless monsters of Shakespeare's day! with what speed

they were seized with remorse! And with what sensitiveness they reflected upon their wickedness! ...

[A]t one point the great Mann somewhat tactlessly remarked, like a character in one of his novels repeating a pat line, that in every Italian there was something of an actor—indeed a touch of the *buffone*, Mann added, as if to be sure that the insult was properly pinned in place and would stick. ... [*This is at home with Borgese!*] The geyser exploded. History was summoned to become a tidal wave of refutation. Was Dante a *buffone*? Was Michelangelo a scalawag of an actor? And what finally was Mazzini—an empty strutter? There was no need for Borgese to bring in Borgese: Mazzini was close enough, for, now that I know Mazzini better, I realize that the best parts of *The City of Man* are pure Mazzini, and all the better for that. The refutation was complete enough to silence an even greater writer than Mann and a more heroic warrior. ... Borgese ... was magnificent.[127]

It comes as no surprise that here, as in comparable reports, Mann's "geistige Persönlichkeit"—the playful, affectionate, ironical "intellectual-spiritual personality" informing his fictions—is thought a good deal "friendlier" than the empirical Mann. But then, as the tag goes, "Quid de te alii loquantur, ipsi videant ..." (Let what others say about you be their concern ...).

The City of Man (1940)

Soon after Munich, in the fall of 1938, I knocked on his door, in Princeton, with the hope of winning his support for a green idea of mine: the City of Man, a free association of philosophers and poets, self-appointed leaders of democracy toward victory and global peace. I won his support and that of several others. Our words, none the less, were to fall on deaf ears, for practically everybody believed at that time—as a few still believe today—that colonels and diplomats know better.

—GIUSEPPE ANTONIO BORGESE

If "firmness" is to be a real policy, it must imply the use, explicit or implicit, of force, and it is here that the advocates of "firmness" were in their quandary.

—ROBERT RHODES JAMES

The "Declaration" of *The City of Man*—to which Mann, Borgese, Broch, and Kahler contributed—is lucidly introduced by the Italian Germanist Ester Saletta, the author of a rich monograph on this project:

Between 1920 and 1940, the Nazi and Fascist totalitarian systems over-
whelmed Europe, enchanting the masses with their dystopian pseudo-
democratic ideology, chiefly philosophical, literary, and mythical in nature.
They were countered by traditional, popular, partisan, and underground
resistance, as well as groups of intellectuals and scholars, both American
and European. The latter, exiled in the United States, planned a new liberal
model in which democracy would once again be a value defending and
safeguarding human rights and dignity in all their diversity. *The City of Man*
is the anti-totalitarian Euro-American response of some of the leading cultural figures of the twentieth century, who did not limit themselves to observing the collapse of Europe and the debasement of the democratic
principle but presented an achievable liberal and anthropocentric utopia.
Hermann Broch and Thomas Mann, Giuseppe Antonio Borgese and
Gaetano Salvemini, Reinhold Niebuhr and William Allan Neilson were
among the utopians who, in *The City of Man*, attempted to promote a Roo-
seveltian New Deal of democracy.[128]

The City of Man represents a call to arms by a group of committed
intellectuals—"The Committee on Europe"—in the face of the Nazi invasion of
Europe. It consists of a Declaration and a Proposal. I shall comment from time
to time, but I mainly want to present the gist of this brilliantly written if quixoti-
cally idealistic manifesto. Mann participated fully in this project: at the group's
first meeting, he read his "Problem of Freedom" lecture with impressive pathos,
and he also chaired one of its sessions (V 32). The document aims to steer a
path—with difficulty—between the pacifist concerns of one half of the Committee and the militancy of the other. Mann was frankly bent on having America
enter the war as the one great hope for "The Coming Victory of Democracy."

The authors judge the prospects for civilization at this moment as dismal.
"'I shall eradicate the thousands of years of human domestication,' said Hitler,
in conversation. 'I want to see again in the eyes of youth the gleam of the beast
of prey. A youth will grow up before which the world will shrink.'"[129] The totalitarian slaughter in Europe is a catastrophe from which even New York cannot be safe. "The Nazi conquerors today manifestly envision the time . . . when
they will be 'ready to take the stride into overseas space'" (15). "The doom of
the Old World will be our doom unless we make a last stand" (18).

It is delusory to suppose that the Nazi triumphs are solely an affair of their
mechanical advantage over less technically equipped nations. It is another
mistake to think that a continual convoy of American war material to

embattled England via "Lend-Lease" will change the outcome by itself. It will not. The Nazis have been

> stronger in arms because they were stronger in heart. It was their fanatical faith that gave them wings and fire; it was the singleness of their purpose that sharpened the spearheads of their march. To the compactness of their religion of darkness the rulers of France and England had nothing to oppose but a dim, Hamlet-like glow. . . . Military defeat was the outcome of moral abdication. (15–16)

Democracy today (in 1940), as we (the authors of the Declaration) declare, has neither wings nor fire: it has fallen into a flaccid "way of life." What was once "a strenuous unity of thought and action," better: "a faith, militant and triumphant," has become a routine of "liberties and comforts" (17). Yet this lazy boon is not available to all, not to the disenfranchised masses, whose deprivation and despair have become means to be shaped to vile ends by a ruthless leader. The present crisis is due in no small way to the betrayal of those *intellectuals* who have preferred to wash their hands of the body politic. This very Declaration constitutes an "atonement."

The authors write in the hope of a human flourishing, the necessary condition of which is peace—universal peace. The enemy of growth and progress is war, which is not a fate or a moral compulsion but a decision.

> Blood feuds, ordeals, and duels were proscribed by collective law; while legalized warfare itself is returning on wings, before our eyes, from standards of epic piety and chivalric honor to the indiscriminate atrocity of primal murder. . . . Peace, universal peace, is the *sine qua non* if man's advance is to be resumed beyond the present threat and ruin. (21–22)

But the peace cannot be produced from a feckless readiness to compromise. Unlike "parasitic pacifism," a strong peace includes a readiness to fight for its own ends. And it will fight best under the one administration it can trust, which "can be founded only on the unity of man under one law and one government."

With Europe under Nazi-fascist rule, however, what can this "fight" mean (this commentator, SC, wonders) if not war? Admittedly, the signatories cannot exclude the prospect of war—a real, fierce, and bloody war; indeed, "'a war to end war' may be, again, the lot of our generation and of ours alone [America's!]." And, here, observe a second loophole: "or of others to come, until the totalitarianism of death or the universality of peace is established on earth."

The latter is alone the freely breathable air of a universal City of Man (23–24). But this Declaration may not be read as an argument for *immediate* American intervention in Europe: "an immediate war of 'liberation and rescue' seems an absurd assignment." And yet a devoutly wished isolation from the destitution of Europe seems even more absurd (14).

The goal, again and again, in impressive capitals, is "the Nation of Man embodied in the Universal State, the State of States." History has made it quite clear that the nation-state—the product of the disintegration of Rome—has no lien on the future: its weakness is evident from the speed with which it has fallen to the Germans. "There can be no peace for the small nations whose feeble freedom is but a gift of the stronger; there can be no peace among the giant states whose size itself bids for the anarchy of violence and conquest" (24). But universal republican unity is not at hand: "The area of destruction must probably spread before the path is clear for the new order" (26).

At this point, I'll note, Mann might very well have recalled the letter he wrote to Erich Kahler on Mann's arrival in Princeton: "The way that history has taken has been so filthy, such a carrion-strewn path of lies and baseness, that no one need be ashamed of refusing to travel along it, *even if it should lead to goals we might commend if reached by other paths*" (EF 17–18; emphasis added). Mann imagined a crisis in which a community of nations would rise up from under Nazi rule. The crucial meetings of the signatories of this manifesto on May 24–26, 1940, and August 24–25, 1940—meetings from which this document sprang—bracket the date of the occupation of Paris by Nazi armies on June 14. On *that day* Mann wrote to Agnes Meyer about "the way that history has taken": "Now, if the monster [Hitler] sleeps in the Tuileries, will that be the culmination of his career—a shameful thing for all of us? We don't know. If all the misery and destruction had a more decent origin than in the pus-filled (*jauchig*) mind of this subject, it would be easier to endure."[130] Conceiving its "higher" origin might allow one to have rational hopes for a higher end—and Mann continued to have such hopes. He wrote to his brother on September 22, after Heinrich had managed to leave France, "There are no doubt many more horrible things to come, but they will necessarily eventuate in a humane new order, which is to say, one not determined by the great gangster of our time" (BR.H. 236).

Henceforth, *The City of Man* will invoke a higher tone. The signatories authorize the invocation of "the teachings of Christ" as a figure of thought in this defense of democracy (28). We are urged to think these two ideals together, for "democracy is nothing more and nothing less than humanism in theocracy and rational theocracy in universal humanism" (33). True, such a society has never before existed: "As there has never been a wholly Christian society in spite of the teachings of Christ and of the loyalty of some of His disciples scattered throughout the ages, so there has never been a total democracy ordering all activities of life over any great area of space and time" (28).

A reader might wonder about the propriety of an invocation of a Christian ethos and a Christian society in a Call to Arms composed by a group of avowed secular humanists. At least one such motive might be the recurrent desire of the émigrés to eliminate the suggestion that in pleading for America's intervention in Europe it meant chiefly to rescue the targeted victims of the Nazis—Communists and Jews—neither group having a stake in a Christian society. Readers today must keep the fact in mind—on noting this Christian appeal and especially Mann's pleadings in own speeches—that America did *not* send soldiers to Europe (discounting Iceland) until a year and a half later, shortly after the Japanese attack on Pearl Harbor and Hitler's declaration of war on the United States.

A militant democracy, such as the one envisioned, needs to pay heed to fundamental principles: "The first is universal participation in government," as through town meetings and elections. The second principle grants to citizens the right to correct or indeed remove elected persons who abuse their office. The third is its own promotion of an educated, disciplined, and cultivated citizenry active in defense of these principles (29). The authors attack a certain liberalism (we have seen Lewis Mumford do this) that entitles unconstrained individualism and leads to a global principle of noninterference: "If a foreign country had freely chosen to forfeit its own freedom or had freely managed to kill the freedom of its neighbor," so be it: there are no *liberal* grounds here for indignation—and this is deplorable. On the other hand, the slave-mongers of Europe are full of conviction; "democracy, they say, 'rests on opinion, it has no conviction'" (31). But that is true only of an enfeebled liberalism. "The democratic concept of freedom"—as it relates to every state—"can never include the freedom to destroy democracy and freedom."

The Broch scholar Michael Paul Lützeler cites, as very likely Broch's contribution to the manifesto, the accompanying justification: "Democracy teaches that everything must be within humanity, nothing against humanity, nothing outside humanity. The dictatorship of humanity, on the basis of a law for the protection of human dignity, is the only rule from which we may hope for life for ourselves and resurrection for the nations that have fallen" (34–35). Ideas from Broch's resonantly titled essay "On the Dictatorship of Humanity within a Total Democracy" of early 1939 "were absorbed," we learn, "into the group's attempt to refine the theory of democracy."[131]

This secular claim is promptly hallowed again by religion and placed on a Christian foundation, which will be constantly invoked throughout the manifesto. Here, it proceeds through an allegory of the Holy Ghost, a "divine spirit of man," assuring, beyond the "dictatorship of humanity," the dignity of all persons and requiring their lawful protection. The learned authors conjure as sureties the main contributors to a universal religion of humanity—the prophets of Israel, Greek poetry and philosophy, Roman law, the Catholic Church, the Protestant revolt, humanism, the Renaissance, the revolutions, and the philosophies of the Enlightenment—in order to conclude that "in all of these particular systems there are humanity and redemption. Each and all of them are comprehended under the all-embracing and all-interpreting religion of the *Spirit*" (37–38; emphasis added). This formulation would have attracted Mann's readiness to sign on; it is the sort of higher rhetoric that irritated the pragmatist James T. Farrell and others (see in this chapter "Contra Thomas Mann the American," *supra*).

The Church in modern times has failed this great goal of a universal religion of man. The fulfillment of that ideal is obstructed as well by what the authors call "most of the Synagogue," meaning, the form of "the Hebraic tradition" professed by many of its orthodox believers. That tradition fails mankind "by the sterility of its unshakable conservatism and by the racial [sic] stubbornness which severed the orthodox Jew from Jesus, highest of Jewish prophets" (39–40). Did Hermann Broch and Erich Kahler and Hans Kohn, three of the signatories, help draft this sentence? Were they glad to read about "the greatness of the Roman Church . . . [and] the glory of its achievement in piloting Western man through the Dark Ages" (40)? What of the "piloting" that brought the savage army of Crusaders through the Rhineland, murdering Jews, and onto Jerusalem, whose streets it filled with blood? Never mind. For the moment, the spirit of this summons aims to be practical and ecumenical (it cannily cites President Roosevelt as an exemplary advocate of "the spirit of the New Testament," 35). One hears especially the voice of Borgese in a caustic enough attack on the behavior of the papacy at this crucial historical juncture: "the Church is tempted to make peace with tyranny and come to terms with Fascism, if Fascism promises not to harm the Church as a historical institution." Its claim to "an absoluteness of veneration," even given its "relativity in history," has been corrupted by the changing play of social and political forces. Even more decisively, he scolds "the docility of the Church toward the powers that be and its readiness not only to compromise but also to collaborate with evil, when collaboration is profitable." We have seen "the Christian pontificate hitch its wagon to the Fascist star" (41–42). Pious Catholics may rue this compact, but their voice has scarcely been heard. Certainly, the Protestant churches offer no healing example. "When . . . the orthodox Lutherans in Germany hastened to grovel before Hitler, the liberal Protestant Churches in the democratic world either shrank in solitary protests . . . or supported a doctrinaire pacifism" (44). The result of both sorts of submission is a peace no different from slavery. Mann would have recalled his summons "To the Civilized World" of late 1938: "Shall we listen only to the enemy who says 'peace' when he means 'war'?" The "liberal Protestant Churches" have "watered Christian charity, *which is a fighting one*, down to the Quaker's entreaty to extend 'love even to Hitler'—Christ's love to the Antichrist" (44; emphasis added). One will wonder, once more, what a "fighting" charity could mean, other than an expression of the conflict of wills behind this document, one ready to fight a war and the other ready to preach patience.

Still, both parties would agree: Neither war nor submission to the threats of its enemies can create the peace of a robust democracy, a "world-humanism and world-democracy," which draws strength from its informing spirit, "a divine intention," for which it is "the spearhead. . . . The direction of this intention is from matter to life and from life to spirit, from chaos to order, from blind strife and random impulse to conscience and moral law, from darkness to light" (46–47). At this historical moment, these values are neither understood nor universally shared. The detachment of the enemies of democracy is worse than indifference, worse than a slumbering conscience: it is an active evil, demanding resistance, "with battle if necessary." What is at stake is nothing less than the fulfillment of a messianic ideal of "the good, under the inspiration of faith, hope, and charity." It is the wish that "Thy kingdom come. Thy will be done *on earth* as it is in heaven" (emphasis added; 48). The signatories of *The City of Man* are inviting a crusade—with or without violence: "This earth of ours is the laboratory where the validity of eternal ideas is tested under the limits of space and time" (49)—and perhaps must be tested by force!

To the robust faith, hope, and charity of a vital democracy, add liberty and its main instrument: economic justice. There is no liberty of thought and action available to the exploited poor. They are the captives of a freebooting, wildcat capitalism, a rugged individualism bent on efficiency whose mongrel dialectical product is the slave societies of Nazi-fascism and Communism. Here, the idea of justice has been suborned by a "scheme of mass-regimentation, with its equality of servitude and its universality of deprivations" (51). With uncanny relevance to the mean-spirited politics of *our* day, these scholars write:

> Barbarism is not a condition that man has left behind him; when the leniency or cowardice of society shirks the daily delivered effort which is needed to conquer the barbarism within it, the result on the local scene is the rule by gangsters and racketeers, the result on the world-scene is the rule by tyrants. Indeed, many of today's tyrants and their henchmen, before their day of glory, had been criminal offenders to whom the liberal era flung open the gates of the prisons of which they were rightful inmates. (51–52)

Marxism, which promised a human good, has been traduced by Hitler's malice and boasting. His Nazism is a Marxism stripped of its salvational potential, a degradation now fully realized by Stalin. They meet halfway into this darkness, and so it is no wonder that they could join both ideologically and *real*-politically in the Nazi-Soviet Nonaggression Pact of 1939. Under their rule, Europe is a slave society: the victors enslaved by madness—"the drunkenness of primacy and the exultation of rapine. . . . [and] the vanquished . . . dissolved . . . in the benumbed felicity of a subhuman bondage." No matter, this difference: victors and vanquished will remain slaves "unless they rise again, *unless we lend our hand that they may rise again*" (54; emphasis added).

Half the signatories are content with a lending that goes no further than lend-lease; others—the German exiles, Mann, Broch, and Kahler especially—want a hand that turns into a fist—an armed fist! This envisioned hand is American, the incorporation of "the human dream, the American dream." The Committee calls for a world in which those who own but do not work no longer oppress those who work but do not own. "All the children of the earth must know that they all have inherited the earth. . . . The problem of production, which was a problem of power, has been superseded by the problem of distribution, which is a problem of justice" (55–56). And again, with incisive relevance to the kleptocracies of our time (2021), "Limits must be set to the accumulation of wealth and its transmission down the generations." The argument for the exemplary character of American democracy is built on an ingenious use of the metaphor of biblical supercessionism. There is a (continually valid) "Old Testament of Americanism," consisting of the key provisions of the Declaration of Independence and Woodrow Wilson's plea for a League of Nations (58–59). But this ethos needs to be improved in a "New Testament of Americanism." The *separation* from the Old World that the Old Testament consecrated has degenerated into *isolationism*: hence the need for a New Testament of "World Humanism," a militant spirit of world unity and interdependence. It alone can "defeat" the Fascism that means to rule the world: the vitality of the space of the entire world is at stake, and we "cannot divide the world with Fascism, which is, by definition, totalitarian" (60–61). England alone, in a spirit of struggle and sacrifice, keeps up the fight, but "no self-sufficient British victory . . . is in sight" (62). It is for America to acknowledge "the dignity and power of her inevitable mission," which is to lead, for "no one is left free and strong enough to show the way toward social reform and universal order except this country" (63). She has been chosen "by the objective circumstances of history for a privilege which is a service, for a right which is a duty. . . . American leadership is world-trusteeship; the *Pax Americana* a preamble to the *Pax Humana*" (64–65).

The authors of this manifesto, they admit, are few in number, and their power is limited. On the other hand, recall that "the destructive upheaval which is now shaking the earth started from humbler origins in conventicles of lost souls in Milan and in Munich some twenty years ago. They had stumbled upon the deeper pathological yearnings of the time" (66). But will not a purposeful Good outlast a transient Evil? Everything depends on this Good, democracy, asserting itself with a primary strength of purpose: it will not survive as "Antifascism or Antinazism." It must rediscover and realize its root power: once more, "the emergency of democracy must be the emergence of democracy" (67).

Here, the pacifist core of the signatories asserts a crucial addendum—but one that is incoherent in light of the militant air of the demands that have just preceded it. The core retreats from a declaration of war by concealing the abusive temper of war under the head of *revolution* and then disowning any revolutionary intent. After all, both warmongers and peacemongers can safely declare that they are opposed to revolution. "No spirit of revolution animates our proposals, since revolution . . . is but the counterpart of war. It is war itself, with fire and steel, with fraud and terror." But another core of the signatories, we know, is hell-bent precisely on this "war itself, with fire and steel," forgetting its necessary accompaniments "fraud and terror," for how else are the fascist armies to be defeated? Aside from the hoped-for effect of a brief in favor of the Good and a renewed adherence to spirit (*Geist*) among the signatories and its readers, what is to be done? This action surely cannot be so jejune as a literal "restatement of Democracy," which, together with the Constitution, "will interpret themselves" and then presumably acquire legs and wings (67). And yet a sort of hope is on the horizon: the present ordeal can and must be made to lead to a "new beginning," the universal City of Man (73).

The memorandum adopts a conclusion that could seem ever so slightly off topic, however uplifting. It is a paean to the American melting pot: "It is good that this country was never allowed to be the exclusive fief of any single stock." This is to say it has encouraged immigration. This claim may be a reflexive acknowledgment of the many ethnic backgrounds of the signatories, in case this variety should itself become the object of concern, even skepticism, by privileged readers of the—named—"English stock, whose language we proudly speak and whose tradition we faithfully share." But this paean borders on the hyperbolic and lacks discrimination: "It is manifest destiny that representatives came here from all races and regions—from Europe and Africa, from Asia and Polynesia—thus lifting the young nation above the level of the old and molding the New World into a scheme of the All-World to come." It is hardly necessary to point out that the forcible transport of African slaves to America and thereafter the sort of hospitality shown to Chinese laborers did not lift the young nation above the level of the old. It is also noteworthy that none of the signatories hailed from Asia or Africa.

The manifesto then goes on to invoke, somewhat surprisingly, "the Jew among us." The citation is meant figuratively: "he" is the "survivor of persecutions [who] warns us by his very presence that anti-Semitism is the entering edge of racism, the dusk of hatred which precedes the totalitarian night." But I would think that this mention at the penultimate end of this plea would also be understood more personally and literally by the Jewish members of this collective. Here, very likely, readers can detect the ideological presence of Hermann Broch, who, a year before, had written, "I foresee a totalitarian England and a totalitarian France and perhaps also a dictatorial America. These will arise of necessity by German example with the help of the pogroms, so that, starting with the annihilation of the Jews, civilization will end in total self-annihilation."[132] Months later, Broch added, "I am absolutely convinced the German penetration of America is entirely possible, that (because of the Negro problem) the idea of racial superiority—and therefore anti-Semitism—could flourish better here than anywhere else."[133] In fact, this mention of "the Jew" concludes with "The Negro himself, [who] helps us by reminding us that our slow progress is a mere token of the justice we pledged " (68–69). This caution is capped by an unacknowledged citation: "There is neither Jew nor Gentile, neither native nor naturalized, neither master nor slave, neither white nor colored" (69–70). This vision is offered as the American credo, which readers can only treasure as an ideal, and blink at with dismayed bemusement at how violently it has been and continues to be betrayed. We have just intuited the strong presence of Broch. Here, perhaps, is Thomas Mann: In America "the treasure of English culture is guarded; . . . along with the treasure and essence of all human cultures. Here, and almost nowhere else is Europe. . . . For here, and almost nowhere else, is man granted the right and duty of being Christian and human" (71). This trope represents a soft taking-back of the previous stress on the exemplary Jew, the canary in the dusky mine of totalitarianism, and could point to the growing Christianizing thrust in Mann's public speeches (see chapter 1). But less soft is the phrase "[the] *duty* of being Christian" (emphasis added). Would neglect of this duty amount to a dereliction on the part of the Jews Broch and Kahler and Kohn? Here, surely, one feels the weight of the heretical Catholic Borgese, the most prominent of the contributors to this Declaration.

The conclusion might well be too stentorian to command a wide assent: "Only those Americans are truly Americans who pledge their lives, their fortunes, and their sacred honor to the creed of universal democracy in the expectation of a world-society for men united to fight their common enemies, the untamed forces of Fate and Evil" (71). Such, according to this manifesto, is America's tragic destiny; but it is a destiny that will become active only after a pileup of empirical horrors a year later: the Japanese attack on Pearl Harbor and Hitler's declaration of war. At the end the signatories reach for a personal note, amplified to a symbol: foregrounding the various ethnicities and backgrounds, they find it (provably) wonderful that, faced with the danger that confronts the civilized world, their "deliberations [have found] a unity which we hardly hoped for. . . . In this consensus we find, with all due humility, a pledge for a more comprehensive unity among all men of good will." These fine words are addressed to the scions of the founders as well as to those newly arrived refugees and exiles. They reach out notably, as we have heard, to "the American youth . . . [who] will reject the guidance of a false education, the teachings of a degraded science, the sophistry of the irresponsibles" (72). These fine words are meant to undo such blemishes on the national character as "the degraded education, the corrupted political machines, the efficiency of the dollar-hunter, the inertia of the forgotten man" (68). Do we hear, now, once more, the voice of Thomas Mann, resonating with his lecture on "Richard Wagner and *The Ring of the Nibelung*" delivered at Princeton University earlier that year (see this section of chapter 3, *infra*). There he spoke of Wagner's parallel rejection of "the bourgeois world of vitiated culture, false educational ideals, sterile scholarship, the reign of money, and the exhaustion of the capacity for feeling."[134]

The Declaration ends here, but it is not the end of *The City of Man*: it is followed by a lengthy, detailed Proposal that aims to give administrative substance to the learned rhetoric of the Declaration. The task of the Committee is to show a world of readers how a world-society might indeed be established, proposing answers to such fundamental questions as, for example, the position of (the one?) religion in such a state. Such a religion would be founded on "an unsectarian liturgy—virtually adequate to a new religion outside the literal fences of each separate faith and embracing the spiritual substance of all" (85). How sweetly quixotic! Like Gandhi's alleged reply to the question of what he thought of Western civilization, "It would be a good idea."

"War and Democracy"

Mann delivered this seminal talk on October 3, 1940, before the Friends of the Colleges at Claremont, California, and thereafter on January 12, 1941, at a town hall event in Washington, D.C. It includes arguments and rhetorical gambits from his other talks, as we shall see, especially *This War*, "The Problem of Freedom," and "The War and the Future." Following his lecture in the Washington town hall, Mann was sternly criticized by Agnes E. Meyer for its militancy and the depth of its political involvement. Like Mann's publisher Alfred Knopf, who wanted Mann to devote himself to the writing of novels—which, not incidentally, would sell profitably in America—his patroness Meyer, who believed in Mann's transcendent genius and, not incidentally, was an isolationist Republican, insisted that Mann was meant for higher and better things. Mann was pained by her charge and replied, in wonderful, dispositive fashion,

> We do not feel the same way about this [world civil war], which for me is a matter of life and suffering, and for you just "politics," which you kindly think beneath me. *Je fais la guerre*—and your kind concern is to want to see me *au dessus de la mêlée*. But this mêlée is a decisive battle of humanity, and everything will be decided by it, *also* the fate of my life's work, which at least for decades may not return to Germany in the order of its tradition [in its proper place in a German literary tradition], when a miserable rabble is victorious, whom for eight years a lazy, cowardly, ignorant world has presented with nothing but victories. You do not know what I've suffered in those eight years, and how my first and last [concern] is that the most

disgusting baseness that ever made "history" will be confounded—and that
I live to experience that satisfaction as well. Did I cut an ill figure during
those years and let myself be degraded and paralyzed by hatred? I have written *Joseph in Egypt, Lotte in Weimar,* and *The Transposed Heads,* works of
freedom and joy, and, if you wish, of superiority. I am a bit proud that I managed to do that instead of joining the ranks of the emotionally shattered, and
I think my friends should see a sign of strength and not of weakness and
humiliation in the fact that I also fight. My engagement in my free work is
not complete: it cannot make me happy unless it is also dictated and accompanied by this acknowledgement and emotional engagement. There is
the saying, "Whoever is not for me, is against me." But whoever is not against
this evil—passionately and with all one's soul against it—*is more or less for
it.* God forbid that your pained concern for my talk has anything to do with
that! It remains the case that I will not give it anymore. (BR.M 254)

In fact, he repeatedly gave the talk, although only after he had tempered its
militancy, partly in light of Meyer's objections. It is remarkable that the key
locution in the letter—the obligatory commitment to political action—would
be put by Mann some five years later, shortly before the German defeat, in a
letter to Hermann Hesse on the topic of "the politicization of the spirit" (*Die
Politisierung des Geistes*): "I believe that no living being today is able to avoid
the political. The refusal is itself politics, and in this way, one advances the
politics of the evil cause."[135]

The basic point of Mann's essay is that a thinker of pacifist inclinations, who
wants nothing more radical than a world structured along democratic socialist
lines, must invoke conditions under which that order must defend itself by
murdering its antagonist in war. How can this be argued?

From the start, the violence of murder (if at first only metaphorically) is
attached to the program of this antagonist—the Third Reich, Hitler, and the
Gestapo—which amounts to "the total dishonoring of humanity and . . . the
murder of freedom."[136] What is at stake is nothing less than "the problem of
man"—of what he is and what he shall become—a destiny that today is being
realized in the *political* field. Today (1940), the philosophical is the political, for
"a matter of ultimate values, of the foundations of civilization, of the very idea
of mankind" is threatened by a certain species of "beast-man . . . dedicated [in
practice] to force and to nihilism." The fight is with us now, "a fight for life or
death"—a fight for democracy, for which "we must be ready to die." Consider
that more than a certain manner of governing, the concept of "democracy"

means "the acknowledgement of truth, freedom, and right as the foundation of our social and political life."

The world is at war—but no longer in the sense of nation against nation: "A World Civil War" is raging, in which two fundamental *Weltanschauungen* stand fiercely opposed (1037). One is, in a word, "democracy"; the other is— Mann does not hesitate to call a spade a spade—the Gestapo mentality, a belief in the efficacy of "force, high-explosive bombs, and bestiality" (1038). What is called for is a supernational united front.

The listener hears a hint of the rhetoric that so upset Agnes Meyer: although Mann is an "alien," he will not renounce the obligation to join the struggle; for, here, where he lives, "in all probability, the future of the Western World will be decided." What is at stake—in plain words that Mann waits to announce—is whether or not this country will go to war in defense of the European democracies. As for the charge that he is, after all, "an alien"—hence, without the right to preach to citizens—Mann dares to suggest "that there are 'aliens' in this country who are more faithful to 'the American way of life' than this or that American." One can imagine Agnes Meyer being taken aback at even the glimmer of the suggestion that isolationists of her ilk are the faithless ones (1038).

Mann is eager to refute the accusation that aliens like him constitute a "Fifth Column," and he will expend a good deal of rhetorical energy on this matter. The latter expression is "not infrequently used in this country as if it meant a conspiracy of aliens to drag America into a war which does not concern her." The listener might expect him to address immediately the second part of this charge as the fundamental issue, but his defense for the moment is weak. He merely asks "us" literally to put aside the question, while appealing to the "many Americans" who share his opinion that the war in Europe concerns America "in the most vital sense." Which is . . . ? Mann will not get lost—I'll note, for the moment—in geopolitical data, which would require talk of trade, army divisions, and submarines. But the more personal charge is for the moment the more compelling. It is vexatious. "In accordance," he declares, "with the old trick of the thief crying, 'Stop thief!' the underminers of every foundation of human understanding have succeeded in bringing into very close connection the concept of the 'Fifth Column' with that of the 'alien.'" It was Franco who coined the expression and set the usage of the term when he said, while marching against Madrid with his four columns, that a fifth column was at work *within the city* preparing for his conquest. Well, Mann declares, there are such traitors active and alive in Europe at the moment—but they are not aliens—they are Norwegians and Dutchmen, Belgians and Frenchmen. If there were a fifth column in America on this pattern, it would consist not of aliens but of Americans.

And there are such specifiable "columns" in America that do not need to sport Nazi emblems to be of use to Hitler: "There is the perhaps natural egotism of the great private business [*sic*] which at a time of universal conscription insists on its own absolute freedom, disparages every regulation as 'sovietization,' and endangers the preparedness of the country by a 'strike of capital.'" Mann knows full well, with Agnes Meyer listening, that he must distribute his anger all across the political field, and invokes, as well, "the Moscow-dependent communism which hates democracy much more than it hates Hitler and whose propaganda joins everywhere with that of the national socialists" (1039–40). But what of an honorable pacifism? Mann has little patience with it if it is of the "orthodox" kind that will not resist "base force from seizing the rule of the world, for that is what the fight is all about" (1040). After all, what does it mean to be a pacifist when one is willy-nilly in the middle of a *fight* that cannot be otherwise defined? Worse, not to realize that the word "peace" is forever on the lips of fascist propagandists as a ruse to weaken the resolve of the democracies is a dereliction that "supports the enemy . . . and belongs to the Fifth Column, whether it knows it or not" (1041).

One also hears with dismay "objective" reasons for giving Hitler's ambition some slack: consider, for example, the cruel, impoverishing effect of the Versailles Treaty. But before one does so, let him note the responsibility of his very own people for allowing these national hatreds to produce the crisis of the moment. At a crucial juncture, the United States might have joined the League of Nations and provided it with the backbone it needed to survive. (The US participation was scuttled by the opposition of the Republican Henry Cabot Lodge, and so this reminder, once more, cannot have gone down well with Agnes Meyer.) Or again, where was America's moral—and armed—force in September 1939, on Germany's invasion of Poland, when, appearing "to tremble before every German scowl," it chose to remain neutral? Meanwhile, the reprehensible stance of France and England in the years between 1918 and 1933 is deplorable but irrelevant to the present crisis. The point is that there is nothing in Germany's behavior since 1933 to merit it "a place in the sun" (1042). It would be truer to say, and Mann will say it repeatedly, that it has rather shrouded the sun in a veil of horror—one, incidentally, produced by a vast outlay of German marks—one hundred billion, to be exact, to cite Adolf Hitler, "in four years for armaments alone."

Mann here reproduces his reflections on the different conceptions of power held by the Germans and the English—the crux being, according to Mann, that Germany's war on England is irrational and based on envy. Its motive goes back to a motive at the time of the First World War: Germany's rage at England's naval superiority. But why on earth—or on the sea—should England's mastery of the oceans ever have stood in the way of the cultivation of culture, wealth, and industry, all of which Imperial Germany possessed till bursting ca. 1914? The answer reads in part: Because, as we recall, for the Germans, power is "a darkly emotional concept; power, in English eyes, implies no emotion, but a function; the 'will to power' is a German invention" (1043). It is a blind, unintelligent drive that pays little attention to empirical reality. England's warships never threatened Germany, but cast a spell over the German soul. And now the Nazi ideology has revived the old Napoleonic idea of keeping England's influence out of Europe, as if a good portion of the world would be, according to Mann, in better hands if it were held by the Germans or the Italians or—Mann adds, prudently—the Russians. There follows a much too celebratory account of England's benevolence to its (vast) colonies that we have criticized earlier (see *This War* in this chapter, *supra*). But at the present painful juncture, England is Mann's last chance for the defense of European values, and he is very grateful.

We are still addressing hypothetical arguments on Hitler's behalf, one of which holds that Hitler has aligned himself with the forces of history at work leveling social and economic differences—in short, that Nazism is the revolutionary avant-garde. Rubbish! Hitler "is in alliance with that revolution; yes, by exploiting it and debasing it to the level of an advance-guard of his nihilistic mania for power. He is not a revolutionary but a free-booting exploiter of the revolution; not a lion but a hyena. He reduces the social revolution . . . to his out-of-date Alexandric expedition for the conquest of the world." This is not history; it is "a froth of blood" (1044). Contrast Hitler with Churchill, who has a different ideal of a comity of nations and has exemplified the ideal by proposing a total "governmental and economic union" with France—which France, by the way, rejected! This germ of a unity of nations in Europe and thereafter throughout the world animates Mann's deepest political imagination.

But the outward unity of a common citizenship matters only as its inner morality is that of democracy, a "social self-discipline under the ideal of freedom." The crux is "discipline," a freedom exercised only under the aegis of a common good. Mann is insistent on what should seem an elementary principle, but one dismissed in quarters of opinion in the United States as an infringement of an absolute, entitled freedom. This insistence is a betrayal of democracy rightfully understood. Mann is not demure: he cites the aperçu: "Let me tell you the whole truth: if ever Fascism should come to America, it will come in the name of freedom" (1045). (How prophetic!)

The contradiction between the concepts of individual freedom and social equality is "merely logical"—a contradiction resolved in the lively (Christian) practice we experience. "In this elemental ideal of Christianity and democracy, the overwhelming majority of the nation is united" (1046). Here, we have the very argument (and the literal text) that concludes Mann's lecture on receiving an honorary degree from Rutgers University in April 1939—namely, "The Problem of Freedom," which is *enfin* not a "problem" but a *desideratum*. "*Social Democracy* [as we might recall] is now the order of the day" (1048). And it is the principle that must be extended if there is to be the saving birth of a new entity—"the European confederation . . . a democracy of states, in which Freedom and Equality have reached a new creative balance" (1049). One aspect of this "problem," which Mann does not discuss here but will stress in his later writings, is the need to revise a traditional German, and disastrous, notion of freedom as the right to untrammeled appropriation of what is not yet German—a freedom to advance *outwards*, while civic freedom lies dormant or repurposed as the inner bliss of reflection.

"I Am an American"

Mann's essay is remarkable for the company it keeps in this short volume of recorded radio broadcasts—heartfelt testaments to their adopted country by distinguished naturalized Americans, produced with admirable intent by the Immigration and Naturalization Service of the US Department of Justice. Mann's paper is accompanied by statements by the likes of Albert Einstein, Gaetano Salvemini—the co-inspirer of *The City of Man*—the conductor and opera composer Walter Damrosch, the actress Claudette Colbert, and other notables.[137] In a rousing introduction, Archibald MacLeish, who had assumed the post of Librarian of Congress and would become a great friend and supporter of Mann, wrote:

> The purpose of the program was in part to reply to those in this and in other countries who make political capital of the differences of race and the suspicion of strangers, in part to remind Americans of all bloods and all origins

that America was once, and must still remain, the land in which the lovers of freedom, the refugees from intolerance, the fighters for liberty of man and mind, can always turn [*sic transit*...].[138]

Mann's rhetorical strategy is to establish the value of the good thing he means to celebrate—his welcome in America—by evoking the loss that it compensates: "familiar surroundings, [which] mean much to a writer. His own desk, his accustomed books and walls, the view from the window of his study, which meets his eyes when he lifts them from his work." These familiar settings describe his home in Küsnacht near Zurich, where he lived before immigrating to the United States. He represents this move as the product of a free choice "to resign all these things and deliberately choose America as [my] future homeland." In fact the choice, as we know, was only partially or not at all free: he was told by his daughter Erika, while he was lecturing in America in early 1938, that his life would be in extreme danger if he were to return to those familiar settings. But it stands to the credit of the object of his choice—his new home—that he represents the choice as based entirely on its merits. Such quiddities aside, he is now certain that in America he can "continue his life's work in peace and freedom" (though he will be horrendously dismayed a decade later, when America will no longer be "hospitable to me and to my ideas as well").

The crux of the value of America is its alter ego: Democracy. Democracy has been put under attack in various quarters but certainly not powerfully enough to rock Mann's "faith in this idea" (30). He has never construed American democracy as the topic of a course in civics—as pragmatic politics: it is endowed with a higher meaning, "the highest human attributes; with the dignity of mankind, with truth and with justice."

Democracy as a life form is beleaguered today (1939) by arguments for the new: the fascist revolution, with its panoply of new values: "force, hate, cruelty, fear" (31).[139] Perhaps aspects of them do work effectively in such spheres of life as world trade—as an answer to technological unemployment (even then!)—or as a vade mecum to solve economic crises. But there is nothing in the present constitution of capitalist democracy to stifle a native ingenuity for devising new solutions; in a word, it is endlessly adaptable (a point we have encountered in *This War*). And surely America stands out as illustrating this facility: consider, in words that Mann does not use, Roosevelt's New Deal. No means are too primitive for use in the needed project of a militant democracy; it can employ propaganda to enlist youth to these new social principles. "Democracy's task is to defend civilization against barbarism. There is no doubt that young people are deeply impressed by the outward successes of the so-called totalitarian governments, and therefore it is imperative that we do all in our power to uphold and strengthen the faith of youth in our American form of government" (32). Its ideals are indispensable for a life lived in dignity and security, with a knowledge of happiness and justice. Consider, by contrast, the abusive indoctrination of young people in the totalitarian countries.

There is a distinctive American character, which is to be found no more embedded in individual members of long-established families than in recent arrivals: the land breeds quick loyalty and a sense of community (32–33). Hence, there should be no resistance to immigration: newly arrived immigrants are eager "to become true Americans as quickly as possible" (33) as—notice—"the Swedes, the Danes, the Germans" who built up the land. Mann will forever suppose his audience to consist of Christian "Aryans," whose tolerance to mentions of Asians, Africans, Jews, and swarthy Mediterraneans can be assumed to be very limited. But, after all, the country is so vast and so underpopulated: would not immigration bring a real economic advantage? Mann would have found arguments in favor of immigration in many of his intellectual sources: it is made very strongly, as we have seen, in Louis Nizer's *Thinking on Your Feet* (see "A Typical Evening's Reading: Nizer and Mumford" in this chapter, *supra*); and Mann provably knew Nizer's book (T4 169).[140] He takes up a familiar theme in answering an imputed question: If the government chose to assign immigrants to a workplace, would it not be interfering with their freedom of choice and movement? That may be the case, but this is not the time for individuals to claim absolute personal freedom. On the contrary, "we should be adjusting individual claims by friendly and willing concessions to the claims of all" (34). And, with little evidence, Mann maintains that Americans have already done so. He may be alluding to the popular support of Roosevelt's social policies, as, for example, the establishment of Social Security some years earlier, in 1935. America's willing "adjustment" of a notion of absolute individuality is sponsored by an underlying Christian sentiment of charity and a pragmatic, "can-do" readiness to institute this change.

Mann's conclusion is familiar from *The City of Man*. The ideal of personal freedom *able* to constrain itself will vanish from the planet if fascism wins. The grave duty of preserving a democratic civilization falls to America. Agreed, the main view of the nation must still be internal—aimed at the social and economic well-being of its citizens; for where there is poverty and misfortune, the soil is ready to foster "the seeds of danger and retrogression" (35). Nonetheless, democracy must triumph on a larger scale: it must participate in the greater idea of a federation—"a Democracy of free peoples who are responsible each one to the other." This is a very plausible idea for Europe: America must help to bring this ideal to fruition as "a preserver of the faith . . . in goodness, in freedom and truth, in justice and peace. Only so is there any hope for the world" (35). Mann has armored himself against the charge of banality or simplicity with the vigor of his address.

"Denken und Leben" (Thinking and Living)

On being inducted into Phi Beta Kappa in March 1941, Mann was eager to acknowledge the honor by promptly publishing a short essay in the *Virginia Quarterly,* which expresses his gratitude in beautiful German. It was also an occasion for him to express his bigger gratitude for life, an ability at the heart of the literary artist. For the writer, thus Mann, does not make things up, he makes something out of things as gifts for the intellect (*Geist*); and it is there that these things come into their intrinsic fullness.[141] The writer returns this gift of things by reflecting on them, by thinking them. The German word *Denken* (thinking) has the root meaning of *Danken* (thanking), thought being a grateful present (*Dankesgeschenk*) to life on behalf of the spirit.

I will note that this etymological *jeu d'esprit* is not original with Mann. It would be too stale a mantra (of Pietist origin) to serve up to a knowledgeable German audience, a fact that did not stop Heidegger from doing so in his university lecture of 1952 "Was heisst Denken?" (What is called thinking? Equally, What *calls for* thinking?). But Americans not deeply at home in German intellectual history, though able to read Mann's elite German, might be an appropriate target audience in 1941.

What is wonderful in the title of this association—which Mann writes as *Philosophia bioy kybernetes* (better: *philosophia biou kybernētēs*, meaning, "Philosophy, Guide of Life")—is the responsibility of thought for life. Mann quotes a line from Goethe's *Faust* spoken by Atropos, the oldest of the Fates: "Viel zu denken, viel zu sinnen / Gibt's beim zarten Lebensfaden" ([There is] much to think, much to meditate in the delicate fiber of life) (370). This epigram, thus Mann, has a fundamentally democratic thrust—it invokes the responsibility of everyone's thought for the well-being of real lived life, an ultimate pragmatism. And just here Mann notes with dismay the dreadful state of Germany, which is due more to a psychological than a political aberration. Nazi Germany is the political outcome of the failure of the German spirit to have exercised its responsibility for the fiber of the common life.

Mann cites with interest "the essay of an Englishman" that formulates this very thought. The author turns out to be Herbert Read, who regards German culture with sympathy and also with despair. "It is as though every road taken by German poets and philosophers led to the edge of an abyss—an abyss from which they could not withdraw, but into which they must fall into headlong . . . abysses of intellect no longer controlled by any awareness of the sensuous realities of life."[142] Both Herbert Read and, above all, Mann are thinking foremost of Nietzsche, who, as Mann writes (now in English translation), "in heroic self-contradiction . . . created a rapturously anti-humane doctrine whose leading concepts of power, instinct, dynamism, supermanhood, naive cruelty, the 'blonde beast' represent the amoral triumphant life force." In years to come, as in his famous 1947 Zurich speech on "Nietzsche's Philosophy in the Light of Our Experience" (see the Preface), Mann would be less inclined, as here, to palliate Nietzsche's literally "fascistic" views by invoking his heroic self-contestation, "a tender, complicated, artistic nature, deeply capable of suffering" (372). He would be less inclined in 1947, on the strength of the "education" flowing from Nietzsche's thought, to miniaturize it, as here, as "an ecstatic-romantic poem" or believe that Nietzsche never for a moment considered its *real*-political consequences (373). This Phi Beta Kappa essay is a rehabilitation of Nietzsche—a romance, even—in which Mann, identifying Nietzsche with himself in a shared detestation of "Brother Hitler" and his work, imagines Nietzsche emigrating to America (for Nietzsche had indeed emigrated from the German Empire) and—given America's native kindness, tolerance, and generosity—receiving an honorary election to Phi Beta Kappa (!).

It is interesting for our purposes to note that this, in places, rather tender, anodyne reading of Nietzsche was well prepared for, a year before, in Mann's engaging Princeton lecture "On Myself" (B 43). (At the end of the full lecture, a number of students were seen leaving the hall "their faces flushed with excitement" [T4 69].) Nietzsche figures as a powerful intellectual and stylistic mentor for Mann's first (and subsequent) writings. But this is not the Nietzsche of Renaissance swagger, "the blond beast," the Antichrist, and so forth: "I took nothing in him literally. . . . [H]is glorification of life at the expense of the spirit" Mann could assimilate in only one way—"as irony . . . [as] a matter of erotic irony and conservative affirmation." Perhaps this "meant making him bourgeois," but oddly "this bourgeois interpretation . . . seems today deeper and of more consequence than all the heroic-aesthetic delirium that Nietzsche fanned up elsewhere." The end result: Mann became "resistant to all the evil romantic charms which can proceed from an *inhuman* valuation of the relationship between life and spirit as happens so often today." That undeniable "inhumanity" figured drastically in Mann's repudiation of Nietzsche *pur sang* in 1947.

The crux in "Thinking and Living" is Mann's felt urgency, in view of the devastation of Europe, that philosophy—thoughtfulness, the spirit—once again guide life. Does a restoration of this relation amount to a "politicization" of thought? Not at all. Mann aims to refresh philosophy's loving responsibility for the common life. But has it ever been the case that thought has functioned in sterile isolation from life? For Mann the answer is evident: this aberration— spiritual arrogance, the mandarin sensibility—lies at the heart of modern Germany's tragic fate, a failure of responsibility for the basic goods of everyday life with its well-known deficit of exaltation. The present moment, above all, has no room for philosophy as *l'art pour l'art*: we have entered a *moral* age, a time for moral seriousness, even for a certain moral simplification, requiring us to say a decisive "No!" to the sheer evil that engulfs the world. In these passages, we now have a direct anticipation of Mann's postwar Nietzsche essay of 1947, where Nietzsche is accused of conjuring the ideal of a life bare of moral constraints: "We are no longer aesthetes to the point of being afraid of our adherence (*Bekenntnis*) to the good and ashamed of such trivial concepts and leading images as truth, freedom, justice."[143] In concluding the current essay, Mann makes this urgent point even more eloquently:

> We have been made aware of evil in so base and formidable a shape that we have resolved on the good—quite simply, without any irony—in a way which, not so long ago, we should not have considered "intellectual." Truth, freedom, humanity, law: intellect [*sic*] ventures to take these words in its mouth once more—a nobler venture than to pour scorn and confusion on them. It is no longer ashamed of them, as it thought it had to be as long as they were taken for granted. Now . . . they must be fought for lest they perish.[144]

An essay *in German* encouraging a fight—meaning, quite literally, America's entry into the war in mid-1941—was hardly commonplace in the print culture of the time, "intensely wary of European influences." But accommodating Mann's militancy was a risk the editors of the *Virginia Quarterly* took from their ardent desire to distinguish Nazism from German culture—altogether a mark of the enormous respect they had shown before to Mann the artist.[145]

Listen, Germany!

Other than daily habits, so-called Life made ever lesser claims: no allurements, no temptations, a fading curiosity. For him, life had now—almost—become like writing, and writing—almost—like life: [it became] the instrument of his psychic resistance to the overpowering challenger in Germany, whom he viewed more and more as his personal adversary, his arch-, his primal enemy.

—KLAUS HARPPRECHT

In autumn 1940, while living in Princeton, Mann agreed to broadcast to Germany, via the BBC, the first of *sixty-one* aggressive, comminatory radio messages—eight-minute "rocks thrown into Hitler's window."[146] The first three were read by a German-speaking employee of the BBC; the rest, with great satisfaction, by Mann himself. They have been criticized—even excoriated—by some German scholars, who have called them the work of "a frigid know-it-all"—"sermons"—even "grievous errors of judgment."[147] Very well, one can find faults in tactics and tone in sixty-one texts—above all, a deficiently imagined target group and Mann's shifting loyalty to an idea of a good, a decent Germany. I shall be evoking the five talks broadcast during Mann's time at Princeton, which I consider by and large admirable in their sacred furor.

In his "Foreword" to the first American edition of these talks, written retrospectively in September 1942, Mann makes the valuable distinction between short-wave broadcasts from America and long- or medium-wave broadcasts from London: only the latter "could be heard on the only type of radio the German people were permitted to have."[148] Here was an opportunity for Mann to speak directly to those who had read him and adulated him and endured the knowledge that his books had been burned[149]—as well as to speak to the greater number for whom he was merely a spokesman of *different* facts and thoughts. Coded messages from Sweden and even from the occupied countries—Holland, the Czech "Protectorate," and Germany itself—proved how great a risk people were willing to run to satisfy their "hunger and thirst for free speech" (vi). (It is possible that Mann underestimated the gravity of the danger to which he was submitting his listeners.) "The most striking proof" that he was listened to, as he observes, is

the fact that my allocutions have been referred to . . . by my Führer himself, in a beer-hall speech in Munich, in the course of which he mentioned me as one of those who attempt to incite the German people against him and his system. But these rabble-rousers, he roared, were greatly mistaken: the German people were not that way, and to the extent that they were that way, they were, thank God, behind lock and key.

Verbum sapienti. The Führer's logic is deficient.

Mann has detected in many of Hitler's statements a more than implicit contempt for the German public: they swallow the "lies" of the powers arrayed against him . . . as well as his own. This being so, one is led to a conundrum: How can a stupid, submissive people "spiritually incapable of ever revolting *even against him* be a master race?" (vii). But is the German nation in truth, in Mann's view, capable of revolting against this tyranny? In the past, in these speeches, one will have more than once wondered whether his arguments and invocations were heartfelt. Here, interestingly—in fall 1942, two years after beginning his broadcasts—Mann puts the matter directly: "To call a people to revolt does not yet mean to believe, deep down in one's heart, in their ability to revolt" (vii–viii). Was Mann prepared to take responsibility for the horrors that might result from a heedless, unstudied incitement to revolution? Examples of the sangfroid of recent governments are well known after their encouragement to *other* peoples to revolt had led to nothing more than brutal repression. But we are thinking now with Mann in 1940 and so are turned inevitably toward Hitler.

On metaphysical and moral grounds, Hitler cannot win the war, which is not the same thing—take note—as believing that the common will, as a *wish* for his defeat, will achieve this end. We are now in a war that will end with a *military* defeat of Nazi Germany, but only through the fiercest practical resolution. Mann detects the stink of fascism in hidden places, hence, the need to resist the delusion of supposing that Hitler cannot triumph—the sense, famously at home in the German mind, that what is not *right* cannot *be*. (Mann had often not been far from espousing this delusion, as in the call "To the Civilized World" that prompted his pragmatic adversary James T. Farrell to refuse to sign on.) This is the idle conception "that the victory of the United Nations [the Allies] is self-evident and assured, and that in view of this self-evidence and this certainty one can afford not only every mistake but also every division of the will, every half-heartedness, every 'political' reservation concerning one's allies [Soviet Russia!] and the kind of peace to be gained." There can be no misjudgments, in light particularly of the diplomatic blunders of the past: "The war has sinister antecedents, whose determining motives are by no means dead, but continue to work underground, endangering the peace and with it the victory" (viii). Be vigilant!

Mann's first address was broadcast in October 1940 when America's war with Germany was still cold, and so Mann can stress only his warning to the Germans that America was poised to fight. It is important that the Germans conjure the enormous weight of people and physical power involved. Mann quotes Henry Luce of *Life*, a magazine "which everybody reads," who responded forcefully "when German troops invaded Holland five months ago, and tens of thousands of human beings were bombed to death in Rotterdam." Luce wrote: "This is the greatest challenge to America, the land of liberty, in eighty years. . . . Mighty and ruthless military nations have attacked the American way of life. . . . We do not know whether we will ever have to fight on England's side; but we know that England's struggle is also our own" (4).[150] Let the Germans reflect that Americans also have roots in the countries that the German armies have pillaged and ruined: "An American is above all an American citizen; yet it is often true that he, or his father or grandfather, was born in Norway, in Holland, in Belgium, in protected Denmark, in the Government General [Poland], in the Protectorate [Czechoslovakia], that he still has relatives in one of these countries, and fond memories of them" (5). Such Americans, Mann maintains—very likely thinking of himself in this mix—are furious to learn of the outrages committed against the peoples among whom they or their families lived.

Let the Germans also keep in mind the three great concerns that occupy Americans now: one is their fond attachment to America, its "immense economic strength, its good and proved leaders." The second is their admiration for the resistance of England, which "carries the banner of freedom, which speaks and fights for all the nations who suffer and who resist only in secret. It wants to help England in its fight" (6). And third—again, Mann is projecting his own desires—is an American faith in the German people: that they will overthrow the tyranny that is coercing them into these horrific deeds. Here, Mann rises to the full pitch of his eloquence, his *j'accuse*: When will the Germans

> finally recognize that their victories are only steps in an endless quagmire; that when their soldiers invade three more countries, when their U-boats sink three more ships full of refugee children, when they drive still more people into misery, exile, and suicide, and heap the hatred of the world upon themselves, they are not one inch closer to the desired goal; that there are many better ways to the goal for which we all long: a just peace for all the world. (6)

It is difficult to imagine what listeners in Germany or occupied Europe hud-
dled over their radio now, at the close of this oration, are supposed to do,
sufficiently grateful that they have not yet been apprehended and sentenced
to prison or, in extreme cases, to death. Are they meant to turn the radio off
and reach into their cache of hidden weapons?

Here are the dated texts of Mann's "allocutions."

November 1940

Mann is elated by the reelection of Roosevelt, whom he passionately admires.
The event is full of world-historical significance, and he wants the Germans to
know what is now in store for them. Roosevelt is exemplary—the bearer of
the ideals foremost on Mann's mind, as we know from Mann's earlier lectures:
he is "the representative of a *fighting* democracy, the true bearer of *a new social
conception of freedom*" (7; emphasis added). This president enjoys the support
of a vast number of Americans ("the masses"); and he, like they, is committed
to the good cause.[151] At this moment "the heroic resistance of England . . .
gives him time to mobilize the enormous latent powers of his country for the
struggle for the future" (8).

Germany, rouse yourselves! Wake up to the awareness that if you persist in
this mad adventure for "another three, another five years" (it would be five),
you will know a misery that the present barely suggests (9). (One wonders
from what source Mann has this information: in 1940 Germany was neither
hungry nor unclothed.) He asks his German listeners: What do you really
want? Surely a world of peace and justice, "a society of peoples with equal
rights and equal duties, free. . . ."

It is vital that this war stop short of mutual military devastation. "If the war
was ended today, and the common work was begun, every nation would have
a better chance for a happier future" (9–10). Lay down your arms . . . and your
credulity and your obedience! This Nazi persuasion—namely, if Germany
were ever to be defeated, Germany as a nation would cease to exist—is alive
even now, in fall 1940, for Mann is clear in his assurances: "In the world which
is to come the German nation must and will have its 'place in the sun' . . . but
a nation does not obtain its place in the sun by shrouding the world in darkness
and horror" (10). In the following, Mann will be less tempted by gracious literary flourishes, as if he were talking chiefly to an audience of his readers, and
his language will be one understood by gangsters and illiterates.

Christmas 1940

There are holiday exceptions to his plain speaking. In a ceremonial mood, Mann asks his unlucky, oppressed listeners—whom he posits as exclusively German, without a Jew among them—to consider that Christmas might be the most German of all festivals. "It is a symbol of your birth as a nation . . . and in the pagan Germanic past it was the festival of the winter solstice, the rebirth of light out of winter darkness, the dawn of a new day" (11). Christ was born, and with him, Mann declares, a new morality came into the world; and, in an intellectually dubious, surely imprudent gesture, he adds that this "transcendental, spiritual, and all-loving God of the universe" arose out of "the folk-bound Jewish race-God" (*"volksgebundene jüdische Rasse-Gott"*; "Thomas Mann Spricht 'Zum Deutschen Volk'" [E 5:145]). The rare Jewish listeners of these words—if they were lucky enough to have this chance to risk their life—would now be hard-pressed to open their heart to this speaker.

Mann is bent on linking German Christmas with the mind and fate of the entire Christian Occidental world. All throughout his radio addresses, "Mann routinely stylizes himself," writes Boes, eloquently, "as a messianic figure speaking on behalf of a Christian ethical tradition brutally abrogated by the Nazis" (TB 267). Now let his German audience marvel at all that "the German spirit has contributed to this Christian Occidental culture . . . the work of Dürer and Bach, the poems of freedom of your Schiller, Goethe's *Iphigenie*, the *Fidelio*, the Ninth Symphony." Mann must be unconsciously addressing a very narrow sector of any conceivable resistance movement: Does he suppose that an appreciative *Bildungsbürgertum* is extant and at hand to cherish these way stations to its culture? That his listener is ready to translate a love of Dürer and Bach into armed rebellion?

Consider this Christmas celebration: What many of you cannot celebrate is the loss of a son or a father dead from your "leaders' . . . assault on neighboring countries." This charge will become acute six months later when, with the Russian invasion, casualties would mount. But these words will find "all of you, surely, with uneasy hearts at the thought of how long all this will still last, whereto it will all lead" (12). Descriptive words falter in the force of Mann's eloquence; his speeches aim to move listeners to action less on the strength of their arguments than on their phatic force:

> You set the tables with Christmas gifts—they will be scanty enough, for
> good things cannot be had though your masters have pillaged the devastated

Continent in your name. But the candles are burning. I want to ask you how, in their light, the deeds appear to you which your leaders made you commit as a nation during the past year, the deeds of insane violence and destruction, in which they assiduously made you their accomplices; all the atrocities which they have amassed in your name; the fathomless misery and human suffering which National Socialist Germany—that means a Germany which is no longer permitted to be either German or Christian—has spread all around it. Can you tell me how these deeds harmonize with the beautiful old carols which you now sing again with your children, yourselves filled with feelings of childhood . . . ?

Mann imagines the public being required to sing, in place of "Silent Night, Holy Night," the Nazi party anthem, the "Horst Wessel Song," with no substitutions allowed. And why would this public disobey? "I do not doubt that you would obey, for your obedience is infinite" and, with time, less and less forgivable (13).

For you go on fighting, with the fury of berserkers, for this sham savior and his "New Order," in which "the observance of the Christmas festival, the festival of peace and love, would be a still greater lie and blasphemy than it is even today." The notion of a Nazi celebration of Christmas is appalling as a violation of everything Christian, indeed, everything human—"all those values . . . which make the human being a human being," now trapped "in a world without truth, freedom, and right" (14).

Mann repeats the metaphor that proves irresistible when the stake is a redeemed Germany's "place in the sun": it is a thing "you cannot conquer by veiling the earth in night and horror" (15). It is there as a new beginning should you throw off your obedience and credulity to this "possessed fiend." He will claim that you are in a pact with him, that "your fate is inextricably bound to his" (14). It is not. He will be wiped out of existence—and not Germany, if "reason and human decency gain the victory" (15). Mann evokes an unsuspected quality of the German character, which he has Goethe attribute to the Germans in *Lotte in Weimar*: this quality is italicized in the text of his speech, precisely because it comes as surprise. It is the German "need to be *loved*" (15). One can, I believe, trust Mann as a psychologist of the German character: who is better? "Underneath all the crimes to which you are seduced, this deep wish [to be loved] always remains alive." Do you "not know that you are not at all happy, that in reality it is a horror and a desperate distress for you to play the enemy of mankind?" (15). This may be much too subtle an appeal, inviting, not a pacifist emotion in his German listeners, but even churlishness and mockery. In fact, Mann strives to rouse contrary emotions, difficult to imagine coexisting: "It is Christmas, German people. Let yourselves be moved [to thoughts of love and peace] and *also roused to wrath* by what the bells mean when they ring out their message of peace, peace on earth!" (16; emphasis added). This message is in line with his hope for a *militant* democracy, with that militancy unspecified—is it a fist-shaking or a bayonet?

February 1941

Here is the crux: In light of President Roosevelt's recent speech declaring an unlimited National Emergency, now consider the consequence: "America is throwing the whole weight of its power and its tremendous resources" onto the side of England and the nations who are at war with Germany. It rejects a negotiated peace with Hitler, "the Hitler peace, the world order of enslavement and cynicism, this conception of a sinister and sick brain." It will not be tolerated (17–18).

And now: What are you Germans thinking, despite the news that you will surely hear of new "victories" by your sick masters, which are in reality criminal acts committed against a world unarmed and unprepared for such onslaughts? You will go on devastating the continent until you yourself are devastated. But in that final devastation is a seed of hope: you will not be subjected to another Treaty of Versailles. You can, if you will, play your part in the genuine destiny of the nations, which includes that of your adversaries, advancing toward a greater measure of social and economic participation in a "future community of free nations" (20). This should be the better thought for you to keep in mind after you have shuffled off your "Hitler and his contemptible dream of world subjugation" (20).

March 1941

Mann is now speaking in his own, very personal voice, and this fact is his entrée. "It is the voice of a friend, a German voice; the voice of a Germany which showed, and will again show, a different face to the world from the horrible Medusa mask which Hitlerism has pressed upon it. It is a *warning* voice" (21). But it is a warning that can already count on an echo in your conscience: you know that you are walking on a path to perdition, and you will not have peace until you have left this path. Keep that thought in mind!

What is the news? The subjugation of Bulgaria? But what, beside the force of weapons, is behind this criminal act? Your leaders speak of "the might of the idea"—the idea of a New Order. And what is that idea? "The idea is violence and vileness . . . but the last resistance against it and against the unbearable degradation of humanity . . . is far from broken." Have you heard of the Lend-Lease Bill? You are at war with America! What do you imagine your end will be? And here Mann shifts course from the preceding talks, when he encouraged the Germans to think of their defeat as an opportunity to enter smilingly into a compact with the victors in a clean new order of peace and harmony—no! "If you are defeated, the vindictiveness of the whole world will break loose against you for all that you have inflicted upon the people and nations" (23).

In a review of Mann's broadcasts, the theologian Reinhold Niebuhr considered this proposition proof of Mann's naiveté "in his grasp of political realities. . . . Since Dr. Goebbels strikes the same note, one may question its value as propaganda against Nazism."[152] Nevertheless, Mann's prophecy would be well and truly accomplished four years later with the Soviet entry into the homeland. What follows, in the book that you—amiable reader—are now reading, is Mann's final warning to the Germans: "As long as Hitler and his regime of arsonists remain, you Germans will not have peace, ever, under any circumstances. Always you will have to go on and on, as now, with the miserable acts of violence, be it only to prevent revenge, be it only to keep a gigantic and constantly growing hatred from devouring you" (24). Here Mann is indeed speaking in his own voice!

Would all this have been worth doing? During the next four years, Mann wavered in his belief that with this polemical effort he had accomplished anything toward the good end of a German defeat and a heightened German awareness of a guilt that brooked no exceptions. His talks were excoriated by the Germans of the "inner emigration," who knew, they alleged, what *they* were talking about, while Thomas Mann, from his perch on Stockton Street in Princeton and then in Pacific Palisades, hadn't a clue as to the reality of the German experience during the Nazi war years. *Their* true state could be put this way: they could not bear very much experience of what they had connived at. I shall reach for one more passage of Mann's rhetoric—his truth!—outside our assigned bounds. On November 30, 1941, he told the Germans,

In German hospitals, the seriously wounded, along with the old, infirm, and mentally ill, are killed by poison gas—two to three thousand, according to a German doctor, in *one* institution. This is being done by the very regime that bellows when Roosevelt accuses it of wanting to destroy Christianity and all religion and pretends to lead a crusade of Christian ethics against Bolshevism—Bolshevism, of which it is only an incomparably meaner variety. The Christian counterpart to the mass gassings are the "mating days," when soldiers on leave are ordered to join girls of the Bund Deutscher Mädel (League of German Girls) for an animalistic marriage-hour in order to produce state-[sanctioned] bastards for the next war. Can a people, a youth, sink lower? Abomination and blasphemy of humanity wherever you look.[153]

Was it an accident or an expression of Nazi viciousness that Mann's Munich villa on the Poschingerstrasse was converted in 1937 into just such a brothel, edulcorated as a *Lebensborn* (a Wellspring of Life)? Not all commentators followed this abuse with speech acts of Mann's quality. Others recalled how his broadcasts lifted their spirits in the worst of times. And Jonas Lesser, a devotee of Mann's work, saw in these speeches an additional qualification suiting Mann for the role of president of the democratic entity that would arise from the ashes of Munich and Berlin.[154]

3

A Roundup of Political Themes

Among modern writers, he possessed the mind most congenial to liberal democracy, which his colleagues to the left and to the right tended to despise.

—ALGIS VALIUNAS

AT THE CLOSE OF CHAPTER 1 and in the Prologue to chapter 2, I spoke briefly of Mann's main themes and preoccupations in his polemical writings—his "war writings in exile," stressing his recurrent moral and political concerns.[1] From the very beginning of his lecture tours in 1938, Mann invoked a "militant humanism," believing that war between the Western democracies and the fascist powers was inevitable; and he could not hide his wish that he thought the war desirable. He deplored the Western nations' policy of appeasement, their delusory isolationism. The task at hand was to crush a perverted Germany and restore it to its genuine condition.

Mann was in no doubt about the cause of the war, which he saw as Germany's naked aggression, retrograde as a refusal of the timely political project of modernity—a federation of European states—and inspired by a mad conception of endless geographical conquest, owed to a dreamt-of superior German morality. Another rubric: this war is a *world* civil war; what is at stake in the German ruin and plundering of other nations is the very destruction of humanity as we know it, a crime in which the totality of the fascist nations of Europe is implicated. All the ideals constitutive of a thoroughly humanized world—its aspiration to goodness, justice, decency—are sacrificed to a national will to power. Recall the early citation, although possibly apocryphal, from Hitler's table talk in *The City of Man:* "I shall eradicate the thousands of years of human domestication. . . . I want to see again in the eyes of youth the gleam of the beast of prey."[2] Or again, "The day will come when I shall hold up against these commandments [the Decalogue] the tables of a new law" (TB 156).

Mann dramatized the disparity between the values of the two powers—the Allies and the Axis—in a higher and a lower sort of propaganda, considering the difference in tone between his lectures across America and his radio broadcasts to Germany.[3] What is central to all of them is the fate of a country he once called "this execrated, indecipherable, fateful Germany" (Br.H 121). Authentic Germany lives on—in exile, in good measure in the genius of German literature, in the traditions conjured there. Its guardian is Thomas Mann—never mind on which continent he dwells; when, disembodied, he speaks on the radio, Germany lives on in a resonant authoritative voice from nowhere. The genuine culture of Germany is no longer the possession of ruling institutions—let alone the institutions of National Socialism, forever bent on culture's opposite, its annihilation in *war*. And so, Mann's polemical and analytical writings and speeches are preoccupied in the first instance with the unfolding of the war—one vile thing after another—while in an undercurrent, the question of "What is German(y)?" receives, in stages, an implicit answer.

One thrust of thought pits good Germans against the bad—the Nazi devotees, cynical sympathizers, and benighted followers. The good make up Mann's audience of daring listeners, who turn on their radios in the dark. This distinction separates the saved—or salvageable—from the damned. Another perspective both precedes and rejects this distinction. In early January 1940, in a published defense of Richard Wagner, Mann wrote: "There is only one Germany, not two, not a bad and a good; and Hitler, in all his wretchedness, is no accident; he would never have been possible without psychological preconditions that are to be found deeper than in inflation, unemployment, capitalist speculation, and political intrigue. But it is true that peoples do not always show the same face, and that the shape their constant properties assume depends on time and circumstances."[4]

The first thrust of thought, which silently exonerates the exiles as good Germans, will be progressively subordinated to Mann's claim to "the continuity and metapolitical identity *of all German culture*."[5] A famous formulation at the end of the war reads: "It is not that there are two Germanies—an evil and a good—but [there is] only one" ("*daß es nicht zwei Deutschland gibt, ein böses und ein gutes, sondern nur eines*"). This postulated unity, however, is swiftly relativized, for "the best part through diabolical cunning turned to evil" ("Deutschland und die Deutschen," E 5:279).[6] But it remains unclear as to the identity of "the best part" and the agent of this cunning.

And so, the question of the German responsibility for the crimes of Nazism remains unsettled . . . and unsettling. Citing Mann's reflections on the *Reichskristallnacht*, the historian Manfred Görtemaker sees Mann as deploring the tendency to "apply the justified revulsion at the present German regime and its evils entirely and in general to Germanness, to German culture, *which surely has nothing to do with that,* and to turn away from German culture as well. On the other hand," our critic writes, Mann declares to another correspondent, as early as 1939, "'that this [violence] had 'always been there . . . more deeply rooted than any humanity.'"[7] The paradox confronts us once again in the concluding lines from the letter cited just above in defense of Wagner's music (as well as of the Western democracies [!]):

> Germany has to be defeated, that is: it has to be forced *to reactivate* as well all the socially friendly elements in its own stock of traditions from earlier centuries so as to be able to fit into the European confederation, the society of states for which Europe is ripe, and which will demand sacrifices of state sovereignty and national selfishness from every people [*etc.*].[8]

Görtemaker continues by asking about the quality of Mann's commitment to the Western democracies: they were "supposed to liberate Germany from National Socialism"; but on the other hand, if we have been following Mann's thoughts, "the type of Germanness for which this regime was responsible remained deeply rooted."[9]

I suggest that the still deeper, probably unfathomable question that runs through all of Mann's political writings—*for us* and for the entire human world—is the precise relation of the "friendly" and the "anti-civilizational" elements in "Germanness." (If this ratio could be specified, then the "time" and "circumstances" Mann refers to in his Wagner essay might be studied and prepared for: the moment when chiefly the one and not the other might make its smiling or grinning appearance. This question had real teeth once again when, during 1990, the unification of East and West Germany was fiercely debated—and feared by many—but then, on October 3, accomplished.)

What survives these dilemmas is the fact that, for Mann, the best part of German culture—its cosmopolitan longings—survives abroad, where it has needed to find safety: German fascism is a *"Verhunzung,"* a "going to the dogs" of these longings in the form of a "petty-bourgeois universalism, cosmopolitanism in a bedcap" turned vicious in numbers.[10] It calls for resistance from within or without. "Against fascism's totalizing political calculus"—thus Boes—"Mann pitted the notion of a 'human totality' that he saw most strongly expressed in

the liberal democratic tradition and in the Judeo-Christian heritage . . . a cultural, intellectual opposition to fascism" presumed to be lively in America and
chiefly dormant in Germany (TB 198). Along the way, he produced a cogent
anatomy of German fascism that has stood the test of time.[11]

We are not by any means clear of the matter of how—and why—the destruction of the better Germany occurred. It will be enlightening to look ahead
to Mann's 1944 essay "What Is German?" written with the prospect of an Allied
victory at hand and with it a new dispensation for Germany. Here, we again
encounter Germans who are neither entirely good nor entirely bad: "These
people have been deluded and seduced into crimes that cry to high heaven. . . .
We [emigrants] . . . cannot deny their responsibility, but we are inclined to
speak of a historic curse, a dark destiny and aberration, rather than of crime and
guilt."[12] A more nearly final précis of the German character, following the full
disclosure of Germany's war crimes, considers, as above, the Germans as a
single entity, in which good and evil coexist: distinctions between those in
whom the good predominates are idle, since all those who have not yet been
murdered for their resistance are responsible for these crimes. And so, if in the
beginning Mann encouraged the good Germans to revolt, he thereafter warns
them *all*—they have not revolted—of the punishment that awaits them. It will
not be otiose to repeat Mann's notorious formulation, which he often repeated:
"It is not that there are two Germanies—an evil and a good—but [there is]
only one."[13] Every German, at "home" or *in exile*, shares in this misfortune.

Meanwhile, the more fortunate country is America (or so Mann alleged in
public): a sustained theme is his faith and hope in America as "the arsenal of
democracy." This phrase was employed by Mann's beloved President Roosevelt in a fireside chat in late December 1940 while canvassing for popular and
congressional support for his Lend-Lease program, which, enacted in
March 1941, amounted to an all but nominal declaration of war against Germany. America's formal declaration of war against Germany on December 11,
1941, *followed* Hitler's declaration of war against the United States. I dwell on
this point in the spirit of Mann's fascination with President Roosevelt and his
passionate hope that he would commit the United States to war. Mann would
inscribe Roosevelt in *Joseph the Provider* as the pragmatic source of the New
Deal in the national distribution of wealth and commodities, the very "deal"
cited by Hitler in his declaration of war against the United States as the "failed"
construction of "Jews and plutocrats."

This question of Germany's fall into barbarism, to which we are inevitably
returned, receives different treatments throughout Mann's talks, as we have seen,

culminating in the clear enough conclusion as "the responsibility of all Germans for the crimes committed in their name as well as the consequences following from it."[14] This proposition is *not* equivalent to a declaration of collective guilt: it allows for the distinction between *culpability*—"a degree of blameworthiness"— and *guilt*—"direct responsibility." With this judgment on Germany's war guilt, we are looking mainly at Mann's later lectures, post-Princeton, notably "Germany and the Germans," delivered at the Library of Congress in 1945; but we will stay a little longer with the currents that precede them.

The lines of influence coming through Mann's readings and into his position papers—in contrast with the Marxist-economic perspective of the Frankfurt School—tend toward "the conservative end of the political spectrum" (TB 141). Here, we are recalling influences that have run through our pages: Kahler, whose work on the German character was decisive for Mann (see chapter 1); (Hermann) Rauschning, whose alleged accounts of Hitler's dyspeptic table talk were cited in *The City of Man*; Giuseppe Antonio Borgese, the militant anti-Fascist (and anti-Papist) along with Gaetano Salvemini the driving force behind *The City of Man* and author of *Goliath: the March of Fascism* (1937). A common thread is the stress these writers lay on anomalies in the German character as the source of Nazism—a culture, precisely, of the avoidance of care for the political body, a thread that Mann himself spun in *Nonpolitical Man* but sought to break in the exemplary lecture "Culture and Politics" (see "Contra Thomas Mann the American," in chapter 2, *supra*). The view that holds the "good" and the "bad" Germany to be one entity can be found in Kahler, Rauschning, and Borgese throughout: the good Germany implicates its destiny in Western, post-Enlightenment civilization, in a Christian, democratic world order; the other, the retrograde Germany, romanticizes its native depth, biological type, and exceptional culture.

Lacking the moral support of his original country, Mann's speeches and papers claim a foothold in the works of great German writers and thinkers of the past, viz. the triumvirate of Schopenhauer and (with provisions) Wagner, and Nietzsche: in this sense authentic Germany is with him. On its problematic side, another Mann scholar—Ernest Bisdorff—regrets a certain sleight of hand in Mann's recourse to tradition: you cannot just put, let us say, Goethe and Marx in the same basket as the avant garde of the democratic Absolute.[15] This ahistorical mixing can be seen as a function of Mann's transcendentalizing, theologically inflected, biblical-prophetic stance that in many cases will have weakened the pragmatic argument of the lecture, namely, the demand that his listeners take up arms against evil! But how? And which of many evils?

This higher tone is also found in the political and anthropological writings Mann was reading at the time, engaged by the unanswerable question, "What Is Man?"[16] But it remains to insist on Mann's bold and original thrust in many of these talks—the privilege of art, through the artist, to speak in its own voice, unbeholden to nations and institutions, in the name of a besieged humanity—a notion not so very distant from the haunting invocation concluding Adorno's *Minima Moralia*: "The only philosophy which would still be accountable in the face of despair would be the attempt to consider all things as they would be portrayed from the standpoint of redemption."[17] Mann's rephrasing of this standpoint will be a declaration of his "faith in goodness, which may exist without faith and may indeed be the product of *art*."[18]

4

Professor Thomas Mann, Nobel Laureate

Enthusiastic audience hears learned author. Speaker reaches height in quoting "Faust" in German with tremendous feeling. . . . Among the listeners was Moe Berg '23, former big-league ball player.

—*DAILY PRINCETONIAN*

WHEN, IN 1938, Mann's wealthy and highly placed benefactor Agnes E. Meyer set out to invite Thomas Mann to Princeton, she had her eye on the Institute for Advanced Study, which had been functioning for several years as a place of academic refuge for several very distinguished European scholars in exile— Einstein, most famously; and thereafter, the prodigious genius John von Neumann, who arrived in 1933; the mathematician Hermann Weyl, who fled Germany because his wife was Jewish (as was Thomas Mann's) and arrived later that year; the very accomplished art historian Erwin Panofsky, who came in 1935; the polymathic archaeologist and historian of Islamic studies Ernst Herzfeld, in 1936; and, of course, other exiles with stunning talents. Klaus Mann is said to have observed of the Institute: Hitler shook the tree, and we picked up the apples.

There was no precedent at the Institute then (or now) for "creative writers" or even for philosophically minded literary critics. Nonetheless, the director, Abraham Flexner, was open to the idea of accommodating Mann. Still, "the Institute is a kind of 'think-tank'; there is no formal lecturing arrangement— and hence no contact with students," and it is precisely that sort of contact that both Meyer—knowing Mann—and Mann thought they wanted (BR.M 40).

Now, as it happened, Harold W. Dodds, the president of Princeton University, was just then bent on fortifying its program in the humanities. With Flexner's help and this quick display of interest by Dodds, a solution could be found. It redounds to Agnes Meyer's passion and diplomatic skill that she contrived in this way to secure an attractive position for Mann at the university and thereafter a suitable residence and a suitable income (T3 228). As an accomplished master of the humanities, Mann would deliver a series of lectures, most of them in capacious Alexander Hall, during the three semesters of his two-and-a half-year stay in Princeton. The appointment was set in motion on May 8, 1938, at a crucial dinner in town.

Mann arrived in Princeton Junction by train from Penn Station, where he would, on occasion, never waste a moment and would spend the time waiting for his train or car to write in his diary; and was then brought by limo, as his diary reads, to a "dinner with Professor Flexner, President Dodds, and 'the Lowe'"—Helen Tracy [H. T.] Lowe-Porter, resident in Princeton and Mann's prolific if often criticized translator, and her husband, the paleographer Elias Avery Lowe, a permanent resident at the Institute for Advanced Study. Mann noted the "important conversation after dinner with the gentlemen" (T3 220).

Not long thereafter he received an official offer for the position of Lecturer in the Humanities with no departmental affiliation but with the expectation that, in addition to the public lectures, he would conduct seminars and preceptorials for the Princeton "boys," an idea that at first would not displease him.[1] In time, as his English improved, he would be a very successful performer even if, in the words of his grandson Frido Mann, "He was no academic; he was an artist."[2] In the end Mann admitted that he had been unnerved by the academic purlieu and would actually have preferred, as we may recall, the company of "the Hollywood gang."

As a choice of academic *Ressort*, Princeton came in just barely ahead of Harvard, which Mann had favored at first. Harvard had awarded him the first of his many American honorary doctorates in 1935 and thereafter invited him, again, to give a series of lectures, an invitation he could not take up. Now, in 1938, Harvard seemed an altogether receptive host, and there was the further attraction of the distinctly cultured cities of Cambridge and Boston. But Harvard failed to act with all deliberate speed. Princeton acquired this jewel at little cost: Mann's salary came not from university monies but mainly from the Rockefeller Foundation, an arrangement produced by Mann's great—if complex and intrusive—friend and sponsor Ms. Meyer, who had conceived the entire plan of his installation as a university professor.[3]

In earlier days, it had never occurred to Mann to play such a role, for which in any case he was, formally speaking, singularly unqualified, having never earned an *Abitur* (an advanced high school diploma), let alone a university degree. Hence, there was the perpetual irony, perceptible in his diaries, of his receiving some eight honorary degrees in America, an arrangement that required a dress-up each time in black robes and mortarboards. Would he have again turned over on his lips the phrases he gave to Dr. Riemer, Goethe's secretary, in his novel *Lotte in Weimar*: "My ideal career was that of university teacher, honorable in itself and affording leisure for the cultivation of the less high-strung, more relaxed (*loser gestimmten*) muses, who have not wholly denied me their favor."[4]

The Princeton appointment was as alluring as it was necessary; with his large family at home, Mann would welcome the solid salary of $6,000 ($116,000 in 2021 dollars; university salaries have kept precise pace with inflation!) for the academic year with limited responsibilities (VA 268). The offer, "impressive and honorable," officially documented in his diary entry for May 14, 1938, called first for four and thereafter for seven public lectures in Alexander Hall, which would include such writers and topics as Goethe's *Faust*, Wagner's *Ring*, Freud, Goethe's *Werther*, Mann himself ("On Myself"), and Mann's work (*The Magic Mountain* and "The Art of the Novel").[5] Mann took his assignments seriously, preparing assiduously for them and practicing reading them aloud to English-speaking listeners. But evidently not always long enough: Professor Bernhard Ulmer, my late colleague in the German Department at Princeton, attended Mann's lectures and recalls that

> his public lectures were of course given to an audience which was mostly composed of people (and even students) who were without any real knowledge of his work but awed by the name of the writer. I felt, and others would agree, that if he had spoken in *German* rather than in "English," at least a *few* of us would have understood him. His German accent garbled the English and made it mostly incomprehensible. (B 14–15)

A hint as to the sorts of incomprehension that both Mann and his audience shared is conveyed by the curious impression Mann had of a coterie of students who had come to hear a lecture delivered earlier that year at the University of California in Berkeley. For Mann, they apparently represented a mysterious "Sakramentum" (a sacramentum is an oath that a Roman might make to his gods, assuring his devotion in the event of his violating it). In truth, as these students explained, they had come from *Sacramento* to hear Mann's lecture (H 994).

After Mann had delivered the first half of his *Faust* lecture on the evening of November 28, 1938, he noted with pleasure that he had been "Introduced by [Dean] Gauss. The lecture, 'Goethe's *Faust*,' manfully delivered [*treulich durchgeführt*, a Goethean trope] to enthusiastic applause. Afterward a group of professors at the club, beer and sandwiches" (D 312, T3 326). We have a lively account of Mann's lecture from the college newspaper, *The Daily Princetonian*, on the following day:

> *Enthusiastic Audience Hears Learned Author*
> *Speaker Reaches Height In Quoting "Faust" In German*
> *With Tremendous Feeling*

> A small, learned man, grey hair neatly trimmed in a short haircut, delivered before an enthusiastic audience of undergraduates, fellow Faculty members and townspeople last night the first lecture of an impressive series. He was Dr. Thomas Mann, who, with his compatriot and good friend Dr. Albert Einstein, is one of Princeton's most famous residents. Speaking careful, precise English with a pronounced German accent, Dr. Mann applied himself to the task of Goethe and his "Faust," interpolating his remarks with a keen sense of humor. His oratory reached its height as he quoted from "Faust" in the original language so feelingly that his audience was able to understand the meaning of the passage without the translation. Dean Christian Gauss, with a few asides directed toward the "Prince," introduced the lecturer ... the applause was long and hearty ... among the listeners was Moe Berg '23, former big-league ball player [!].[6]

The text of Mann's lecture was reprinted in German in the exile journal *Mass und Wert*, where Mann's son Golo was active as an editor, and thereafter in English translation in Mann's *Essays of Three Decades*.[7] In the section below on *Lotte in Weimar*, I shall cite the conclusion of this talk in connection with Mann's portrait of Goethe: they are at odds with one another in their view of Goethe's politics—humanist champion of the German bourgeois versus autocratic conservative-reactionary.

Mann was once again elated by his delivery on January 17, 1939, of his Wagner lecture—"Richard Wagner and *The Ring of the Nibelung*"—on which he had taken great pains:

> At 7.30, a snack with Kahlers and then to Alexander Hall, the auditorium full. The "Wagner" lasted an unpredictable 1½ hours, which I noticed only from the fatigue that I had to fight with towards the end. Great attentiveness

and warm applause. Afterwards, together with the Kahlers in our dining room. Tea and beer restored me after my exhaustion. The athletic performance was basically remarkable in view of my very significant nervous exhaustion considering the vast transplantation and the indefinable impositions of the climate. (T3 348–49)

Erich Kahler was notably present at both the beginning and conclusion of the event: it was customary for Kahler to accompany Mann on all such occasions.

The Wagner lecture was based on Mann's 1937 lecture in Zurich titled "Richard Wagner und der *Ring des Nibelungen*"; it is *not* the notorious Wagner lecture, delivered in 1933 in Munich and titled "Sufferings and Greatness of Richard Wagner," that so distressed Nazi ideologues and local cultural fascists and led to Mann's flight from Germany.[8] The Princeton speech is an abridged version of the 1937 Zurich talk, with a good deal of intellectual and cultural context left on the auditorium floor (see *infra*, "Richard Wagner and *The Ring of the Nibelung*"). Mann was to comment that in his Princeton talks he had tried "not to be too good."

Mann's lecture on Freud, on February 13, 1939, gave him some trouble—at first. "After tea, to Mrs. Lowe: studied the Freud-lecture with her ['Freud and the Future'], which she praised highly but considers too difficult" (T3 359.) It was an English translation of a lecture delivered in German in Vienna on May 8, 1936, at a celebration of Freud's eightieth birthday. But the result, however strenuous it had been for him to speak this long and intricate piece in English, was again very satisfying:

Evening dress. Dinner at 7:15. To Alexander Hall with the children: Freud lecture. Very large audience and a good performance in spite of some nervousness. Extremely attentive and highly appreciative. Gauss there . . . and he told me in the anteroom that it was "the most interesting lecture in my experience." Back home, rolls, tea, and beer with the family and Kahler. At first quite exhausted, but then grew calmer and better. Lively discussion of the lecture, the political picture, Schiller's ballads, German poetry in the world. The Princeton astronomer [Shenstone] denounced Nazism in a recent speech with clenched fists. Contented and relieved, *rebus bene gestis* [things well done]. Return engagement likely.[9]

Mann was overly optimistic in translating his elation into the certainty of a renewed offer. In fact, he was hired by Princeton to lecture (informally) at half-pay for only the second semester of the following school year and not thereafter. He must have been hurt, and his letter acknowledging the latter decision conveyed to him by a Princeton dean, Robert Root, was reserved, even beyond Mann's usual manner.

Mann's "Introduction to *The Magic Mountain* for Students of Princeton University," although beginning "Gentlemen," was presented in German to advanced students and enriched by an idea sent to Mann by a precocious Harvard student (see the relevant section, *infra*). An English version of Mann's talk would appear as an introduction to the American translation of the novel.

Finally, Mann's penultimate lecture, a year later on May 2, 1940, "On Myself," is the most original and engaging of Mann's Princeton talks—an intimate reflection, without parallel in his writings, on himself as artist and on his work. It would be grand to retrace all its constructed memories, ranging from his earliest beginnings as a devotee of the play instinct—enhanced by a spiritual maturity—to the contemporary composition of *Lotte* (with Goethe "Manned"), but to do so would, perhaps sadly, burst the bounds of this chapter.[10] It would involve, at the very least, a salute to *Buddenbrooks* (with Schopenhauer and "spirit as a product of biological decline"); to *Tonio Kröger* (with "its Hamlet-melancholy and disgust of knowledge [*Erkenntnisekel*]"); to *Death in Venice* (with its "enslavement to sensuality"); to *The Magic Mountain* (with *Reflections of a Nonpolitical Man* as a source), and more. I have cited several of the lecture's high points in other chapters; meanwhile, observe how deeply Mann enjoyed his performance:

> Spoke in a lively way for an hour and had tremendously attentive listeners among the young, who ended up applauding. Mrs. Shenstone claimed that some faces were flushed with excitement (*einige hätten rote Köpfe gehabt*). What a joy it is to have given people [such] satisfaction! (T4 69)

It is irresistible to refer these words to "On Myself," the lecture that Mann had just delivered, in which he cites his own essay "Goethe and Tolstoy":

> Nobody has ever loved his own ego . . . in the sense of conceiving of his own ego as a cultural task and toiling early and late in pursuance of it, without reaping, almost as though by accident, educational influence in the outer world, and the joy and dignity of a leader and former of youth. The harvest never comes save at the height of life, and the moment of his realization of it is the sublime moment in the life of the productive human being. (B 53)

Mann had less-grand obligations to the college: he needed to "precept" at discussion groups and hold classroom lectures; and by now the sum of these additional tasks was taking a toll. His publisher Alfred Knopf had attempted to discourage him from the start from this "university idea" as it would interfere with his writing, and Knopf would have been very glad to have yet more of Mann's work to print and sell. Nonetheless, Mann was at first altogether taken with the "honorable" idea of a professorship—but certainly not forever. One reason for his leaving Princeton for California in March 1940 was his boredom with seeing the "same professors"; but the absolutely binding one was that funds for a continuing Princeton lectureship had dried up. By now, this predicament was not unwelcome: a sign of how burdensome his teaching duties had become was his assigning the writing of most of his last lecture, on "The Art of the Novel," to an amanuensis, Hans (James) Meisel.[11]

Meanwhile, Agnes Meyer, hard at work for her protégé, soon found an alternative source of income for him. It turned out to be a bountiful arrangement with the Library of Congress. Between the years 1942 and 1949 Mann delivered five new lectures at the library: "The Theme of the Joseph Novels," "The War and the Future," "Germany and the Germans," "Nietzsche's Philosophy in the Light of Contemporary Events," and "Goethe and Democracy."[12] Fortunately, we have been able to adumbrate much of this rich material even while keeping with Mann's years at Princeton.

It will come as no surprise that Mann's stay in Princeton was shaped in a major way by his lectureship at the university and all that this entailed: the preparation of the seven-odd lectures, for the most part in English, and personal contact with deans, professors, and students. The effect was real even if, on closer inspection, he was employed at the university for only the three semesters (he was called upon to lecture on *Werther* during a "free" month in fall 1939). But the earlier university obligations in 1938 and 1939 and for half of 1940—his public lectures, classroom talks, and question-and-answer sessions (which he especially disliked)—far exceeded the remit that he thought he had subscribed to.

Herewith an attempt to sum up the advantages and the disadvantages of these entailments for Mann in the vital years 1938–41.[13] What is crucial, first of all, is that Mann's association with the university and the town provided him with the first secure station of his American exile: we recall his finding it "a good thing to follow the vicissitudes and terrors [of the war] in my Princeton library" (T3 472). This comment followed by four months his remarks to the audience at the award of an honorary doctor of letters: "Yes, the homeless one has found a home. A new home in Princeton, in America. His gratitude is great. And since the desire to give is inseparable from such abundant taking, I shall pray my good genius that my gratitude may bear fruit."[14]

Mann's prayer was answered. For starters, his lectures produced five new essays—on *Faust, The Sufferings of Young Werther,* and *The Magic Mountain;* "On Myself"; and the partly written "The Art of the Novel." There was the indefinable boon of an appointment, leading, as we noted, to paroxysms of delight if only from the distance of a podium. Again, at the university, he would have a vivid experience of what at least those involved would consider Americans doing what they do best at an elite institution of learning (minus the politically motivated impassiveness of the German Department).[15] Finally, at Princeton, Mann would acquire a readiness to speak freely of important things—though far more readily in German, of course. This linguistic point underscores Mann's pain at needing to express himself in a language which he did not master and in which, in the best of cases, could never convey the nuanced elegance, the "erotic irony," of his native rhetoric. But surely in these various senses Princeton was an "education," if not the academic education he had never had.

Lotte in Weimar: "A German Curiosity of a Nobler Sort"

Lotte in Weimar is one of Mann's many works that exhibit the social monstrousness of the artist-nature. . . . Goethe's mission, like Nature's [and like Mann's—SC], is transformation. He consumes his friends and himself that the material may turn into spirit.

—PAUL ROSENFELD

When Mann came to America in 1938, it was not with the intention of becoming a university professor or, for that matter, serving as "the emperor of all German emigrants, the patron saint of the tribe of writers," let alone of contemplating the sometime attribution to him of the post of president of the next German republic, though all these unforeseen events did come true.[16] In early 1938 he accepted an invitation to give a series of antifascist lectures throughout America, fully intending to continue his literary work on his safe return to Switzerland. He needed to finish his "Goethe-novel," *Lotte in Weimar* (in dubious English translation, *The Beloved Returns*),[17] this "German curiosity of a nobler sort" (Br. M 144), and thereafter, the fourth part of his *Joseph* tetralogy.[18] As we have noted, the dangers of returning to Küsnacht outweighed his attachment to his home; and in May 1938, he made his formal application to immigrate to America. And so, it was in Princeton, New Jersey, later that year, that he resumed work on the novel, although it took him until the following summer and fall to finish it in Holland, in Sweden, and then, finally, on October 26, 1939, in Princeton.

The product of these several adventures is *Lotte in Weimar*, an elegant and richly informative work that easily satisfies the Horatian standard of pleasure and instruction. The novel springs out of the visit on September 22, 1816, of a certain Frau Councilor Charlotte Kestner of Hanover, to Weimar, where Goethe lived and served as the privy councilor to the duke. In the popular view, it was she—née Charlotte Buff—who, as a young woman, Goethe had immortalized as Werther's beloved in his sensational first novel *The Sufferings of Young Werther*. There is little doubt that Goethe embedded in his fiction a great many factual details of his friendship with Lotte, along with the shocking inventions they inspired—a misuse that, according to Mann, would haunt Lotte for much of her life. For one thing, the occasionally (unwitting?) seductive behavior of the fictive Charlotte Buff toward the fictional character Werther surely contributed to his lurid, lovesick suicide. Now, many decades later, the "real" Lotte has come to Weimar at once to visit her sister but, more importantly, to speak very seriously to Goethe (now, the very superior *von* Goethe) about his right to have used her life, at some cost to her, to produce the extravagant pathos of *Werther*. As the critic Morton Dauwen Zabel observes, from the moment of her arrival in Weimar, "she is treated to the deserts of a fame she has struggled a lifetime to evade."[19]

That postulated "right of fair use" reverts to the fact that the young Goethe, in 1772 a lawyer in Wetzlar, did often visit her and walk with her in the once idyllic village of Garbenheim; and it prompts Mann, in his Princeton lecture "On Myself," to pose the "old agonizing question: why that [fictionalized] 'love for a betrothed woman'?–for at that time Lotte was already engaged to . . . [another] man. . . . And what was it actually, which drove the young 'storm-and-stresser' [Goethe] to her and then abruptly into flight?" The reader receives no answers, although Mann suggests that they might be worked out from this novel; but the fictive Goethe certainly does not supply them (B 77).

Mann had written the first six of nine chapters of *Lotte* in Switzerland and France, beginning on November 11, 1936. After a rare writer's block and intense reflection on a possible form for a crucial seventh chapter, he succeeded in "finishing" it, he believed, in a beach chair in Noordwijk, Holland, on July 24, 1939. (In the matter of unforeseen events, *Lotte* began life as the thought of a story or at best a novella—and not as the 450-page novel it was to become.) Some weeks later, in early September, in Sweden, finding chapter 7—Goethe's dramatized monologue—"stiff," Mann began rewriting it, again, and truly finished it—or, let's say, "abandoned" it—as part of the whole only in late October 1939. Its intellectual content has been well put by Zabel:

> Goethe's reverie . . . gives unforgettable expression to Mann's lifelong researches into the meaning of art, the role of the artist as mediator between idealism and resolution, the androgynous temper of the creative vision, the fatal nature of a sympathy for universal truth, the unremitting struggle against disillusion that must accompany the aging man, and the expanding consciousness of his conceiving mind.[20]

One crucial refrain remains throughout its versions: Goethe "murmurs," in a more casual idiom, the self-regarding phrase Mann had written on the first day of 1937 to the dean of the Faculty of Philosophy of the University of Bonn on having his honorary doctorate revoked. It was a phrase that mattered enough for Mann to repeat it in a letter to Einstein (L 198). In "Goethe's" slight variation, it reads, "The thing is, that I was born to be a representative and absolutely not a martyr."[21]

Such personal interventions into "Goethe's" stream of consciousness did not escape the delighted critical eye of Erich Kahler, who wrote to Mann of the connection he had seen "between your own nature and Goethe's, on the hiding places and underground corridors that you have so cunningly found for highly personal statements" (EF 29). Mann was well aware of this identification: indeed, he practiced it. In his diary for December 2, 1938, he noted the "ever-increasing recurrence of the connection of my name with Goethe's and how my identification game prevails in [others'] minds" (T3 327).

A notorious instance of this equation caught the equally delighted though errant critical eye of Sir Hartley Shawcross, the British Chief Prosecutor at the Nuremberg Trials. This mirroring (*Widerspiegelung*) of Goethe and Mann would take on world-historic proportions several years later than our story but cries out for mention now. In 1945, in his final summation, Shawcross cited powerful lines from the English translation of *Lotte in Weimar,* assuming that they had been composed by Goethe himself. In fact, they were words that Mann had written in Princeton, in the winter of 1938, for his *fictive* Goethe. They were indeed fighting words—and the German so-called national conservatives took fierce umbrage. Shawcross's language—which is to say, Mann's!—deserves to be cited.

> Years ago, Goethe said of the German people that someday fate would strike them, "would strike them because they betrayed themselves and did

not want to be what they are. It is sad that they do not know the charm of truth, detestable that mist, smoke and berserk immoderation are so dear to them, pathetic that they ingenuously submit to any mad scoundrel who appeals to their lowest instincts, who confirms them in their vices and teaches them to conceive nationalism as isolation and brutality." With what a voice of prophecy he spoke—for these are the mad scoundrels who did those very things. . . . And so, after this ordeal to which mankind has been submitted, mankind itself . . . comes to this Court and cries: "These are our laws—let them prevail." Then shall those other words of Goethe be translated into fact, not only, as we must hope, of the German people but of the whole community of man: "thus ought the German people to behave— giving and receiving from the world, their hearts open to every fruitful source of wonder, great through understanding and love, through mediation and the spirit—thus ought they to be; that is their destiny."[22]

It was not long before erudite journalists in Britain observed that Shawcross had cited not Goethe but Thomas Mann's pastiche of Goethe,[23] although Shawcross's rendition did miss out two of the original *aesthetic-ecstatic* features of "Goethe's" argument. Mann did not write "mist, smoke [*Rauch*] and berserk immoderation" but "mist, intoxication [*Rausch*] and berserk immoderation"; not "mad [*verrückte*] scoundrels" but "ecstatic [*verzückte*] scoundrels." And thus, Shawcross's speech "disfigured formulations intended [by Mann] to elevate aesthetically the political factum brutum" (LW 170).

Shortly after Shawcross spoke, Mann received a worried letter from the British ambassador in Washington, Lord Inverchapel, inquiring

whether you put the words into Goethe's mouth or whether they are an actual quotation from the latter's works. If they do represent an actual quotation, I should be very glad if you could let me know in which work they appear. It is, of course, possible that they are a passage from a contemporary or later commentator. Should this be the case, perhaps you would be good enough to say where you got them from.[24]

Mann replied to the ambassador, "It is true, the quoted words do not appear literally in Goethe's writings or conversations; but they were conceived and formulated strictly in his spirit and although he never spoke them, he might well have done so."[25] "But I could warrant," he then added—in *The Story of a Novel: The Genesis of Doctor Faustus*—"that if Goethe had not really said the words the prosecutor attributed to him, he might very well have said them. In

a higher sense, therefore, Sir Hartley had quoted correctly." How had this curious contretemps ever come about? Mann explained:

> Even during the war, copies of the novel had been smuggled into Germany
> from Switzerland and circulated widely. In the long monologue of the sev-
> enth chapter there occur authentic and documented sayings of Goethe side
> by side with apocryphal matter of my own invention, to which, of course,
> I gave a Goethean cast. Opponents of the regime had extracted from this
> monologue a number of dicta, which analyzed the German character in
> unfavorable terms and warned that it might lead to evil; these passages had
> been collected and distributed as a leaflet under the camouflage "From
> Goethe's Conversations with Riemer." A copy or a translation of the curious
> forgery fell into the hands of . . . Sir Hartley Shawcross. In good faith, im-
> pressed by the topical forcefulness of the remarks, he quoted extensively
> from it in his charge.[26]

There is a double irony in all this. We return to 1938 in Princeton and
Kahler's observation of the many ways that Mann, in *Lotte in Weimar*, had
equipped Goethe with his own concerns and with features of his own personality. It is equally true that *Goethe's* concerns and features of his personality
stimulated Mann to a kind of higher mimicry in this very matter of making
another's words one's own. In chapter 3 of *Lotte,* in the course of a long (and
long-winded) conversation between Lotte and Dr. Riemer, Goethe's factotum,
Riemer ridicules the notion that his activity, as Goethe's secretary, might be
dismissed as that of a merely vulgar copyist: "Actually, for years I have carried
on his correspondence, not only to dictation but also quite independently, or
rather as though I were he, in his place and in his name and spirit" (in the
original, in italic, *as he himself, "als er selbst"*).[27] In chapter 7 of *Lotte,* we find
Mann asserting the power he has attributed to his literary creation: as Mann's
Riemer may duplicate Goethe's voice, so Mann may imitate his Riemer. Indeed, for Mann's biographer, Klaus Harpprecht, this pushy factotum is even
more: "an unplanned, unconscious, perhaps even unwanted alter ego of
Thomas Mann" (H 1097).

However, all literary-theoretical justifications to one side, Shawcross's citation of an inauthentic document, a *quasi*-forgery, was horrendously malapro-
pos at Nuremberg, in a proceeding that could condemn the Nazi conspirators
only on the strength of proven facts and legitimate documents.[28] Mann could
hardly foresee that a work of his, whose substance he had once considered
better suited to a stage comedy, would play a world-historical role of such

gravity (GW 3:167). In a situation ripe with tense ironies, there is also the jotting Mann made in his diary years before—on April 28, 1939—while still in the throes of composing *Lotte*: "[I spoke] with Erika about a plan to bring the writings (*Literatur*) of émigré authors into Germany" (T3 400).

This novel, a *tour de force*, cries out for extended literary appreciation, which it would be a joy to undertake; but we must stay with our idea of looking at Mann's writing in the special context of his preoccupations in Princeton. He fuses his own worldviews with Goethe's as his views take shape under the pressure of Nazi madness: his Goethe is appalled by the anti-Napoleonic *German* fervor, a patriotism auguring nothing better than "chaos and the reign of barbarism: . . . When hysterical citizens revel metaphorically in the shedding of blood, because the historic hour has given the rein to their evil passion, the sight is painful to behold" (LWA 187–88). More: all throughout one's reading of *Lotte*, the place-name in the title of the novel—*Weimar*—will work its effect. It surely did for Mann, as he read his pages aloud to Kahler and Katia and others in his family, and, as he might hope, for his readers in Germany. Recalling the *collapse* of the Weimar Republic, and in its aftermath the Nazi seizure of power, one scholar reflects on

> "Weimar" as the symbol of the failed republic, of Germany's political catastrophe; and "Weimar" as the epitome of its cultural greatness. In the manner almost of an exorcism, *Lotte in Weimar* confronts National Socialist Germany with the greatness of German intellectual culture, epitomized by Goethe as its chief representative, a position to which Mann aspired and which in exile he even attained.[29]

This confrontation is never realized more concretely than when Charlotte Kestner takes up lodging in Weimar in the Hotel Elephant, which, as many contemporary readers knew, had become the very headquarters of the Nazi presence in Weimar.[30] Hitler was received there! Moreover, years before Hitler, Weimar had been the last resort, not only of Goethe but also of Nietzsche. These details are part of what we shall see as Mann's frontal attack on the post-1933 Nazi incorporation of Goethe—the "German genius"—into its cultural politics.

During the writing of these final chapters, Mann was convulsed with hatred of Hitler and his satraps and the credulous German masses. And so, we have in several places in *Lotte* the fictive Goethe's furious attack on the misbegotten German stock, which does not know what it is about in succumbing to the deceptions of a criminal misfit. We even have as well "Goethe's" defense and celebration of the Jewish character. Let us look at these matters in slower motion.

Words attributed by Mann to Goethe (henceforth, the fictive Goethe is meant) parallel several of Mann's polemical political statements, as do those sentences, par excellence, excerpted by Sir Hartley Shawcross. Here is a fuller account of their context, part of a monologue in which Goethe "murmurs" a pageant of his past, stressing the Roman character of his maternal line:

> Their early seat . . . lay close to the Roman wall . . . where the blood of ancients and barbarians has always mingled. Thence it comes . . . your aloofness from the Germans, your perception of their vulgar strain; that scurvy misbegotten race, out of it, in spite of it, you take your life, your antipathy for it gnaws at a thousand roots that feed your very being. So, you lead this unspeakably precarious, painful life, called to their instruction, isolated not only by your station but from the very outset by your instinct; grudgingly respected and honoured, picked flaws in wherever they can! Don't I know they find me a burden, one and all? How could I appease them? I have moments when I would so gladly do so. It should be possible—sometimes it has been. For in your bones there is so much Sachs and Luther marrow; you even take a defiant pleasure in the fact, yet the very stamp and seal of your mind drives you to lift and lighten it with all your gift of irony and charm of words. So, they mistrust your German soul and you, they feel it an abuse, your fame is a source among them of hate and anguish. Sorry existence, spent wrestling and wrangling with my own blood—yet after all it is my blood, it bears me up. It must be so, I will not whine. That they hate clarity is not right. That they do not know the charm of truth, lamentable indeed. That they so love cloudy vapouring and berserker excesses, repulsive; wretched that they abandon themselves credulously to every fanatic scoundrel who speaks to their baser qualities, confirms them in their vices, teaches them nationality means barbarism and isolation. To themselves they seem great and glorious only when they have gambled away all that they had worth having. Then they look with jaundiced eyes on those whom foreigners love and respect, seeing in them the true Germany. No, I will not appease them. They do not like me—so be it, I like them neither, we are quits. What I have of Germany I will keep—and may the devil fly away with them and the philistine spite they think is German! They think they are Germany—but I am. Let the rest perish root and branch, it will survive in me. (LWA 329–31)

Well and good, this is splendid polemic—it is Mann's Goethe (and Mann!) at his independent best. But—crucial question—is Goethe prepared to grant these enabling virtues to others, his fellows . . . the "freedom, culture, universality, love" that make for such development? In his murmurings, yes, he is democratic for all the world, in principle, but. . . .

In this novel, we will soon see the "real" Goethe of fictive Weimar. Chapter 8 paints a portrait of Goethe on his feet—and thereafter, at the table with guests—which is at odds with Mann's pathos on behalf of a bourgeois democratic sharing of opportunity and respect. In Mann's public speeches during his Princeton years, we hear again and again of his love of democracy, a spiritual thing, and of the striving for personal freedom *and* political equality possible only in a socialist democracy. It is the sole political form enabling the full development of the individual. But his portrait of Goethe in *Lotte* will challenge—even brutally—both ideals: first, the ideal of full self-realization, which Mann once saw accomplished in Goethe, the *Bildungsbürger* (the cultivated citizen) par excellence; and second, the ideal of social and political democracy. Mann's earlier essays portray Goethe as exemplary, as one who fulfilled his creative possibilities, a personal greatness in harmony with one's community, indeed with the great world—benevolent, universalist, and democratic in principle. In "Goethe as Representative of the Bourgeois Age," we read, "The great sons of the bourgeoisie, who grew out of it into the spiritual and the ultra-bourgeois, are witnesses to the fact that in the bourgeois there are boundless possibilities, possibilities of unlimited self-liberation and self-overcoming." And what Goethe's novel of his old age, *Die Wanderjahre*, is actually about is "the self-conquest of individualistic humanity and a visionary bold departure from it in favor of human and educational principles and volitions" (E 3:341, 339).

Mann's earlier Princeton lecture on *Faust* establishes even more dramatically this opposition between Mann's early representations of Goethe and his portrait of Goethe in *Lotte*, for the former is all on the side of Goethe's "goodness." In the lecture we hear at length of Goethe's now entrenched belief in the goodness of all mankind—its intuitive knowledge of "the right way." Mann cites a startling line from a poem that Goethe wrote while young, at the time of his first "betrothal."[31] It reads: "I, a good boy" (*Ich guter Junge*) (!). Mann comments:

It is touching to hear Goethe so address himself; and whatever the intellectual heights he reached, however reverend he became to himself, it remained to the end a good description. We know how mild he was, how tolerant, what universal benevolence he possessed. We know his lifelong wish, "to do good to men," "to teach them to live"; we know his confession, that after every flight into solitude he needed but to see a human face "to love again." And the man of the Faustian strivings and efforts, he too is "a good boy." Just as he means well by himself, and feels that he can be saved, so also he means well by humanity: he wants its good, would have it assisted, positively, lovingly, reasonably; would not have it bewildered, would have it satisfied. In a Paralipomenon Faust says to Mephistopheles:

> So hearken now, if thou hast never heard:
> The human hearing's very keen,
> And glorious deeds can follow one clear word.
> Man knows only too sore his human need,
> And gladly counsel he will heed.

And again:

> Nothing of all is granted thee.
> Then how canst thou men's longing read?
> Thy warped nature, bitter, curst,
> What can it know of human need?

Nothing could be more Goethean, nothing more Faustian. Its conception of man, its attitude towards the human being, are a part of the Everlasting Goodness; and no differently speaks the Eternal Goodness itself, God the Lord, in the Prologue, whose characterization of man is young Goethe's characterization of himself: in it self-love grows till it embraces humanity:

> Though still he serve me with a darkened mind
> Soon to the light of truth I'll lead his feet.
> Knows not the gardener when the tree is green
> That flower and fruit the coming year shall greet?

And then that primal word of the Eternal Goodness:

> For man must err, so long as man must strive.

And that final pronouncement of God, which in its lofty and trusting mildness has become proverbial for all mankind:

> And stand abashed, when you at last must say,
> The good man, howsoever dark his striving,
> Is ever mindful of the better way.

A good man, a good boy. For our time, which seems to have fallen helpless prey to evil and cynicism,[32] how welcome were some kindly greatness, which should know what man needs and instead of offering him mocking sophisms, could give him serious advice in his necessities! A "clear word," and a benevolent, pointing out the better course, seems powerless today; world events pass all such over with brutal disregard. But let us hold fast to the anti-diabolic faith, that mankind has after all a "keen hearing," and that words born of one's own striving may do it good and not perish from its heart.[33]

At the very moment of delivering this *Faust* lecture to his Princeton students—credulous "boys," good boys and bad—Mann was *taking back* this ideal picture of his hero. The Goethe of *Lotte in Weimar* is a stiff, unreachable autocrat—an aged monarch dominating court and table, an arch-conservative and least of all a spokesman for the individual freedom of others. "'Liberation? That was simply freedom to go under' [*Das sei eine Befreiung zum Untergehen*], Goethe bitterly said" (LW 190; LWA 185). Mann was evidently practicing Goethe's maxim that certain hard truths must be told only to the wise few— and not to a "gang" of undergraduates: "Tell it to no one, only to the wise / Because the mob will immediately mock it."[34]

In *Lotte,* to the delight of Goethe's sycophantic dinner guests, on the one occasion on which he has any contact with Lotte at all, he pronounces an allegedly Chinese proverb: "The great man is a national misfortune" (LWA 418). Lotte has been hoping throughout for moral edification, quite particularly in this matter of a life—her own—being put brazenly to the uses of art. But on hearing this *bon mot,* carelessly declaimed by the speaker, and odd in the mouth of someone who is indubitably a "great man," Charlotte, who is our perspective on the scene, "sat alone on the defensive, stiffly upright, her . . . eyes wide with alarm. She felt cold" (LWA 418). When Goethe next entertains his company with a story about an Italian singer who became "the brightest star in the musical firmament" and yet repeatedly abandoned her art so as to care for her shiftless father (LWA 421), Charlotte broods, "There was something painful and disquieting in the story."

> She had been hoping—for her own gratification but also for the speaker's sake as well—that some moral edification would be the issue of this instance of filial piety. But he [Goethe] had given a disappointing turn to the gratifying sentiment, it was at best psychologically "interesting"; it showed an approbation of this example of the artist's contempt for his art—and

that chilled and frightened Charlotte, again for his sake as well as for her own. (LWA 423)

Throughout the novel, we hear echoes from Goethe's lips of one of the great topics in Mann's political speeches: the German striving for universality. For a brief moment in the novel their views are in synch. In the fifth chapter of *Lotte in Weimar,* "Adele's Tale," the fictive Adele Schopenhauer cites a fictive Goethe: "Our civic life," she has him say,

> is very different from that of the ancients, our relation to the State is quite other than theirs. The German, instead of confining himself to himself, must take in the whole world in order to have an effect on the world. Our goal must be, not hostile separation from other peoples, but rather friendly association with all the world, cultivation of the social virtues, even at the expense of our inborn feelings or even rights. (LWA 160–61)

A comment on this matter by Hans Rudolf Vaget is very apt. Despite the fact that

> Mann's consciousness of being "a German writer and servant of the German language"[35] was and always remained the deepest root of his exile-existence, it comported perfectly with American citizenship, since America, as he wrote admiringly, was a country whose "foreign-born citizens . . . always sought to become true Americans as quickly as possible" (GW 13:708). What in Germany and otherwise would be an impossibility: to have grown up in a foreign language and yet be able to become a "true German" is, in the United States—which is "shaped by a providential [*glücklich*] history" [GW 3:729], a country undamaged by nationalism—a normal matter. . . .
>
> Resistance from the side of his original national identity—damaged and disgraced, as it now was—could oppose this drift, but all the less so given that, since 1922, Mann had acknowledged a transnational concept of Germanness, one, namely, that strove for universality, such as was presupposed in the late work, especially in the case of *Doctor Faustus*. It is a universal Germanness, as he displayed it in essays on Goethe, Nietzsche and Wagner. It is fair to claim that Thomas Mann was the first German after them who in his work and in his public activity would showcase such a universalism. The historical context in which this elevation and extension of his existence was accomplished was his American exile.[36]

On the other hand, one of the more startling items in Goethe's table talk in chapter 8, with Charlotte present, is his harrowing report of a medieval pogrom in the city of Eger. (The city had been mentioned earlier in the chapter rather harmlessly as the source of the very good mineral water that Goethe drinks before offering it to Charlotte.) "Lowering his voice and sticking out his lips, with a portentous expression that had something epically humorous about it, as when one tells frightening stories to children, he [Goethe] talked about a night of blood that remarkable town had experienced in the late Middle Ages, an uprising against the Jews, a sudden and violent attack like a paroxysm" (LWA 410). Following a furious speech by a "barefoot friar," who fulminates against the Jews as Christ-killers, a soldier cries out to the congregation to follow him into the ghetto and slaughter the Jewish inhabitants. Blood runs down the alleyways. Only one man survives: during the massacre, he hides in a chimney, in which he very nearly chokes to death.

How would news of that horror be received in Mann's homeland—in a novel that would be read, among other readers, by its anti-Semitic, fascist-minded element? On the one hand, it could be seen as establishing a kind of precedent, a subliminal justification for the Judeocide in progress. On the other hand, the wildly irrational grounds for the slaughter—"theological" and not racist—might give even some Nazis pause. And as if the latter point, just barely inviting sympathy for the murdered Jews of Eger, might need underpinning, Goethe afterwards speaks at length of the merits of the Jewish people, even positing the inflammatory thesis that the Germans and Jews are deeply allied in their nature; and just as the Jews have lived for centuries as a scattered, wandering people, so (as he had murmured earlier) it shall be the fate of the German people:

> Unhappy folk! They will end in a smash! [They] do not understand themselves ["their pig-headed craving to be a unique nation"] that makes the rest of the world laugh at them, at first; but after a while the world hates them for it, and that is dangerous. Fate will smite them, for betraying themselves and not wanting to be what in fact they are. She will scatter them over the earth like the Jews, and justly. For their best always lived in exile among them; and in exile only, in dispersion, will they develop all the good there is in them for the healing of the nations, and become the salt of the earth. (LWA 339)

The "smiting" will be terrible. Goethe persists in this analogy at the dinner table with Charlotte, her family, and his obsequious retinue of acquaintances, declaring:

> Most remarkable, and hard to fathom in view of the considerable contribution they [the Jews] have made to civilization in general, was the ancient antipathy forever smouldering in the other peoples of the world against the

figure of the Jew, forever threatening to blaze up into active hatred, as was amply instanced in the tale of the disorders at Eger. This antipathy, this aversion, only heightened by the feeling of respect inseparable from it, could be compared with that felt in the case of only one other people: the Germans. And the destined rôle of the Germans and their inward as well as outward situation among the other peoples showed the most extraordinary likeness to that of the Jews. He would not venture to enlarge upon the point, that would be foolish; but he confessed that sometimes he was conscious of a fear that almost took away his breath lest one day the concentrated world hatred against that other salt of the earth, the German stock, would be released in a historic uprising of which that medieval night of butchery was but a rehearsal in miniature. (LWA 417)

According to the savant Klaus Harpprecht, there are no authenticated reports of the historical Goethe having actually conjured so frightful a prophesy. But as Harpprecht and other scholars have well known, Goethe was addicted to comparisons between the Germans and the Jews. In one instance, in a conversation with his friend Friedrich von Müller, Goethe remarked, "The Germans must be transplanted and scattered throughout the world like the Jews in order to develop fully and for the salvation of all nations the mass of good that lies in them."[37]

Other tropes and phrases attributed to Goethe that develop the likeness are citations from Mann's speeches and writings. In a 1934 letter to Bertram, for one, Mann writes: "Unhappy, unhappy [German] people! For a long time now, I have reached the point of begging the Weltgeist [lit., "world spirit"] to liberate it from politics, dissolve it, and scatter it in a new world like the Jews, with whom so much related tragedy connects it."[38]

The sinister connection of laughter and hatred in the response of "the others," a link that Goethe earlier murmured in his monologue, now makes a virtual reappearance at the dinner table. We recall Goethe's *bon mot* "The great man is a national misfortune" (which had actually been coined by his brother Heinrich) and which Goethe attributes fancifully to the Chinese. Coming from this great man, the epigram elicits paroxysms of laughter:

Here came another outburst of laughter, even more boisterous than before. That word [*das Wort, bon mot*] from those lips, caused a perfect storm of merriment. They threw themselves back in their chairs, they bowed over the table, they struck it with the flat of their hands—shocked into self-abandonment by this nonsensical dogma and possessed by the wish to show their host they could appreciate his quoting it and at the same time to convince him what a monstrous and blasphemous absurdity they considered it.

Charlotte is once again hardly amused. She feels a chill—and then more than that—passes into an anxious trance, triggered by the word "Chinese": she has a loveless vision of

> a train of people, repulsively sly and senile . . . in pigtails . . . they hopped first on one foot and then on the other, then lifted a shrunken long-nailed finger and in chirping voices pronounced words that were, utterly, fatally, and direfully, the truth. This nightmare vision was accompanied by the same dread as before, running cold down her back, lest the too loud laughter round the board might be hiding an evil something that threatened in a reckless moment to burst forth: somebody might spring up, overturn the table, and scream out: "The Chinese are right!" (LWA 419)

This reader is negatively fascinated by the "evil" that Charlotte (and Mann) can have had in mind. The expression Mann uses that is translated as "an evil something" is *"ein Böses"* (LWA 412), which can have a vast range of (negative) implications, as relatively trifling as "naughty" or "mischievous," as in the expression *"ein böser Bub"* ("a bad boy"), or as grievous as in the title of Nietzsche's *Jenseits von Gut und Böse* (Beyond good and evil), where it represents the triumph of slave morality and the repulsive impoverishment of Western humankind. Something of this range of judgment emerges in the commentaries of expert readers. The premier *Lotte* commentator Werner Frizen inclines to a moderate view of sorts, thinking that the evil that threatens is "the loss of self" (*"die Preisgabe des Selbst"*), to which Frizen adds the somewhat cryptic remark, "an experience touching both oneself and one's fellows that was part of everyday life in 1938" (LW 738). Is he referring to the widespread political catastrophe of self-abnegating devotion to political masters, or, indeed, something more intimate, such as Mann's sensation of self-alienation in exile under the weight of intractable external demands ("I am afraid of my new life")? The eminent Mann scholar Herbert Lehnert makes his comment perfectly clear. In a grand essay on *Lotte*, on reproducing this passage, he is moved to add in respect of "this evil": "This was written in October 1939, two and a quarter years before the Wannsee conference," which sought the murderous annihilation of the Jews of Europe.[39]

The leading, if implicit, question running throughout this account calls for a direct answer. What explains Mann's reluctance in *Lotte* to recruit Goethe for the democratic ideal that Mann cared about so deeply at the time of writing the novel? *Lotte*'s Goethe is an icon of esoteric conservatism, bare of any respect for the mass of "the Germans." We have a glimpse of Goethe's politics in Mann's lecture on *The Sufferings of Young Werther* delivered to a Princeton University audience on November 17, 1939, just weeks after the signal date October 26, 1939, when he finished writing *Lotte in Weimar*.[40] According to Mann, Goethe, still in his early days when writing *Werther*, filled his surrogate with social revolutionary fervor. Werther is a Rousseauist in his animus against the aristocracy. One cannot avoid the theme of class conflict in Werther's "encounter with snobbish aristocratic society: this humiliating and provoking collision with the despised class is too characteristic of ... [the book's] basic revolutionary tendency to be passed over." Goethe has taken pains to inject an element of social revolt into a story of unrequited love. Mann then wonders whether Goethe, "as a conservative Olympian, might even have been embarrassed" in later life "by that episode in which the novel's latent revolutionary quality ... becomes socially manifest: ... *Werther's Leiden* (The sufferings of Werther) must be numbered among the books which prophesied and prepared the French Revolution" (B 132–33).

In light of our discussion until now, Goethe, as represented in his fictive counterpart—his "vice-exister" (to speak with Samuel Beckett)—is neither that of a democratic bourgeois (Werther revolts against "bourgeois narrow-mindedness") nor a devoted antagonist of democracy (B 113). There is certainly no talk in the lecture of Werther's or Goethe's *nationalism*, which would have been historically incoherent. Goethe's later Olympian conservatism is hostile to revolution and to the revolutionary tendencies of *Werther*. But precisely for this reason, this view of Goethe would be of very little use to the Nazis' self-representation as an anti-bourgeois party of revolution: the Goethe of Mann's *Werther* lecture stands far offside any contribution to Nazi ideology. The account of Goethe in this lecture, however, is replete with ironies.

Goethe claims to have reread his *Werther* only once and then in his old age. Thomas Mann comments:

This re-reading must have taken place ... in the year 1816. By an odd coincidence, that year brought to him at the age of 67, a memorable ... reunion of a personal nature. An old lady, only four years younger than he, came on a visit to Weimar, where one of her sisters was settled in marriage, and announced her presence to him. It was Charlotte Kestner, formerly Buff, the

Lotte of Wetzlar, Werther's *Lotte*. They had not seen each other for forty-four years. She and her husband had at one time suffered severely from the inconsiderate exposure given to their affairs by the writing of *Werther*. Now, however, as matters had developed, the good woman was rather proud of her especial character as the model for the heroine of a youthful work by a man now become so great. Her appearance in Weimar awakened an interest, by no means welcome to the old gentleman. His Excellency invited the titled lady (the Frau Hofrat) to dine with him at mid-day, and treated her with a stiff courtesy, which is reflected in the letter about the reunion she wrote to one of her sons. It is a tragi-comic human document, that belongs to literary history. "I have," she wrote, "made the acquaintance of an old man, who,—had I not known he was Goethe, or even knowing it—made no pleasant impression upon me."

It is my opinion, that a thoughtful tale might be based on this document—or even a novel. It might comprehend much on the subjects of art and the emotions, the dignity and the decline of age, and form the occasion for a penetrating portrait of Goethe and of genius itself. Perhaps a writer may be found to undertake it. (B 134–35)

Mann's last sentence is sumptuously ironical—in more ways than one. The more obvious is that he is of course that writer who has been found: just some months before, as we have noted, on October 26, 1939, he wrote in his diary, "[I] introduced corrections into the finished copy of the final chapter, put the complete manuscript of the novel in order, and laid it aside" (T3 494). There is an additional resonance to this jest. Many years before, in his *Reflections of a Nonpolitical Man*, Mann set down the same conceit, though with a change of name. He wrote, "I've often felt that Nietzsche's philosophy might be able to become the good fortune and the lucky find of a great writer. . . . Unlike Schopenhauer, Nietzsche has not found or not yet found his artist."[41] But it is hard to believe that at this moment Mann was not supposing that the project of completing Nietzsche would be his and no one else's. Now he repeats the trope, saying that the artist—the novelist—who would portray Lotte's late visit to Weimar has still not been found. But the implication of the first occasion of this trope, in the *Reflections of a Nonpolitical Man*, might still be very much in play. True, *Lotte* does not complete *all* of Nietzsche, by any means, but it has a good deal to say to Nietzsche's great aperçu: "A Homer would not have created an Achilles nor a Goethe a Faust if Homer had been an Achilles or Goethe a Faust."[42] *Lotte* addresses the public disparity between the putative greatness of the author and the masterworks he has written. But Mann's Goethe is still great as long as he is alone—and thinks.

It is finally true that the representation of Goethe in Mann's Princeton lecture on "Goethe's *Werther*" in no way completes Mann's idea of Goethe in the earlier essays, which show him, as an exemplary bourgeois, standing ready to serve the ideal of a universal humanism. The view of Werther as a revolutionary and of the later Goethe as a nay-saying Olympian conservative neither adds to nor detracts from Mann's earlier view of the author of the novels of *Wilhelm Meister*. What is crucial, historically speaking, is the Nazi reinvention of Goethe as the embodiment of nationalist racial energies—as a militarist and anti-Semite. "None other than Goethe and Schiller," declared the Nazi Goethe scholar Julius Petersen, "were forerunners of an ideal National Socialism."[43] Mann's Goethe in *Lotte* is a narcissist *decadent* ("reactionary and self-indulgent"), altogether unique, with passionate and unpredictable sympathies: Mann sacrifices him as the very model of a fulfilled personal *Bildung* for the sake of a strike against the Nazi cultural front. In this sense, the "incommensurable" Goethe in *Lotte* leaves intact Mann's wider program of a militant universalist democracy at war with totalitarian Nazism.[44]

It will be interesting—and surprising—to pursue for a moment the attention in America that this recondite novel (in its very stilted translation) received. It is unlikely that many American readers would have perceived the polemical implications of his Goethe portrait as contributing to the Allies' burgeoning war effort. An amiable review in *The New Yorker* by the excellent critic Clifton Fadiman gives the gist of the general understanding:

> Goethe has written more sympathetically than Mann about himself, but not with more acuteness. There are a number of things one can say of the book, the most important of which is also the simplest: it seems like a convincing portrayal of a great man. It is, in addition, an oblique disquisition on the two perennial Germanys, Goethe's and Bismarck-Hitler's; a charming period piece, re-creating, without the fuss of literary archaeology, the post-Napoleonic Weimar of 1816; and a portrait gallery drawn with that odd, exhaustive humor peculiar to Thomas Mann.[45]

There is little here that would displease Mann, and something to please him very much—that the term "exhaustive" is quickly modified by the "humor" that Mann so much wanted to be the hallmark of his fiction. The reception of *Lotte* in New York would leave very little to be desired in the matter of a

welcoming American readership at a time when his German readership was
so contracted. Agnes Meyer described the scene of his "translation":

> Scribners bookstore on Fifth Avenue has turned its big show window into
> a tribute to you. They have photographed the front page of the Times Book
> Review and of the Tribune Book Review and enlarged them to a size of five
> or six feet so that every letter is about a half an inch in height. In the middle
> of the window are great piles of "The Beloved Returns," and all your other
> books are stacked in groups on both sides. (BR.M 231)

Few members of the nation of exiles in those years can even have imagined
such a reception of their work, especially of work accomplished during the
period of exile. Mann's neighbor Erich Kahler lived hand to mouth by journalism; his house was bought for him by Einstein; and his future tenant Hermann
Broch was literally close to penury.

Richard Wagner and *The Ring of the Nibelung*

Mann's Wagner lecture on January 17, 1939—itself a music-drama—opens with
a ringing declaration of his admiration for Wagner and the "greatness and significance" of his works. Mann's "love and admiration [is] still untarnished and
untouched by time," a time that includes, importantly, the Nazi botching of
German culture by the abuse of Wagner's main motif—the evocation of a
primeval Germanic greatness. The strength of Mann's attachment to Wagner
is increased from his having resisted "disillusionment by the perversion to evil
ends to which, *perhaps,* this art affords an opening" (emphasis added).[46] Recall
that "the ideological message of Nazism," in the words of Saul Friedländer,
"constantly evoked a longing for the sacred, the demonic, the primeval."[47]
Mann was well aware of the intimate connection between what his biographer
Klaus Harpprecht calls "the Bayreuth magic and the mythic surgings of National Socialism"—in a word, the consanguinity of Wagner and Hitler (H 1121).

Mann is on safer ground when his topic turns to "admiration" pure and
simple as the best attitude one can have to *life*—a receptiveness that prompts
the desire to communicate to others a portion of that life personally, artisti-
cally, or intellectually. He may be thinking, along with Nietzsche, of the "art of
communication [that is] commanded in the highest degree by the Dionysian
type, marked by the ease of metamorphosis; it is impossible for him to over-
look any sign of an affect."[48]

Wagner is such a Dionysian—a passionate communicator and revolutionary artist who created a new kind of drama fusing music and myth (87). But this revolution alone does not do justice to his character, which informs his art: alive to his passions, he knows the temptations of power and pleasure yet struggles for catharsis, "a process of cleansing, clarification, sublimation," and we will glimpse its artistic realization in the *Ring* (88).

The younger, the once-naive Mann is spiritually at home with Wagner in describing Wagner's aversion to politics:

> He never concealed his profound antagonism to the activities of politicians. He acquiesced in the revolution of 1848, he took part in it; but that was hardly out of interest in its concrete aims, it was rather due to his general revolutionary sympathy, his aspirations and dreams, which went far beyond the political program. Indeed, they went far beyond the bourgeois age itself. (89–90)

Operagoers protested, for they continued to feel attached to the high bourgeois art of "German classicism and humanism from which this new art was disassociating itself. . . . But from a social and ethical point of view . . . [Wagner's work] looked far beyond any bourgeois capitalistic society: he envisaged a world freed from delusions of power and domination by money; a world based on justice, love and brotherhood" (90–91).

Wagner recurs to myth, the putative first story of a people, the "folk-song" lodged in its "folk-soul." It is there at the very beginning, before the accretions of debasing experience and a factitious culture. The "folk-song" expresses in elevated simplicity what Wagner calls "the purely human"—humankind's original feeling and behavior. Wagner is driven by a passion for first things, by "a compulsion to go back to the beginnings of all things; to the first cell, the E-flat of the double basses of the prelude to the prelude" (92). How many in Mann's Princeton audience of undergraduates, listening to Mann's Teutonically darkened English, would have made much sense of this "beginning"? But if they were patient, they would soon see it come to light—"the beginning, the source of all things and the music thereunto appertaining! For [in the *Ring*] it was at the bottom of the Rhine and the gleaming hoard of gold round which the Rhine maidens sported and played—that was the still untarnished, primeval state of the world, guiltless of greed, untouched by the curse." (The dwarf Alberich, a Nibelung, cursed the gold he stole; his prophecy was fulfilled: everyone touched by it is destroyed.) Wagner's return to origins—to a fleeting innocence and then to crime and a curse—is at the same time a return to an original music: as *Das Rheingold* begins, we have "the representation of how . . . [music] was built up from the E-flat chord in the major key of the flowing Rhine into a rich and varied world of musical symbols" (103–4).

Mann is once again present *in propria persona* in addressing Wagner's exile in Switzerland, where a good part of the *Ring* was composed. (Wagner had been "implicated in the Dresden upheaval of 1849 and became overnight a political refugee" [93]). His fate is uncannily close to Mann's own, who had also been "implicated" in the hostile critical reaction in Munich to his 1933 lecture on the "Sufferings and Greatness of Richard Wagner." Mann's children persuaded him not to return to Germany and instead choose exile, like Wagner himself, in Switzerland. Mann reflects on "the whole political development of Germany up to 1870" from Wagner's standpoint and concludes that "the worship of facts [the failure of the Revolution of 1848 and thereafter the establishment in 1870 of a Prussian hegemony] is not such a high-minded historical attitude; nor is history so glorious an affair that we should cease to respect the hopes cherished by high-minded men, simply because the event failed to justify them" (94). This will be Mann's own axial stance all throughout his years of exile until the destruction of Nazi Germany in 1945.

The lecture studies in detail the gradual maturation of Wagner's plan for the *Ring*, which feeds on ancient Norse mythology and the German *Nibelungenlied*. Wagner is a devotee of the myth of the purely human; and the *Ring* enacts the return to the best part of the purely human after its terrible excursus through the greed of gold and power. That best, saving power is love, in its especially privileged form for Wagner, eagerly affirmed by Mann as the eternal feminine, "*das ewig Weibliche*," which Mann's translator terms, none too felicitously, the "woman-soul."

In writing of Wagner's passion "for the primitive poesy of the emotions, . . . prior to the social and the conventional" (however incoherent the notion of such a priority), Mann takes the opportunity to advance his own major historical thesis: the uniquely *German* character of this obsession. The great French and English artistic productions of the nineteenth century are novels of the social world. Not so the German mind, which, in principle, "knows and wishes to know nothing of social values; the social, it feels, is not musical, and will not lend itself to musical treatment. Only the legendary, the purely human, the timeless, unhistorical primitive poetry of nature and the heart, lends itself to art; it is, indeed, art's refuge from the social" (106–7). That flight from the social will have—indeed, has had—dreadful repercussions in the sleepwalking acceptation of the values of the ruling clique. Mann is not hesitant about making this point; if the "German spirit" is fundamentally apolitical and asocial and yet found nurture in this attitude for its production of great works of art, still, in the year 1938, "such a lack . . . leads to conflict with the world-spirit," for this is an age imperiled by grave social and economic injustice. The peril flows from an unnamed country—of course, it is Germany—in whose "social and political experiment just such a myth-substitution" of the "legend, the fairy-tale"—Wagner's material—has taken place. "Alas, in the realm of politics, the fairy-tale becomes a lie" (108).

At the end we hear, finally, of Mann's distress at the Nazis' use and misuse of Wagner. This passage is carried over without cuts from his 1937 Zurich talk: it is the bitter complaint, once more, about the Nazi appropriation of Wagner's mythic world for totalitarian purposes. Mann means to take back Wagner from the Nazis and attach him to Goethe—to *Faust,* a tragic poem that concludes with the same thought as Wagner's *Götterdämmerung* (*The Twilight of the Gods*). Both works celebrate the power of love to lift men above their obsessions with mastery and display, with wealth and treacherous treaties. Valhalla, the great monument to factitious grandeur in Wagner's opera, is flooded and consumed in flames. One implication, since Wagner is a prophet, is that the same fate awaits the Nazi empire. And Mann, not unlike Wagner, who wrote from exile, may see himself, in Mann's words, as a prophet, for he has forecast the "Coming Victory of Democracy"; and "more than one prophet has already turned away with shuddering from the realization of his prophecy and preferred to bury himself in a strange land, rather than be honored in the country where his prophecy has come true." It is interesting that the original phrasing in the typescript of Mann's lecture reads: "More than one prophet has already resigned himself to a grave in a strange land rather than death in a country where such a realization has taken place." Mann's key changes from the original typescript heighten the dreadful emotional cost—fear and loathing, literally, "shudderings"—at the thought of exile and death in a foreign land. These changes foreground the present vile turmoil—the realization of the prophet's warning—in his native country. The possibility remains (though it is probably owed only to Mann's weak English diction) that "burying oneself" in a foreign land might attenuate the thought of a literal death and mean only "to live deeply in, to immerse oneself in the business of" the foreign land. But this doubt is erased by the very plain introduction of the notion of the "honor" owed to the prophet in his own country, which, however, as an exile, he must do without. All these changes underscore the impression that in the moment

Mann is presenting *himself and his own predicament* as Wagner's. The rousing conclusion deserves a full citation:

Folk, and swords, and the heroics of the Nordic myth—all these, on certain lips, are only contemptible pilferings from Wagner's vocabulary. The creator of the *Ring* emancipated himself from the age of bourgeois culture, for the sake of his artist infatuation with the past and the future. But he never meant to accept in exchange a form of political totalitarianism destructive of all spiritual values. For these were everything to him, the German state just nothing at all. The keynote of the *Meistersinger* is struck in the lines: . . . "Were the Holy Roman Empire to vanish like a cloud, / we still should have our holy German art." In the *Ring* Wagner exemplified the curse of gold; the lust of power he converted into a feeling so pure that it could love its own destroyer. His heart's true prophecy is . . . "Not goods nor gold nor pomp nor might; not lying bonds nor wrongful pacts"; rather it is the heavenly melody which at the end of the *Götterdämmerung* (Twilight of the Gods) rises from the burning citadel of earthly power, and proclaims in the accents of music the same message as that in the closing words of our other cosmic German poem [Goethe's *Faust*]: . . . "The Woman-soul leadeth us / Upward and on." (109)

On reflection, we have a double stance in this lecture in the matter of the admiration that is owed to Wagner. It is consistent with Mann's views on Wagner as they emerge from an exchange with Peter Viereck, notable as the author of *Metapolitics: From the Romantics to Hitler* (1941), which Mann read and admired. Later in 1939, the year of Mann's Princeton lecture, Viereck published an article in the journal *Common Sense,* treating Wagner as an extraordinarily influential modern artist and at the same time a proto-Nazi pamphleteer, a primary source of Nazi ideology. Because the piece mentions Mann respectfully though regrettably as an admirer of Wagner's work, including even his polemical screeds, Mann was interested in replying; and here, in mid-1939, he redoubled his case *against* Wagner, declaring his almost thoroughgoing agreement with Viereck and, as Hans Rudolf Vaget notes, going even one step further: it is not only Wagner's writings that paved the way to Nazism but the entirety of his production. Wagner's works, including the operas, are a "precise, intellectual-spiritual preformation of the 'metapolitical' movement that today terrifies the world" (Mann). Mann still wished to hold on to his appreciation of the "love" that somehow survives the *Götterdämmerung,* but this by and large unequivocal disclaimer remains his last word on Wagner (VA 338–39).

"Freud and the Future"

The most interesting lecture in my experience . . .

—CHRISTIAN GAUSS

The first version of Mann's Princeton lecture on Freud was delivered in German in Vienna on May 9, 1936, in honor of Freud's eightieth birthday.[49] The following month—*mirabile dictu*—Mann visited Freud on the Berggasse in Vienna and read his speech to him![50] On July 25, a mere month later, Mann published an abridged English translation in *The Saturday Review of Literature*. I mention this fact to highlight the alacrity with which Mann's words were received in his soon to be adopted land.[51]

The opening of the Vienna lecture is at once eloquent and mistaken; after making the correction, showing that Mann is wrong to deny Freud's early awareness of Nietzsche, I will segue to Mann's Princeton lecture of February 13, 1939, which was very likely based on his essay in *The Saturday Review* (the original typescript has not been preserved). The thrust of Mann's approach can be summed up with an early and trenchant phrase from both lectures: he will address the "moral aspect of a psychology of the unconscious" while celebrating "mythical thinking."

The Vienna talk profiles the choice of a creative writer and not a scientist to speak on behalf of Freud's life and work. Although Mann finds the choice remarkable, he quickly admires the suggestion of an intimate relation between literature and psychoanalysis.[52] When Freud embarked on his lonely journey of discovery, Mann continues, he did not know that he could find corroboration of his main ideas in the works of creative writers and philosophers, foremost Nietzsche. (Mann strikes this allusion to Nietzsche from the abridged Princeton lecture, as a mention of Nietzsche, regarded at that time as a wild thinker and even as a proto-Nazi, was unlikely to be welcomed by an audience uninitiated in German intellectual history.)

We know that Mann's general claim of Freud's ignorance of Nietzsche is untrue, although the matter of this relation is a tangled one. Freud records that he did indeed read Nietzsche in the 1880s and then again ca. 1909 but thereafter maintains that he had always been reluctant to read Nietzsche—uneasy, perhaps, that one would find in Nietzsche the very truths that Freud was engaged in establishing. Nietzsche would have been Freud's very capacious precursor, robbing him of originality.[53] But, as Mann makes plain, thinkers other than Nietzsche would corroborate Freud's findings, especially the importance

of the unconscious as a prime motivator, an agency corresponding to Schopenhauer's Will. And with this mention of Schopenhauer, who as yet carried
no negative political charge for an American audience—an impression Mann
would erase in a subsequent article two years later ("Culture and Politics"; see
"Contra Thomas Mann the American," in chapter 2, *supra*)—we have returned
to the Princeton speech.

Schopenhauer is pertinent as the original source of Mann's *own* initiation
into "that region of the soul which we have learned to call the unconscious, a
realm whose discovery and investigation, whose conquest for humanity, are
precisely . . . [Freud's] task and mission." Mann elaborates: This metaphysics—
shared by Schopenhauer and Freud—shifts the time-honored Enlightenment
primacy of reason to instinct. "It recognized the will [in Freud, the unconscious
Id] as the core and the essential foundation of the world . . . and the intellect as
secondary and accidental, servant of the will and its pale illuminant."[54]

This discovery of the primacy of the unconscious follows from psychoanalysis's striving for the truth of man's (and woman's) psychic life: indeed,
for Mann, psychological truth is truth itself, which is to say, a truth that humankind can evade only at its peril. Like Freud, Mann is a devotee of "a psychological interpretation of knowledge and truth . . . for the psychological
will to truth [is] a desire for truth in general . . . in the most actual and courageous sense of the word" (413). The question of courage arises in light of the
resistance, which this "revolution"—this is Mann's word—encounters from
a would-be hegemonic Ego.

Psychoanalysis takes as its chief object of study the phenomenon of disease,
mainly in the form of neurosis; and that knowledge points to its second kinship
with the activity of creative artists and philosophers. Along with an intuition of
the unconscious, "science and the creative impulse [share] the understanding
of disease, or, more precisely, of disease as an instrument of knowledge" (414).
Mann never fails to stress, in this lecture and indeed all throughout his work,
man's unlucky position between the regimes of spirit and flesh. The human
being is "*das kranke Tier*," the sick animal suffering from the strain of brutish
impulses and both conscious and unconscious shackles. This struggle leaves
traces of pain; and psychoanalysis has made its greatest discoveries by exploring the abnormal—neurotic symptoms and troubled dreams!—that inheres
in every assumed normality: this "study of disease . . . has revealed itself as a
first-class technique of anthropological research" (414). Disease is once again
forever an object of attraction for creative writers, at whose forefront Mann
has every right to place himself. Consider, I'll add, such leading figures in

Mann's fiction as the pederast Gustav Aschenbach, the tubercular patient Hans Castorp, and the half-mad syphilitic Adrian Leverkühn.

The discovery of the dominance of the unconscious has historical implications in light of the irrational politics of the day, from which Mann distances himself: the metaphysics of the Id has been preached "not in malice, not in the anti-human spirit of the mind-hostile doctrines of to-day . . . but rather in the mood of a truth-loving bitter irony and anguished pessimism" (415). At the end of his talk Mann will elaborate the tough humanistic value of the discoveries of psychoanalysis.

Freud's view on the unconscious is vivid and tendentious: "it is a chaos, a melting-pot of seething excitations . . . it is not organized, produces no collective will, merely the striving to achieve satisfaction for the impulsive needs operating under the pleasure-principle" (416). This situation can be enlarged to address masses of men, the unnamed fascism of the day: "a whole mass-Ego" has been annihilated, "thanks to a moral devastation which is produced by worship of the unconscious, the glorification of its dynamic as the only life-promoting force. . . . For the unconscious, the Id, is primitive and irrational, is pure dynamic. It knows no values, no good or evil, no morality."[55]

The unconscious harbors imperturbable wishes, ancient and actual. Psycho-analytical therapeutics identifies these longings as part of the patient's past: they disturb the neurotic and can be erased only on being "recognized as belonging to the past, devalued and robbed of their charge of energy, by becoming conscious through the analytic procedure" (3). This procedure is anathema to the Ego, especially under current historical conditions, which, in the fascist masses, "is intoxicated by a worship of the unconscious to the point of being in a condition of subterranean dynamic" (3). This allusion to the contemporary German psyche is perspicuous when Mann writes of the Ego as "deaf to analysis: . . . the name of Freud must not be mentioned in its hearing" (4).

Mann's novelistic powers are on display in his presentation of *"seine Wenigkeit"*—the Ego—which asks to be cited at length. It begins harmlessly—and eloquently—enough: "As for the Ego itself, its situation is pathetic, well-nigh alarming. It is an alert, prominent, and enlightened little part of the Id." But the proposition is promptly enlarged by a simile that today would be considered a reprehensible stereotype of the Orientalist mind, "defined as the West's patronizing representations of 'The East.'"[56] Mann situates the rational Ego vis-à-vis the libidinal and aggressive Id *"much as Europe is a small and lively province of the greater Asia"* (emphasis added). This conceit has a date stamp on it, preceding by some forty years Edward Said's *Orientalism* of 1978.[57]

Mann's own embeddedness in this racialist sensibility calls for a full-scale treatment, which can be found in a luminous work by Professor Todd Kontje titled *Thomas Mann's World: Empire, Race, and the Jewish Question*, a study of Mann as "a writer whose personal prejudices reflected those of the world around him . . . and whose autobiographical fiction expressed not only the concerns of the German nation, as he liked to claim, but also of the world in an era of imperial conquest and global conflict."[58] The actors in the world of conquest and conflict of 1938 have changed, but Mann's orientalist stereotypes have varied little. He continues:

> The Ego is that part of the Id which became modified by contact with the outer world; equipped for the reception and preservation of stimuli; comparable to the integument with which any piece of living matter surrounds itself. . . . The relation with the outer world, Freud says, is decisive for the Ego, it is the Ego's task to represent the world to the Id—for its good! For without regard for the superior power of the outer world, the Id, in its blind striving towards the satisfaction of its instincts, would not escape destruction. The Ego takes cognizance of the outer world, it is mindful, it honorably tries to distinguish the objectively real from whatever is an accretion from its inward sources of stimulation. It is entrusted by the Id with the lever of action; but between the impulse and the action it has interposed the delay of the thought process, during which it summons experience to its aid and thus possesses a certain regulative superiority over the pleasure principle which rules supreme in the unconscious; correcting it by means of the principle of reality. But even so, how feeble it is? [*sic*] Hemmed in between the unconscious, the outer world, and what Freud calls the super-Ego, it leads a pretty nervous and anguished existence. Its own dynamic is rather weak. It derives its energy from the Id and in general has to carry out the latter's behests. It is fain to regard itself as the rider and the unconscious as the horse. But many a time it is ridden by the unconscious; and I take leave to add what Freud's rational morality prevents him from saying, that under some circumstances it makes more progress by this illegitimate means.

With horse and rider, Mann employs a time-honored metaphor from Plato's dialogue *Phaedrus* in order to evoke the unconscious inspirations known, from time to time, by other writers "of European rank." A good many members of the audience will have appreciated this trope.

The relation of the unconscious to myth and mythical imitation forms a vital bridge to Mann's literary concerns of the time: the imitable life depicted in Mann's epic *Joseph and His Brothers* and his own imitation of Goethe in *Lotte in Weimar*, a work he was just completing. Indeed, Mann's own life can be seen as an imitation of the recurrent ancient Near Eastern myth of the exiled hero.[59] The present essay proceeds by developing the idea that the apparently contingent conditions of one's life are unconsciously produced: one is oneself "the giver of all givens." Indeed, Mann claims this "perception of the apparently objective and accidental as a matter of the soul's own contriving [to be] the innermost core of psychoanalytic theory" (4). Ergo, one's unconscious is one's fate; and insofar as one is also the "secret theater manager" of the unconscious, then one is oneself the author—and not merely, on the best of occasions, the hard-pressed master—of one's fate. Something like this idea is Schopenhauer's gift to Mann; and thus inspired, Mann delights in discovering in an essay by "a scholar in the Freudian school" the related idea that the story of one's own life conforms to established conventions of "biography" (4).[60] This notion links one's unconscious with the fates of exemplars; one's "own" unconscious is in fact the residue of the enacted lives of others. *Laudatores temporis acti.* Finally, the goal of these remarks is to have Mann cite illustrative passages from his own *Joseph and His Brothers*—at this point a trilogy, although Princeton would see Mann's foray into a fourth volume, *Joseph the Provider.* The point about one's creating one's own conditions becomes in *Joseph* a "psychological theology." Abraham co-endows the God of the Hebrews with the properties of the divine; hence, they are reciprocal creators of divinity: "He [Abraham] perceived and brought Him forth." Self and world are one. Next, characters in the novels—for example, Eliezer—are not so much owners of their own lives as reproductions of their predecessors. Again, Self and world are one. This link was put nicely by a reader of *Joseph*: "Looking at his tutor, Jacob's chief servant, Eliezer, Joseph in his dreamy way sees him as a long row of historic Eliezer-figures, right-hand man to the head of the family, going back centuries; all the Eliezers speak through the mouth of the contemporary Eliezer."[61] This phenomenon—for "the typical is actually the mythical"—Mann calls "*Mythus*" and mythic captivation: "the mythus as lived is the epic idea embodied in my novel" (14). Mann ties up these strands elegantly: "The myth is the timeless schema, the pious formula into which life flows when it reproduces its traits out of the unconscious." Again: "This life as reanimation" of the prototype, the schema, "is this life as myth" (15).

Is the following statement true? According to Mann, "Christ's word on the Cross, about the ninth hour, that *Eli, Eli, lama sabachthani* was evidently not in the least an outburst of despair and disillusionment; but on the contrary a lofty messianic sense of self. For," Mann continues, "the phrase is not original, not a spontaneous outcry. It stands at the beginning of the Twenty-second Psalm, which from one end to the other is an announcement of the Messiah." Mann is satisfied that "Jesus was quoting Psalm 22, and the quotation meant: 'Yes, it is I!'" This reading figures as a requirement for the coherence of Mann's *idée fixe* but is scarcely acceptable to Jewish scholars of the Hebrew Bible, who will claim that the text has been falsified by Christian apologists to support a *prophecy* nowhere present in the psalm.[62]

Mann's lecture ends on a surprisingly auspicious note, seemingly inspired by the joy he feels writing this paean to the unconscious and Freud its "diviner." This joy would be an efflux of the joy he explicitly invokes while composing the mythoi of his *Joseph* novel:

> The Joseph of my novel is an artist, playing with his *imitatio dei* upon the unconscious string; and I know not how to express the feelings which possess me—something like a joyful sense of *divination of the future*—when I indulge in this encouragement of the unconscious to play, to make itself fruitful in a serious product, in a narrational meeting of psychology and myth, which is at the same time a celebration of the meeting between poetry and analysis. (15; emphasis added)

This joyful fusion of the activities of the conscious and unconscious agents— the first the subject of psychology, the second the creator of myth—strikes Mann as harbinger of a new humanism—the "third humanism" of Mann's credo "I Believe." For, "in the light of psychology [at] play upon the myth, there lie hidden seeds and elements of a new and coming sense of our humanity." Here Mann conceives the centerpiece of a new anthropology and with it a new humanism, "which we dimly divine and which will have experienced much that the earlier humanism knew not of. It will be a humanism standing in a different relation to the powers of the lower world, the unconscious, the Id: a relation bolder, freer, blither, productive of a riper art than any possible in our neurotic, fear-ridden, hate-ridden world." It is not crystal clear just how this mythopoeic agency of the conscious self will contribute to "The City of Man," but then again Mann explicitly imagines this new order as quite possibly "a poet's utopia." Perhaps, in some dark, devious, and wonderful manner, thinking it so will make it so. *That* activity in any case is a better alternative than acceding to the pathology of mass behavior.[63] It is as Blake's Los proclaims: "I MUST Create a System [which we may very well call "Myth"], or be enslav'd by another Man's."[64]

Introduction to *The Magic Mountain* for Students of Princeton University

Mann's introductory lecture to *The Magic Mountain* was delivered on May 10, 1939, in German, to advanced students of Princeton, who, afterwards, did respond with engaged questions, which speaks mightily in their favor, since this is not an easy text (GW 11:602–17). Readers may be familiar with an English version with the title "The Making of the *Magic Mountain*," which was printed in *The Atlantic* some fifteen years later.[65] One can follow the traces of its composition through Mann's own papers; and indeed scholars have done so quite thoroughly, identifying the contributions to Mann's essay by the erudite professor of German at Yale, Hermann Weigand, who had sent Mann his study of *The Magic Mountain* years earlier.[66] And something quite wonderful: a nineteen-year-old Harvard undergraduate named Howard Nemerov, who was to fulfill his talents as literary critic and poet, sent Mann a term paper that Mann found extraordinary.[67] It has been noted that if Mann had realized that one of these "curious fellows," as he termed his Princeton audience in a following diary entry—namely, an *undergraduate*—had been the author of the paper, he would hardly have cast even a cold eye on it. But as it was, it gave him all the mythic depth he needed to conceive of Hans Castorp's pursuit of the "mystery of man" as a search for a Holy Grail.

Although a quarter of the lecture is owed to Mann's borrowings from secondary literature, it nonetheless throws an intermittent bright light on his innermost concerns—intermittent, because the invocation of the categories of "*Steigerung*" (intensification) and alchemical "transubstantiation" to describe the hero's growth requires more than the odd paragraph to make good sense. But the talk is otherwise very much alive—for, one thing, with a piece of history. Swiss sanatoria for the treatment of tuberculosis, such as the Berghof of *The Magic Mountain*, tended to disappear in the years after World War I. Fewer families could afford the costs of keeping patients there for decades at a time. "Perhaps it is a general rule that epics descriptive of some particular phase of life tend to appear as it nears its end," Mann notes with historical precision, since most fin-de-siècle Swiss sanatoria have since been repurposed as "sports hotels" (42). It is a phenomenon, I'll add, parallel to the refitting of luxurious oceangoing liners as World War II troopships.

Mann wants it known that his life's work is a totality; to appreciate any given work, you must look backwards and forwards in his oeuvre. For example: "*Death in Venice* portrays the fascination of the death idea, the triumph of drunken disorder over the forces of a life consecrated to rule and discipline. In *The Magic Mountain* the same theme was to be humorously treated" (42). Here, of course, Mann's "looking backwards" in 1912 to *Death in Venice* with an antithetical intention did not produce a "forward" movement consistent with his plan. In *The Magic Mountain* the "death idea" is only occasionally a subject for humor. With Mann as one's "educator," one could exclaim, "How ironical!" I think it admirable that Mann gives priority to the energy of the work itself over the intentions of the author. "It is possible for a work to have its own will and purpose, perhaps a far more ambitious one than the author's. . . . The work must bring it forth and compel the task to completion" (42–43). How very timely—this work-intentional poetics!

Much of that new energy flowed in from another project that Mann undertook in the midst of writing *The Magic Mountain*, interrupting it: the notorious *Reflections of a Nonpolitical Man*. There we have the stimulus to the intellectual debates of Ludovico Settembrini the humanist and Leo Naphta the totalitarian. To Mann's alleged surprise, *The Magic Mountain* acquired a dazzling success among German readers. "The national crisis [of the years post–World War I] had produced in the general public precisely that alchemical 'keying up'" in response to the burning questions of the time that Castorp suffers and which bring about his adventures.

The book's deepest subject is time: "It is in a double-sense a time-romance." First, it means to represent the soul of an historical epoch—Europe before World War I. But its concern with time occurs at a deeper level through the hero's immersion "within the timeless" element of the "magic mountain" and the book's very form, "which attempts to give complete presentness at any given moment to the entire world of ideas which it comprises . . . in other words, to establish a magical *nunc stans*" (44).[68] Well, these are indeed other words, but what do they mean? Mann adds, not all-too-helpfully, "its aim is always and consistently to *be* that of which it speaks." If Mann were to accomplish this fusion of being and articulate linguistic conception on the page, he would be, in the perspective of contemporary literary theory, the first to have done so: he would have escaped the depredations of universal *différance*—an irrepressible agent of difference and delay with respect to the full accomplishment of any verbal meaning, not to mention the alleged raising up to full presentness of the very being of the thing signified. Still, that mode of *being* that Mann awards to his work might be understood as the aura of newness accompanying the thing or concept invoked, for him, in the very act of putting pen to paper. It is a subjective thrill, although Mann would have this parousia objectively accomplished—*nunc stans.* Furthermore, it would be additionally difficult to establish the *being* or *presentness* of such characters as Joachim Ziemssen, Claudia Chauchat, Mynheer Peeperkorn, Ludovico Settembrini, etcetera, when, in Mann's words, they "are nothing but exponents, representatives, emissaries from worlds, principalities, domains of the spirit" (44). Mann admitted that it would be hard for him to write in 1939 about the novel he wrote in the years between 1912 and 1924, being accustomed, after letting his pen drop, to consign his finished work to the better eternity of readers' reception . . . and move on. Boes observes that this would be an extraordinarily counterintuitive claim to make in 1939, with Nazi publicists striving to excel in abusing his productions—the "decadent" *Magic Mountain,* and add on: the "Jewish" *Joseph* and the furiously treasonous Goethe of *Lotte in Weimar* (TB 113).

The crucial adventure in *The Magic Mountain* is the hero's and necessarily the engaged reader's journey into "the dark, mysterious side of life," which includes death, disease, seances, Romantic music, and sexual intercourse. "There are," Hans Castorp once says, "two ways to life: one is the regular, direct, and good way; the other is bad, it leads through death, and that is the way of genius" (44). This second way involves the time-honored experience of *initiation*—a concept whose relevance Mann has from Professor Hermann Weigand. Mann devotes even more space to the contribution of the Harvard sophomore Howard Nemerov, which turns on the figure of the Quester Hero. Here is Mann-Nemerov:

> The hero, be it Gawain or Galahad or Perceval, is the seeker, the quester, who ranges heaven and hell, makes terms with them, and strikes a pact with the unknown, with sickness and evil, with death and the other world, with the supernatural, the world that in *The Magic Mountain* is called "questionable." He is forever searching for the Grail—that is to say, the Highest: knowledge, wisdom, consecration, the philosophers' stone, the *aurum potabile,* the elixir of life. (45)

Here we have a sublime echo of Mann's doctrine of the coming new humanism outlined in "I Believe" (see chapter 2, *supra*)—but a belief in man hard to come by, as Mann well knows, in the universe of atrocity burgeoning in 1939. And so, *en bonne pédagogue,* he will suppress what was the case in Europe in 1914, when Castorp is "snatched downwards" from *The Magic Mountain* to death in a muddy battlefield; or in Germany, in 1923, when, writing of Castorp's destruction, he witnesses the debasement of "humanism" by hyperinflation and the Nazi Beer Hall Putsch; or, in Princeton, in 1939, when, speaking to an audience of America-first undergraduates who wanted nothing of war, he would conceal the spectral materialization in *The Magic Mountain* of Castorp's dead cousin, bearing prophetically the scars of war, in uniform and wearing the *Stahlhelm*—the iconic steel helmet that was not produced until 1916, two years after the novel's fictional end.[69] Instead, Mann will insist on a famous conclusion, rich in humanistic faith:

> If he [Castorp] does not find the Grail, yet he divines it, in his deathly dream [in the chapter called "Snow"] before he is snatched downwards from his heights into the European catastrophe. It is the idea of the human being, the conception of a future humanity that has passed through and survived the profoundest knowledge of disease and death. The Grail is a mystery, but humanity is a mystery too. For man himself is a mystery, and all humanity rests upon reverence before the mystery that is man. (45)

It is the last word of a tragic humanism. The horror was in (temporary) remission in the classroom that day.

The Transposed Heads—A Legend of India

While writing this surrealistic Indian story in Princeton between January and August 1940, Mann considered it an "intermezzo" in his life's work, but afterwards he thought it quite wonderful.[70] Part of his liking for it might well be the past associations it invokes. In a novella that opposes and then transposes heads and bodies, we have an obsession from Mann's earlier stories.[71] There, heads and bodies were forever opposed as objects, in the best case, of *reciprocal* longing. But more often than not it was the head that did all the longing—recall the cerebral Tonio Kröger and Gustav von Aschenbach, heroes of what Mann, in *Joseph and His Brothers*, will call "the romance of the soul, its love affair with matter and the 'melancholy sensuality' that inspired it."[72] The soulless bodies of the other (the naive Hans Hansen and the ephebe Tadziu) did not need to long for anything, and that is their charm. Mann's eudaemonic Indian legend gives the head the grace of figuring as an object of longing as well.

For our concern, the main point about this enterprise is that it *departs* from the deeply entrenched, *history*-based writing of *Lotte in Weimar* and bears on Mann's political environment as its dialectical negative—a dance out of time.[73] Mann had his own doubts about this adventure, as we might recall: "A reading like 'Eheglück' [Tolstoy's "Family Happiness"] in its realistic and moral seriousness of course does not encourage it. [One] feels the gap between this healthy-serious sphere and frolicsomeness and fantasy, which is much more afflicted [*leidend*, also "ailing"] than that naturalism" (T4 16). But Mann will continue the attempt: at the time he craved to breathe an atmosphere far removed from the toxic political climate of 1940.

This story tells of the intense friendship between two young men—one, Shridaman (in the American translation; Schridaman in the German), a cerebral, slightly higher-caste, paler merchant with a soft body; and Nanda, a blacker, "goat-nosed" blacksmith's apprentice with a hard body—both of whom love the same young woman. The story arises as an act of friendship as well between the author and his source. Mann was taken with the account of this tale in Heinrich Zimmer's unfinished *Die Geschichte vom indischen König mit dem Leichnam* (a volume subsequently enlarged and edited by Joseph Campbell as *The King and the Corpse: Tales of the Soul's Conquest of Evil*).[74] The title page of American translation of *The Transposed Heads* reads: "To Heinrich Zimmer, The Great Indian Scholar, Returned with Thanks." It is Mann's grateful retelling of Zimmer's tale.[75]

Each of the friends—*mirabile dictu*—will chop off his own head: Shridaman first in an act of contrition and devotion to the goddess Kali; Nanda out of mimetic desire for his decapitated friend. Sita, who, although Shridaman's wife, loves both men, is distraught; but she is empowered by Kali to restore the heads to the trunks to which they belong. In her excitement—by an accident owed to "blind chance"—she attaches the head of each to the body of the other. The result is to establish the superiority of the head to the body, because "between sobs and laughter," it is the head of each that she addresses, confessing her mistake. And what is wonderful and to my mind most telling in the tale is the fact that "it was manifest that neither of them was angry at Sita for her mistake, but both actually found pleasure in their new guise."[76] Rarely has a text more openly acknowledged its substance to be an effect of the very act of writing. The pleasure the friends take in this transposition of identities is at once the pleasure that Mann takes in this transposition of *forms*: here, his dominant aesthetic drive elects a (novelistic) form that until recently was reserved, by and large, for a "realistic and morally serious" substance. True, Mann was at pains—somewhat against the grain—to underline the comedic elements as well of *Lotte in Weimar*. But *Transposed Heads* is a "first approach to the French-surrealistic sphere [Cocteau], to which . . . I [Mann] have long been drawn" (T4 16).

Shridaman exults in his wholeness:

I count myself the happiest of men. I have always wished I could have a
bodily form like this; when I feel the muscles of my arms, look at my shoul-
ders and down at my magnificent legs, I am seized with unrestrained delight, and say to myself that from now on I shall hold my head high, in quite
a new way; first in the consciousness of my new strength and beauty, and
second because my spiritual leanings will now be in harmony with my
physical build.[77]

It is not long, however, before Mann's irrepressible play of contradictions appears. "Of course, my dear friends," continues Shridaman, "there is a certain
sadness in this, that the strange is now become my own and no longer an object of desire and admiration" (121–22). Mann-Shridaman knows the erotic
flair of the ascetic artist's *longing* for wholeness, that decadent ecstasy: sex in
theory. His longing will become more marked; it will prove his undoing: "His
intelligent mind straightway found something sad in the fact that the strange
had now become his and was no longer an object of admiration—in other
words, that he was now himself that after which he had yearned" (168). But we
are not yet at the tipping point.

Shridaman is content for the moment, but what now will poor Nanda—if
it is still Nanda—think of his lot: the goat-shaped nose joined to a flabby
trunk? He—and his narrator—have decided to refine the adjective: the body
that has been represented as soft ("*weich*") and indeed puffy ("*schwammig*")
and rounded, no less, with belly fat ("*mit einigem Schmer*") is now, though still
fatty ("*speckig*"), suddenly slender ("*fein*") and even "new and finer" ("*neu und
feiner*"); and so Nanda declares, to the incredulity, surely of all, that he has
always wanted such a body (8, 116, 123, 126).[78] But this transposition, which
cannot really be imagined as happy for him—gluing his goat's nose onto a
plump trunk with weak arms—is an opportunity, in a scene requiring elation,
for him to have a wonderful thought. Consider, first, that on entering the
temple where the bloodshed had taken place, Sita observes that "the attraction
between heads and trunks was not so strong as one might have expected"
(114). Of course, she is relaying Mann's droll suggestion that one's head might
be just as glad to abandon its body for the body of a friend as remain attached
to its old trunk. And so, Nanda, commenting generously on his transposition,
observes that the very force that has so perfectly united his head to Shridaman's body is the force of their original friendship: otherwise, the weld could

not have taken. Through Sita's mischief, both have achieved a happy incorporation of the other as a marriage of two minds.

Now, however, a worrisome complication arises: Sita is pregnant from the body of her husband, the once soft body of the original Shridaman. But that body now belongs to the Nanda-head, and it is Nanda who suddenly asserts his paternity: bodies, not heads, make children. So, what can the outcome of this misology be? One answer is brilliant and involves Mann's recourse to an event in Goethe's *Elective Affinities*. The mother Charlotte loves the Captain but is pregnant by her husband Eduard. The birth is miraculous, and the child bears the features not of the man she slept with but the man she imagined. The Nanda-head on the Brahman's soft body declares, "Sita of the lovely curves [is] my wife and her fruit of my begetting," to which Shridaman replies: "Is it really? I should not have dared to assert it, when your present body was still mine and slept at Sita's side. For it was not that body that she *really* embraced . . . instead it was the one I now call my own" (125; emphasis added). Problem solved; unity obtained. And the real Nanda, the Nanda-head, would appear to have lost everything. But no: Sita now makes plain that even before the transposition, she had looked with love, not at Nanda's body, but to his head and into his eyes. However, feeling forever his great loyalty to Shridaman, Nanda had not returned her gaze and held his eyes downcast. It is proven: without his head, even his magnificent body is nothing—"pathetic and insignificant," declares Sita, who nonetheless loves its present possessor, Shridaman, as well; and so, the dispute reigns as to who now is Sita's proper husband and will give her the affection she inspires. Only a sage can save them.

Finding the savant Kamadamana in the dark wood will not be easy, especially as Nanda, who had found him once before, "had done so in another body, and this hampered his intuition and sense of locality" (an additional suggestion that his transposition has not rewarded him with the best of both bodies) (135). Now, it is true that once before Nanda had sought the counsel of this wise man "on the subject of the solitary life." So, the question arises: Will Kamadamana recognize Nanda? He seems to: "'At least I might recognize your face; but your form seems in the meantime to have gone through a certain refining process, *which I suppose I may ascribe to your former visit.*' 'It did me a great deal of good,' Nanda answered evasively" (138; emphasis added).

The wise man's incomprehension is richly significant for the reader—and I will venture, for the author as well. In writing these sentences, Mann quietly exults in producing a genuinely funny moment. This is no trifling matter: it belongs to Mann's repeated claim that at the very least his own writing had provided the world with a bit of elegant entertainment. But the wise man's incomprehension also comes as a shock: it is the sense of the yawning disparity between what has taken place—the transposition, with its very serious consequences—and his casually produced ignorance. It is not difficult to feel that disparity as an efflux of Mann's ever-present awareness that this "intermezzo" does not bear, except "evasively," on the world outside his library—a world threatened with barbaric ruin, murder, and despair.

The wise man, isolated from life (and however farcically portrayed), emerges as a noble parody of the author in his asceticism and pretense to a higher wisdom. "In short," declares Kamadamana pertinently, "asceticism is a bottomless vat, because the temptations of the spirit are mingled therein with the temptations of the flesh, until the whole thing is like the snake that grows two heads as soon you cut off one" (141). These temptations are especially familiar to *this* author. Again, like any author of a certain complexity, Kamadamana invites "all life's manifold uncleanliness" into his "study"—a hollow tree!—but not for his entertainment: he will resist it, promptly refining it into a linguistic nullity by the power of his aesthetic indifference. A stunning phrase follows, which will return us, for a moment, to Mann's preceding work, *Lotte in Weimar*: "Here he [Kamadamana] bade [his two] guests sit down, which they hastened to do, in all modesty, well knowing that they were here only for his asceticism, so to speak, to sharpen his teeth on" (143). They are like Lotte, when she comes to realize that she had once "sat" with the young Goethe only for the "ascetic" exercise of his writing *The Sufferings of Young Werther*; and it is to make Goethe aware of this illicit appropriation of her being that she has made the trip to Weimar. Further, as if to intensify the association of author and sage, Kamadamana proceeds to describe in lush verse the copulation of bodies in rhyme, in phrases seemingly torn from a Wagner libretto, with the contrary intent of despising it and encouraging in its place—renunciation! Here is Mann, once again, in *his* chosen medium. And Nanda, let it be stressed again, draws the short straw as Kamadamana judges the man who wears the better head to be the rightful husband. Now Nanda must confront his only fate: the hermetic asceticism of a neophyte.

Shridaman and Sita, lawfully wedded husband and wife, enjoy a paradisiacal affection. But this paradise is, once again, only a dream, "for in paradise, surely, that which is forbidden and that which is granted, so diverse here below, must there become one. The lovely forbidden must be crowned with legality, while the legal attains to all the charms of the forbidden" (154).

This fusion cannot last. The head of Shridaman begins to assert its absolute prerogative to shape anew the strange body to which it has been yoked; and it is not long before the body has assumed the worst of Shridaman's original features—his skinny arms, narrow chest, and even a bit of belly fat. To pile Pelion on Ossa, his face decays as well—it is unclear by what logic—for it gets fleshy, droopy, indeed, goat-like (!) "The final product was a Shridaman with a finer Nanda-body and a coarser Shridaman head; there was no longer anything right about him at all" (169–70). What, the reader might ask, are Nanda-features now doing on the head of Shridaman, when the head, we've been told, holds all the reins of change? Never mind. What is especially deplorable for Shridaman about his transmogrification, on the spiritual side, is that it invites Sita to begin to consider the sort of changes that would now have taken place in Nanda, whom she once loved to distraction. "She definitely suspected that a refining process must have taken place in the loyal friend-head which now sat atop the husband-body, corresponding to the refinement of the friend-body now owned by the husband-head" (170). This thought drives her out of paradise, out of a settled embrace in her husband's arms.

After the birth of her son Samadhi-Andhaka, whose paternity, to her mind, remains in dispute, this piercing thought turns to action, and Sita resolves to find Nanda in his forest hideaway and show him the boy—"show him his delightful offspring, that he too might have his joy in him" (174). Nanda, it should be noted, in line with his original constitution, has not taken the vows of the ascetic very seriously. Despite his sadness, he has been gorging on the forest fruits abundantly at hand and will even eat a fire-roasted bird. "In short, he was merely contemplative [while eating] after the fashion of any disappointed and dejected man" (178). Now, on Sita's miraculous reappearance, his response is full of the yearning of "body and soul" that he has never stopped feeling: *they* consummate their "wedded bliss." But this bliss will not outlast its consummation. Shridaman himself is suddenly there, bringing a terrible wisdom, indeed a shadow from the world of Mann's other great concern: it is put beautifully, in the language of this story, but its basis is recognizable in the horrors of the Nazi conquest: "For in the madness and divisions of this life," intones Shridaman, "it is the lot of human beings to stand in one another's light, and in vain do the better-constituted long for an existence in which the laughter of one would not be the weeping of another" (185). In *The City of Man*, we read, "There is, indeed, no liberty but one: the right, which is a duty, of making oneself and others free through absolute allegiance to the final goal of man. All other liberties are the rewards of battle. There is no comfort but one: pride in the duty performed. All other comforts are the ornaments of victory" (C 31–32).

The outcome for the three lovers is the devastating truth that no worldly arrangement exists to satisfy them. (It is important to rule out the sacrilege of polyandry.) And so, continues Shridaman, "Since you [Sita] cannot live with both of us, I am certain that . . . Nanda will agree with me that neither of us can live, and nothing remains but to put off the division we have exchanged and unite our essences once more with the All"—in death! in sacrifice! in the flame of a funeral pyre! (187). Nanda is of one mind with Shridaman: "You know too that I was always resolved not to outlive you" (189): proof is his voluntary beheading after Shridaman had beheaded himself. Sita, who has warrior blood in her veins and will not be left behind, demands, quite grandly, "that Nanda build the funeral pyre for three. As I have shared the couch of life with you both, so shall also death's fiery bed unite us three" (190). The festival proceeds, but not until each of the friends, pretending to duel, has stabbed the other through the heart; whereupon Sita, now properly a widow, lies down between them and burns away, but even "the heat was cool to her in the joy of being united with her two beloveds" (194). In a real world of murder, here death regains its dignity.

As an attempt to humanize a myth, this "Legend of India" shares the same intention as *Joseph and His Brothers*.[79] Writing to Karl Kerényi, the renowned scholar of mythology, Mann declared, "It is essential that myth be taken away from intellectual fascism and transmuted for humane ends. I have for a long time done nothing else" (TB 104).

Joseph in Princeton

On vacation from Princeton in Brentwood, California, on October 5, 1940, Mann wrote the last pages of *The Transposed Heads*. He then felt obliged to find (*finden*) or—better—"contrive" (*erfinden*) the "lust and love" he needed to complete his Hebrew epic, which he had tentatively begun two months before (T4 129, 160).

Joseph and His Brothers retells in elegant, imaginative detail—one scholar writes "lusciously detailed"—the stories of the lineage of Jacob and Joseph from chapters 27–50 of Genesis, silhouetting the topics of exile and the Jewish and Pharaonic finding of the One God.[80] An incisive digest of its themes lists "love, hate, trickery, sibling rivalry, vengeance, reconciliation" against "the contrast between the relatively simple life of Joseph's people and the sophisticated civilization of imperial Egypt; the notion of progress; the idea of consciousness as something evolving and of the covenant between the human and the divine. . . ."[81]

The first two volumes are titled, respectively, *The Stories of Jacob* and *Young Joseph*, the third, *Joseph in Egypt*, which Mann regarded as his masterpiece. Now his task was to improve on what he had written with a fourth volume called *Joseph the Provider* (*Joseph, der Ernährer*) and fulfill a "grand edifice" of myths, about myths, and of mythic proportions, responding, as he acknowledged, to the tetralogy of Wagner's *Ring*. In recalling the intermittent composition of *Joseph*, Mann describes being

> highly motivated to complete this narrative . . . and my desire to do so was only strengthened by certain mythic memories, playful parallels not inappropriate to the subject matter. I stood [*though not physically!*] where Wagner had once stood when, after the grand interpolation of *Tristan* and *Meistersinger,* he again took up work on his dramatic epic, the vast fairy tale of *The Ring of the Nibelung.* True, my method of dealing with myth was in essence closer to the humor of Goethe's "Classic Walpurgisnacht" than to Wagnerian pathos; but the unanticipated evolution that the story of Joseph had taken had, I am certain, always been secretly influenced by memories of Wagner's grand edifice of motifs, was a successor to its intentions. Playing with themes invented long before, I needed to reshape and elaborate them all for a crowning convergence and conclude my three previous fairy-tale operas with a *Götterdämmerung* of high delight. I was looking forward to it—and yet I hesitated to begin. . . . The reason for my timidity was simply that I feared an anticlimax.[82]

Mann overcame his trepidation and closed down this vast project on January 4, 1943.

At Princeton, Mann was never fully detached from the work; a vast audience of engaged readers would not let him be. They wrote to him soon after his arrival, questioning him, for one thing, about anachronisms. Here, promptly, is one such "luscious" detail. Mann had presented Jacob and Joseph preparing a Passover festival some four centuries before the Israelites had fled to Egypt. But Passover celebrates their manumission from Egypt and their return from exile. Mann, tireless, would not fail to answer his correspondents, in this one instance explaining that

> the so-called modern Passover had its precursor in a much older celebration of semi-pagan character, which was known even before Joseph's time. This fact has been borne out by scholars of ancient mythology and history, who have confirmed the correctness of my contention. The old Passover had to do with astral bodies and the worship of the stars. Nergal,

whom Joseph mentions, was a solar deity in Babylonia who represented the sun of noon time and summer solstice[!].[83]

Here, Mann defends against anachronism; in other moods, he effortlessly accommodates anachronisms to his story.[84]

In spring 1941, after having left Princeton for good, Mann completed parts 1 ("The Second Pit") and 2 ("The Summons") of the seven parts constituting the fourth and final volume. (In the original these "parts" are called "Hauptstücke"—not merely "Chapters" but more nearly "Principal Parts"— even, grandly, "Centerpieces.") Much has been made of the fact that this volume was written entirely in America and is steeped in allusions to American life, especially to the works and personality of Mann's much-loved Franklin Delano Roosevelt. Mann explicitly shaped the mature Joseph, who suggests to Pharaoh the meaning of his notorious dreams of famine and plenty, "in the image of 'the American Hermes and highly skilled messenger of wisdom whose New Deal is reflected in the magic administration of the economy,' which includes Social Security law and dam and irrigation projects on the model of the Tennessee Valley Authority."[85] (One still needs to point out, as does the critic Clement Greenberg, that this redistribution of wealth was made under the auspices of a dynastic tyranny and certainly not under the conditions of an American democracy!)[86]

Since Mann's exile also involves a reconstruction of his identity, with many hardships on its path, critics have been inclined to see negative features of what Adorno called "the damaged life" ("*das beschädigte Leben*") embedded in *Joseph the Provider*. For one thing, the volume begins, after a Goethean fugue, with Joseph condemned to many years in prison and concludes with his exclusion from the "leadership" of Jacob's tribes.[87] Just as Joseph is punished for the crime of ogling Potiphar's wife Zuleika, which he did not commit, Mann, in nervous sympathy, might have had a frisson of fear—Boes writes—of being interned at this time despite his "impeccable antifascist credentials" (TB 196).

This grim view, however, is not every reader's experience of the novel, which is rich in intellectual play, and, for the most part, is sunlit, cheerful, and truly funny, conceived in the radius of the two Egyptian sun-gods Amun and Atôn. In Mann's words, echoing Nietzsche's *Gay Science*, it is is "translucent, cheerful . . . and serene."[88] These judgments confirm Hermann Broch's opinion of Mann's second volume *Young Joseph*, which he found "charming, enchanting, clever."[89] Our frame requires us to limit our discussion to the two Princeton "Centerpieces," but they should give us a pleasant taste of the whole.

Prelude in Higher Echelons

The fourth *Joseph* opens with an extraordinary feat of theological wit and imagination in a Prelude reminiscent of Goethe's "Heavenly Prologue" to *Faust*.[90] Mann locates his narrator among the "Higher Echelons" of the cosmos and describes the conversations of these higher officers, who are angels, concerning God's creation of the extraordinary creature man, a being equipped, like themselves, with a higher consciousness but, like animals, with the power to procreate: "We will create man—in the image of the angels, and yet fruitful!"[91] Is that a wise creation? From early on, Mann had located man, this troublesome figure, between the angels and the beasts, and in fact had done so explicitly in his essay "I Believe." For with man, the creation of nothing less than the possibility—and thereafter the reality—of evil is achieved. But man's evildoing is not without its wider facility: it gives the Almighty—so the fable goes—endless new forms of activity hitherto unknown: pardoning, raising on high, etcetera. "One needed only to think of the exercise of grace and mercy, of judgment and correction, of the emergence of merit and guilt, of reward and punishment" (1043).

Ergo, with evil comes its dialectical opposite, goodness—a term occupying a very high place in God's—and Mann's—moral vocabulary; and in this light there comes a larger invention, a commitment not without its dark side: the Almighty is devilishly persuaded to grant unique favor to the "sacred body politic" (*"göttliches Volksleib"*) of Israel, a people who will nonetheless suffer greatly from the evil they do and the evil inflicted on them. (This divine attraction to fleshly embodiment is a prelude to the Fall—with the implicit parallel, as Eve to the apple, so God to the nation of Israel.) Mann's awareness of the Judeocide in 1943, however lightly and loftily recast, haunts this scene: "The ambition, the attempt [of the Almighty, on the devil Sammael's advice] to be a tribal god, through the union of the cosmic God with one tribe, could never come to a good end—or at best might come to a good end only after lengthy detours, after much embarrassment, disappointment, and embitterment" (1049).

Joseph, Part One: "The Second Pit"

Joseph Recognizes His Tears

At the outset we find Joseph—"a favorite, a piece of conceit, a dreamer of dreams, a little fruit from the tree of him [Abraham] who had first hit upon the notion of being a means of self-awareness . . . fallen into the pit, into the dungeon, into the hole . . . because his stupidity has run wild, because he has let love, just as he had once let hate, run wildly out of control" (1045). How will he be rescued and—having suffered the slander contrived by Potiphar's wife—be raised on high? For Joseph is forever accompanied "by a lofty awareness of destiny" and was not meant to be lying forever in the bottom of an oxen barge on the Nile—dressed in a slave's loincloth, his elbows tied together—en route to prison, to Hell (1053). This descent, though gradual, is a mythic reprise of his first disgrace when, in volume 2—*Young Joseph*—"Joseph is Cast into the Well." In that scene, we have, by a general reader's agreement, a taste of the mob violence raging in Germany at the time the chapter was written, from January 1931 to June 1932. Joseph's brothers

> all leapt up in savagely precise simultaneity and hurled themselves at him. They fell on him like a pack of starved wolves on their prey; . . . they looked as if they were about to tear him into at least fourteen pieces. . . . "Off, off, off!" they gasped and shouted, and it was clear they meant the *ketônet*—the robe of symbols, the veiled garment—it had to come off him. (451)

They beat him bloody and toss him into the bottom of a well. But the coloring of this second fall into "The Second Pit" is that of the sunlit "Egyptian heaven"—very different from the "rot and horrors" of the bottom of the well.

———

It can be convenient and enticing to draw wisdom sentences from *Joseph*— they abound and hit home as Mann's truths. We are on the barge with Joseph and the flunkey who guards him but whom Joseph treats with scorn. Joseph has imagined that in this *barge,* heading for Lower Egypt and a dungeon, he is no longer the boy who was beaten and buried but, in some sense, *is* once again Atum-Rê—the deity, the "finisher of the world," journeying together with the great Usir (Latin, Osiris: "King of the Underworld") in their *barque*; and he makes free with this comparison. The watchman—Kha'ma't of the house of books and the pantry—is appalled, but never mind:

> Take it however you must [thus Joseph]. I did not beg you to sit down beside me, for I am just as happy alone, perhaps even a bit happier, and know how to entertain myself without you. . . . That a man can entertain himself and not spend his life like some dumb beast is really the point after all, and the heights to which he can bring his diversion are what matter (1060).

Such a height can be measured as the *mythic* dimension, the force of the factor of allusion. Joseph has been described as marked "by a meditative play of thought . . . the dearest and sweetest form of . . . [which] was allusion; and whenever events in his carefully monitored life grew rich with allusion and circumstances proved transparent for a higher correspondence, then he was happy" (1053).

The Warden of the Prison

There were times when Mann considered his Indian novella *The Transposed Heads* time misspent, a diversion from his chief predilection of completing *Joseph,* the centerpiece of his literary career. The composition of *Lotte,* with its insistent narrative complications, also stood in the way. But it would be wrong—Manichean—to put the shorter novels on the side of dilettantism and Joseph on the side of a countable life work, for *Joseph the Provider* is devoted to literary strategies tried out in *Lotte* and in *The Transposed Heads.* In this sense, *Joseph* is not a wings-away from work that had occupied Mann in Princeton.

Consider: Joseph is marched to the prison citadel and brought before a susceptible prison head, Mai-Sakhme, who, for one thing, is "dreamily" disturbed by Joseph's self-confidence and personal beauty—"the handsomest twenty-seven-year-old in the Two Lands" (1066). The captain's thoughts flow into the channel running through Joseph's letter—a charge sheet: Joseph, it says, has cast lascivious looks at "a woman in the house of a stranger—[Potiphar]." How can that have happened? the captain wonders. Hasn't Joseph read the precepts of the great Imhotep, physician and scribe, which forbid "such foolishness"—this sage who understands incomparably well "how to comfort those who toss and turn . . . [who] understands the body's pleasures and pains, its fluids and functions, toxins and talents"—all of which are circumspect ways of designating the body in lust? Joseph does not hesitate to declare that he knows these precepts by heart. The erudite captain is inclined to be lenient:

> It takes two for any love affair, which always leaves the question of guilt rather opaque, and although its resolution may appear quite clear to the outside world—because one party, the man of course, takes the entire guilt upon himself—it may also be advisable yet again to discriminate in private between speech and reality. When I hear of a woman's being seduced by a man, I chuckle to myself, for I find it rather droll, and think: . . . [O]ne knows all too well who has been charged with the art of seduction since the

days of the god. . . . Do you know "The Tale of the Two Brothers"? he asked Joseph directly . . . (1069)

This is another text that Joseph knows by heart. And here we have an echo of the pleasure Mann had truly taken in the writing of the Indian novella: he loved the applause and laughter in his library when he read the most extravagant parts aloud. Now, in *Joseph*, the narrator, Mann's mythy-minded "vice-exister," proceeds to summarize "The Tale of the Two Brothers"—this "excellent piece of fiction" that, like *The Transposed Heads*, has all the flair of the archaic fable of transformation. At one point "the queen is impregnated by a splinter of persea wood that flies into her mouth." At another, one of the brothers, Bata, having been ravished by "the wife of Anup," uses the leaf of a bulrush," even before the eyes of his unnamed brother, "to cut off his manhood [!], giving it to the fish to eat [!]." Bata is then transformed into Hapi the bull who, after declaring his majesty, reveals himself to be Bata intact: "I am Bata! Behold, I still live and am god's holy bull!"

In recounting the legend, Mann's mythic imagination is free to contrive a happy correspondence, in the world of the novel, between the present and the past, the at-hand and the sacred. He supports his practice with the device of the leitmotif, also a way to satisfy his longing to overcome in his literary work "the laws of time and continuity"; for this "magic formula"—the leitmotif works both ways, linking the past with the future . . . to preserve the inward unity and abiding presentness of the whole at each moment."[92]

The mention of Potiphar's wife could bring us to Mann's engaging portrayal of her in his Princeton lecture "On Myself," composed shortly after her appearance in volume 3. He has been describing the success of his first published story, "Little Mr. Friedemann," whose core theme runs through all his work, indeed "holding it together":

> The main character is a person neglected by Nature, but he finds himself able to come to terms with his fate in a wisely gentle peaceful philosophic way, and he has attuned his life entirely to repose, contemplation, and peace. The appearance of a remarkably beautiful and yet cold and cruel woman means the invasion of passion into this guarded life, which upsets the whole structure and annihilates the quiet hero himself.

Now what has this catastrophe to do with Potiphar's wife? Answer: Everything. *She* has not been neglected by Nature: Her name, in Jewish and Muslim scripture, is Zuleika—a word of Pashtun origin, meaning "The Radiant One." Furthermore, as *nomen est omen* (for Mann, at least), she is very "mindful . . .

of her beauty" (891). "The strange God"—Eros-Dionysus—"stretches the bow" of its presence through Mann's oeuvre, reaching even to *Joseph*, for "what is the passion of Potiphar's wife for the young foreigner other than again the crash, the collapse of a highly cultivated poised attitude, laboriously won by judgment and renunciation: the defeat of civilization, the howling triumph of the suppressed world of instinct?" (B 34).

We return to the book-intoxicated prison warden, who in turn is moved to tell the story of his "first love, who at the same time was also his second" (1070). Here, we encounter again the elating correspondence of different temporal orders, recounted within an injected story. This is the device—the "ring" structure—that readers of *Lotte* will recall from chapters 4 and 5, in which Mann inserts Adele Schopenhauer's lengthy account of the louche love of August Goethe for Agnes's friend Ottilie von Pogwisch, who is better than he. This story of the commandant's first, second, and virtual third love concludes this round of mythic recurrences: these women whom Mai-Sakhme adores from afar are all part of a single line, the daughters being, as it were, mothers of the women who bore them.

In a following give-and-take with Mai-Sakhme, Joseph answers challenging questions dealing with domestic economy and the building trades: his answers are confident and precise, whereupon, his talent being recognized—and now appropriately exploited—he is promoted to oversee a bunch of men who, like oxen and asses, will have to haul stone so hectically that they are in perpetual danger of dying of dehydration. If Joseph is himself mythy-minded, he is also analytical.

Of Goodness and Cleverness

We are plunged at once into a witty Old Egyptian medicinal fugue, replete with worms and odd electuaries. It appears that Mai-Sakhme—prison warden, scribe, and lover—is also a physician running a bizarre laboratory in the citadel tower of Zawi-Rê. It is an occasion for Mann to display his twofold passion for medicine and archaic vocabularies. Before long, Mai-Sakhme intuits that Joseph—this "I am he" who is now called Osarsiph, an Egyptian paraphrase of Joseph's epithet—is *blessed*: he wears the mantle of the divine. And to a real extent, Joseph fulfills the expectation aroused by this semi-divine newcomer as one who will usher in a new epoch. This expectation redounds to the hermeneutic imagination of Mai-Sakhme:

[E]ven the gentlest traces, memories, and hints in the traits of some phenomenon were sufficient for him to see in it the fullness and reality of what
was merely hinted at—and in Joseph's case that was the figure of this long-
expected bringer of salvation, who comes to put an end to all that is old and
boring and, amid the jubilation of all mankind, to establish a new epoch.
About such a figure, of which Joseph showed some traces, there hovers the
nimbus of the divine. (1082)

Joseph brings order into the quarries and granaries and kitchens and in-
stitutes a fairer system of punishments and rewards. Whereas under the old
regime slave workers who fainted were obliged to faint twice more before
qualifying for medical treatment—merely to have fainted once or twice
meant being suspected of malingering—under Joseph's new and benevolent
regime, they had only to faint twice before being carted off to the infirmary.
Furthermore, in the evening hours he acts as literary advisor to Mai-Sakhme,
who has written a story telling how he loved the "same" woman twice (and
then, a virtual third time) and now needs to get it into the best possible form
for inscription, in stunning black and red, into papyrus. Hearing of these joint
literary and "apothecarial pursuits," we are confirmed in our earlier surmise:
Mai-Sakhme's affection for his educator—the physician and scribe Imhotep,
who is expert on the "toxins and talents" of the body—has an erotic bias. "For
Mai-Sakhme was particularly interested in this newcomer [Joseph] as a student of love" (we recall Joseph's "personality and fate"); and inasmuch as love
is "the primary playground for all gratifying literature"—the commandant
being absorbed in the mystery of falling in love with the same woman once,
twice, and in principle a third time—"the commandant felt [for this 'field'] a
warm and deep . . . sympathy" (1084).

Here, Mann makes a final conceptual point, which could come as a surprise: this chapter is titled, after all, "Of Goodness and Cleverness." You would
think that this phrase forecasts renewed praise of Joseph, who is no stranger
to these qualities. But in fact, they are assigned to Mai-Sakhme on subtle
grounds: his goodness is proved by his having been clever enough to perceive
the nimbus of the divine surrounding Joseph. The distinctive exercise of cleverness that intuits signs of the divine "with reverence" confirms the goodness
of the observer (1082). We will let this claim float on the Nile of Mann's fiction.
"Goodness" is a key term in Mann's moral lexicon; he welcomes the opportunity to set it down; and this section of Joseph deepens the idea.

The Gentlemen

In November 1940, Mann wrote in his diary, thinking of the pages of *Joseph the Provider*, that "the worldly adventures that come"—namely, the convulsions of Europe—"must not disturb their calm and their cheerfulness." His intention is on display in this section, the most playful piece we have so far seen in volume 4. To feel the play, one must remember, in the first instance, that "irony" is the jack-of-all-trades narrative mode that Mann claims for himself—it is his authorial signature. And now we are prepared and ready to delight in his smile in the following.

Mai-Sakhme has instructed Joseph how he is to treat the two newly arrived gentlemen: they are Pharaoh's baker, who has been accused of baking his master's bread with chalk; and Pharaoh's wine steward, who has been accused of pouring out his master's wine with flies. They once bore very grand titles as noblemen of a high rank, although their future in Zawi-Rê is hardly auspicious. Joseph is urged by Mai-Sakhme to "keep a happy medium. Respect tinged with gloom would be about right, in my opinion." "'I'm not much of a master of gloom,' Joseph said. 'Perhaps one could lend the respect a tinge of irony.'" "'That might be good too,' the captain replied."

And so, the two captives are supplied with some of the necessities of the courtly life they had led. Mascara, of course, is indispensable: "Some very good eye makeup will be made available, black but with a greenish cast, which the commandant himself prepares" (1091). Behind this gift giving—and there are a few other exiguous amenities, like *one* easy chair to be shared by *both*—lurks an ironical abuse of the pleasure principle: the prisoners, having "lacked for everything in these first few hours, from now on . . . will not lack for at least some few things, and after such complete deprivation, this will seem to . . . [them] more pleasant. . . . You see, then, my lords . . . what good intentions lay behind your having been in temporarily straitened circumstances" (1090–91). True, think of the pleasure of cherished things when you've been so long deprived of them: of strolling once again after long confinement. Joseph regales these prisoners with the logic of the bliss of arrested pain.

The baker and sommelier are a pair of comedians—Mann loved comedians in movies, and he laughed easily at them.[93] On being asked by Joseph to explain how they have fallen so low, the sommelier, the fat cheerful one, makes sense. The other, the thin, pensive baker, tangles himself in a madcap Rabelaisian rhetoric. He cannot say what he intends to say; he is soon lost in his own florid blather. He is very funny—and Mann loved his work to be found funny when he meant it to be funny. His journal records his bliss at the laughter he produced especially on reading the comparable palaver of the ascetic priest in *The Transposed Heads*.[94]

At the close both truants are desperate to know how long their case will take. Joseph can only guess: forty days.

"'Oh, that long!' the butler wailed." (He is the sensible one.)

"'Oh, that's short!' the baker cried, but was immediately and terribly alarmed by his cry and assured them that he also had intended to say, 'That long!'"

The Sting of the Serpent

An ancient legend tells of the rivalry between the goddess Isis and the sun god Rê. There had been no quarrel with his rule—as king of the Two Lands—until he had grown old and frail, whereupon, realizing that his time on earth had passed, he "deemed it a good idea" to retire into "the upper sphere." A warrant for his decision was the fact that "his bones had become silver, his flesh gold, his hair . . . the purest lapis lazuli—a very beautiful form of senescence, but nonetheless accompanied by all manner of pain and illness" (1097).

Might Mann, aged sixty-five while writing these lines, have delighted in their resonance with his own knowledge of pain and illness but with a view onto the symbolic translation of his own body into the silver, gold, and lapis lazuli of literature—of the very prose he was writing and which would survive him in "the upper sphere" of a putative cultural immortality? So many times, in his confessional writings—in his diaries and letters—he had dismissed even the rewarding excitements of the day as a "life" he did not wish to be bothered with, and called his craving to reenter the "higher sphere" of solitary writing as powerful an instinct as any other.

And yet, as Mann also knew, this readiness to die—even upwards—was bound to be countered with a bodily "Not yet!" and so it was with the king. For "even in this state, the aged Rê had continued to cling to his sovereignty over earth, although he should have realized that it had begun to free itself from his old and enfeebled grip and that fearlessness, indeed insolence was gaining the upper hand on all sides" (1098). I suggest that Mann's word "insolence"—that quality, in this situation—indicates a masterful knowledge of human nature.

The legend has an additional appeal because it is being invoked to support its mythic repetition in the present affair of the arrest and humiliation of a baker and a butler. We learn to our surprise that they are in fact figures in a plot to murder Pharaoh, one that will employ the wiles of Isis, who prepared a serpent to sting and kill the sun king and be done with him. In the absence of a suitable serpent, however, the revolutionary cadre, headed by Tiy, Pharaoh's once favored concubine ("this Isis of the House of Women"), has adopted poison as a pharmakon, with the goal of installing Tiy's bastard son Noferka-Ptah on the throne of the murdered king. Mann is droll: the plot involves seventy-two—no more or less—conspirators, "a promising number dictated by tradition. . . . So then, whenever a conspiracy takes place in this world, it is customary, indeed necessary, for the conspirators to be seventy-two in number. And if the coup fails [and this one will fail!], one can be certain that had that number not been adhered to, the failure would have been far worse" (1100).

The plan involves poison, then, and here the baker and the wine butler are key players, for the idea is indeed to insert chalk in Pharaoh's bread and flies in his wine and in the ensuing commotion—presumably ending in his murder—for a gang of armed upstarts to proclaim the new king of the Two Lands. But, as we now know, the plan has foundered, owing perhaps to the treachery of one of the plotters, who "at the last moment . . . was seduced by the promise of lovely inscriptions for his grave if he chose to remain loyal" (1100). Pharaoh's revenge is swift; the discovery of the plot is followed by a wave of stranglings, but the fate of the baker and the wine butler remains uncertain; and in the prison far from the court, where Joseph is also incarcerated, they await their punishment . . . or their pardon.

Joseph Assists as an Interpreter

In the morning, Joseph finds the two accused plotters—the baker and the wine butler—in hermeneutic distress: both have dreamt vivid dreams, and there is no one on hand in their prison cell to tell them the meaning. Whereupon Joseph volunteers as a dream interpreter, reminding the prisoners of his own and his clan's special familiarity with strong dreams. The convicts respond vigorously, insisting on the difference between the experience of dreaming and the experience of interpreting dreams, of which Joseph has not spoken. Joseph, an implicit reader of Freud, points out that dreams and their own interpretation constitute a whole: the (right) interpretation is embedded in the dream. This Joseph is an astute theoretician of hermeneutics, arguing further that in fact the interpretation *precedes* the dream; otherwise, how would the dreamer accept an interpretation, declaring it to be right, if he did not already possess that understanding—the cognition of the dream depending on its recognition?

Joseph interprets the dream of the wine butler, and it is auspicious. The hands glimpsed on a giant stalk are the three days leading to his manumission:

he will once again be raised on high in Pharaoh's court; and there, in appreciation of the good news that Joseph has brought him, on Joseph's asking for this
favor, the butler promises to praise Joseph in Pharaoh's presence and bring him
into Pharaoh's good graces. Joseph's reading of the baker's dream, on the other
hand, is not auspicious; true, he too will be raised on high ... but on a cross,
for birds to peck at; whereupon Joseph attempts to console him, arguing that
the world is a great circle—it includes the sphere above and the sphere
below—and even in death the baker will not fail to participate in the great ring
of life and death.

This latter decree of the interpreter would appear to be decisively opposite
to the good tidings he has brought to the butler: but that is not quite the case,
for we learn that the butler would in fact forget Joseph, just as Joseph prophesied, and fail to praise him, not wanting to be reminded of the prison in which
the promise had been made.

Joseph, Part Two: "The Summons"

Neb-nef-nezem

For another two years, Joseph remained captive of the prison at Zawi-Rê, unable to witness but having heard tell of a celebration following the mourning
of the death of the old Pharaoh, who had ruled while the baker and the butler
were awaiting their fates, and the crowning of the new Pharaoh, nicknamed
Neb-nef-nezem, Lord of Sweet Breath, as he loved to smell the flowers. Not
incidentally, "a child of the Egyptian nobility named Nefertiti ... had now
become his Great Consort and Mistress of the Two Lands, and on ... [her] he
had bestowed the radiant second name of Nefernefruatôn, 'Beautiful Beyond
All Beauty Is the Atôn'" (1111). But the gentle epithet of her young master
should not imply that he was content with a pastoral passivity: he is driven to
fix the pantheon and to construct, though in unseemly haste, a new House of
the Sun in honor of the god Rê-Horakhte in his aspect as a heavenly body, as
the sun. The radical doctrines of the new king are narrated, not dramatized,
and can be economically summed up:

> As a heavenly body [the god Rê-Horakhte] ... was threefold: in his birth
> out of night, in the zenith of his manliness, and in his death in the west. He
> lived a life of birth, of death, and of regeneration. ... Pharaoh's doctrinal
> message did not want the god's life to be viewed in that same way, not as a
> coming and going, a becoming, perishing, and becoming again ... but
> rather as pure being, as the changeless source of light subject to neither rise

nor fall, from whose image both the human and the bird were henceforth to be removed, so that only the pure, life-radiating solar disk remained, and its name was Atôn. (1113)

The Courier

A barque with purple sails arrives at the fortress of Zawi-Rê, and a lithe messenger, Pharaoh's First Runner, leaps out. Breathless, or feigning breathlessness, he rushes past the guards to the inner sanctum of the prison warden. On his cap and at the back of his sandals are gold-foil wings signaling the authority of the royal court. He finds Mai-Sakhme and asks that Joseph be brought to him for immediate delivery to the court of Pharaoh on Pharaoh's express— indeed "beautiful"—command. Joseph appears, unkempt and wearing coarse linen, unfit to make an appearance at "the House of Re-Horakhte, who invented the solar year" (1116). That is no matter: he will be groomed and dressed "aboard ship while we fly." Furthermore, the commission at hand is of such urgency that Pharaoh is actually prepared to meet Joseph halfway at his beloved palace at On "at the tip of the Delta" (1126).

Pharaoh has had a dream whose meaning has baffled "Pharaoh's greatest experts and magicians, . . . seers, prophets, and interpreters" (1116). And given his dissatisfaction and distress (if this is something that can be said of Pharaoh), he has consented to the wine butler's tardy recommendation of Joseph as an interpreter of dreams, for the latter has approved Joseph's skill on his own body, as it were: Joseph might be worth the fetching. And now, on the barque with purple sails, Joseph is given a rough accounting of Pharaoh's dream, in which seven cows were seen "eating seven ears of grain, and on a second occasion seven cows being eaten by seven ears of grain." This (nonsensical) reckoning sets Joseph thinking, and throughout the journey, he "plays with images of nourishment, famine, and precaution" (1119). Is there any reader who does not know what Joseph will inspire Pharaoh to think?

Light and Darkness

This chapter owes its special richness to the fine and subtle resonances it contains of Mann's most intimate experience in America. As the young Pharaoh is torn in two by his twin functions as a devotee of the sun god Atôn and ruler and pragmatic administrator of the Two Lands, so was Thomas Mann in America torn in two by his twin functions as a devotee of literature and—in Klaus Mann's phrase—the ambassador to America of the nation of exiles.

The portrait of Pharaoh is finely realized: he is a mystic lover of beauty, as his nickname Lord of the Sweet Breath suggests, but prey to migraines and epileptic seizures, which are not without their value: for "he himself explained these attacks as an instant visitation by his father, the god, and rather than fearing them, looked forward to them . . . because he returned . . . into the light of day enriched with authentic doctrines and revelations concerning the beautiful and true nature of the Atôn" (1122–23). At the same time, he is a lover of the works of the god Ptah, the source of beautiful images, the original begetter of taste, skill, and "worldly ornamentation"; in short, Pharaoh is an aesthete.

Mann is surely speaking *in propria persona* in reminding the reader— through a knowledge attributed to Joseph!—that the world is one: the activity of art does not stand apart from religion or, for that matter, politics (1123). Mann spells out this belief, as it is one he shares with Joseph:

> Joseph knew quite well that the young Pharaoh . . . had made the pictorial ornamentation of the world the object of his eager, indeed zealous attention, had done so, in fact, in complete accord with the efforts he expended in conceiving and advancing the god Atôn in all his truth and purity. (1121)

For Pharaoh's artistic devotion to the god Atôn, read, in this fluid allegory, Mann's devotion to democracy in all its "truth and purity." We know of his repeated insistence in his political speeches on awakening the conscience of the artist: the awareness of his embeddedness in the life-worlds of religion and politics in his time, which require, however onerously, the artist's participation.

As an artist, Mann has fulfilled his task with a very clear awareness, especially in dark times, of the non-distinction of the spheres of art and politics. I am recalling his words from "The War and the Future," "In whatever sphere . . . truth and freedom are denied, violated, trampled upon; there art and every decent artist must be gravely affected. He cannot live, cannot breathe, cannot work; he must degenerate, or he must flee"[95] (241). And so, Pharaoh, quite apart from his intimate devotions, being the son of the true sun god Atôn, must also protect his avowed lineage from the machinations of a rival priest Beknechons, who is a devotee of the older, the chauvinistic god Amun, "the hidden One."

These burdens—of rule and religious politics—are grievous, and they make themselves felt on Pharaoh's body with morbid effect: whenever he hears of the imperial business required of him, his face turns green. His body suffers the contradiction between his theological devotions and his responsibilities as the king of Egypt for the material prosperity of his lands—the conflict between "the creed of Isis of the Black Earth . . . that black Egyptian loam . . . fertile with the impregnating flood . . . [and the disciple's] passion for pure light, for the golden youth of the sun at its zenith" (1127). Yet Pharaoh must beware any failure "in the realm of the Black Earth": if "the black workings of fertility" were to fail under his reign, it would be the very creed of Atôn that would suffer the costs (1128).

Pharaoh's Dreams

Pharaoh has dreamt a vivid and terrifying dream that might well have a bearing on the fertility of the black earth: it is unlike the nonsense Joseph was told on the journey to On. Mann has wasted none of his skill in recounting Pharaoh's vision:

> he was standing at a lonely spot, a place of swamp and reeds . . . ; he heard splashing . . . and out of the flood seven shapes emerged—climbing on land were seven cows that must have been lying in the river . . . and they walked past, one after the other in single file. . . . Splendid cows—white, black with a paler back, gray with a paler belly, and two dappled ones, splotched with markings—such beautiful, sleek, fat cows, with bulging udders and heavily lashed eyes . . . and tall, curving lyre-shaped horns; and they began to graze contentedly among the reed grass. (1131)

Their contentment—and more importantly, Pharaoh's contentment—would not last, for they are soon assaulted by a terrible apparition. Seven more cows emerge from the water, but

> they were the ugliest, leanest, gauntest cows he had ever seen in his life— their bones stuck out from under their wrinkled hide, their udders were empty sacks with teats like cord; the sight was terrifying and thoroughly demoralizing, for . . . their behavior was shamelessly impudent, viciously hostile . . . it was the savagery of starvation. . . . The wretched herd attack[s] the sleek one: the hideous cows climb onto the beautiful ones . . . the wretched animals devour the splendid ones, wolf them down, simply wipe the meadow clean of them—but afterward stand there as emaciated as before, showing no sign whatever of having eaten their fill. (1132)

The pattern is no different with the stalk and the seven ears of grain,

> fat, plump ears of grain, bursting with richness and nodding in the golden fullness of their yield. . . . but what follows is more sprouting . . . another

seven ears of grain emerge, miserable ears, barren, dead, and sere, blighted by the east wind, blackened by smut and rust, and as they emerge in their shabbiness below the fat ones, these then dwindle, as if vanishing into the others, and it's as if the blighted ears are devouring the plump ones, just as before the wretched cows devoured the sleek ones, and this time, too, grow no fatter and fuller than before. (1132–33)

These scandalous dreams cry out for interpretation; but none of the sage scholars of the court, the mooted experts and prophets, can produce a satisfactory explanation. Nor can the hurriedly summoned dream experts and magicians from a neighboring court—the house of Djehuti, of Thoth, of "priests consecrated to the white baboon"—do any better. They cannot produce an understanding that will answer to Pharaoh's inner voice. He is furious: "Fraud and falsehood!" he calls after them. And yet these dreams are imperial dreams of national importance: they cry out for right interpretation. The stakes are immense: "Light was endangered by a threat from the blackness, weightless spirituality menaced by danger from the material world" (1133). If they bode ruin, then it is Atôn who will suffer apostasy—and all profit will go to the older, the crueler god Amun. These visions cannot be left to interpret themselves. With the urgency of a saving arrival of the prophetic foreigner, the chapter ends.

We leave *Joseph in Princeton* with bated breath, its dreams only mangled and misinterpreted. Mann-Joseph needed the Egyptian sunlight of Pacific Palisades, California, to bring Pharaoh to a right understanding of the seven fat and seven lean cattle, the seven golden ears of grain and the seven sere, blighted ears. After reading the pages of *Joseph the Provider* that Mann composed in Princeton, one is well inclined to judge "the Princeton years . . . a stunningly productive period [for Mann] as writer and public intellectual."[96]

5

Toward a Conclusion

MUCH OF Mann's life at Princeton was shaped by his obligations to the university: he had to focus very often on the preparation—the content and the delivery—of seven formal lectures, for the most part in English. His performances at Alexander Hall were attended by an audience of nearly 1,000 people. Before long, he was drawn into personal contact with deans, professors, and students, and not all such encounters were life-enhancing. He was chiefly glad that only part of his years in Princeton belonged to the university: he was gainfully employed for just three semesters although, at the same time, offended that his contract for a full second year was not renewed.[1] Nonetheless, his university obligations in 1938 and 1939 and for half of 1940 far exceeded the *pensum* that he thought he had signed on to.

Despite his immersion in auditoriums and classrooms, Mann rarely failed to rise intellectually—and often practically—to the next critical political occasion. He continually published his defense of what might be called a tragic humanism and broadcast his thoughts during strenuous lecture trips throughout the country. Moreover, as "the ambassador of a nation of exiles," together with his wife Katia, he did what his energies allowed in giving practical help to persecuted intellectuals in Europe and America.

He needed to set an example: in the face of the "botched" European reality, he declared that an authentic Germany lived on—elsewhere. It lodged in the spiritual plenty of German literature, kept alive by writers in exile—by Mann and those whom he inspired to carry on. This source of life persisted, but it could not dissolve the sorrow of the loss of one's own country—home, wealth, friends, readership all gone. The fatigue of melancholy could be irresistible. Still,

> There were two things . . . he considered inadmissible, indeed, contemptible for an émigré writer: one, to change his language like a piece of worn-out

clothing and write in an inappropriate, hence, arrogantly assumed one. And two, not to write anymore. It was our duty—he, I, all those to whom the German language had been given—to write in it. We had no choice. We too were obliged to serve, and this—it was his expression—would be our "wartime service"; we too had to fight a war against Hitler with the weapon of the German word, which did not by any means have to be polemical but instead must hold fast to what had to be preserved.[2]

In the years of Mann's stay, Princeton supported other humanist scholars, several of them neighbors with whom he lived in heady, although occasional, relation—foremost, Erich Kahler; the homeless Hermann Broch, to whom Einstein, in the summer of 1939, lent his house;[3] and Einstein himself, who was better friends with Kahler and Broch than with Mann, whose pedantic-patrician ways irked him.[4] There were also lively visits from his son-in-law Giuseppe Antonio Borgese, who came in from Chicago. This is to list only the savants of the Inner Circle. A key question: What did all this fellowship and kinship matter for Mann's creative work?

Mann's fiction writing was *not* permeable to influence. We can try to evoke that protected relation. Mann's own fiction is a brilliant resource: consider Joseph's reflections in *Joseph the Provider*, the opening chapters of which were written in Princeton and continually display signs of Mann's American experience. Joseph's beliefs are often Mann's beliefs, one of which, as follows, he steadily realized even in his Princeton exile.

At the outset of *Joseph the Provider*, we may recall, Joseph is in chains on a barge sailing up the Nile to prison, for he has been slandered by Potiphar's wife. In some sense, Joseph feels he is repeating the mythic journey of Atum-Rê— the deity, the "finisher of the world"—journeying in his barque. On announcing the reference to his keeper, this satrap is scornful; Joseph, unperturbed, rejects him. He never did beg his keeper to share his company, telling him that

> I am just as happy alone, perhaps even a bit happier, and know how to entertain myself without you, as you yourself have noticed. But if you knew how to entertain yourself as I do, . . . then you would not look so askance at the diversions I allow myself. . . . That a man can entertain himself and not spend his life like some dumb beast is really the point after all, and the heights to which he can bring his diversion are what matter.[5]

That height is, once more, the *mythic* dimension, the factor of allusion. Joseph has been described as forever "accompanied by . . . a meditative play of thought . . . the dearest and sweetest form of . . . [which] was allusion; and whenever events in his carefully monitored life grew rich with allusion and circumstances proved transparent for a higher correspondence, then he was happy."[6] And so Mann was often happy during his morning hours, devoted to the "main business" (Goethe) of writing fiction, even sequestered in the happy prison of his American exile.

Although Mann had important conversations with other writers in Princeton, chiefly about the political questions of the day, each maintained, at the same time, a personal isolation, though one not always "splendid." The hallmark of their exchange is a German rich with allusion. It is on display in the beauty and subtlety of their language: they do not forget their art even in politics, to which it is superior. "In the identification of language with life, the subject knows itself to be authentic."[7] It is a matter of keeping intact one's personal dignity even in a wilderness (it is easy to forget how strange and even threatening they found this country)—and, in principle, holding to the dignity of others in a chiefly imagined community.

The substantial gist of the Princeton humanism is summed up in the short book *The City of Man*, to which Mann and Kahler but especially Broch and Borgese contributed. It reads impressively to this day (see the discussion in chapter 2). Note the texture of its language, the breadth of its concerns, its foundational knowledge of history and political thought; and one will grasp what *homo humanitatis* might amount to. In his reflection on the views of the Thomist philosopher Mortimer Adler, Mann added detail to this ideal: "We cannot and should not return to the Middle Ages" (unlike, I will add, Mann's powerful anti-humanist contemporary T. S. Eliot); "and that necessary, ultimate authority can scarcely be located in a transcendental order but has to enter into humanity itself and be based on the feeling for the human, its distinction, difficulty, dignity and mystery" (Br.M 246). That difficulty and mystery also make it impossible for Mann to answer with a resonant Yes or No some of the key questions facing him in the years 1938–41: Is the Nazi hegemony an aberration or an organic expression of "Germanness"? Is every German, at "home" or in exile, culpable for its monstrous crimes? It is not hard to show that at various moments Mann thought differently on the matter. His wavering could be reckoned a shortcoming—and there has been no shortage of scholars and observers ready to punish him for it, and equally, no shortage of scholars and observers ready to praise him precisely for his "Civilized Uncertainty." The recent appearance of an essay on Mann's life and work with this title suggests his eternal presentness: Algis Valiunas's reflections on Mann's "higher irony" are apposite.

Drawing on Mann's readiness in *Joseph* to grant the pharaoh Atôn-Rê and not the Jews alone a measure of theological wisdom, Valiunas comes to a political conclusion, for the questions raised above are political.

> The political lesson for Mann's own time, and for the time to come after him, is patent. The only persons to be trusted with the souls of a people are not those who claim exclusively to possess the truth but rather those who acknowledge their own tentativeness as they continue to seek the truth wherever it may be found. . . . Mann is not intellectually fickle, like someone who does not know his own mind and who is susceptible to every argument that crosses his path; nor is he belligerently timorous, like one who considers it gross presumption for him—or anybody else—to claim he knows anything at all. . . . He is unwilling to reduce profound moral complication to hapless formulae. Art is required to render truth adequately. . . . Philosophical argument or theological contention is unfailingly partial, in both senses of that word: The whole eludes it. In Mann's hands moral instruction is of a piece with the account of the whole, and in this account the mystery of life remains mysterious.[8]

Mann would conclude his lecture on *The Magic Mountain* to the young "gentlemen" of Princeton University with the same sentiment: "The Grail is a mystery, but humanity is a mystery too. For man himself is a mystery, and all humanity rests upon reverence before the mystery that is man."[9]

The humanism of the Princeton émigrés—militant and exalted—faced off against Nazi-fascism. We have a few vicious types in office here and now around the world, but so far, they do not seem capable of crushing, on a worldwide scale, humanists and humanist thought. Should things get worse, humanism will take on a new force in an inspired language; but *until* America went to war with Germany, "democracy"—which, for Mann especially, was another word for humanism—was an enfeebled idea. It is a pity that we must always wait for things to get worse before they can get better.

With respect to "The City of Man," this project of Mann, Kahler, Broch, and Borgese to articulate a vision of a unity of nations, two Yale-trained historians writing about the Hapsburg Empire eighty years later make a similar point:

> As nationalism regains momentum in Europe, it is worth considering the underappreciated benefits of being part of something larger, and the limited answers offered by "going it alone." Without falling into nostalgia for a fundamentally conservative Hapsburg empire, or seeing it as a forerunner to

the European Union, it is possible to acknowledge that a multinational state is not necessarily doomed to failure. And neither, for that matter, is the nation-state the only "natural" form of political organization.[10]

Had Mann lived to read these words, he would have noted his approbation in his diary and an increase in his confidence that the country of which he was a citizen might yet take the right path. This putative happiness might be reckoned "political." His greater happiness would be artistic, and it is at hand. He dreamt with respect to *Joseph and His Brothers* that "some measure of endurance" might be "innate" to this book.[11] With justification, his dream might be wider: in light of what we now know, there appears to be a good measure of endurance innate to Mann's entire life and work.

ACKNOWLEDGMENTS

I AM GRATEFUL to Ms. Ashley Horn, who, on behalf of the ProQuest Publishing Company, allowed me to reprint sections of issues of the *New York Herald Tribune* in the period December 23–December 29, 1938, in which Thomas Mann's appeal "To the Civilized World" was criticized. The staff of Fischer Verlag Permissions allowed me to reprint Thomas Mann's essay "Culture and Politics" and extended sections from his appeal "To the Civilized World." Several scholars have aided this project in important ways. Tobias Boes's detailed study of Mann's political reception in America—*Man's War*—came into my hands just as I was completing the manuscript of this book and sharpened my awareness of many of the matters at hand. The late Klaus Harpprecht's biography of Thomas Mann in 2,253 pages, leavened by mature wit and judgment, was a joy to read. Hans Rudolf Vaget's unparalleled knowledge of Mann's life and works nurtured this book throughout. Hans is the author of a rich panoply of books and articles, foremost to my mind and for the sake of this research *Thomas Mann, der Amerikaner* (VA), and "'The Best of Both Worlds': Thomas Mann in Princeton" (V)—works that pointed the direction and accompanied me all along the way. Under straitened circumstances (sleepless at Orly), Hans also read and improved the lecture on "Thomas Mann in Princeton" that I delivered in fall 2018 at the Eidgenössische Technische Hochschule in Zurich, which houses the Thomas Mann Archive; this lecture was the seed of the book that, in whatever form it takes, you kindly hold in your hands.

For this initial invitation to lecture on Thomas Mann in Zurich, I am grateful to my friends Andreas Kilcher and Christian Jany. The scintillating political philosopher Mark Francis of Canterbury University supplied the title of this book! Walter Hinderer, a close companion for many decades and eminent scholar of German literature, accompanied the years of the production of this book with sympathy and interest. The graciously offered encouragement of Heinrich Detering came at a crucial juncture, for which I am again very grateful. The admirable Christopher Phillips was a gracious friend of the editing process. Rafaël Newman and Caroline Wiedmer attended the Zurich lecture and supplied me with the joy and comfort of their friendship and hospitality. The staff of the Thomas Mann Archive at the Eidgenössische Technische Hochschule of Zurich was most gracious in arranging my lecture—foremost Dr. Katrin Bedenig, who seconded the invitation; and Kathrin Keller, always cordial and efficient, who made the task of obtaining publishing rights and manuscript material a very nearly pleasant one—as pleasant as ever such a procedure can be. The staff at Princeton University Press brought this book into being: they have been brilliant and capable. Especially, Jodi Beder's copyediting was a marvel of care and critical perception: her work is the education in writing and thinking that I would wish for every author. It goes without saying that the faults of form and rhetoric that remain are entirely my own. I am once again dedicating a book—this one!—to my wife, the inexpressibly wonderful Regine Üllner.

NOTES

Preface

1. Mann left Princeton on March 17, 1941, a day before Liverpool was badly bombed, part of the "Liverpool Blitz" beginning in August 1940. Some weeks later, in early May 1941, London suffered the worst aerial bombardment it had known.

2. The phrase in quotes is the title of a speech Mann gave often in 1938 in the months preceding his move to Princeton.

3. *The Letters of Thomas Mann, 1889–1955*, tr. Richard and Clara Winston (New York: Knopf, 1970), 642.

4. Thomas Mann, letter to Klaus Mann (May 12, 1938), *Die Briefe der Manns, Ein Familienporträt*, ed. Tilmann Lahme, Holger Pils, and Kerstin Klein (Frankfurt am Main: S. Fischer, 2016), 180.

5. The German title "Nietzsches Philosophie im Lichte unserer Erfahrung" is misleadingly translated in its current English version as "Nietzsche's Philosophy in the Light of Contemporary Events." The original is found in *Nietzsches Philosophie im Lichte unserer Erfahrung, Vortrag am XIV. Kongress des Pen-Clubs in Zurich am 3. Juni 1947*, ed. David Marc Hoffmann (Basel: Schwabe, 2005), 11–41. The talk was famously delivered in English on April 29, 1947, at the Library of Congress. *Thomas Mann's Addresses Delivered at the Library of Congress, 1942–1949* (Washington, DC: Library of Congress, 1963), 69–103.

6. In 1942, Mann drafted a telegram to President Roosevelt, "feeling that something must be done about the 'enemy alien' matter and asking Einstein to add his signature together with that of Giuseppe Borgese, Bruno Frank, Count Sforza, Toscanini, Bruno Walter, and himself." The conclusion reads, "We, therefore, respectfully apply to you, Mr. President, who for all of us represent the spirit of all that is loyal, honest, and decent in a world of falsehood and chaos, to utter or to sanction a word of authoritative discrimination to the effect that a clear and practical line should be drawn between the potential enemies of American democracy on the one hand and the victims and sworn foes of totalitarian evil on the other" (*Letters*, 389–90).

7. This view of Nietzsche was only the latest in Mann's life-long preoccupation with the philosopher (cf. my "Mann as a Reader of Nietzsche," *boundary* 2 9, no. 1 [Fall 1980]: 47–74). It departs radically from the rather more judicious, even benevolent picture of Nietzsche that Mann presented during his years at Princeton, as in the March 1941 essay on Mann's induction (and Nietzsche's virtual induction!) into Phi Beta Kappa, years before the disclosure of the worst Nazi crimes. See the section on *Denken und Leben* in chapter 2.

8. *Goethe's Faust*, tr. Walter Kaufmann (New York: Random House, 1961), 189.

9. Two years after my writing these lines, things have changed little. "Modern journalism, even before the internet, makes it almost impossible to form a realistic picture of what is going on in the world. It breaks knowledge up into uncoordinated categories and ignores context and connection, which are the soul of historical understanding." Eli Zaretsky, "The Big Lie," *London Review of Books Blog*, February 15, 2021.

10. Here Mann is very likely reading Michael Ivanovich Rostovtzeff, *Gesellschaft und Wirtschaft im römischen Kaiserreich*, tr. Lothar Wickert (Leipzig: Quelle & Meyer, 1929). Rostovtzeff is very much alive at Princeton. Princeton University Press publishes the annual Rostovtzeff Lectures delivered at New York University, named "after the great ancient historian . . . whose prodigious energies and sprawling interests led him to write on an almost unimaginable range of subjects." https://press.princeton.edu/series/the-rostovtzeff-lectures.

11. Claude Lévi-Strauss, *Tristes Tropiques*, tr. John and Doreen Weightman (New York: Penguin, 2012), 29.

12. Erich Kahler, "Memorandum to the Ohio State University Seminar, March 1961." Cited in David Kettler, "The Symbolic Uses of Exile: Erich Kahler at the Ohio State University," in *Exile and Otherness: New Approaches to the Experience of the Nazi Refugees*, ed. Alexander Stephan (Bern: Peter Lang, 2005), 278n14.

13. See chapter 2, endnote 1.

14. The sincerity of this "conversion"—the degree of positive affect behind it—is a matter of dispute, for Mann was above all wedded to an ironical disposition.

15. Private communication.

16. *An Exceptional Friendship: The Correspondence of Erich Kahler and Thomas Mann*, tr. Richard and Clara Winston (Ithaca, NY: Cornell University Press, 1975), 49.

17. Ibid, 71.

18. *Thomas Mann der Amerikaner, Leben und Werk im amerikanischen Exil, 1938–1952* (Frankfurt am Main: S. Fischer, 2011), 342. It turns out that Sontag, while nominally a teen-ager, was not the high-school student who paid Mann a visit in 1947 but actually an undergraduate—and the visit took place in 1949. See Kai Sina, "Die Lehren vom San Remo Drive: Susan Sontag trifft Thomas Mann," *Thomas Mann in Amerika*, ed. Ulrich Raulff and Ellen Strittmatter (Marbach am Neckar: Deutsche Schillergesellschaft, 2019), 63.

19. Thomas Mann, *Tagebücher 1937–1939*, ed. Peter de Mendelssohn (Frankfurt am Main: S. Fischer, 1982), 64.

20. I cite this binary without prejudice from the taxonomy devised by the *Partisan Review* intellectual Philip Rahv in 1939 and thereafter richly elaborated by the Americanist Leslie Fiedler. See Philip Rahv, "Paleface and Redskin," *The Kenyon Review* 1, no. 2 (Summer 1939): 251–56, and Leslie Fiedler, *Love and Death in the American Novel* (1960). On its ongoing propaedeutic vitality, see Sanford Pinsker, "Philip Rahv's 'Paleface and Redskin'—Fifty Years Later," *Georgia Review* 43, no. 3 (Fall 1989): 477–89. In 2008, addressing a controversy about the qualities that the best novelists exhibit, Barry Gewen concluded, "the Rahvian dichotomy is alive and well." "Paleface vs. Redskin," *The New York Times*, August 20, 2008. https://artsbeat.blogs.nytimes.com/2008/08/20/paleface-v-redskin/. *Verbum sat.*

21. I actually heard Levin lecture (on *Finnegans Wake*) one afternoon in 1950 when I was still in high school, as I was allowed to visit my brother Noel at Harvard, who was studying for a doctorate in physics and still found time to listen to Harry Levin. I shall never forget his manner of reading the closing sentences and then the opening sentences with no break between them.

22. Harry Levin, "Dr. Mann versus a Teutonic Mephisto," a review of *Doctor Faustus* by Thomas Mann, *The New York Times* (October 31, 1948): 5.

23. "Time sucks things away into oblivion. . . . What the historian does is hold things against the flow of time, resisting oblivion for some duration." Thus, the former Princeton undergraduate and now professor of history Graham Burnett. https://humanities.princeton.edu/2021/02 /27/2020-rapid-response-grant-pan-explores-attention-economy/

24. Broch wrote of Victor Lange (1908–1996): "As a teacher he is certainly to be recommended; he knows his stuff, is excited by the material, and is surely a good lecturer." Hermann Broch, letter to Kahler (December 7, 1948) in *Hermann Broch: Briefe an Erich von Kahler (1940– 1951)*, ed. Paul Michael Lützeler (Berlin: de Gruyter, 2010), 91. Ralf Frodermann, a wit and author rarely given to praise, notes apropos of Lange's collection of essays *Illyrische Betrachtungen* (1989), "His views on life and scholarship were those of a great teacher." *Lichtenthaler Tagebuch, Sommer 2020.*

25. It has not enjoyed the good fortune of Mann's residence in Pacific Palisades, California. The Princeton house was bought and renovated by private persons with little interest in preserving the interior of the site as Thomas Mann's dwelling, whereas the house in California was bought by the German government (for $13 million!). Its original interior has been respected, and it now serves as a study center for younger German intellectuals.

26. "Mann, Thomas," in Alexander Leitch, *A Princeton Companion* (Princeton, NJ: Princeton University Press, 1978), 312–13.

27. Cited from R.W. Stallman, in Angel Flores, *Franz Kafka Today* (Madison: University of Wisconsin Press, 1958), 61. The story has been variously recirculated.

28. *Thomas Mann: 1875–1975*, ed. Stanley Corngold and Richard Ludwig (Princeton, NJ: Princeton University Library, 1975).

29. The student is Alexander Lin, his unpublished thesis, "The Friendship of Narration in *Doktor Faustus* and *Hōjō no umi.*" The latter title is *The Sea of Fertility*, a tetralogy by Mishima Yukio. Both Mann and Mishima share the distinction of having written tetralogies—both widely regarded as their personal masterpieces—Mann's, of course, being *Joseph and His Brothers.*

30. Alexander Wolff, *Endpapers: A Family Story of Books, War, Escape, and Home* (New York: Atlantic Monthly Press, 2021), 93 (translation by AW). Kurt Wolff's review was originally cited in a Harvard doctoral thesis by Steven John Schuyler, *Kurt Wolff and Hermann Broch: Publisher and Author in Exile* (May 1984). Wolff was Kafka's very first publisher—meaning, primus inter pares of those who recognized Kafka's genius early on.

Chapter One: Thomas Mann in Princeton

1. This chapter expands considerably an earlier version published in German, "Thomas Mann im Lichte unserer Erfahrung: Zum amerikanischen Exil," *Thomas Mann Jahrbuch* 32 (2019): 169–81.

2. See "Contra Thomas Mann the American" in chapter 2.

3. Mann was now at home in an elegant suburb of Los Angeles. It was not Brentwood, as he had hoped, but Pacific Palisades.

4. This judgment is entirely consistent with Mann's view of the *writer's* attitude, as such: "Writing itself always appeared to me as the product and expression of a problematic—of the Here and yet There, the Yes and No, the two souls in one breast, the bad richness of inner

conflicts, antitheses, and contradictions." The passage continues: "Why or whence such a thing as writing at all, if it is not the intellectual and moral concern for a problematic self." (Few readers of Mann's work would consider the richness of his inner contradictions bad.) Thomas Mann, *Betrachtungen eines Unpolitischen*, GW 12:20.

5. Mann arrived in New York on February 21, 1938, having been engaged by "an efficient agency [Brandt and Brandt] for a series of highly-paid lectures" (H 972). Marquis Childs supplies the actual number of the many public lectures Mann delivered in the following months. See Marquis Childs, "Thomas Mann: Germany's Foremost Literary Exile Speaks Now for Freedom and Democracy in America," *Life*, April 17, 1939, 16.

6. This is the conclusion of Hans Rudolf Vaget, who has meticulously edited the 1,200-page Mann–Agnes Meyer correspondence.

7. Harvard was interested; but at a critical moment, James Conant, the president, was away from his desk and out of town.

8. Bade, whose book is most informative, refers to Herbert Lehnert, "Thomas Mann in Princeton," *The Germanic Review* 29, no. 1 (1964): 16, and Hans Rudolf Vaget, "Schlechtes Wetter, Gutes Klima," in *Thomas-Mann-Handbook*, ed. Helmut Koopmann (Frankfurt am Main: S. Fischer, 1990), 70. For further information concerning Meyer's efforts to secure Mann a university position, see BR.M 37–51. In an introduction to the current Princeton website for the German Department, one reads: "From 1938 to 1940 the German faculty also included the distinguished writer Thomas Mann, who had an appointment as Lecturer in German." That is not true. It is worth stressing that Mann's appointment was as Lecturer in the Humanities; in fact, he and the then Department of Germanic Languages and Literatures had very little to do with one another. His existence as an embittered exile *from* Germany played into this distance.

9. "Moving through the warm stillness along Snowden Lane, I beheld the trees, radiant as if illuminated from within, kindled by long, low-angled shafts of 5 o'clock sun into fire-fangled yellows, oranges, and reds." From Patrick Walsh's paean to the trees of Princeton, some eighty years later, in "Princeton, My Enclave of Green," https://www.scene4.com/1119/patrickwalsh1119.html. Describing Princeton as "dignified" is Mann's own preference. Erich Frey writes, "He [Mann] confided in a letter to his son Klaus on May 12, 1938: 'East or West? Princeton, where we were the other day, is very pretty. But I'm a bit afraid of the scholarly atmosphere, and I basically prefer the movie gang in Hollywood. Both options have their strong advantages and disadvantages. We'll have to see. Princeton, of course, is *more dignified* [in English, though not in italic, in original], and then New York and Europe are nearby. But Beverly Hills or Santa Monica would be more fun and the climate beneficial.'" Erich Frey, "Thomas Mann's Exile Years in America," *Modern Language Studies* 6, no. 1 (Spring, 1976): 84.

10. The Munich Agreement was signed at 1:00 a.m. on September 30, 1938, at a meeting of Hitler with Chamberlain, Daladier, and Mussolini in Hitler's headquarters in Munich, the so-called Führerbau. No representative of Czechoslovakia was present at the signing.

11. Hans Rudolf Vaget has remarked in conversation that the German word "Excitation" is Mann's code word for a sexual dream and/or a surprising erection on awakening.

12. Thomas Mann, *Briefe III, 1924–1932*, ed. Thomas Sprecher, Hans Rudolf Vaget, and Cornelia Bernini (Frankfurt am Main: S. Fischer, 2011), 166, cited in Vaget, "Schlechtes Wetter," 69.

13. Mann's friend, the mathematician Hermann Weyl, wrote, in a tribute to his wife Helena Weyl, an accomplished philosopher, upon their emigration from Göttingen and from Zurich,

with evident pertinence to the situation of Thomas Mann: "Hella and I enjoyed a long, happy time in Princeton. . . . We were met with much friendliness. We had the feeling, after only one year in Princeton, of being more accepted, with fewer reservations, than we had been after seventeen years in frosty old Switzerland [Mann's presence in Switzerland in the years before Princeton was barely tolerated by the authorities tasked with regulating—better, prohibiting—foreign entry]. We were happy [Weyl continues] to be in a place where the greatest willingness was shown to aid the victims of Nazism among European scientists. Nonetheless, the lot of the immigrant is harder on the soul than the majority of our American friends realize, however good the material circumstances may be. Nothing can replace our mother tongue, in which our environment first articulates itself, which accompanies us in all our experiences from early childhood on. This fracture could never heal in us." Hermann Weyl, "In memoriam Helene Weyl: A sketch not so much of Hella as of our life together, written at the end of June 1948," tr. and introduction David Hyder, *Leo Baeck Institute Year Book 2019* (New York: Oxford University Press, 2019), 249.

14. "But," writes Donald Prater, "the extent to which he was now trying to close his mind to Europe's crisis was shown by his lack of reaction to the sensational news that broke next day: the infamous Kristallnacht of widespread organized pogroms in Germany and Austria, and revenge for the murder, by a young Jewish émigré, of a German embassy official in Paris, with the systematic destruction of almost all synagogues and over 7,000 Jewish-owned businesses, and the arrest of more than 30,000 Jews. Saul [sic] Liptzin [this eminent scholar of Yiddish is Sol Liptzin] vividly recalls his visit to Stockton Street on 11 November, with one of his students, to seek Mann's views on these ghastly events, and how taken aback they were by his unemotional remarks. Measuring his words as if from a rostrum, the lofty Lübeck patrician considered that for Germany—which he described in his familiar phrase as the meeting-point of Viking civilization and Graeco-Roman classical culture, of Western rationalism and Eastern mysticism—the horror was really no more than a temporary aberration, and he seemed loath to be too critical." Donald Prater, *Thomas Mann—A Life* (Oxford: Oxford University Press, 1995), 290. Prater's account is shaped by his view, all throughout his biography, that it is easier to admire Mann than to love him. On the other hand, it is quite incorrect to see Mann's reaction to events in Europe as by and large a flight. And his diary for the very day of Liptzin's visit begins with the words: "Excessive ["auschweifend": even "wild, debauched"] organized pogrom of Jews in Germany and Austria following the killing of the Embassy member in Paris." And, conceivably as a result, or partly as a result, we read: "Attempted to work, almost without success. Extraordinarily dull" (T3 319).

15. The text of this speech, back-translated into German by Peter de Mendelssohn, is found in GW 13: 491–94.

16. In a superb new monograph on the philosopher, historian, theologian, and sociologist Ernst Troeltsch—until his death in 1923 Germany's outstanding spokesman for democracy, especially *during* World War I—Robert E. Norton presents Mann and Troeltsch as kindred spirits. As evidence, Norton cites Mann's crucial lecture *"Von deutscher Republik,"* his "bold affirmation of the new democratic state." Surprising his listeners, Mann declared (in words cited and translated by Norton), "my intention is to win your support for the republic and for what is called democracy and what I call humanity" (GKFA 15.1:522). Robert E. Norton, *The Crucible of German Democracy: Ernst Troeltsch and the First World War* (Tübingen: Mohr Siebeck, 2021), 572.

17. The Nazis seized power on January 30; February 13, 1933 was the fiftieth anniversary of Wagner's death. Michael H. Kater, *The Twisted Muse: Musicians and Their Music in the Third Reich* (New York: Oxford University Press, 1997), 42.

18. https://www.pro-europa.eu/europe/mann-thomas-god-help-our-darkened-and -desecrated-country/. In an interview with Otto Fuerbringer, a young American journalist, Mann expressed with pride the fact that his biting letter to the dean of the Faculty of Philosophy of the University of Bonn now belonged to the literature of the German antifascist underground. Many young Germans, Mann declared, had even memorized the letter so that they could not be discovered with so subversive a text in their possession. From an interview published in the *St. Louis Post-Dispatch* (March 18, 1939), in *Frage und Antwort: Interviews mit Thomas Mann 1909–1955*, ed. Volkmar Hansen and Gert Heine (Hamburg: Albrecht Knaus, 1983), 243. American readers of *The Nation*, which reprinted Mann's reply, would also have taken notice of the admiration that Ernest Bisdorff, a connoisseur of Mann's political writings, felt for Mann's "Ernst und Eleganz" (gravity and elegance). *Thomas Mann und die Politik* (Luxembourg: Imprimerie Centrale, 1966), 8.

19. Note especially Ernst Krieck, "Agonie: Schlußwort zu Thomas Mann," *Volk im Werden* 5 no. 3 (March 3, 1937), 121–25.

20. Dean Gauss was also well acquainted with Erich Kahler and richly supportive of Hermann Broch.

21. Jacques Lacan, *Le séminaire sur la lettre volée* (1955), cited in J. Hillis Miller, *For Derrida* (New York: Fordham University Press, 2009), 118.

22. Cited in *Thomas Mann, Briefe 1937–1947*, ed. Erika Mann (Frankfurt am Main: Fischer Taschenbuch, 1992), 768.

23. Thus Janet Flanner, in her witty and incisive early profile of Mann, the two-part "Goethe in Hollywood." Here, Janet Flanner, "Profiles: Goethe in Hollywood—I," *The New Yorker*, December 13, 1941, 31.

24. Frido Mann, Mann's grandson, has it right when he declares that he knows for a fact that his grandfather's contacts with Einstein in Princeton were few and far between. Frido Mann, "'Er war kein Akademiker, er war Künstler,' Ein Gespräch mit dem Schriftsteller Frido Mann über seine Großeltern und ihr Leben am Pazifik," interviewed by Jan Bürger in *Thomas Mann in Amerika*, ed. Ulrich Rauff and Ellen Strittmatter (Marbach am Neckar: Deutsche Schillergesellschaft, 2018), 19.

25. Mann wrote to Caroline Newton, who had made him a gift of the poodle: "I have made certain that he feels he belongs especially to me." For more of his first impressions and adventures with Niko, see his letter of thanks (N 69).

26. "There have been a series of dearly loved dogs in his life; indeed, the only story he ever wrote with a happy ending was one about a dog." Janet Flanner, "Profiles: Goethe in Hollywood—I," 38. For the poodle's confusion and return, see T3 502.

27. *Goethe's Faust*, tr. with intro. by Walter Kaufmann (New York: Random House, 1961), 153.

28. This item shares equal space with the notation that Mann took tea with Giuseppe Antonio Borgese, Hermann Broch, and others to discuss, for the first time, a "collective work to prepare for a restoration of the West," which would become, a year later, the small book *The City of Man* (C). See the sections of chapter 2 titled "A Typical Evening's Reading: Nizer and Mumford" and "*The City of Man*." As Paul Michael Lützeler notes, Mann had sought an occasion to bring Borgese and Broch together on the strength of their shared accomplishments and

goals—both were highly cultivated authors of novels and essays; both were vigorous antifascist universalists. See Paul Michael Lützeler, *Hermann Broch: A Biography*, tr. Janice Furness (London: Quartet Books, 1987), 188.

29. N 69. The book was presumably laid out in the open because Mann was reading Cassirer's writings on Goethe at the time.

30. Ernst Lothar, *Das Wunder des Überlebens: Erinnerungen und Erlebnisse* (Vienna and Hamburg: Paul Zsolnay Verlag, 1961), 141.

31. *The New York Times*, November 10, 1938. Bracketed text represents corrections to the *Times* report drawn from the actual text Mann read, which is reprinted in his *Diaries 1937–1939* (T3 889–93).

32. David Brooks, "The Glory of Democracy," *The New York Times*, December 14, 2017, https://www.nytimes.com/2017/12/14/opinion/democracy-thomas-mann.html.

33. The phrase is taken from Mann's letter to Caroline Newton, March 13, 1941 (N 76). By way of comparison and illustration, the most extreme requirement for "order" by a philosopher might be Socrates's "bouts of stillness. . . . He could all of a sudden revert to such a state at the most unexpected moments. . . . On such occasions, Socrates was in no retreat from mortal concerns, yet he isn't addressing or encountering them in typical space-time either. . . . Imagine the incredibly intensive state of mental activity that can come only from within a self-concocted cocoon of stillness and silence." And meanwhile, the life of the *polis* is crashing about one's ears, thankfully unheard. Christopher Phillips, *Soul of Goodness: A Philosopher's Path* (Amherst, NY: Prometheus Books, 2022).

34. Translation revised. Kahler's chef d'oeuvre is titled *Der deutsche Charakter in der Geschichte Europas* (The German character in the history of Europe) (Zurich: Europa Verlag, 1937). A revised, abridged version was published in English as *The Germans*, ed. Robert and Rita Kimber (Princeton, NJ: Princeton University Press, 1974). Hans Rudolf Vaget was the first to point out the importance to Mann of Kahler's *Der deutsche Charakter*. See "Kaisersaschern als geistige Lebensform. Zur Konzeption der deutschen Geschichte in Thomas Manns *Doktor Faustus*," in *Der deutsche Roman und seine historischen und politischen Bedingungen*, ed. Wolfgang Paulsen (Bern: Francke, 1977), 200–235.

35. The outcome of a conversation with Caroline Newton, one of his muses, and her mother.

36. Alice Kahler and Tom Edgar, "Einstein Chastised Kahler for Obtaining Visa Without Difficulty," *The Princeton Recollector*, September 1990, 7.

37. Frido Mann, "'Er war kein Akademiker,'" in *Thomas Mann in Amerika*, 22.

38. Hans Rudolf Vaget, *Thomas Mann, der Amerikaner. Leben und Werk im amerikanischen Exil 1938–1951* (Frankfurt am Main: S. Fischer, 2011); citations coded as VA plus page number. Klaus Harpprecht, *Thomas Mann, Eine Biographie* (Reinbek bei Hamburg: Rowohlt, 1995); citations coded as H plus page number.

39. Walter Kaufmann, *Critique of Religion and Philosophy* (Princeton, NJ: Princeton University Press, 1978), 423.

40. Frido Mann, "'Er war kein Akademiker,'" in *Thomas Mann in Amerika*, 20.

41. See Martin Heidegger's account of boredom in *The Fundamental Concepts of Metaphysics: World, Finitude, Solitude*, tr. William McNeill and Nicholas Walker (Bloomington: Indiana University Press, 1995), esp. 74–164. Jensen Suther comments, "Heidegger gave those lectures in 28/29, having read Mann's novel in 1925. He then heaped praise on the novel's treatment of time

and history in a letter to a young Hannah Arendt in July of that same year. There is a deep connection between the form of *Langweiligkeit* [boredom] described by the narrator and the second form of boredom analyzed by Heidegger" (which Suther calls "subjective boredom"). "Even Heidegger's example of such subjective boredom—a party at which time flies by—smacks of *The Magic Mountain*, which is phenomenologically quite rich in its engagement with the notion of being bored, both on the narrative level and on the level of the form (the narrator is preoccupied with the idea of a work that makes the time pass quickly, that is 'long on diversion' and 'short on boredom,' which arguably exemplifies the very notion of boredom he is trying to avoid)." Private communication, February 18, 2021. See also Kevin P. Eubanks, "Heidegger Reading Mann, or What Time *Is* It, Hans Castorp? Death, *Bildung*, and the Possibility of Time in *The Magic Mountain*," *College Literature* 44, no. 2 (spring 2017): 256–87.

42. Br.M 258; emphasis added.

43. Inge and Walter Jens, *Frau Thomas Mann: Das Leben der Katharina Pringsheim* (Hamburg: Rowohlt, 2003), 327.

44. Thomas Mann, "Sixteen Years: Reprinted from the 1948 American Edition of *Joseph and His Brothers*," *Joseph and His Brothers*, tr. John E. Woods (New York: Knopf, 2005), xxxix; T4 160.

45. *Thomas Mann Diaries 1918–1939*, 244. The date of the diary entry was June 29, 1935, the same evening as his visit. On the depth of Mann's admiration of Roosevelt, see VA 19.

46. Mann commented afterward on the extraordinary resemblance of the protagonist, Raymond Massey, to Lincoln, as known from his portraits—a very plausible judgment (T3 352).

47. The telegram was cosigned by Albert Einstein and Bruno Walter.

48. Gerhard Lauer, *Die verspätete Revolution. Erich Kahler: Wissenschaftsgeschichte zwischen konservativer Revolution und Exil* (Berlin: de Gruyter, 1995), 288. Lauer is citing Frank Fechner, *Thomas Mann und die Demokratie* (Berlin: Duncker & Humblot, 1990).

49. (EF 29). *Briefwechsel,* Kahler and Mann, 24.

50. In a letter to Schiller (July 9, 1796), Goethe wrote, "So werde ich immer gerne inkognito reisen [. . .], zwischen mich selbst und zwischen meine eigene Erscheinung stellen" (I will always like traveling incognito [. . .], situated between myself and my appearance). In a letter to Carl Friedrich von Reinhardt (June 22, 1808), Goethe adds that "es mir von jeher Spaß gemacht hat, Versteckens zu spielen" (I have always enjoyed playing hide and seek). Cited by Prof. Hellmut H. Ammerlahn, in an email to the Goethe Society of America, February 21, 2021.

51. Thomas Mann, *Buddenbrooks: The Decline of a Family,* tr. John E. Woods (New York: Knopf, 1993), 648.

52. C 15. Along with sixteen formidable intellectuals, including his friends and acquaintances Giuseppe Antonio Borgese, Erich Kahler, Hermann Broch, and Lewis Mumford, Mann helped to compose *The City of Man, A Declaration on World Democracy.*

53. Robert Galitz, "Family against a Dictatorship: Die Rundfunkstrategien der Familie Mann," in *Thomas Mann in Amerika*, ed. Ulrich Raulff and Ellen Strittmatter (Marbach am Neckar: Deutsche Schillergesellschaft, 2018), 50.

54. Ibid., 41.

55. Britta Böhler, *The Decision,* tr. Jeannette K. Ringold (London: Haus, 2015). On Mann's "towering complexity," see "America and the Refugee," in chapter 2.

56. This paragraph and the two paragraphs that follow draw on an essay on Mann as "a model of the writer in exile" by the Sorbonne professor Gérard Schneilin: "Thomas Mann: un modèle

d'écrivain en exil?" in *Exil et Résistance au national-socialisme 1933–1945*, ed. Gilbert Krebs et Gérard Schneilin (Asnières: Publications de l'Institut d'Allemand d'Asnières, 1998), 319–39.

57. Ibid., 323.

58. Ibid., 331. The dilemma, if it is one, continues to engage contemporary social philosophers. One reads of the philosopher Elizabeth Anderson that she is "a champion of the view that equality and freedom are mutually dependent, enmeshed in changing conditions through time. Working at the intersection of moral and political philosophy, social science, and economics, she has become a leading theorist of democracy and social justice." Nathan Heller, "Annals of Thought: The Philosopher Redefining Equality," *The New Yorker,* January 7, 2019, https://www.newyorker.com/magazine/2019/01/07/.

59. Ulrich Rauff and Ellen Strittmatter, "Einleitung," in *Thomas Mann in Amerika*, ed. Raulff and Strittmatter (Marbach am Neckar: Deutsche Schillergesellschaft, 2018), 6.

Chapter Two: Reflections of a Political Man

1. "Thomas Mann is ranked by many thoughtful critics as the finest of living imaginative writers. There are some rasher spirits—the editor of this book [Clifton Fadiman] is one—who believe he will eventually take his place among the very greatest novelists the race has produced." Clifton Fadiman, "Thomas Mann," in *I Believe: The Personal Philosophies of Certain Eminent Men and Women of Our Time* (New York: Simon and Schuster, 1939), 188. The appellation stuck. According to the journalist Alex Ross, who draws on Boes's *Thomas Mann's War*, it was Mann's American publisher, Alfred A. Knopf, who "remade a difficult, quizzical author as the 'Greatest Living Man of Letters,' an animate statue of European humanism." "Exodus: The Haunted Idyll of Exiled German Novelists in Wartime Los Angeles," *The New Yorker* (March 9, 2020), 42. The encomium wasn't entirely an American affair. In 1946, the well-known German writer Erich Kästner wrote in the newspaper *Weser-Kurier*, "Thomas Mann is not God . . . ; he is only, as I have said, the greatest and most famous living German author." Cited in Harry Pross, "On Thomas Mann's Political Career," *Journal of Contemporary History* 2, no. 2 (April 1967): 79.

2. Hans Rudolf Vaget cites a remark by Donald Prater from the latter's *Thomas Mann—A Life* (Oxford: Oxford University Press, 1995) to the effect that Mann is "sometimes undervalued as a political writer and thinker." Prater goes on to say that "though his ideas were often vague, and sought-after less for their content than for the authority of his standing as an artist, they were far from being those of a merely careerist conservative [*sic*]" (p. 525). Indeed! Vaget then lists Klaus Harpprecht and Anthony Heilbut as commentators who "would undoubtedly agree [with *different* parts of this judgment], the former stressing Mann's dangerous incompetence in this field, the latter extolling the liberal and emancipatory spirit of much of Mann's writing. . . . Prater and Heilbut . . . thus join the ranks of those who are prepared to take Mann's political writings seriously—among them Kurt Sontheimer, T.J. Reed, and Inge Jens. Harpprecht, on the other hand, while devoting ample space to Mann's politics, would probably prefer to take a place alongside Erich Heller, Joachim Fest, Marcel Reich-Ranicki . . . [and I will add Manfred Görtemaker, the author of *Thomas Mann und die Politik* (Frankfurt am Main: S. Fischer, 2005)], who argue that Mann's political ideas were amateurish and therefore need not be taken seriously." Hans Rudolf Vaget, "Mann and his Biographers," *Journal of English and Germanic*

228 NOTES TO CHAPTER TWO

Philology 96, no. 4 (October 1997): 599. In the two decades since Vaget wrote, both sides have acquired numerous reinforcements.

3. T. J. Reed, *Thomas Mann: The Uses of Tradition* (Oxford: Clarendon Press, 1974, 1996), 308. Reed's assessment was the same in 1974 as in 1996.

4. Görtemaker, *Thomas Mann und die Politik,* 7–8. Görtemaker's brief account of Mann's stay in Princeton is unreliable. Mann lectured at the university and not at the Institute for Advanced Study; Erich Kahler was not living in Princeton when Mann arrived; Hermann Broch did not settle in Princeton until 1942 and hence not "soon thereafter"—ergo, Görtemaker has failed to consult the correspondence of Mann and Kahler or the very rich introduction to Vaget's edition of the Thomas Mann–Agnes Meyer correspondence. These faults do not inspire confidence in Görtemaker's large, skeptical judgments, which are also based, after all, on a selection of details.

5. (H), Klaus Harpprecht, *Thomas Mann: Eine Biographie;* Anthony Heilbut, *Thomas Mann: Eros and Literature* (New York: Knopf, 1996).

6. Emphasis added. Tobias Temming is the author of a focused monograph on Mann's critique of German fascism during his years of exile: *"Bruder Hitler"? Zur Bedeutung des politischen Thomas Mann. Essays und Reden aus dem Exil* (Berlin: Wissenschaftlicher Verlag, 2008), 16.

7. The Munich Agreement was signed at 1:00 a.m. on the early morning of September 30, 1938, and was broadcast. The time difference between the continents meant that Mann had the news on the evening of September 29, the evening following his arrival in Princeton.

8. At least in the view, with which I concur, of Klaus Harpprecht; see *Thomas Mann: Eine Biographie,* 1405.

9. Gerhard Lauer, *Die verspätete Revolution, Erich Kahler: Wissenschaftsgeschichte zwischen konservativer Revolution und Exil* (Berlin: de Gruyter, 1995), 277–78.

10. Thomas Mann, *Tagebücher 1933–34,* ed. Peter de Mendelssohn (January 18, 1934) (Frankfurt am Main: S. Fischer, 1977), 293.

11. Here, at the risk of conflating great things with small, I evoke for my own purpose Wittgenstein's use of a Kierkegaardian trope. Kierkegaard wrote, in Johannes Climacus's *Concluding Unscientific Postscript,* "It is thus left to the reader himself to put two and two together, if he so desires; but nothing is done to minister to a reader's indolence." Now it has been said.

12. Gilles Deleuze, *Cinema 2: The Time-Image,* tr. Hugh Tomlinson and Robert Galeta (Minneapolis: University of Minnesota Press, 1989), 1.

13. In his diaries, Mann recorded a potent observation by the philosopher Max Horkheimer in the notable *Zeitschrift für Sozialforschung* in New York. Horkheimer had assumed ("rightly," thus Mann) that he, Mann, did not feel altogether easy with the philosophical-political message that had been "put into his custody." Horkheimer, as Mann notes, "speaks of the transparent coloring (*Lasurfarbe*) of irony, which the experienced reader still detects in my political compositions." "Horkheimer [. . .] nimmt mit Recht an, daß ich mich bei der zugesprochenen philosophisch-politischen Botschaft nicht wohl fühle. Spricht von der Lasurfarbe der Ironie, die der Erfahrene noch über meinen politischen Kompositionen entdeckt . . ." (T3 361–62).

14. About the emergence of *Death in Venice,* Mann wrote: "In truth, every work is of course fragmentary—but a *self-contained* realization of our nature, and here many things combined and crystallized to yield an image, which, hovering midst manifold associations, could well start an artist dreaming. Association: I love this word: when I ponder it, it falls together in my mind

with the conception of the significant—indeed, I would equate that which is significant with that which is rich in associations" ("On Myself," B 49).

15. The sequence in which these lectures and essays appear follows Mann's own collection in *Order of the Day: Political Essays and Speeches of Two Decades*, as well as the informative bibliography compiled by Walter Reichart ("Thomas Mann: An American Bibliography," *Monatshefte für Deutschen Unterricht* 37, no. 6 [Oct. 1945]: 389–408). The hotly desired volume 18 of the *Große kommentierte Frankfurter Ausgabe—Werke, Briefe, Tagebücher* (GKFA), which would contain Mann's political and ethical writings during these years, 1938–41, in best philological form, is still underway. The collection of Mann's political and essayistic writings that follows is as representative as I could have it, given page limits, and in this way means to be useful to the project of the GKFA.

16. "That Man Is My Brother," *Esquire*, March 1939, 31, 132–33; *"Bruder Hitler," Das Neue Tage-Buch*, March 25, 1939, 306–9.

17. In Mann's own words, "The ineffable disgust this man has always inspired in me is here held in check by an ironic approach which seems to me to bring the little study closest to the artist sphere." *Order of the Day: Political Essays and Speeches of Two Decades*, tr. H. T. Lowe-Porter, Agnes Meyer, and Eric Sutton (New York: Knopf, 1942), xiii–xiv. Citations from this work will be assigned a page number in parentheses.

18. "'Die Diktatoren werden am Ende doch verlieren,' sagt der von den Nazis vertriebene Schriftsteller" ("In the end the dictators will lose," says the writer, driven out by the Nazis). An interview with Clifford Epstein, *Detroit News* (March 3, 1938), in *Frage und Antwort: Interviews mit Thomas Mann 1909–1955*, ed. Volkmar Hansen and Gert Heine (Hamburg: Albrecht Knaus, 1983), 236.

19. "Bruder Hitler," GW 12:849, 852.

20. Mann, "A Brother," xiv. Mann notes in the "Foreword" to *Order of the Day* that the essay first appeared "in German, in the Paris refugee paper *Das Tagebuch* [in 1939] and in English in *Esquire*, under the title 'This Man Is My Brother'" (xiv). In fact, it appeared in *Esquire* first, with the title "That Man Is My Brother," and thereafter in the Paris weekly, *Das Neue Tage-Buch*.

21. In the words of Mann's biographer Klaus Harpprecht, Mann tends to employ irony as a general philosophical principle—one "to which he was willing to subordinate almost everything if it seemed helpful to him—often a kind of fetish he carried before him" (H 1122). Algis Valiunas describes Mann's "characteristic mode of thought as the ironic" and cites Mann's description of this mode from his 1922 essay "Goethe and Tolstoy": "Beautiful is resolution. But the really fruitful, the productive, and hence the artistic principle is that which we call reserve. . . . In the intellectual sphere we love it as irony: that irony which glances at both sides, which plays slyly and irresponsibly—yet not without benevolence—among opposites, and is in no great haste to take sides and come to decisions; guided as it is by the surmise that in great matters, in matters of humanity, every decision may prove premature; that the real goal to reach is not decision, but harmony, accord. And harmony, in a matter of eternal contraries, may lie in infinity; yet that playful reserve called irony carries it within itself, as the sustained note carries the resolution. . . . Irony is the pathos of the middle . . . its moral too, its ethos. . . . We [Germans] are a people of the middle, of the world-bourgeoisie; there is a fittingness in our geographical position and in our mores." "Thomas Mann's Civilized Uncertainty," *Humanities* 41 no. 3 (summer 2020). https://www.neh.gov/article/thomas-manns-civilized-uncertainty

22. In *Why the Germans? Why the Jews? Envy, Race Hatred, and the Prehistory of the Holocaust* (New York: Henry Holt, 2014), the historian Götz Aly identifies a generalized dislike of energetic "foreigners"—read: the Jews—by the Germans, a politically unstable people, and comments: "During the Great Depression, two Nazi slogans proved particularly resonant: 'Don't forget you're German' and 'Germany, awaken'! Slogans like these seem more appropriate to a people who are disoriented and lethargic than to muscle-flexing hypernationalists." Kindle version, loc. 3661.

23. See chapter 4, "Freud and the Future," *infra*, which Mann read in shortened form to the Princeton community on February 13, 1939.

24. https://gutenberg.spiegel.de/buch/der-mann-ohne-eigenschaften-erstes-buch-7588/14.

25. Morten Høi Jensen, in "The Unbearable Pathos of Thomas Mann," *Los Angeles Review of Books,* March 25, 2016, https://lareviewofbooks.org/article/the-unbearable-pathos-of -thomas-mann.

26. Mann, "A Brother," xiv.

27. Cited in an interview with Curt Riess, "Thomas Mann—Interview: The Writer on His Work, the War, and America on the Occasion of His 65th Birthday," *Aufbau* (June 7, 1940), in *Frage und Antwort: Interviews mit Thomas Mann 1909–1955,* 257.

28. Neil Ascherson, "Hitler as a Human: Hopping in His Matchbox," a review-essay of *Hitler: Ascent, 1889–1939* by Volker Ullrich, tr. Jefferson Chase (London: Bodley Head, 2016). *London Review of Books* 38, no. 11 (June 2, 2016): 23–24.

29. Thomas Mann, "I Believe," in *I Believe: The Personal Philosophies of Certain Eminent Men and Women of Our Time,* tr. H. T. Lowe-Porter, ed. Clifton Fadiman (New York: Simon & Schuster, 1939), 191. Citations from this work will be assigned a page number in parentheses. Mann reprinted this essay under the head of "Living Philosophies VI: The Coming Humanism," in *The Nation,* December 10, 1938, 617–18. It is again collected in *Order of the Day: Political Essays and Speeches of Two Decades,* 162–66.

30. Friedrich Hölderlin, "Der Rhein,"

> Denn weil
> Die Seligsten nichts fühlen von selbst,
> Muß wohl, wenn solches zu sagen
> Erlaubt ist, in der Götter Namen
> Teilnehmend fühlen ein Andrer,
> Den brauchen sie . . .

31. Albert Einstein, foreword to Rudolf Kayser, *Albert Einstein, A Biographical Portrait, by Anton Reiser* (New York: A. & C. Boni, 1930), v. "Anton Reiser" is not the author of this work. He is a fictional character—a soulful wanderer and outcast—the protagonist of an eponymous fictionalized biography by Karl Phillip Moritz (1756–1793)—introduced into the title of this portrait of Einstein by Kayser for inscrutable reasons.

32. Thomas Mann, *Joseph and His Brothers,* tr. John E. Woods (New York: Knopf, 2005), 1044.

33. Morton Dauwen Zabel, "Lotte in Weimar," a review in *The Nation,* August 31, 1940, 176.

34. Jeremy Adler, cited in Benjamin Balint, "The Witness," a review of Peter Filkins, *H. G. Adler: A Life in Many Worlds* (New York: Oxford University Press, 2019), and H. G. Adler, *Theresienstadt 1941–1934: The Face of a Coerced Community,* tr. Belinda Cooper (Cambridge, UK:

Cambridge University Press, 2019), *The Jewish Review of Books,* June 2019, https://jewish
reviewofbooks.com/articles/5409/the-witness/.

35. *"Mankind, Take Care!" The Atlantic Monthly,* August 1938, 178–84. The phrase "school for
barbarians" plays on the title of a book by Erika Mann, for which her father Thomas Mann wrote
a rousing introduction: Erika Mann, *School for Barbarians* (New York: Modern Age Books,
1938). Citations from Mann's *Atlantic Monthly* article will henceforth be assigned a page number
in parentheses.

36. Hendrik Ibsen, *The Wild Duck,* in *Four Great Plays* (New York: Simon & Schuster, n.d.),
Kindle location 2834–49.

37. Ibid., 3022–42. It is a telling fact that in Munich in 1895 Mann himself played the role of
Gregers Werle in the first German performance of *The Wild Duck*!

38. Martin Heidegger, "The Word of Nietzsche: 'God Is Dead,'" in *The Question Concerning
Technology and Other Essays,* tr. William Lovitt (New York: Harper & Row, 1977), 112 (originally
published in 1952).

39. Peter Sloterdijk, *Regeln für den Menschenpark: Ein Antwortsschreiben zu Heideggers Brief
über den Humanismus* (Frankfurt am Main: Suhrkamp, 1999), cited in Mark Greif, *The Age of the
Crisis of Man: Thought and Fiction in America, 1933–1973* (Princeton, NJ: Princeton University
Press, 2015), 103.

40. In the late 1940s, Mann recalls writing this essay "out of profound despondency, which
was not without outrage." He continues by stressing—perhaps excessively—its description as
"a bitter indictment of how the policies of Western nations were being debased *by a fear of Russian socialism*" (emphasis added). From the essay "Sixteen Years," describing the composition
of the grand tetralogy *Joseph and His Brothers,* composed for the 1948 American edition and
cited in *Joseph and His Brothers,* translated by John E. Woods (New York: Knopf, 2005), xxxvii.
Mann's insistence on a fear of Russian socialism would be heightened by the national mood of
his recollection, as described by Heinrich Detering: "Mann was disappointed . . . that in America, a new populist mass movement emerged in the form of the Cold War almost seamlessly
after Germany's Nazis were triumphantly vanquished. In 1947, he wrote in his diary that 'rule of
law was declining' and observed a creeping new form of 'fascist violence,' with all the charac-
teristics of populism, agitation against the media, anti-intellectualism, recurring racism, and so
forth—it was something he was horrified to watch. Everything connected to the name 'Mc-
Carthy' was a mess of authoritarian and anti-democratic movements that Thomas Mann experienced and countered in word and text." https://www.dw.com/en/thomas-mann-was
-disappointed-by-americas-populism/a-44238143.

41. Thomas Mann, *This Peace* (New York: Knopf, 1938), 7. Citations from this work will be
assigned a page number in parentheses.

42. James T. Farrell, "Mann's Manifesto against Fascism: James T. Farrell Writes That He
Cannot Accept It," *New York Herald Tribune,* December 23, 1938, 14.

43. Jerome Frank, *Save America First: How to Make our Democracy Work* (New York and
London: Harper and Brothers, 1938), 28–29.

44. Britannia certainly played its hand along with the other culprits on both sides. In an
essay titled "Downfall: The Flawed Heroes of Anti-Hitler Resistance," a review of Paddy Ash-
down and Sylvie Young, *Nein! Standing Up to Hitler, 1935–1944* (London: William Collins, 2019),
Deborah Vietor-Engländer discusses "a memorandum written by one of the few people who

did see through Hitler very early on: Sir Robert Vansittart, the Chief Diplomatic Adviser to the British Government. He wrote to the Foreign Secretary Anthony Eden in 1937, relaying the warnings of Carl Goerdeler against Hitler. The memo remained on Eden's desk and was later found in Vansittart's private papers with a note, 'Suppressed by Eden.'" *The Times Literary Supplement*, July 19, 2019, 13.

45. Mann's refrain "Fear not!" (*"Fürchtet euch nicht!"*) is an echo of Luke, the angel's glad tidings to the frightened shepherds heralding the birth of Christ. It would have been well known to Mann and his musically aware listeners from the familiar choral refrain by Johann Michael Bach, not to mention Handel's *Messiah,* and is of a piece with Mann's exalted tone throughout many of these lectures. In *Thomas Mann's War*, Boes observes that "attentive readers [of 'This Peace'] . . . would have discovered foreshadowings of the same prophetic diction that Mann [would] so systematically employ in his BBC broadcasts" titled "German Listeners" (186; see the section "Listen, Germany!" in chapter 2, *infra*). Anglophone commentators will hear in Mann's phrase an echo of Roosevelt's impressive trope from his 1933 inaugural address, "[T]here is nothing to fear but . . . fear itself."

46. Ian Buruma, "Winston Churchill Would Despise Boris Johnson," *The New York Times,* July 27, 2019. Churchill declaimed, in a speech beginning "I wish to speak about the tragedy of Europe," "Yet all the while there is a remedy which, if it were generally and spontaneously adopted by the great majority of people in many lands, would as by a miracle transform the whole scene. . . . What is this *sovereign* remedy? It is to recreate the European fabric, or as much of it as we can, and to provide it with a structure under which it can dwell in peace, safety, and freedom. We must build a kind of United States of Europe." Winston Churchill, "A Speech Delivered at the University of Zurich, 19 September 1946," https://rm.coe.int/16806981f3; emphasis added.

47. See Nigel Hamilton, *War and Peace: FDR's Final Odyssey, D-Day to Yalta, 1943–1945* (New York: Houghton Mifflin Harcourt, 2019). What Mann did not live long enough to see—and what we see today—is the "botched" version of the supranational state. Sovereignty dissolves when the plutocrats of the various nations lodge their wealth and cunning in a giant offshore virtual state. As George Monbiot writes, "As economic life has been offshored, so has political life. The political rules that are supposed to prevent foreign money from funding domestic politics have collapsed. The main beneficiaries are the self-proclaimed defenders of sovereignty who rise to power with the help of social media ads bought by persons unknown, and thinktanks and lobbyists that refuse to reveal their funders. A recent essay by the academics Reijer Hendrikse and Rodrigo Fernandez [in the journal of the TNI (Transnational Institute)] argues that offshore finance involves 'the rampant unbundling and commercialization of state sovereignty' and the shifting of power into a secretive, extraterritorial legal space, beyond the control of any state. In this offshore world, they contend, 'financialized and hypermobile global capital effectively is the state.'" "From Trump to Johnson, Nationalists Are on the Rise—Backed by Billionaire Oligarch: The Ultra-Rich Are Benefitting from Disaster Capitalism as Institutions, Rules and Democratic Oversight Implode," *The Guardian,* July 26, 2019, https://www.theguardian.com/commentisfree/2019/jul/26/trump-johnson-nationalists-billionaire-oligarchs.

48. Eric Hobsbawm writes, "What National Socialism certainly achieved was a radical purging of the old Imperial elites and institutional structures. After all, the only group which actually launched a revolt against Hitler—and was consequently decimated—was the old aristocratic

Prussian army in July 1944. This destruction of the old elites and the old frameworks, reinforced after the war by the policies of the occupying Western armies, was eventually to make it possible to build the Federal Republic on a much sounder basis than the Weimar Republic of 1918–33, which had been little more than the defeated empire minus the Kaiser." *The Age of Extremes: A History of the World, 1914–1991* (New York: Vintage, 1996), 128.

49. Ascherson, "Hitler as a Human: Hopping in His Matchbox," 24. The sense of a common German identity of which Ascherson speaks has been gravely challenged by the recent immigration into Germany of a million refugees.

50. From an interview with Fletcher Wilson, published in the *Minneapolis Morning Tribune* of February 15, 1940, in *Frage und Antwort, Interviews with Thomas Mann, 1909–1955*, 251.

51. Winston Churchill, "Iron Curtain Speech," in Philip White, *Our Supreme Task: How Winston Churchill's Iron Curtain Speech Defined the Cold War Alliance* (New York: Public Affairs, 2012), 198.

52. Robert Rhodes James, *Churchill: A Study in Failure, 1900–1939* (Cleveland: World, 1970), 361.

53. Ferdinand Mount, "Nasty, Brutish, and Great," a review of *Churchill: Walking with Destiny* by Andrew Roberts (New York: Viking, 2019). *The New York Review of Books* 66, no. 10 (June 6, 2019): 24.

54. Boes's *Thomas Mann's War* (TB) traces Mann's shifting fortunes as an American icon.

55. "Scheußliche Schmähkarte unter der Post, jüdelnd, mit der Vermutung, daß ich das Bombardement von Weimar durch die Engländer veranlasst hätte,—wie [Martin] Gumpert mir erzählte; ich hätte es nicht gelesen, sondern nur, daß der Sender mir 'verachtungsvoll ins Gesicht spucke'" (T4 144).

56. It can be read in typescript in the Thomas Mann Archive of the Eidgenössische Technische Hochschule in Zurich, Reference Code A-I-Mp IV 55 Ue1.

57. As early as Mann's notorious 1918 essay "Thoughts in War" (*Gedanken im Kriege*), Mann links *Geist* with intellectuality. But in that text, intellectuality, which organizes civilization, is considered inferior to the drives that inform and empower culture (E 1:189). Mann's second round of thoughts in wartime, the time of the Second World War, assigns *Geist* to the first rank in the arsenal of weapons to counterattack Hitler's botching of an authentic German culture.

58. Quite possibly an echo of Mann's beloved President Roosevelt's best-remembered encouragement, spoken at his inauguration in 1933: "The only thing we have to fear is fear itself."

59. James T. Farrell, "Mann's Manifesto against Fascism: James T. Farrell Writes That He Cannot Accept It," *New York Herald Tribune*, December 23, 1938, 14.

60. "Gedanken im Kriege" is the first essay in the volume correctly titled *Friedrich und die große Koalition* (Berlin: S. Fischer, 1915).

61. In 1952, Harry Slochower became a cause célèbre for taking the Fifth Amendment under political duress, whereupon he was fired from his teaching job at Brooklyn College though subsequently (briefly) reinstated. He went on to a distinguished scholarly career while teaching at the New School for Social Research.

62. Harry Slochower, "Sees Mann Misunderstood," *New York Herald Tribune*, December 29, 1938, 16.

63. In "A Power of Facing Unpleasant Facts," Fussell writes: "I have [those] authors especially in mind . . . who, not liking the reviews their books receive, feel obliged to insist publicly that

the comment of the reviewer is, variously, unfair, perverse, stupid, irresponsible, or otherwise not at all what it should be—that is, laudatory." He cites "Samuel Johnson's classic observation, in his *Life of Pope* . . . 'An author places himself uncalled before the tribunal of criticism,' says Johnson, 'and solicits fame at the hazard of disgrace.' Or as E. M. Forster puts it: 'Some reviews give pain. This is regrettable, but no author has the right to whine. He was not obliged to be an author. He invited publicity, and he must take the publicity that comes along.'" Paul Fussell, *Thank God for the Atom Bomb and Other Essays* (New York: Summit Books, 1988), 112–13.

64. Bernard Rosenberg, "The Threat of Fascism," *New York Herald Tribune*, December 29, 1938, 16.

65. Thomas Mann, *Order of the Day: Political Essays and Speeches of Two Decades*, 228–37; Thomas Mann, "Culture and Politics," *Survey Graphic* 28 (February 1939): 149–51. This journal ceased publication in 1952. The German is in GW 12:853–61.

66. Janet Flanner, "Profiles: Goethe in Hollywood—II," *The New Yorker*, December 20, 1941, 22–35.

67. Ibid., 22.

68. Thomas Mann, "In My Defense," *The Atlantic Monthly*, October 1944, 101–2. The original German is found in GW 13:206–12.

69. Luis Araquistáin, "Good Germans?" in Letters to the Editor, *The London Times Literary Supplement*. August 21, 1943, 403.

70. Enid Starkie makes a brief and spectacular appearance in Terry Eagleton's *The Gatekeeper: A Memoir* (New York: St. Martin's Press, 2001). Instancing the inhuman wit of Oxford dons in the late 1950s, he notes that "Maurice Bowra . . . observed of the gaudily dressed French scholar Enid Starkie that she had appeared at one of his parties 'in all the colours of the Rimbaud.'" Kindle version, loc. 1791. Starkie's complaint in her *Flaubert: The Making of a Master* that Flaubert had been dismayingly incoherent in representing Mme. Bovary's eye color differently on different pages is dismissed as ignorant by Julian Barnes (through his fictional spokesman Geoffrey Braithwaite) in *Flaubert's Parrot*, Kindle version, loc. 1182. (New York: Knopf, 1985).

71. *The Spectator*, September 10, 1943, 12.

72. Thomas Mann, "What Is German?" *The Atlantic Monthly*, May 1944, 78–85. This article became the basis of a famous lecture Mann delivered at the Library of Congress on May 29, 1945, under the title "Germany and the Germans," in *Thomas Mann's Addresses Delivered at the Library of Congress 1942–1949* (Washington, DC: Library of Congress, 1963), 47–66.

73. Henri Peyre, "Thomas Mann and the Germans," *The Atlantic Monthly*, July 1944, 26.

74. Thomas Mann, "In My Defense," *The Atlantic Monthly*, October 1944, 100–102; the original German in GW 13:206–12.

75. Thomas Mann, "In My Defense," 102; GW 13:212.

76. The various citations bearing on Mann's motive to return to Europe are found in Erich Frey, "Thomas Mann's Exile Years in America," *Modern Language Studies* 6, no. 1 (Spring, 1976): 91–92.

77. Morten Høi Jensen, "The Unbearable Pathos of Thomas Mann," *Los Angeles Review of Books*, March 25, 2016, *https://lareviewofbooks.org/article/the-unbearable-pathos-of-thomas-mann/#!* The book under review is Britta Böhler, *The Decision*, tr. Jeannette K. Ringold (London: Haus, 2015).

78. *New Republic,* November 8, 1939, 38–39.

79. Readers will have long noted Mann's insistent and inconsiderate use of exclusively male pronouns in such reflections, which are in fact about and addressed to a more capacious humanity, foremost including women. This being so, one would wish that Mann had explicitly addressed the women in his reflections by their pronouns. But the fact that this courtesy is an evident requirement has taken a long time to come to people's awareness.

80. Professor Todd Kontje is one of these commentators: see *Mann's World: Empire, Race, and the Jewish Question* (Ann Arbor: University of Michigan Press, 2011). Mann's own embeddedness in a racialist sensibility calls for full-scale treatment, which is found in Kontje's luminous work. This is a study of Mann as "a writer whose personal prejudices reflected those of the world around him . . . and whose autobiographical fiction expressed not only the concerns of the German nation, as he liked to claim, but also of the world in an era of imperial conquest and global conflict." The actors in a world of conquest and conflict in 1938 have changed, but many of Mann's stereotypes survive as fossils.

81. Thomas Mann, "This War," tr. Eric Sutton, in *Order of the Day, Political Essays and Speeches of Two Decades* (New York: Knopf, 1942). The concluding portion of this long essay was originally published in a different translation as "Looking Abroad: Two Visions of Peace," *The Nation,* February 10, 1940, 174–77. Thereafter the full essay appeared as a small book, *This War,* tr. Eric Sutton (New York: Knopf, 1940).

82. Mann, "This War," 186. Citations from this work will be assigned a page number in parentheses.

83. Erich Kahler, *Man—the Measure: A New Approach to History* (New York: George Braziller, 1956), 532–33.

84. On the other hand, in "This War," Mann does employ the adjective "civilized" (*zivilisiert*), as in the genitive expression "der zivilisierten Menschheit" (of civilized humanity)—in a looser sense, in opposition (God forbear!) not to Nazi *Kultur* but to Nazi barbarism.

85. This colonization by renaming is brilliantly dramatized in Brian Freel's *Translations,* described by the author as "a play about language and only about language." Freel is correctly discussed in https://en.wikipedia.org/wiki/Translations.

86. Thomas Mann, "Foreword," tr. H. T. Lowe-Porter, in *Order of the Day,* xiv–xv.

87. Thomas Mann, "Mediators between the Spirit and Life: Address before American Booksellers' Association in May 1939," *Publishers Weekly,* May 27, 1939, 1886. Citations from this work will henceforth be assigned a page number in parentheses.

88. See Nietzsche, who writes in *Götzen-Dämmerung* of what Germans lack: namely, an understanding that *pulchrum est paucorum hominum.* Nietzsche, *Werke, Kritische Gesamtausgabe,* ed. Giorgio Colli and Mazzino Montinari (Berlin: Walter de Gruyter, 1969), VI-3: 6.

89. Mann lectured on "The Problem of Freedom" in various versions and at various venues. The fullest version, replete with many literary references (to Benjamin Constant, Goethe, Heine, et al.) was to be delivered, in German, at the meeting of the 17th International P.E.N. Congress in Stockholm in September 1939, but the outbreak of the war annulled the event. The text of "Das Problem der Freiheit" can be found in E 5:54–74 and, in English, as "Freedom and Equality" in *Freedom: Its Meaning,* ed. Ruth Nanda Anshen (New York: Harcourt Brace, 1940), 68–83. I will be excerpting and commenting on the compact version delivered, in English, at the April 1939 commencement exercises at Rutgers University, New Brunswick, New Jersey.

This translation was made by Agnes E. Meyer, thereafter shortened and improved by Erika Mann, and then certainly approved by Mann himself. The American Mann scholar Russell Berman, invited in 2017 to deliver the first international Thomas Mann Lecture at the ETH (Zurich), astutely chose as his subject matter "Thomas Mann—Literatur und Freiheit" (Literature and freedom).

90. Mann is not alone in an effort to resolve the tension between the two ideals: the freedom of individuals and their participation, as equals, in a community. In short, the seemingly innocently-phrased ideal of "a society of equals" is in fact explosively tense. I am taken with the anecdotal rephrasing of this issue by the Harvard scholar Sarah Dryden-Peterson, who wrote, in her vita, "My English teacher . . . assigned me [at age 12] a project on the meaning of a word. I chose the word 'community' and riffed on what I saw as the two essential parts of this idea: common and unity. I began to think about a big question that still preoccupies me: How much needs to be common to have unity?" https://www.gse.harvard.edu/news/ed/16/01/making -assistant-professor-sarah-dryden-peterson-edd09.

91. *The Problem of Freedom, an Address to the Undergraduates and Faculty of Rutgers University at Convocation on April the 28th, 1939* (New Brunswick, NJ: Rutgers University Press, 1939), 4. Citations from this work will be assigned a page number in parentheses.

92. Irving Singer, *The Nature of Love*, vol. 2, *Courtly and Romantic* (Chicago: University of Chicago Press, 2009), 439.

93. Christian Morgenstern, *Die unmögliche Tatsache*, in *Palmström. Alle Galgenlieder* (Zurich: Diogenes, 1981), 164.

94. Walter A. Kaufmann, *Time Is an Artist*, the second book of *Man's Lot: A Trilogy* (New York: Reader's Digest Press/McGraw-Hill, 1978), 58.

95. From an interview published by Otto Fuerbringer in the *St. Louis Post-Dispatch* (March 18, 1939), in *Frage und Antwort: Interviews with Thomas Mann*, 245. How prescient! In maskless America today, the fascist watchword, whether explicit or not, is "Give me freedom, *and* give me death!"

96. On Mann's further prescience: in the very interview cited above—published by Otto Fuerbringer in the *St. Louis Post-Dispatch* (March 18, 1939)—Mann is quoted as contemplating, as an eventuality, "the possible connection or even union of Germany and Russia in the coming years . . . referring to the external similarities of the two systems, which could lead to such an event." And he then outlines the "moral" distinction between the two systems that we have heard him making in his Rutgers speech, exactly one month later: "Although they are somewhat similar in their technical methods . . . in reality the two systems are quite different. Communism is in certain respects connected with the idea of humanity. Although it may make use of wrong methods that are inconsistent with human nature, its goal, despite everything, is to improve the conditions of humanity. Fascism is exclusively destructive and admires power only." Ibid., 244. It was not to be a matter of "coming years": four months later, on August 23, 1939, Germany and Russia concluded the German-Soviet Nonaggression Pact.

97. http://holocaustonline.org/significant-events/kristallnacht/insurance-payments/.

98. Thomas Mann, "The Dangers Facing Democracy," an address broadcast by the NBC on behalf of "The United Jewish Appeal for Refugees and Overseas Needs," in GW 13:491.

99. David Brooks (of *The New York Times*) might once again have been reading Mann (see *supra*, chapter 1) when Brooks wrote: "A society is healthy when its culture counterbalances its

economics. That is to say, when you have a capitalist economic system that emphasizes competition, dynamism and individual self-interest, you need a culture that celebrates cooperation, stability and committed relationships." "The Rise of the Haphazard Self," *The New York Times,* May 13, 2019, https://www.nytimes.com/2019/05/13/opinion/working-class-men.html.

100. Thomas Mann, "Foreword," in *Order of the Day: Political Essays and Speeches of Two Decades,* xiii.

101. Mann, *Order of the Day.* Citations from this work will be assigned a page number in parentheses. In a foreword, Mann notes that he considers this lecture, "written in 1940, . . . a 'better job' than *This War . . .*" (xv).

102. "Hobart Confers Degree on Mann: Makes Him Doctor of Letters after His Commencement Address Assailing Nazis," *The New York Times,* May 30, 1939.

103. Erich Kahler, "The Basic Problem of Our Time," in *Man—the Measure: A New Approach to History* (New York: Braziller, 1956), 3. The work was originally published by Pantheon in 1943 but had been long in preparation. Mann saluted the work on its cover: "Of all the minds at work today, his is one of the cleverest, finest and richest. This work, a composition broad and towering as a mountain-range, evidences once more the magnificent propensity of this mind for the comprehensive and the universal. It is no more and no less than the novel of humanity."

104. Louis Nizer, *Thinking on Your Feet: Adventures in Speaking* (Garden City, NY: Garden City Publishing Co., 1944; originally, New York: Liveright, 1940).

105. Janet Flanner, "Profiles: Goethe in Hollywood—I," 31.

106. Nizer, *Thinking on Your Feet,* 53–55.

107. Juan Vicente Gomez died on December 17, 1935. For twenty-seven years he had been dictator of Venezuela and crushed the voices of the opposition.

108. Nizer, *Thinking on Your Feet,* 228–31.

109. Ibid., 238–41.

110. Lewis Mumford, *Faith for Living* (New York: Harcourt, Brace and Company, 1940).

111. Ibid., 88–90.

112. Thomas Mann, letter to Count Carlo Sforza (August 13, 1941), originally written in French and quoted here in English (L 370).

113. Lewis Mumford, *The Culture of Cities,* 3rd ed. (New York: Harcourt Brace, 1970; originally 1938), 290–91.

114. I am grateful to VA 234 for its illuminating references to Mumford's autobiographical writings.

115. Mumford locates the event in "Smithfield," a part of Amenia. Lewis Mumford, *My Works and Days, A Personal Chronicle* (New York and London: Harcourt Brace Jovanovich, 1979), 329.

116. *Sketches from Life: The Autobiography of Lewis Mumford, The Early Years* (New York: Dial Press, 1982), 194.

117. Ibid., 467–68.

118. Mumford, *Works and Days,* 390; emphasis added.

119. C, *The City of Man, A Declaration on World Democracy* (New York: Viking Press, 1940).

120. Ibid., 67; emphasis added.

121. Ibid., 73.

122. Mumford, *Sketches,* 486–87.

123. Mumford, *Works and Days,* 391.

124. *City of Man*, 71.

125. "After the guests had gone, I read in Laski's 'Where do we go?'" (*sic*; T4 194).

126. Mann, *Briefe 1937–1947* (January 28, 1941), ed. Erika Mann (Frankfurt am Main: Fischer Taschenbuch Verlag, 1992), 177.

127. Mumford, letter to Josephine Strongin, November 13, 1941, *Works and Days*, 329–30.

128. Ester Saletta, "*The City of Man*: The Political-Ideological Contribution of Giuseppe Antonio Borgese and Gaetano Salvemini to Hermann Broch's Democratic Utopia," *Research* October 2015, DOI: 10.13140/RG.2.1.2748.7441. Her monograph has been translated by Catherine Bolton in *Teoria Politica*, vol. 5 (Ariccia [Rome]: Aracne, 2015). This not quite "forgotten manifesto," as the historians Adi Gordon and Udi Greenberg describe it, continues to exercise a hold on the political imagination. The title of their detailed essay, "*The City of Man*, European Émigrés, and the Genesis of Postwar Conservative Thought," gives their slant away, which finds in it the germ of Cold War ideology—an extravagant thesis, as witness Paul Michael Lützeler's countering essay, "Visionaries in Exile: Broch's Cooperation with G. A. Borgese and Hannah Arendt," in *Hermann Broch: Visionary in Exile*, ed. Paul Michael Lützeler (Rochester, NY: Camden House, 2003), 67–88. Lützeler sees in this document the germ of a neoliberal world economy.

129. *City of Man*, 12. Citations from this work will be assigned a page number in parentheses. This quotation, though uncredited here, is taken from a work by Hermann Rauschning, *The Voice of Destruction*, a book of conversations with Hitler. I owe this information to Mark Greif's *The Age of the Crisis of Man*. Greif goes on to observe that "indications of Rauschning's reception and influence are widespread in the discourse of the crisis of man but not always conspicuous. . . . Thomas Mann, then the leading voice of the anti-Nazi exiles in the United States, included Rauschning among a select group of authors—along with himself, his brother Heinrich, and the likes of Stephan Zweig, Paul Tillich, and Erwin Schrödinger—who he hoped would write pamphlets to smuggle back into Germany so its citizens would hear the voice of 'intellectual Germany on the outside.' He outlines the plan in a letter to Heinrich Mann of May 14, 1939 [BR.H 223–24] . . ." (341n28). Rauschning's presence in *The City of Man* is confirmed by a letter of Broch to Borgese on March 3, 1940: "The book *Conversations with Hitler* gives a complete and in my opinion absolutely authentic picture of Hitler's concept of world politics, the concept he serves and cherishes in his mind, heart and soul, the concept of a new universal slavery." Cited in Michael Paul Lützeler, *Hermann Broch: A Biography*, tr. Janice Furness (London: Quartet Books, 1987), 191. Lützeler notes that Rauschning's book had appeared at the beginning of 1940, revealing that "Hitler intended not only to subjugate all of Europe but had plans to conquer the whole world" (191). Awareness of this "concept" is acute all throughout *The City of Man*. According to Boes, Rauschning's citations did their work despite the fact that "nowadays [2019] most historians regard Rauschning's Hitler quotes as fakes" (TB 307).

130. BR.M 210. Cf. Claude Lévi-Strauss, in a social optic, describing the cruelty he faced from Vichy-allied French Forces on landing in Martinique on his passage to New York: "This was not the first occasion on which I had encountered those outbreaks of stupidity, hatred and credulousness which social groups secrete like pus when they begin to be short of space." *Tristes Tropiques*, tr. John and Doreen Weightman (New York: Penguin, 2012), 29.

131. Lützeler, *Broch: A Biography*, 195.

132. From a letter to Stephen Hudson, ca. December 7, 1938, cited in ibid., 189.

133. From a letter to William Stewart, December 28, 1938, cited in ibid., 189–90.

134. Thomas Mann, "Richard Wagner and *The Ring of the Nibelung*" (B 89). Mann delivered this lecture on January 17, 1939. See the section of this name in chapter 4, *infra*.

135. Cited in Ulrich Raulff and Ellen Strittmatter, "Einleitung," *Thomas Mann in Amerika*, ed. Ulrich Raulff and Ellen Strittmatter (Marbach am Neckar: Deutsche Schillergesellschaft, 2018), 11.

136. Thomas Mann, "War and Democracy" (T4 1036). Further citations from this work will be assigned a page number in parentheses.

137. Thomas Mann, "[I Am an American,] By Dr. Thomas Mann," in *I Am an American, by Famous Naturalized Americans*, ed. Robert Spiers Benjamin, with an introduction by Archibald MacLeish, foreword by Francis Biddle, Solicitor General of the United States (New York: Alliance Book Corporation, 1941), 30–35.

138. Archibald MacLeish, introduction to ibid., vii.

139. "Cruelty" as a value in politics? Does this make any sense at all? Evidently, it does, in recent times, for more than one thoughtful observer. Peter Wehner writes, "Beyond that, in their ferocious defense of the president, Trump supporters are signaling that decency is a form of weakness, that cruelty is a welcome and highly effective political weapon and that the low road is the preferred road." "Trump Is Betting That Anger Can Still Be Power," *New York Times*, June 19, 2019, https://www.nytimes.com/.

140. Louis Nizer, "Let Them In," in *Thinking on Your Feet: Adventures in Speaking* (New York: Liveright, 1940), 238–41.

141. "*Denken und Leben*: Reflections on Being Received into Phi Beta Kappa." *Virginia Quarterly Review* 17, no. 3 (Summer 1941): 370–75. This essay was subsequently translated by H. T. Lowe-Porter and republished in Mann, *Order of the Day: Political Essays and Speeches of Two Decades*, 257–63.

142. Mann does not give the source of this quote, but it is Herbert Read, "The Politics of the Unpolitical," subsequently published as the lead essay in *The Politics of the Unpolitical* (London: Routledge, 1943), 36.

143. Thomas Mann, "Wir sind nicht mehr Ästheten genug, uns vor dem Bekenntnis zum Guten zu fürchten, uns so trivialer Begriffe und Leitbilder zu schämen, wie Wahrheit, Freiheit, Gerechtigkeit." *Nietzsches Philosophie im Lichte unserer Erfahrung, Vortrag am XIV. Kongress des Pen-Clubs in Zurich am 3. Juni 1947*, ed. David Marc Hoffmann (Basel: Schwabe, 2005), 40.

144. I rely here on H. T. Lowe's translation of "Thinking and Living," 261.

145. For the rich historical context, see the essay by Mary Beth Lineberry, "Thomas Mann in VQR: How the Nobel Laureate came to publish an anti-Nazi essay in VQR—in German." https://www.vqronline.org/vqr-vault/thomas-mann-vqr.

146. Thomas Mann, from a letter to Felix Braun, July 31, 1943, cited in the valuable study by Sonja Valentin, "*Steine in Hitlers Fenster*": *Thomas Manns Radiosendungen "Deutsche Hörer!*" (*1940–1945*) (Göttingen: Wallstein, 2015), 7.

147. Valentin, "*Steine in Hitlers Fenster*," 9.

148. Thomas Mann, "Foreword," *Listen, Germany! Twenty-Five Radio Messages to the German People over BBC* (New York: Knopf, 1943), v.

149. See http://www.lib.cam.ac.uk/collections/departments/germanic-collections/about -collections/spotlight-archive/burning-books. The Wikipedia article on Thomas Mann (as of

May 2021) falsely asserts that Mann's books were not burned; the author can have been misled by the fact that, curiously, his books continued to be sold in Germany through 1936.

150. Mann was one of the "everybody" that reads *Life* magazine. He was aware of the extensive, very positive account of his pro-democratic activities described by Marquis Childs in "Thomas Mann: Germany's Foremost Literary Exile Speaks Now for Freedom and Democracy in America," in the April 17, 1939, issue of *Life*; and on October 14 of that year, together with Einstein, he attended in Princeton a performance of the play *Margin for Error* (which, by the way, he considered execrable), written by Clare Boothe Luce, Henry Luce's wife. He chatted amiably with her on stage after the performance.

151. Mann preferred not to speak here of the "America First," isolationist, and even rampant pro-Nazi currents in the "masses," let alone, in a good part of them, perfervid anti-Semitism and hostility to the refugees. I shall cite Eric Rauchway's description of this countercurrent, deriving from the work of Bradley W. Hart. Rauchway identifies the explicitly pro-fascist organizations at home in America: the German American Bund and the Silver Shirts, among others. "Some adherents of these organizations hoped to establish a National Socialist government in Washington; essentially all aimed to stop the United States from joining the war on the side of the Allies. They claimed tens of thousands of members and many more sympathizers. The general enthusiasm for Nazi racial views and American isolationism was even more evident, inspiring espionage, sabotage, propaganda and political activism intended to assist the advance of Nazism throughout the world." Eric Rauchway, "Selling to Suckers: Nazi Sympathies in American Souls," a review of Bradley W. Hart, *Hitler's American Friends: The Third Reich's Supporters in the United States* (New York: St. Martin's Press, 2018) in *The Times Literary Supplement*, July 5, 2019, 13.

152. Reinhold Niebuhr, "Mann Speaks to Germany," *The Nation*, February 13, 1943, 244. Mann was to hold all Germans and everything German responsible to some extent for the crimes of the Nazi government; Niebuhr resisted this charge.

153. "In deutschen Lazaretten und Krankenhäusern werden die Schwerverwundeten zusammen mit Alten, Gebrechlichen, Geisteskranken durch Giftgas zum Tode gebracht—zwei tausend von drei tausend, so erzählte ein deutscher Arzt, in *einer* Anstalt. Das tut dasselbe Regime, das aufbrüllt, wenn Roosevelt es beschuldigt, es wolle das Christentum und alle Religion vernichten, und das vorgibt, einen Kreuzzug christlicher Gesittung gegen den Bolschewismus zu führen,—den Bolschewismus, von dem es selbst nur eine unvergleichlich gemeinere Abart ist. Das christliche Gegenstück zu den Massen-Vergasungen sind die 'Begattungstage,' wo beurlaubte Soldaten mit BDM- Mädchen zu tierischer Stunden-Ehe zusammenkommandiert werden, um Staatsbastarde für den nächsten Krieg zu zeugen. Kann ein Volk, eine Jugend, tiefer sinken? Greuel und Lästerung der Menschlichkeit, wohin ihr seht" (GW 11:1020–21).

154. Alfred Tyrnauer, "German Leaders-in-Exile Ponder Country's Postwar Fate," *Washington Post*, July 4, 1943. The article was discussed in Br.M., 498 and 980–81. See Valentin, *"Steine in Hitlers Fenster,"* 314.

Chapter Three: A Round-Up of Political Themes

1. My approach to Mann's political writings has been enriched throughout by Hans Rudolf Vaget, "Zu Thomas Manns Kriegsschriften im Exil," in *Exil im Krieg 1939–1945*, ed. Hiltrud Häntzschel, Inge Hansen-Schaberg, Claudia Glunz, and Thomas F. Schneider (Göttingen:

Vandenhoeck & Ruprecht, 2016), 89–98; and by two critical studies: Gérard Schneilin, "Thomas Mann: un modèle d'écrivain en exil?" in *Exil et Résistance au national-socialisme 1933–1945*, ed. Gilbert Krebs and Gérard Schneilin (Asnières: Publications de l'Institut d'Allemand d'Asnières, 1998), 319–39, and, once again, TB 188–93.

2. *The City of Man*, 12.

3. In elaborating these points, I will have an eye on Vaget's and Boes's organization of these topics.

4. Thomas Mann, "Zu Wagners Verteidigung: Brief an den Herausgeber des 'Common Sense,'" GW 13:358.

5. Emphasis added. Hans Rudolf Vaget, "Mann and his Biographers," *Journal of English and Germanic Philology* 96, no. 4 (October 1997): 601.

6. At a virtual conference on Mann's essay "Germany and the Germans" held on December 3, 2020, several commentators reproved Mann for this formulation, among them the literary scholar Kai Sina, who declared, "Mann's assertion that the 'best' in the German tradition has been transformed into 'evil' through 'devilish cunning' puts metaphysics in the place of acting people—probably the most irritating point in his reasoning." "Sincerity and Modesty: A Plea for Hermeneutic Fairness," https://mutuallymann.vatmh.org/all-contributions-germany-and-the-germans/.

7. Emphasis added. Manfred Görtemaker, *Thomas Mann und die Politik* (Frankfurt am Main: S. Fischer, 2005), 113. The first Mann citation is taken from his letter to Anna Jacobson, a professor of German at Hunter College in New York. It is found in *Thomas Mann Briefe*, 65, and is shaped by its context: Mann had been informed of the resistance that students of German in Jacobson's department had begun to feel toward their subject matter. The second citation is taken from a letter to Alexander M. Frey (February 2, 1939), which exists only in paraphrase in *Die Briefe Thomas Manns: Regesten und Register*, vol. 2, *1934–1943*, ed. Hans Bürgin and Hans-Otto Mayer (Frankfurt am Main: S. Fischer, 1980), 76.

8. Mann, "Zu Wagners Verteidigung," 358; emphasis added. Mann goes on to conjure, in the spirit of *The City of Man*, "a pacified, a depoliticized Europe, in the sole atmosphere of which Germany can be great and happy, because it returns a political innocence to its works and a good conscience to the admiration of them, so that it [Europe] no longer has to sigh: It [Germany] is great, it is wonderful, but it is 'against civilization.'" Ibid., 359.

9. Görtemaker, *Thomas Mann und die Politik*, 119.

10. "Deutschland und die Deutschen," E 5:262.

11. Tobias Temming, *"Bruder Hitler"? Zur Bedeutung des politischen Thomas Mann. Essays und Reden aus dem Exil* (Berlin: Wissenschaftlicher Verlag Berlin, 2008).

12. Thomas Mann, "What Is German? *The Atlantic Monthly,* May 1944, 80.

13. "Deutschland und die Deutschen," E 5:279.

14. Vaget, "Zu Thomas Manns Kriegsschriften im Exil," 94.

15. Bisdorff, *Thomas Mann und die Politik*, 46.

16. See Greif, *The Age of the Crisis of Man*.

17. Theodor Adorno, *Minima Moralia: Reflections from the Damaged Life*, tr. Dennis Redmond (Scotts Valley, CA: CreateSpace Independent Publishing Platform, 2011), 274.

18. Emphasis added. From a radio broadcast, "Thomas Mann's War," BBC Radio 4 FM, December 5, 2005, 0.15.

Chapter Four: Professor Thomas Mann, Nobel Laureate

1. Robert Goheen, foreword to *The Letters of Thomas Mann to Caroline Newton* (Princeton, NJ: Princeton University Press, 1971; N 1).

2. Frido Mann, "'Er war kein Akademiker, er war Künstler': Ein Gespräch mit dem Schriftsteller Frido Mann über seine Großeltern und ihr Leben am Pazifik," in *Thomas Mann in Amerika*, ed. Ulrich Rauff und Ellen Strittmatter (Marbach am Neckar: Deutsche Schillergesellschaft, 2018), 13.

3. T3 245; Vaget, "Schlechtes Wetter, Gutes Klima: Thomas Mann in Amerika," in *Thomas-Mann-Handbuch*, ed. Helmut Koopmann (Stuttgart: Alfred Kröner Verlag, 1990), 70.

4. "Die Laufbahn als Universitätslehrer, ehrenvoll und mit Freizeiten geschmückt, die Raum bieten für den erfrischenden Umgang mit loser gestimmten Musen, deren Gunst mir nicht völlig abgeht—lockte mich über alles," L 67–68. Abridged English translation in LA 62.

5. Goethe's "Faust" (11/28/1938)

Richard Wagner and "The Ring of the Nibelung" (1/17/1939)

Freud and the Future (2/13/1939)

An Introduction to "The Magic Mountain" (5/10/1939)

Goethe's "Werther" (11/17/1939)

On Myself (5/2/1940)

The Art of the Novel (5/9/1940)

6. https://theprince.princeton.edu/princetonperiodicals/?a=d&d=Princetonian19381129 -01.2.12&srpos=4&e=20-11-1938-01-12-1938--en-20--1--txt-txIN-Thomas+Mann. One can only imagine a conversation between these two Faustian figures after Mann's lecture; but unlike Mann, Berg was reticent and publicity-shy. Their fates would become entangled some years later when Christine, the daughter of Werner Heisenberg, would marry Mann's grandson Frido. Christine was born the very year, 1944, that Berg was recruited by the OSS to assassinate Heisenberg if circumstances warranted.

7. "Aus dem Princetoner Kolleg über *Faust* von Thomas Mann," *Mass und Wert* 2 no. 5 (May– June 1939): 590–612. "Goethe's *Faust*, 1938 [*Delivered in English as a public lecture in Princeton University in 1938*]," in *Essays of Three Decades*, tr. H. T. Lowe-Porter (New York: Knopf, 1971), 3–42.

8. Thomas Mann, "Sufferings and Greatness of Richard Wagner," in *Essays of Three Decades*, 307–52. The more anodyne Princeton speech is found in James Bade's illuminating compendium of Mann's Princeton lectures (B); it is, again, not at all the same lecture, as Bade points out, as the essay in English titled "Richard Wagner and the *Ring*," which appeared in 1971 in Mann's *Essays of Three Decades* and is a translation of the original 1937 Zurich lecture (B 16).

9. D 319. Vaget notes that "language did not constitute a barrier to the unfolding of Mann's vast publicistic activity in America. For where his knowledge and pronunciation of the English language left something to be desired, the aura of his personality and his experience as a performer stood him in good stead. He was an effective reader in English: the recordings prove it. His public appearances—the lecture tours all over the country, the mass events on the East as well as on the West Coast, the countless articles, summons to action, broadcasts, testimonial dinners, and fund raisers—represent a field of activity so wide-ranging that it cannot be completely reconstructed even on the basis of the diaries" ("Schlechtes Wetter," 73). But here is a

typical addendum: after completing a tour in January 1941 at the University of Georgia in Athens, Georgia, Mann notes: "It was an exhausting tour; I'm glad to have done it, with the usual nervousness and anxiety—in spite of it. Hope for a few quiet weeks with a return to the work on Joseph" (T4 112).

10. The full text of "On Myself" is available in an excellent, revised translation in Bade's monograph, B 23–79.

11. For more about Meisel, see Br.M 855–56.

12. *Thomas Mann's Addresses Delivered at the Library of Congress,* ed. Don Heinrich Tolzmann (Bern: Peter Lang, 2003).

13. This account is enriched by the reflections of Hans Rudolf Vaget throughout his writings on Thomas Mann in America, especially (V).

14. Thomas Mann, "Address to Princeton University Convocation, upon receiving honorary degree of Doctor of Letters [May 18, 1939]," box 1, folder 9, series 1: *Works,* Rare Books Room, Firestone Library, Princeton University.

15. For a full account of the meretricious tolerance for Nazi Germany throughout the 1930s provided by the major German departments at universities across the United States—when they were not, indeed, Nazi-leaning (Harvard perhaps the worst)—see Stephen H. Norwood, *The Third Reich in the Ivory Tower: Complicity and Conflict on American Campuses* (Cambridge: Cambridge University Press, 2009), and Laurel Leff, *Well Worth Saving: American Universities' Life-and-Death Decisions on Refugees from Nazi Europe* (New Haven: Yale University Press, 2019).

16. The attribute in quotes is the coinage of Ludwig Marcuse, cited in Erich Frey, "Thomas Mann's Exile Years in America," *Modern Language Studies* 6, no. 1 (Spring 1976): 84.

17. An anonymous reviewer, who is undoubtedly right, wrote: "As usual, those who can read the original text will find it vastly better than the translation." *The American Mercury,* February 1941, 248.

18. Thomas Mann, *Lotte in Weimar—Roman* (Frankfurt am Main: S. Fischer, 2013), henceforth LW; *Lotte in Weimar (The Beloved Returns),* tr. H. T. Lowe-Porter (New York: Knopf, 1940), henceforth LWA.

19. Morton Dauwen Zabel, "*Lotte in Weimar,*" a review of LWA in *The Nation,* August 31, 1940, 176.

20. Ibid.

21. Mann did not say "The thing is" ("Das aber ists" [LW 327]) or add the word "absolutely" ("garnicht" [LW 327]) when writing to the dean at Bonn. See Werner Frizen, "Nachwort" (LW 447). The extraordinary allusiveness of the chapter, the fullness of embedded Goethe citations, creates an exceptional problem for the translator, as Mann himself notes (T3 439). On the other hand, this difficulty scarcely justifies H. T. Lowe-Porter's mangling the entire phrase in translation as "But the thing is, I was born far more apt for appeasement than for tragedy" (LWA 331).

22. The Nizkor Project: Remembering the Holocaust (Shoah), Nuremberg, War Crimes, Crimes against Humanity, "The Trial of German Major War Criminals. Sitting at Nuremberg, Germany 16th July to 27th July 1946; One Hundred and Eighty-Eighth Day: Saturday, 27th July 1946 (Part 8 of 8)," http://www.nizkor.com/hweb/imt/tgmwc/tgmwc-19/tgmwc-19-188-08.shtml.

23. Their discovery was made on the strength of the first revelation of the piece as a fiction by Eugen Kogon in the *Frankfurter Hefte.* See TB 229.

24. *Thomas Mann Tagebücher 28.5.1946–31.12.1948*, ed. Inge Jens (Frankfurt am Main: S. Fischer, 1989), 415. Cited in Stephan Braese, "Juris-Diktionen. Eine Einführung: 'Goethe' im Nürnberger Zeugenstand," in: *Rechenschaften: Juristischer und literarischer Diskurs in der Auseinandersetzung mit den NS-Massenverbrechen*, ed. Stephan Braese (Göttingen: Wallstein, 2004), 9–10.

25. Mann, *Tagebücher 1946–1948*, 869, cited in LW, *Kommentar*, 170–71.

26. Thomas Mann, *The Story of a Novel—The Genesis of Doctor Faustus*, tr. Richard and Clara Winston (New York: Knopf, 1961), 193–94.

27. "... durch lange Jahre einen großen Teil seiner Korrespondenz nicht etwa nur diktatweise, sondern ganz selbständig für ihn, oder richtiger gesagt, *als er selbst* geführt habe ..." LW 81; LWA 75. As he begins to immerse himself in preparations for his lectures at the university, Mann notes that he is reading about Riemer—again! Riemer's loquacious conversation with Lotte had made up the entirety of the third chapter, completed in July of the previous year.

28. Braese, "Juris-Diktionen. Eine Einführung,"10.

29. Yahya Elsaghe, "Lotte in Weimar," in *The Cambridge Companion to Thomas Mann*, ed. Ritchie Robertson (Cambridge: Cambridge University Press, 2002), 193.

30. Alexander Honold, "Falsche Freunde und 'heilige Identität,' *Lotte in Weimar,* Thomas Mann bei Goethe," in *Goethe als Literatur-Figur,* ed. Alexander Honold, Edith Anna Kunz, and Hans-Jürgen Schrader (Göttingen: Wallstein, 2016), 166n. Honold refers to Gesa Dane, "Lotte im 'Hotel zum Elephanten.' Zur Codierung des Historischen in Thomas Manns *Lotte in Weimar*," in *Jahrbuch der Deutschen Schillergesellschaft* 43 (1999), 358f.

31. The following citation, two pages long, concluding with the words "may do it good and not perish from its heart," is taken from Mann's lecture, "Goethe's *Faust*, 1938," *Essays of Three Decades*, 40–42.

32. Mann published the German version of his Princeton talk as "Aus dem Princetoner Kolleg über *Faust*" in the émigré journal *Mass und Wert*. The German version adds a trenchant phrase to its translation of the original English words, "For our time, which seems to have fallen a helpless prey to evil and cynicism" (page 42 of the English text). The added German phrase reads: "hilfloser verfallen ... als viele frühere" (page 612); in English, "more helplessly than many an earlier one." The phrase adds a contemporary polemical thrust, expressing dismay at the present absence of political will, which Mann evidently did not want in his Princeton speech, so as not to ruffle the waters of a supine neutrality.

33. Hans Rudolf Vaget sees "an implicitly political thought in linking Goethe's [here] benevolent view of mankind to what Mann took to be a core element of the American character and, more precisely, a basic element of the eminently American character of Franklin Delano Roosevelt. . . . This becomes apparent when we link the character traits that he highlights in the *Faust* lecture to what Mann thought about America—'the land of good will'—and to what he thought about FDR—who desires the good—or at any rate the better" (V 20–21).

34. "Sagt es niemand, nur den Weisen, Weil die Menge gleich verhöhnet" are the opening lines of Goethe's celebrated short poem, "Selige Sehnsucht" (Blessed longing).

35. Thomas Mann, *Briefe III 1948–1955*, ed. Erika Mann (Frankfurt am Main: S. Fischer, 1965), 166.

36. Here are omitted parts of Hans Vaget's rich comment: "Mann immigrated to the United States through Toronto in May 1938 and gained American citizenship in June 1944: just a few years after arriving, he felt, with surprising ease, like an American; and he said, as a matter of course, 'we' and 'us' when it became a question of America and its military victories against the

former, now thoroughly corrupted fatherland. A contradiction? A case of hypocrisy and treacherous opportunism? Not at all. The consciousness of being 'a German writer and servant of the German language' (Br III [*Thomas Mann: Briefe 1948–1955*, ed. Erika Mann (Frankfurt am Main: S. Fischer, 1965), 166]) was and always remained the deepest root of his exile-existence. It comported perfectly with American citizenship, since America . . . was a country whose 'foreign-born citizens always sought to become true Americans as quickly as possible' (GW 13:708). . . . Thomas Mann joined that drift to Americanization in a confident and grateful manner, attracted by the 'indescribable beneficence of an atmosphere of moral health that at first breath was so exhilarating next to the dull, poisoned air of Europe overflowing with the miasmas of hatred' (GW 13:729)." "'Schlechtes Wetter, gutes Klima'—Thomas Mann in Amerika," in *Thomas-Mann-Handbuch*, ed. Helmut Koopmann (Stuttgart: Alfred Kröner, 2001), 69.

37. 'Verpflanzt und zerstreut wie die Juden in alle Welt müssen die Deutschen werden, um die Masse des Guten ganz und zum Heile aller Nationen zu entwickeln, die in ihnen liegt.' *Goethes Werke: Herausgegeben im Auftrage der Großherzogin Sophie von Sachsen* (Weimar: H. Böhlau, Weimar, 1887–1919), 5.2: 231–32. For this lead I am indebted to Professor Karin Schutjer, author of the excellent study *Goethe and Judaism* (Evanston, IL: Northwestern University Press, 2015), 98. The passage, slightly varied, is also included in H 823: it was noted by Mann himself in his diaries for 1934 (!).

38. H 823, citing *Thomas Mann an Ernst Bertram: Briefe aus den Jahren 1910–1955*, ed. Inge Jens (Pfullingen: Neske, 1960), 184–85. Mann's attention to this parallel—the problematic similarity of the Germans and Jews—would have been intensified by his reading of Kahler's *Israel unter den Völkern*.

39. Herbert Lehnert, "Dauer und Wechsel der Autorität: 'Lotte in Weimar' as a Work of Exile," in *Internationales Thomas-Mann-Kolloquium 1986, in Lübeck, Thomas-Mann-Studien*, ed. Thomas-Mann-Archiv der ETH in Zürich, vol. 7 (Bern: Francke Verlag, 1987), 49.

40. Thomas Mann, "Goethe's *Werther*," in B 111–35. In the collection of Mann's writings, *Altes und Neues, Kleine Prosa aus fünf Jahrzehnten* (Frankfurt am Main: S. Fischer 1953), Mann notes that this lecture, a translation of the German essay *Goethes Werther* printed on pp. 198–214 of this volume, "is one of the lectures (*Lesungen*) that I held in the years 1938 and 1939 in Princeton for advanced students" (B 14). While this statement is perfectly accurate, it could give the impression that it was delivered in 1938, *before* Mann had finished writing *Lotte in Weimar*. Why is this fact important? Please return to the text and read on.

41. Thomas Mann, *Betrachtungen eines Unpolitischen*, GW 4:84. The great artist found by Schopenhauer was . . . Thomas Mann himself, author of *Buddenbrooks*. His German readers would know that!

42. Nietzsche, *On the Genealogy of Morals* and *Ecce Homo*, tr. Walter Kaufmann and R. J. Hollingdale (New York: Vintage [Random House], 1967), 101.

43. W. Daniel Wilson, *Der Faustische Pakt: Goethe und die Goethe-Gesellschaft im Dritten Reich* (Munich: dtv, 2018), 71.

44. In this respect, Mann, in 1939, enlarges the view, a decade and a half later, informing Walter Benjamin's impressive 1924–25 essay on Goethe's novel *Die Wahlverwandtschaften* (Elective affinities). Benjamin's essay repudiates, early on, the standpoint of the hagiographic Goethe biography written by Friedrich Gundolf with the blessing of Stefan George (whom both Benjamin and Mann intensely disliked). As Márton Dornbach writes, "Gundolf's glorification of Goethe accords with various currents of post-Nietzschean vitalist irrationalism. . . . An attempt

to appropriate Goethe in the name of such a deeply conservative agenda, in a country whose unstable identity had all but become bound up with that author's legacy, was bound to be perceived by a left-leaning intellectual [Benjamin] as an ominous development." Márton Dornbach, *The Saving Line: Benjamin, Adorno, and the Caesuras of Hope* (Evanston, IL: Northwestern University Press, 2021), 21. On Benjamin and Mann as coordinated thinkers, we might note Benjamin's admiration, avowed to Gershom Scholem, for *The Magic Mountain* (1924!) and Mann's printing Benjamin's essay "What is Epic Theater?" (1939!) in the journal Mann edited, *Mass und Wert* (Measure and value).

45. Clifton Fadiman, "Mann on Goethe" (a review of *Lotte in Weimar*), *The New Yorker*, August 31, 1940, 52. In a letter to Agnes E. Meyer (September 3, 1940), Mann indeed described Fadiman's review as "nice and intelligent"; BR.M 232.

46. Thomas Mann, "Richard Wagner and *The Ring of the Nibelung*" (B 81). Subsequent references to pages in this text will be assigned a page number in parentheses.

47. Saul Friedländer, *Nazi Germany and the Jews: The Years of Persecution, 1933–1939* (New York: HarperCollins, 1997), I:191.

48. Friedrich Nietzsche, in *The Portable Nietzsche*, ed. and tr. Walter Kaufmann (New York: Viking, 1954), 519–20.

49. Mann's Princeton lecture on Freud is an abridged English version of the speech he delivered at the Wiener Akademischer Verein für medizinische Psychologie on May 9, 1936, in honor of Freud's eightieth birthday. It has not been possible to find the typescript of the Princeton lecture. The opening of this chapter follows the English translation of the original 1936 lecture made by H. T. Lowe-Porter, "Freud and the Future," in *Essays of Three Decades*, 411–28.

50. See G. Hummel, "A Summer Afternoon in Grinzing: Thomas Mann Visits Sigmund Freud," *Luzif Amor* 19, no. 38 (2006): 76–101.

51. Thomas Mann, "Freud and the Future," *The Saturday Review of Literature*, July 25, 1936, 3–4, 14–15.

52. For a fresh look at the parallelism—better, the intertwinededness—of modern literature, literary analysis, and psychoanalysis as disciplines intent on reading the signs of meaning in the absence of physical evidence, especially in the shadow of world war, see John Zilcosky, *The Language of Trauma: War and Technology in Hoffmann, Freud, and Kafka* (Toronto: University of Toronto Press, 2021). Kindle version loc. 316–73.

53. "Freud admired the degree of penetration in Nietzsche's self-knowledge but at the same time denied having read him, so how could he have come to any conclusion about Nietzsche? If, now, at the same time, Freud 'ran himself down' as being in no way of comparable 'nobility,' that judgment must be seen, according to [Walter] Kaufmann, as an unconscious expression of guilt for having denied what had really happened: Freud had read a good deal of Nietzsche, especially in the 1880s and then circa 1909." Stanley Corngold, *Walter Kaufmann: Philosopher, Humanist, Heretic* (Princeton, NJ: Princeton University Press, 2019), 544–45. See also Walter Kaufmann, *Discovering the Mind*, volume 3, *Freud, Adler, and Jung* (New Brunswick, NJ: Transaction, 1992), 266, 272; originally published as *Freud versus Adler and Jung* by McGraw-Hill (New York) in 1980.

54. Thomas Mann, "Freud and the Future," translated by H.T. Lowe-Porter, *Essays of Three Decades*, 414–15. Citations from this translation will be assigned a page number in parentheses.

55. Thomas Mann, "Freud and the Future," *Saturday Review*, 3. Citations from this version will be assigned a page number in parentheses.

56. Cf. Edward W. Said, *Orientalism* (New York: Pantheon, 1978). https://www.google.com /search?client=safari&rls=en&q=edward+said+orientalism&ie=UTF-8&oe=UTF-8.

57. Ibid.

58. Todd Kontje, *Mann's World: Empire, Race, and the Jewish Question* (Ann Arbor: University of Michigan Press, 2011). https://www.press.umich.edu/2456281/thomas_manns_world.

59. Edward L. Greenstein, "Moses and the Fugitive Hero Pattern," *The Torah*, December 27, 2018: 2.

60. The reference is to the unnamed Viennese scholar who wrote "Zur Psychologie älterer Biographik," *Imago*. But Mann almost certainly had in mind the article of this name written by Ernst Kris, "Zur Psychologie älterer Biographik: (dargestellt an der des bildenden Künstlers)," *Imago* 21, no. 3 (1935): 320–44.

61. Fredericka A. Schmadel, "Mythic Time in Thomas Mann's Novel *Joseph und seine Brueder*," https://www.academia.edu/6346710/Mythic_Time_in_Thomas_Manns_Joseph _und_seine_Brueder.

62. I discuss this logomachy in my *Walter Kaufmann: Philosopher, Humanist, Heretic*, 401–2.

63. Boes notes that many readers have found in "Mann's description of the episode in which Joseph's brothers throw him into a well . . . a trenchant analysis of the fascist mob mentality" (TB 78).

64. William Blake, *Jerusalem*, "The Words of Los," f. 10, lines 20–21, http://www.bartleby.com /235/307.htm.

65. Thomas Mann, "The Making of 'The Magic Mountain,'" tr. H. T. Lowe-Porter, *The Atlantic Monthly*, January 1953, 41–45. Citations from this translation will be assigned a page number in parentheses.

66. *Thomas Mann's Novel "Der Zauberberg": A Study* (New York: D. Appleton-Century, 1933). See V 281–82 and TB 111–13.

67. The paper was titled "The Quester Hero: Myth as Universal Symbol in the Works of Thomas Mann." Nemerov was the brother of the great photographer Diane Arbus and was twice appointed United States Poet Laureate.

68. Here, in an incisive critical refutation of Mann's claim to have awarded a sort of out-of-time-ness to Castorp's life at the Berghof sanatorium, Jensen Suther (Yale) writes, "In an argument that has exercised a considerable influence on *Magic Mountain* scholarship, Paul Ricoeur understands the time of the mountain and in the 'Snow' chapter in particular as a form of eternity that transcends the finite, empirical time of the flatlands (Paul Ricoeur, *Time and Narrative*, tr. Kathleen Blamey and David Pellauer [Chicago: University of Chicago Press, 1988], 2:129–30). By contrast, I [JS] will argue that, far from being a form of eternity, the time on the mountain is perfectly continuous with the finite time of the flatlands, giving expression to its qualitative specificity, its essential emptiness. While Mann's technique of narrative contraction (of gradually shrinking the *narrative* time in inverse proportion to the length of *narrated* time) gives the temporality of the mountain the appearance of existing beyond history, it actually captures our normative relation to time: our experience of time as empty in a historical form of life in which there is no self-conscious relation to the past (who we have been) and to the future (who we are trying to be)." From an unpublished paper, "The Bildung of the Beautiful Soul: On Thomas Mann's *The Magic Mountain*," 19n11, delivered as a talk on October 25, 2019, at a Dartmouth College conference, "Mann Family: Lives and Fictions."

69. John Zilcosky, *The Language of Trauma: War and Technology in Hoffmann, Freud, and Kafka* (Toronto: University of Toronto Press, 2021), 5.

70. Thomas Mann, *Die vertauschten Köpfe: Eine indische Legende* (Stockholm: Bermann-Fischer, 1940); *The Transposed Heads: A Legend of India*, tr. H. T. Lowe-Porter (New York: Knopf, 1941). Mann described this novella as "keine Haupt- und Staatsaktion, sondern ein Divertissement und Intermezzo." Letter to Agnes B. Meyer, July 27, 1940, in *Thomas Mann Briefe II (1937–1947)*, ed. Erika Mann (Frankfurt am Main: Fischer Taschenbuch Verlag, 1992), 152.

71. It was certainly not hard for Mann himself, who wrote the extraordinary note, "Ja, Tonio, Hans und Inge sind nun im Flammengrabe vereinigt. Friede ihrer Asche" ("Yes, Tonio, Hans, and Inge are now united in a grave of flames. Peace to their ashes"). *Dichter über ihrer Dichtungen II*, vol. 14/ I–III: *Thomas Mann*, ed. Hans Wysling (Frankfurt am Main: S. Fischer, 1975–81), 590. Cited in Helmut Koopmann, "*Die vertauschten Köpfe*. Verwandlungszauber und das erlöste Ich," in *Liebe und Tod—In Venedig und Anderswo, Die Davoser Literaturtage 2004*, ed. Thomas Sprecher, *Thomas-Mann-Studien 33* (Frankfurt am Main: Vittorio Klostermann, 2005), 211–12.

72. Thomas Mann, "Prelude in Higher Echelons," *Joseph and His Brothers*, tr. John E. Woods (New York: Knopf, 2005), 1047.

73. In a strenuous, exalted, and thoroughly incoherent essay on "Thomas Mann's Fable for Today," Mann's sponsor, Agnes E. Meyer, argues that we have here an antifascist thrust draped in the dhoti of "an ancient Hindu legend." What is said to be antifascistic about it is that it conjures, with approbation, the eternal longing of spirit for body and body for spirit in an agon that must never be abandoned *or* completed. But here the fusion is humorously accomplished. Let that be a warning to the Axis. This allegory will win no wars.

74. Princeton, NJ: Princeton University Press, 1948.

75. This story, which Mann read in 1935, tells of the woman Sita and her two husbands. Zimmer supplied more than one inspiration: Mann was "reminded of it when, in November 1939, he read 'Die indische Weltmutter' (The Indian Mother of the World, 1938), also by Zimmer. In his book and in the earlier essays, Zimmer had retold the story 'Kathasaritsagara' (The Transposed Male Heads) from the *Vetalapancavimshati*." For this information and more on Mann's sources, see Jens Rieckmann, "The Gaze of Love, Longing, and Desire in Thomas Mann's 'The Transposed Heads' and 'The Black Swan,'" in *A Companion to the Works of Thomas Mann*, ed. Herbert Lehnert and Eva Wessell (Rochester, NY: Camden House, 2004), 246.

76. *The Transposed Heads*, 120. Subsequent citations from this work appear in the text as page numbers in parentheses.

77. According to Hans Rudolf Vaget, on re-reading Gore Vidal's homosexual novel *The City and the Pillar*, Mann especially liked the presentation of the main figure, Jim Willard, who is at once a well-built athlete and a man of delicate sensibility, which makes him an outcast among his young contemporaries. Vaget comments: "Seen in cold daylight" [e.g., when you come right down to it], what we have here is "Tonio Kröger in the body of Hans Hansen—so to speak, a Hans Hansen with a transposed head!" Hans Rudolf Vaget, "Thomas Mann und die amerikanische Literatur: Eine Skizze," in *Thomas Mann in Amerika*, ed. Ulrich Rauff and Ellen Strittmatter (Marbach am Neckar: Deutsche Schillergesellschaft, 2019), 35.

78. *Die vertauschten Köpfe*, 15, 139, 146, 151.

79. Hans Rudolf Vaget stresses how *The Transposed Heads* and *Joseph and His Brothers* share the same intention of humanizing myth but treat the matter differently. The narrator of *The Transposed Heads* is sovereign, "saucy," even sarcastic; the narrator of *Joseph*, despite his

forays into sublime humor, is stately and reverential ("Neuedition der späten Erzählungen Thomas Manns," an on-line lecture broadcast on June 1, 2021, for the Thomas-Mann-Forum München e.V.).

80. Steven Toby Weinberg, "The Passover in *Joseph und seine Brüder*: Midrash or Exegetical Biblical Criticism?" An unpublished paper delivered at a Harvard conference on "Midrashic Interpretations of Thomas Mann's *Joseph und seine Brüder*," April 2018.

81. On the 2005 retranslation of the *Joseph* tetralogy by John E. Woods (following the first translation by H. T. Lowe-Porter in 1948), Merle Rubin wrote this appreciative review: "A Joseph for Modern Times, for All Time, " https://www.latimes.com/archives/la-xpm-2005-aug-14-bk-rubin14-story.html.

82. Thomas Mann, "Sixteen Years," reprinted from the 1948 American edition, *Joseph and His Brothers*, tr. John E. Woods (New York: Knopf, 2005), xxxvii–xxxviii.

83. Mann to Robert R. Smith, March 2, 1939, cited in Steven Toby Weinberg, "Vayeshev," episode 9 of the podcast "*The Schrift—Ancient Teachings for Modern Times*," https://podcasts.apple.com/us/podcast/vayeshev-twins-tamar-zarathustras-overcoming-nihilism/id1538122133?i=1000501946449.

84. Weinberg, unpublished paper delivered at a Harvard conference, April 2018. Weinberg foregrounds Mann's 1936 letter to the Hungarian philologist, Karl Kerényi, in which Mann defends his anachronisms in *Joseph*: "Anachronism no longer bothers me in the least—as a matter of fact, this was already so in the earlier volumes. In the third volume, Egyptian, Jewish, Greek, even medieval elements, both linguistic and mythological, make a colorful mixture." Weinberg observes, "Indeed, the opening lines of the epic get at the idea that time is a mystery and that time is inherently unknowable: 'Deep is the well of the past. Should we not call it bottomless? ... [For] the deeper we delve and the farther we press and grope into the underworld of the past, the more totally unfathomable become those first foundations of humankind.'" Thomas Mann, "Prelude: Descent into Hell," *Joseph*, 3.

85. Erich Frey, "Thomas Mann's Exile Years in America," *Modern Language Studies* 6, no. 1 (Spring, 1976): 89.

86. Greenberg's criticism is discussed in TB 262.

87. Julia Schöll, *Joseph im Exil: zur Identitätskonstruktion in Thomas Mann Exil-Tagebüchern und -Briefen sowie im Roman "Joseph und seine Brüder"* (Würzburg; Königshausen & Neumann, 2004); Ehrhard Bahr, "Exil als 'beschädigtes Leben,' Thomas Mann und sein Roman *Joseph, der Ernährer*," in *Exilerfahrung und Konstruktionen von Identität 1933–1945*, ed. Hans Otto Horch, Hanni Mittelmann, and Karin Neuburger (Berlin: de Gruyter, 2013), 245–55.

88. *Joseph*, xxxviii–xxxix.

89. Paul Michael Lützeler, "Einleitung: 'Optimische Verzweiflung: Thomas Mann und Hermann Broch im Exil," in *Freundschaft im Exil: Thomas Mann und Hermann Broch*, ed. Paul Michael Lützeler (Frankfurt am Main: Vittorio Klostermann, 2004), 16.

90. Wagner scholars also find a structural parallel with the Prelude to the *Götterdämmerung*, the fourth opera in Wagner's *Ring*. Jan Assmann, Dieter Borchmeyer, and Stephan Stachorski, *Kommentar* to Thomas Mann, *Joseph, der Ernährer, Große kommentierte Frankfurter Ausgabe* (Frankfurt am Main: S. Fischer, 2018), 8.2: 1296.

91. Thomas Mann, "Prelude in Higher Echelons," *Joseph*, 1041. Citations from this work will be assigned a page number in parentheses.

92. Thomas Mann, "The Making of 'The Magic Mountain,'" tr. H. T. Lowe-Porter, *The Atlantic Monthly*, January 1953, 41.

93. Mann's notation after seeing Charlie Chaplin's *The Great Dictator* reads: "Pleasant but all too nonsensical farce and parody with very funny details, at which I laughed a lot" (T4 181). And we might recall his seeing the "very funny" Marx Brothers movie on Broadway in 1938 (D 309).

94. "After dinner a lengthy reading aloud from *The Transposed Heads* for Katia and the children (sacrifice- and goddesses-scene). Laughed at a lot of things" (T4 70). "Reading aloud from *The Transposed Heads*, temple scenes, aroused great admiration and emotion that had to be curbed. The sensuous-supersensuous element a strong stimulant, eroticism with keen-witted intelligence, lust, and clarity, humor" (T4 109). "In the evening *a reading from The Transposed Heads to K[atia], Eri[ka], Loewenstein, Kahler, and Broch: A portion of the Temple scene and the hermit chapter.* Great high spirits (*Heiterkeit*). I had to laugh a lot while reading" (T4 95).

95. Mann, "The War and the Future," in *Order of the Day: Political Essays and Speeches of Two Decades*, tr. H. T. Lowe-Porter (New York: Knopf, 1942), 241.

96. "Die Princetoner Jahre markieren eine literarisch und publizistisch erstaunlich produktive Periode." "Einleitung," BR.M 38.

Chapter Five: Toward a Conclusion

1. He was induced to lecture (on *Werther*) during a "free" month in fall 1939.

2. Thus Ernst Lothar, an émigré Austrian novelist and theater director who visited Mann in Princeton. *Das Wunder des Überlebens: Erinnerungen und Erlebnisse* (Vienna and Hamburg: Paul Zsolnay Verlag, 1961), 141.

3. Broch lived in Einstein's house on Mercer Street from August 15 until September 15, 1939, while Einstein was on vacation.

4. Michael Grüning, *Ein Haus für Albert Einstein* (Berlin: Verlag der Nation, 1990), 248–49.

5. Thomas Mann, *Joseph and His Brothers*, tr. John E. Woods (New York: Knopf, 2005), 1060.

6. Ibid., 1053.

7. Further: "The [German] language of the exile, like his life, is a service bare of ornament, objective and sans illusion as to the extent of the catastrophe—authentic, because not fallen prey to the world of reification but rather: guarantor of utopia." Gerhard Lauer, on Mann and Kahler, in *Die verspätete Revolution: Erich Kahler, Wissenschaftsgeschichte zwischen konservativer Revolution und Exil* (Berlin: de Gruyter, 1995), 301.

8. Algis Valiunas, "Thomas Mann's Civilized Uncertainty," *Humanities* 41 no. 3 (summer 2020), https://www.neh.gov/article/thomas-manns-civilized-uncertainty.

9. Thomas Mann, "The Making of 'The Magic Mountain,'" tr. H. T. Lowe-Porter, *The Atlantic Monthly*, January 1953, 45.

10. Paul Miller-Melamed and Claire Morelon, "What the Hapsburg Empire Got Right: Derided as the "Prison of Nations," the Sprawling, Multiethnic State Was in Fact Surprisingly Progressive," *The New York Times*, September 30, 2019, https://www.nytimes.com/2019/09/10/opinion/hapsburg-empire-austria-world-war-1.html.

11. Thomas Mann, "Sixteen Years: reprinted from the 1948 American edition of *Joseph and His Brothers*," *Joseph and His Brothers*, tr. John E. Woods (New York: Knopf, 2005), xl.

INDEX